50% OFF Online Social Work AS Prep Course!

Dear Customer,

We consider it an honor and a privilege that you chose our LMSW Study Guide. As a way of showing our appreciation and to help us better serve you, we have partnered with Mometrix Test Preparation to offer you **50% off their online Social Work ASWB Masters Prep Course**. Many LMSW courses are needlessly expensive and don't deliver enough value. With their course, you get access to the best LMSW prep material, and **you only pay half price**.

Mometrix has structured their online course to perfectly complement your printed study guide. The LMSW Prep Course contains **in-depth lessons** that cover all the most important topics, **20+ video reviews** that explain difficult concepts, over **1,000 practice questions** to ensure you feel prepared, and more than **400 digital flashcards**, so you can study while you're on the go.

Online Social Work ASWB Masters Prep Course

Topics Included:	*Course Features:*
<ul><li>Human Development, Diversity, and Behavior in the Environment</li><li>Assessment and Intervention Planning</li><li>Interventions with Clients/Client Systems</li><li>Professional Relationships, Values, and Ethics</li></ul>	LMSW Study Guide<ul><li>Get content that complements our best-selling study guide.</li></ul>Full-Length Practice Tests<ul><li>With over 1,000 practice questions, you can test yourself again and again.</li></ul>Mobile Friendly<ul><li>If you need to study on the go, the course is easily accessible from your mobile device.</li></ul>LMSW Flashcards<ul><li>Our course includes a flashcard mode with over 400 content cards to help you study.</li></ul>

To receive this discount, visit them at mometrix.com/university/aswbm or simply scan this QR code with your smartphone. At the checkout page, enter the discount code: **LMSW50TPB**

If you have any questions or concerns, please contact them at support@mometrix.com.

SCAN HERE

 in partnership with

FREE Test Taking Tips Video/DVD Offer

To better serve you, we created videos covering test taking tips that we want to give you for FREE. **These videos cover world-class tips that will help you succeed on your test.**

We just ask that you send us feedback about this product. Please let us know what you thought about it—whether good, bad, or indifferent.

To get your **FREE videos**, you can use the QR code below or email freevideos@studyguideteam.com with "Free Videos" in the subject line and the following information in the body of the email:

- a. The title of your product

- b. Your product rating on a scale of 1-5, with 5 being the highest

- c. Your feedback about the product

If you have any questions or concerns, please don't hesitate to contact us at info@studyguideteam.com.

Thank you!

LMSW Exam Prep
2023 - 2024

3 Practice Tests and ASWB Masters Study Guide for Social Work Licensing

[5th Edition]

Joshua Rueda

Interested in buying more than 10 copies of our product? Contact us about bulk discounts:
bulkorders@studyguideteam.com

ISBN 13: 9781637752845
ISBN 10: 1637752849

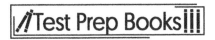

Table of Contents

Welcome

Dear Reader,

Welcome to your new Test Prep Books study guide! We are pleased that you chose us to help you prepare for your exam. There are many study options to choose from, and we appreciate you choosing us. Studying can be a daunting task, but we have designed a smart, effective study guide to help prepare you for what lies ahead.

Whether you're a parent helping your child learn and grow, a high school student working hard to get into your dream college, or a nursing student studying for a complex exam, we want to help give you the tools you need to succeed. We hope this study guide gives you the skills and the confidence to thrive, and we can't thank you enough for allowing us to be part of your journey.

In an effort to continue to improve our products, we welcome feedback from our customers. We look forward to hearing from you. Suggestions, success stories, and criticisms can all be communicated by emailing us at info@studyguideteam.com.

Sincerely,
Test Prep Books Team

FREE Videos/DVD OFFER

Doing well on your exam requires both knowing the test content and understanding how to use that knowledge to do well on the test. We offer completely FREE test taking tip videos. **These videos cover world-class tips that you can use to succeed on your test.**

To get your **FREE videos**, you can use the QR code below or email freevideos@studyguideteam.com with "Free Videos" in the subject line and the following information in the body of the email:

- a. The title of your product
- b. Your product rating on a scale of 1-5, with 5 being the highest
- c. Your feedback about the product

If you have any questions or concerns, please don't hesitate to contact us at info@studyguideteam.com.

Quick Overview

As you draw closer to taking your exam, effective preparation becomes more and more important. Thankfully, you have this study guide to help you get ready. Use this guide to help keep your studying on track and refer to it often.

This study guide contains several key sections that will help you be successful on your exam. The guide contains tips for what you should do the night before and the day of the test. Also included are test-taking tips. Knowing the right information is not always enough. Many well-prepared test takers struggle with exams. These tips will help equip you to accurately read, assess, and answer test questions.

A large part of the guide is devoted to showing you what content to expect on the exam and to helping you better understand that content. In this guide are practice test questions so that you can see how well you have grasped the content. Then, answer explanations are provided so that you can understand why you missed certain questions.

Don't try to cram the night before you take your exam. This is not a wise strategy for a few reasons. First, your retention of the information will be low. Your time would be better used by reviewing information you already know rather than trying to learn a lot of new information. Second, you will likely become stressed as you try to gain a large amount of knowledge in a short amount of time. Third, you will be depriving yourself of sleep. So be sure to go to bed at a reasonable time the night before. Being well-rested helps you focus and remain calm.

Be sure to eat a substantial breakfast the morning of the exam. If you are taking the exam in the afternoon, be sure to have a good lunch as well. Being hungry is distracting and can make it difficult to focus. You have hopefully spent lots of time preparing for the exam. Don't let an empty stomach get in the way of success!

When travelling to the testing center, leave earlier than needed. That way, you have a buffer in case you experience any delays. This will help you remain calm and will keep you from missing your appointment time at the testing center.

Be sure to pace yourself during the exam. Don't try to rush through the exam. There is no need to risk performing poorly on the exam just so you can leave the testing center early. Allow yourself to use all of the allotted time if needed.

Remain positive while taking the exam even if you feel like you are performing poorly. Thinking about the content you should have mastered will not help you perform better on the exam.

Once the exam is complete, take some time to relax. Even if you feel that you need to take the exam again, you will be well served by some down time before you begin studying again. It's often easier to convince yourself to study if you know that it will come with a reward!

Test-Taking Strategies

1. Predicting the Answer

When you feel confident in your preparation for a multiple-choice test, try predicting the answer before reading the answer choices. This is especially useful on questions that test objective factual knowledge. By predicting the answer before reading the available choices, you eliminate the possibility that you will be distracted or led astray by an incorrect answer choice. You will feel more confident in your selection if you read the question, predict the answer, and then find your prediction among the answer choices. After using this strategy, be sure to still read all of the answer choices carefully and completely. If you feel unprepared, you should not attempt to predict the answers. This would be a waste of time and an opportunity for your mind to wander in the wrong direction.

2. Reading the Whole Question

Too often, test takers scan a multiple-choice question, recognize a few familiar words, and immediately jump to the answer choices. Test authors are aware of this common impatience, and they will sometimes prey upon it. For instance, a test author might subtly turn the question into a negative, or he or she might redirect the focus of the question right at the end. The only way to avoid falling into these traps is to read the entirety of the question carefully before reading the answer choices.

3. Looking for Wrong Answers

Long and complicated multiple-choice questions can be intimidating. One way to simplify a difficult multiple-choice question is to eliminate all of the answer choices that are clearly wrong. In most sets of answers, there will be at least one selection that can be dismissed right away. If the test is administered on paper, the test taker could draw a line through it to indicate that it may be ignored; otherwise, the test taker will have to perform this operation mentally or on scratch paper. In either case, once the obviously incorrect answers have been eliminated, the remaining choices may be considered. Sometimes identifying the clearly wrong answers will give the test taker some information about the correct answer. For instance, if one of the remaining answer choices is a direct opposite of one of the eliminated answer choices, it may well be the correct answer. The opposite of obviously wrong is obviously right! Of course, this is not always the case. Some answers are obviously incorrect simply because they are irrelevant to the question being asked. Still, identifying and eliminating some incorrect answer choices is a good way to simplify a multiple-choice question.

4. Don't Overanalyze

Anxious test takers often overanalyze questions. When you are nervous, your brain will often run wild, causing you to make associations and discover clues that don't actually exist. If you feel that this may be a problem for you, do whatever you can to slow down during the test. Try taking a deep breath or counting to ten. As you read and consider the question, restrict yourself to the particular words used by the author. Avoid thought tangents about what the author *really* meant, or what he or she was *trying* to say. The only things that matter on a multiple-choice test are the words that are actually in the question. You must avoid reading too much into a multiple-choice question, or supposing that the writer meant something other than what he or she wrote.

3

5. No Need for Panic

It is wise to learn as many strategies as possible before taking a multiple-choice test, but it is likely that you will come across a few questions for which you simply don't know the answer. In this situation, avoid panicking. Because most multiple-choice tests include dozens of questions, the relative value of a single wrong answer is small. As much as possible, you should compartmentalize each question on a multiple-choice test. In other words, you should not allow your feelings about one question to affect your success on the others. When you find a question that you either don't understand or don't know how to answer, just take a deep breath and do your best. Read the entire question slowly and carefully. Try rephrasing the question a couple of different ways. Then, read all of the answer choices carefully. After eliminating obviously wrong answers, make a selection and move on to the next question.

6. Confusing Answer Choices

When working on a difficult multiple-choice question, there may be a tendency to focus on the answer choices that are the easiest to understand. Many people, whether consciously or not, gravitate to the answer choices that require the least concentration, knowledge, and memory. This is a mistake. When you come across an answer choice that is confusing, you should give it extra attention. A question might be confusing because you do not know the subject matter to which it refers. If this is the case, don't eliminate the answer before you have affirmatively settled on another. When you come across an answer choice of this type, set it aside as you look at the remaining choices. If you can confidently assert that one of the other choices is correct, you can leave the confusing answer aside. Otherwise, you will need to take a moment to try to better understand the confusing answer choice. Rephrasing is one way to tease out the sense of a confusing answer choice.

7. Your First Instinct

Many people struggle with multiple-choice tests because they overthink the questions. If you have studied sufficiently for the test, you should be prepared to trust your first instinct once you have carefully and completely read the question and all of the answer choices. There is a great deal of research suggesting that the mind can come to the correct conclusion very quickly once it has obtained all of the relevant information. At times, it may seem to you as if your intuition is working faster even than your reasoning mind. This may in fact be true. The knowledge you obtain while studying may be retrieved from your subconscious before you have a chance to work out the associations that support it. Verify your instinct by working out the reasons that it should be trusted.

8. Key Words

Many test takers struggle with multiple-choice questions because they have poor reading comprehension skills. Quickly reading and understanding a multiple-choice question requires a mixture of skill and experience. To help with this, try jotting down a few key words and phrases on a piece of scrap paper. Doing this concentrates the process of reading and forces the mind to weigh the relative importance of the question's parts. In selecting words and phrases to write down, the test taker thinks about the question more deeply and carefully. This is especially true for multiple-choice questions that are preceded by a long prompt.

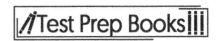

9. Subtle Negatives

One of the oldest tricks in the multiple-choice test writer's book is to subtly reverse the meaning of a question with a word like *not* or *except*. If you are not paying attention to each word in the question, you can easily be led astray by this trick. For instance, a common question format is, "Which of the following is...?" Obviously, if the question instead is, "Which of the following is not...?," then the answer will be quite different. Even worse, the test makers are aware of the potential for this mistake and will include one answer choice that would be correct if the question were not negated or reversed. A test taker who misses the reversal will find what he or she believes to be a correct answer and will be so confident that he or she will fail to reread the question and discover the original error. The only way to avoid this is to practice a wide variety of multiple-choice questions and to pay close attention to each and every word.

10. Reading Every Answer Choice

It may seem obvious, but you should always read every one of the answer choices! Too many test takers fall into the habit of scanning the question and assuming that they understand the question because they recognize a few key words. From there, they pick the first answer choice that answers the question they believe they have read. Test takers who read all of the answer choices might discover that one of the latter answer choices is actually *more* correct. Moreover, reading all of the answer choices can remind you of facts related to the question that can help you arrive at the correct answer. Sometimes, a misstatement or incorrect detail in one of the latter answer choices will trigger your memory of the subject and will enable you to find the right answer. Failing to read all of the answer choices is like not reading all of the items on a restaurant menu: you might miss out on the perfect choice.

11. Spot the Hedges

One of the keys to success on multiple-choice tests is paying close attention to every word. This is never truer than with words like almost, most, some, and sometimes. These words are called "hedges" because they indicate that a statement is not totally true or not true in every place and time. An absolute statement will contain no hedges, but in many subjects, the answers are not always straightforward or absolute. There are always exceptions to the rules in these subjects. For this reason, you should favor those multiple-choice questions that contain hedging language. The presence of qualifying words indicates that the author is taking special care with their words, which is certainly important when composing the right answer. After all, there are many ways to be wrong, but there is only one way to be right! For this reason, it is wise to avoid answers that are absolute when taking a multiple-choice test. An absolute answer is one that says things are either all one way or all another. They often include words like *every*, *always*, *best*, and *never*. If you are taking a multiple-choice test in a subject that doesn't lend itself to absolute answers, be on your guard if you see any of these words.

12. Long Answers

In many subject areas, the answers are not simple. As already mentioned, the right answer often requires hedges. Another common feature of the answers to a complex or subjective question are qualifying clauses, which are groups of words that subtly modify the meaning of the sentence. If the question or answer choice describes a rule to which there are exceptions or the subject matter is complicated, ambiguous, or confusing, the correct answer will require many words in order to be expressed clearly and accurately. In essence, you should not be deterred by answer choices that seem

5

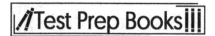

excessively long. Oftentimes, the author of the text will not be able to write the correct answer without offering some qualifications and modifications. Your job is to read the answer choices thoroughly and completely and to select the one that most accurately and precisely answers the question.

13. Restating to Understand

Sometimes, a question on a multiple-choice test is difficult not because of what it asks but because of how it is written. If this is the case, restate the question or answer choice in different words. This process serves a couple of important purposes. First, it forces you to concentrate on the core of the question. In order to rephrase the question accurately, you have to understand it well. Rephrasing the question will concentrate your mind on the key words and ideas. Second, it will present the information to your mind in a fresh way. This process may trigger your memory and render some useful scrap of information picked up while studying.

14. True Statements

Sometimes an answer choice will be true in itself, but it does not answer the question. This is one of the main reasons why it is essential to read the question carefully and completely before proceeding to the answer choices. Too often, test takers skip ahead to the answer choices and look for true statements. Having found one of these, they are content to select it without reference to the question above. Obviously, this provides an easy way for test makers to play tricks. The savvy test taker will always read the entire question before turning to the answer choices. Then, having settled on a correct answer choice, he or she will refer to the original question and ensure that the selected answer is relevant. The mistake of choosing a correct-but-irrelevant answer choice is especially common on questions related to specific pieces of objective knowledge. A prepared test taker will have a wealth of factual knowledge at their disposal, and should not be careless in its application.

15. No Patterns

One of the more dangerous ideas that circulates about multiple-choice tests is that the correct answers tend to fall into patterns. These erroneous ideas range from a belief that B and C are the most common right answers, to the idea that an unprepared test-taker should answer "A-B-A-C-A-D-A-B-A." It cannot be emphasized enough that pattern-seeking of this type is exactly the WRONG way to approach a multiple-choice test. To begin with, it is highly unlikely that the test maker will plot the correct answers according to some predetermined pattern. The questions are scrambled and delivered in a random order. Furthermore, even if the test maker was following a pattern in the assignation of correct answers, there is no reason why the test taker would know which pattern he or she was using. Any attempt to discern a pattern in the answer choices is a waste of time and a distraction from the real work of taking the test. A test taker would be much better served by extra preparation before the test than by reliance on a pattern in the answers.

Bonus Content

We host multiple bonus items online, including all three practice tests in digital format. Scan the QR code or go to this link to access this content:

testprepbooks.com/bonus/aswbmasters

The first time you access the page, you will need to register as a "new user" and verify your email address.

If you have any issues, please email support@testprepbooks.com

Introduction to the ASWB Masters Exam

Function of the Test

An Association of Social Work Boards (ASWB) Master's exam is used for licensure as a master social worker, or the equivalent, in all fifty U.S. states as well as the District of Columbia, the U.S. Virgin Islands, Alberta, and British Columbia. The Master's exam is typically taken by a new graduate of a master's degree program in social work as part of the licensing process, but can also be taken by someone already in the field with an eye toward a new or upgraded license.

In 2016, 15,442 people took the ASWB Master's exam, and 81.2 percent of those test takers passed. The passing score is determined nationally, and not on a state-by-state or board-by-board basis.

Test Administration

ASWB exams are given by computer. They are not administered on any particular fixed dates. Instead, tests are given by appointment at Pearson Professional Centers worldwide. Students must first register for the test, then visit Pearson VUE's website to schedule an exam sitting.

Candidates with disabilities can receive appropriate accommodations while taking the ASWB Master's exam by applying for accommodations through the ASWB website. Candidates whose first language is not English can also seek arrangements for alternate language exams in most jurisdictions.

Candidates must wait 90 days before retaking the exam, although exceptions can be made when there is a serious, documented malfunction with the initial attempt, or if employment is at stake and the initial score was within five correct answers of passing.

Test Format

Each examination lasts four hours and contains 170 four-option, multiple-choice questions in four categories of practice. 150 of the 170 items are scored, while the remainder is used for test validation purposes. Candidates have four hours to complete the electronically administered test.

The four categories of practice for the Master's exam are as follows: Human Development, Diversity, and Behavior in the Environment; Assessment and Intervention Planning; Interventions with Clients/Client Systems; and Professional Relationships, Values, and Ethics. Each section comprises roughly one quarter of the exam. Details are contained in the Knowledge, Skills, and Abilities statement (KSA) published by ASWB.

Here's a table of the sections:

Category	Subcategories	% of Exam
Human Development, Diversity, and Behavior in the Environment	Human Growth and Development	27%
	Concepts of Abuse and Neglect	
	Diversity, Social/Economic Justice, and Oppression	
Assessment and Intervention Planning	Biopsychosocial History and Collateral Data	24%
	Assessment Methods and Techniques	
	Intervention Planning	
Interventions with Clients/Client Systems	Intervention Processes and Techniques for Use Across Systems	24%
	Intervention Processes and Techniques for Use with Larger Systems	
Professional Relationships, Values, and Ethics	Professional Values and Ethical Issues	25%
	Confidentiality	
	Professional Development and Use of Self	

Scoring

Like all ASWB exams, the Master's exam is scored pass/fail, with a certain number of correct answers required in order to pass. The pass point varies from exam to exam based on the difficulty of a given test, but it generally ranges somewhere between 93 and 107 correct answers out of 150 scored questions. There is no penalty for guessing, as the total number of correct answers is the only factor in a test taker's raw score.

Although different states and jurisdictions have different numbers in their rules as a required passing score, the performance required to pass the exam is actually no higher or lower in any one state than in any other. Instead, the score reported by ASWB to each state is scaled to that state's required score. In other words, a test taker who gets exactly the score needed to pass nationally would have that score

9

reported as a 70 in a state that requires a 70 to pass, and reported as a 75 in a state that requires a 75 to pass.

Recent/Future Developments

The content of the ASWB exams is constantly being updated to incorporate new information from the field of social work, such as changes in the new *DSM-5-TR*. However, no other structural or testing procedure changes have been announced for the immediate future.

Study Prep Plan for the ASWB Masters Exam

1 **Schedule -** Use one of our study schedules below or come up with one of your own.

2 **Relax -** Test anxiety can hurt even the best students. There are many ways to reduce stress. Find the one that works best for you.

3 **Execute -** Once you have a good plan in place, be sure to stick to it.

One Week Study Schedule		
Day 1	Human Development, Diversity...	
Day 2	Assessment and Intervention Planning	
Day 3	Interventions with Clients/Client Systems	
Day 4	Professional Relationships, Values, and Ethics	
Day 5	Practice Tests #1 & #2	
Day 6	Practice Test #3	
Day 7	Take Your Exam!	

Two Week Study Schedule			
Day 1	Human Development...	Day 8	Practice Test #1
Day 2	Parenting Skills and Capacities	Day 9	Answer Explanations
Day 3	Concepts of Abuse and Neglect	Day 10	Practice Test #2
Day 4	Assessment and Intervention Planning	Day 11	Answer Explanations
Day 5	Interventions with Clients/Client Systems	Day 12	Practice Test #3
Day 6	Intervention Processes and Techniques for...	Day 13	Answer Explanations
Day 7	Professional Relationships, Values...	Day 14	Take Your Exam!

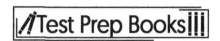

One Month Study Schedule						
Day 1	Human Development, Diversity and Behavior in the Environment	Day 11	Assessment Methods and Techniques	Day 21	Self-Disclosure Principles and Applications
Day 2	Normal and Abnormal Physical, Cognitive...	Day 12	Diagnostic and Statistical Manual of...	Day 22	Professional Development and Use of Self
Day 3	Physical, Mental, and Cognitive Disabilities...	Day 13	Practice Questions	Day 23	Practice Questions
Day 4	Parenting Skills and Capacities	Day 14	Interventions with Clients/Client Systems	Day 24	Practice Test #1
Day 5	Systems and Ecological Perspectives and...	Day 15	Methods of Conflict Resolution	Day 25	Answer Explanations
Day 6	Theories of Trauma-Informed Care	Day 16	Case Management	Day 26	Practice Test #2
Day 7	Concepts of Abuse and Neglect	Day 17	Intervention Processes and Techniques for Use with Larger Systems	Day 27	Answer Explanations
Day 8	Practice Questions	Day 18	Governance Structures	Day 28	Practice Test #3
Day 9	Assessment and Intervention Planning	Day 19	Practice Questions	Day 29	Answer Explanations
Day 10	Information Available from Other Sources	Day 20	Professional Relationships, Values...	Day 30	Take Your Exam!

Build your own prep plan by visiting:

testprepbooks.com/prep

12

Human Development, Diversity and Behavior in the Environment

Human Growth and Development

Human Development Throughout the Lifespan

There are a number of theories on human growth and development. The most important theories are addressed in this section.

Freud's Model of Development

Freud is known for his research on stages of human development and his assertion that there were five stages of psychosexual development:

- Oral Stage (birth to 18 months)
    - An infant's focus of gratification involves the mouth.
    - The primary need is security.
    - Security needs are met when caretakers provide baby with essentials, such as food, shelter, warmth, and cleanliness.
- Anal Stage (18 months to age 3)
    - A child's focus of gratification involves the anus and the bladder.
    - These organs represent sensual satisfaction.
    - Internal conflict arises when the child begins the process of toilet training.
- Phallic Stage (age 3 to age 6)
    - The child engages in exploration of their body with greater interest in genitals.
    - Oedipus and Electra complexes may occur.
    - There is a pseudo-sexual attraction to the parent of the opposite gender.
    - Conflict arises when the child realizes he/she has failed to win control over the parents' bond with one another.
- Latent Stage (age 6 to puberty)
    - The child's sexual interests become subdued or dormant.
    - Energy is focused on school, hobbies, athletics, and mastering social skills.
- Genital stage (puberty until death)
    - The teen becomes aware of physical changes and onset of sexual feelings.
    - The individual is less egocentric and more compassionate.
    - There's a motivation to seek relationships that are emotionally and sexually satisfying.
    - Success in this stage lays groundwork for future relationships that are healthy and long lasting.

13

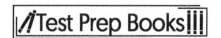

Erikson's Model of Development

Erikson devised eight stages of psychosocial development. He emphasized the importance of social context, asserting that family and environment are major contributors to child development:

- Trust vs. Mistrust (birth to 18 months)
  - The primary goal is to learn to trust others.
  - Trust occurs when a caretaker appropriately responds to a need in a timely, caring manner.
  - Mistrust occurs when caretakers fail to meet the infant's basic needs.
- Autonomy vs. Shame and Doubt (18 months to age 3)
  - The primary goal is the development of self-control without loss of self-esteem.
  - The toddler develops cooperation and self-expression skills.
  - Failure to reach this goal leads to defiance, anger, and social problems.
- Initiative vs. Guilt (age 3 to age 6)
  - Initiative means confidently devising a plan and following it through to completion.
  - Guilt is generated by fear that actions taken will result in disapproval.
  - Failure to achieve initiative can lead to anxiety and fearfulness in new situations.
- Industry vs. Inferiority (age 6 to age 11)
  - Industry refers to purposeful, meaningful behavior.
  - Inferiority refers to having a sense of unworthiness or uselessness.
  - The child focuses on learning skills, such as making friends and self-care activities—e.g., dressing or bathing.
  - Failure in this stage could lead to negative social or academic performance and the lack of self-confidence.
- Identity vs. Role Confusion (age 12 to age 18)
  - This stage involves the desire to fit in and to figure out one's own unique identity.
  - Self-assessment of sexual identity, talents, and vocational direction occurs.
  - Role confusion is the result of juggling multiple physical changes, increased responsibility, academic demands, and a need to understand how one fits into the greater picture.
- Intimacy vs. Isolation (age 18 to age 40)
  - This stage pertains to an ability to take risks by entering the workforce, finding a long term relation, and possibly becoming a parent.
  - Failure to navigate this stage leads to isolation, loneliness, and depression.
- Generativity vs. Stagnation (age 40 to age 60)
  - This stage involves developing stability in areas of finance, career, and relationships, as well as a sense that one is contributing something valuable to society.
  - Failure to achieve these objectives leads to unhappiness with one's status and feeling unimportant.
- Ego integrity vs. Despair (mid-sixties to death)
  - Important life tasks, such as child rearing and career, are being completed.
  - Reviewing and evaluating how one's life was spent occurs.
  - Success in this stage provides a sense of fulfillment.
  - Failure emerges if one is dissatisfied with accomplishments, which leads to depression or despair.

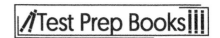

Erikson's Psychosocial Stages of Development

Stage	Age	Psychosocial Crisis	Basic Virtue
1	Infancy (0 to 1½)	Trust vs. mistrust	Hope
2	Early Childhood (1½ to 3)	Autonomy vs. shame	Will
3	Play Age (3 to 5)	Initiative vs. guilt	Purpose
4	School Age (5 to 12)	Industry vs. inferiority	Competency
5	Adolescence (12 to 18)	Ego identity vs. role confusion	Fidelity
6	Young Adult (18 to 40)	Intimacy vs. isolation	Love
7	Adulthood (40 to 65)	Generativity vs. stagnation	Care
8	Maturity (65+)	Ego integrity vs. despair	Wisdom

Piaget's Model of Development

Piaget is best known for his concept that children's minds are not just smaller versions of adult minds, but that they also grow and develop in different ways. His work has been influential within academic settings and has helped educators better determine what and how children can learn at various stages of their educational process. The following are the key ideas related to his research into the way cognition develops in children:

- **Assimilation**: A process by which a person accepts and organizes information then incorporates new material into existing knowledge
- **Accommodation**: A process by which old ideas must be changed or replaced due to obtaining new information from the environment
- **Schemas**: A set of thoughts, ideas, or perceptions that fit together and are constantly challenged by gaining new information and creating change through knowledge

Piaget also recognized and defined the following *four stages of cognitive development*:

- Stage 1: Sensorimotor Stage (birth to age 2)
    - The infant becomes aware of being an entity separate from the environment.
    - Object permanence occurs as the baby realizes that people or objects still exist, even if they are out of sight.
    - Object permanence builds a sense of security as the baby learns that though mommy has left the room, she will still return.
    - This reduces fear of abandonment and increases their confidence about the environment.

15

- Stage 2: Pre-operational Stage (age 2 to age 7)
  - The child moves from being barely verbal to using language to describe people, places, and things.
  - The child remains egocentric and unable to clearly understand the viewpoint of others.
  - The process of quantifying and qualifying emerges, and the child can sort, categorize, and analyze in a rough, unpolished form.

SENSORIMOTOR STAGE

•constantly learning about their environment via their senses

0-2

PREOPERATIONAL STAGE

•can use symbols

•egocentric

•has trouble using logic & understanding differing viewpoints

2-6 or 7

CONCRETE OPERATIONAL STAGE

•can understand differing viewpoints & use logic
•has trouble dealing in the abstract

7-11 or 12

FORMAL OPERATIONAL STAGE

•can think in the abstract   •can solve problems systematically

12 - Adulthood

- Stage 3: Concrete Operational Stage (age 7 to age 11)
  - The ability to problem solve and reach logical conclusions evolves.
  - By age 10 or 11, children begin to doubt magical stories, such as the Tooth Fairy or the Easter Bunny.
  - Previously-held beliefs are questioned.
- Stage 4: Formal Operational Stage (age 12 through remaining lifetime)
  - More complex processes can now be assimilated.
  - Egocentrism diminishes.
  - One assimilates and accommodates beliefs that others have needs and feelings too.
  - New schemas are created.
  - The individual seeks their niche in life in terms of talents, goals, and preferences.

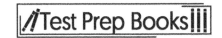

Ivan Pavlov (Classical Conditioning)

Another important concept of development has to do with learning and the way in which humans learn new behaviors. A famous psychologist, **Ivan Pavlov**, conducted research with dogs that proved to be ground-breaking in the field of classical conditioning. In his experiment, a ringing bell was paired with the presentation of food, which produced salivation in the dog. The ringing sound eventually produced salivation from the dog even in the absence of food. Salivation then became the conditioned response to hearing a bell, and thus, the theory of classical conditioning was developed. The important finding of this research is that we learn by association.

B.F. Skinner (Operant Conditioning)

Skinner also did important research in the field of learning, specifically operant conditioning. **Operant conditioning theory** focuses on behavioral changes that can be seen or measured. The basic concept is that behavior that is reinforced will increase and behavior that is punished will decrease. There are several key concepts integral to an understanding of this form of learning:

- **Positive Reinforcement**: Anything that serves as a form of reward, including food, money, praise, or attention

- **Negative reinforcement**: An unpleasant stimulus that is removed when behavior is elicited, such as a man finally cutting the grass to stop his wife from nagging him about it

- **Punishment**: An unpleasant response from the environment—e.g., a slap, an unkind word, or a speeding ticket—that when encountered, increases the likelihood that a behavior will cease. Two problems arise with using punishment. Once the negative stimulus is removed, the behavior is likely to continue. Punishment can also cause humiliation, anger, resentment, and aggression.

- **Superstition**: An incorrect perception that one stimulus is connected to another. Skinner found that when teaching a rat to press a lever for food, if the rat chases its tail before pressing the lever, it will mistakenly believe that the tail chase is required and will do both behaviors each time it wants food.

- **Shaping**: The process of changing behavior gradually by rewarding approximations of the desired behavior, e.g., first rewarding a rat for moving closer to the lever

Skinner found that there are different **schedules of reinforcement** and that some work better than others. These include the following:

- **Continuous rate**: Person or animal is rewarded every time a behavior is demonstrated

- **Fixed ratio**: Reward is given after a fixed number of attempts

- **Variable ratio**: Reward is forthcoming at unpredictable rates, like a slot machine

- **Fixed interval**: Reward is given only after a specific amount of time has passed

- **Variable interval**: Reward is given after an unpredictable amount of time has passed

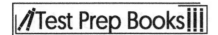

- **Extinction**: Occurs when a behavior disappears or is extinguished because it is no longer being reinforced. To stop tantrum behavior in toddlers, ignoring the behavior will decrease or stop the tantrum if the desired reward is parental attention or parental aggravation.

Seasons of Life Theory (Levinson)

This theory of adult development is classified by development stages, with each stage defined by different, yet meaningful and developmentally necessary, tasks. There are transition periods where stages overlap.

The **pre-adulthood stage** ends at age twenty-two. Beginning at birth, this is the stage when a person develops and prepares for adulthood. It is a time of major growth and transition as the individual develops a state of independence.

The **early adulthood transition** occurs roughly from the age of seventeen to the age of twenty-two. Pre-adulthood is ending and early adulthood is beginning, but the time of transition is actually part of both periods. Physical development is completed, but this time of transition can be compared to the infancy of a new period of development. During this stage, adolescence ends and the individual begins to make decisions about adult life. He or she further develops independence and separates from the family of origin.

Early adulthood stage is roughly age seventeen to forty-five. This stage begins with the early adult transition. From a biological perspective, an individual's twenties and thirties are at the peak of the life cycle. This stage can be the time during which individuals have their greatest energy but are also experiencing the greatest amount of stress as they try to establish families and careers simultaneously.

Midlife transition is roughly age forty to forty-five. This is a time of transition that bridges the end of early adulthood and the beginning of middle adulthood. At this time of life, people tend to become more reflective and compassionate and less concerned with external demands. Values may change, and it is possibly a time where crisis is experienced due to limited time to reach goals. Individuals become aware of death and leaving a legacy.

Middle adulthood stage is roughly age forty to sixty-five. There is a diminishment of biological capacities, but only minimally. Most individuals are able to continue to lead fulfilling and relatively energetic lives. Many take on a mentoring role and responsibility for the further development of young adults. Choices must be made about livelihood and retirement.

Late adulthood is at roughly age sixty. A transition period occurs from around sixty to sixty-five. Late adulthood is a time of reflection on other stages and on accomplishments. During this stage, retirement takes place and the individual gives up their role in the workplace. Crisis occurs at this stage due to declining power and less accolades of work performed.

Social Clock Theory (Bernice Neugarten)

Neugarten proposed that every society has a **social clock**: an understood expectation for when certain life events should happen (e.g., getting married, buying a home, having children). When individuals do not adhere to this timeframe, they often experience stress, the sense of disappointing others, or the experience of an internal "clock ticking" and reminding them that time is running out.

Normal and Abnormal Physical, Cognitive, Emotional, and Sexual Development Throughout the Lifespan

Typical and Atypical Physical Growth and Development

It is important to understand normal developmental milestones. Not all children progress at the same rate, but there are some guidelines that help determine whether the child has any developmental delays that might prevent them from reaching goals by a certain age.

Infancy Through Age Five

During the first year of life, abundant changes occur. The child learns basic, but important, skills. The child is learning to manipulate objects, hold their head without support, crawl, and pull up into a standing position. The toddler should be able to walk without assistance by eighteen months. By age two, the child should be running and able to climb steps one stair at a time. By age three, the child should be curious and full of questions about how the world works or why people behave in certain ways. The child should have the balance and coordination to climb stairs using only one foot per stair. By age four, the child is increasingly independent, demonstrating skills like attending to toilet needs and dressing with some adult assistance.

School Age to Adolescence

By age five, speech is becoming more fluent, and the ability to draw simple figures improves. Dressing without help is achieved. By age six, speech should be fluent and motor skills are strengthened. The youth is now able to navigate playground equipment and kick or throw a ball. Social skills, such as teamwork or friendship development, are evolving. The child must learn to deal with failure or frustration and find ways to be accepted by peers. They become more proficient in reading, math, and writing skills. Towards the end of this phase, around age twelve, secondary sexual characteristics, such as darker body hair or breast development, may occur.

Adolescence

This is a period of extraordinary change. The process of *individuation* is occurring. The teen views themself as someone who will someday live independently of parents. More time is spent with peers and less with family. Identity formation arises, and the teen experiments with different kinds of clothing, music, and hairstyles to see what feels comfortable and what supports their view of the world. Sexuality is explored, and determinations are being made about sexual preferences and orientation. Sexual experimentation is common, and some teens actually form long-term intimate relationships, although others are satisfied to make shorter-term intimate connections. There is often a period of experimentation with drugs or alcohol. As the thinking process matures, there may be a questioning of rules and expectations of those in authority. Moodiness is common, and troubled teens are likely to "act out" their emotions, sometimes in harmful ways.

Typical and Atypical Cognitive Growth and Development

Cognitive development refers to the development of a child's capacity for perception, thought, learning, information processing, and other mental processes. The *nature vs. nurture* debate questions whether cognitive development is primarily influenced by genetics or upbringing. Evidence indicates that the interaction between nature and nurture determines the path of development.

Some commonly recognized milestones in early cognitive development:

- One to three months: focuses on faces and moving objects, differentiates between different types of tastes, sees all colors in the spectrum

- Three to six months: recognizes familiar faces and sounds, imitates expressions

- Six to twelve months: begins to determine how far away something is, understands that things still exist when they are not seen (object permanence)

- One to two years: recognizes similar objects, understands and responds to some words

- Two to three years: sorts objects into appropriate categories, responds to directions, names objects

- Three to four years: Demonstrates increased attention span of five to fifteen minutes, shows curiosity and seeks answers to questions, organizes objects by characteristics

- Four to five years: Draws human shapes, counts to five or higher, uses rhyming words

The **zone of proximal development** is the range of tasks that a child can carry out with assistance, but not independently. Parents and educators can advance a child's learning by providing opportunities within the zone of proximal development, allowing the child to develop the ability to accomplish those actions gradually without assistance.

Typical and Atypical Social Growth, Development, and the Socialization Process

Social development refers to the development of the skills that allow individuals to have effective interpersonal relationships and to contribute in a positive manner to the world around them.

Social learning is taught directly by caregivers and educators, but it is also learned indirectly by the experience of various social relationships.

Social development is commonly influenced by extended family, communities, religious institutions, schools, and sports teams or social groups. Positive social development is supported when caregivers do the following:

- Attune to a child's needs and feelings

- Demonstrate respect for others

- Teach children how to handle conflict and solve problems encountered during social experiences

- Help children learn to take the perspective of another person and develop empathy

- Encourage discussion of morals and values and listen to the child's opinions on those topics

- Explain rules and encourage fair treatment of others

- Encourage cooperation, rather than competition

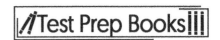
Social development begins from birth as a child learns to attach to their mother and other caregivers. During adolescence, social development focuses on peer relationships and self-identity. In adulthood, social relationships are also important, but the goal is to establish secure and long-term relationships with family and friends.

Social institutions, such as family, church, and school, which assist people in realizing their full potential, also contribute to social development. **Lev Vygotsky** was a pioneer in this field with his concept of cultural mediation. This theory emphasizes that one's feelings, thoughts, and behaviors are significantly influenced by others in their environment.

Typical and Atypical Emotional Growth and Development

Emotional development encompasses the development of the following abilities:

- Identifying and understanding the feelings that one experiences
- Identifying and understanding the feelings of others
- Emotional and behavioral regulation
- Empathy
- Establishing relationships with others

Caregivers who are nurturing and responsive enable children to learn to regulate emotions and feel safe in the environment around them.

- By age two to three months, infants express delight and distress, begin smiling, and may be able to be soothed by rocking.

- By three to four months, infants communicate via crying and begin to express interest and surprise.

- Between four to nine months, infants respond differently to strangers in comparison to known individuals, solicit attention, show a particular attachment for a primary caregiver, and have an expanded range of expressed emotions that include anger, fear, and shyness.

- At ten to twelve months, babies show an increase in exploration and curiosity, demonstrate affection, and display a sense of humor.

- Children at age twelve to twenty-four months often demonstrate anger via aggression, laugh in social situations, recognize themselves in a mirror, engage in symbolic play, and have a complete range of emotional expression.

- Around age two, children begin using different facial expressions to show their emotions, begin to play cooperatively, and may transition from being calm and affectionate to temperamental and easily frustrated.

- At age three, children engage in more social and imaginative play, show interest in the feelings of others, begin to learn to manage frustration, and are often inconsistent and stubborn.

- Children at age four show improved cooperation, express sympathy, and may exhibit lying and/or guilty behavior.

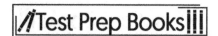

- At age five, children can play rule-based games, often want to do what is expected of them, express emotion easily, and choose friends for themselves.

- Children at age six typically describe themselves in terms of their external attributes, have a difficult time coping with challenges and criticism, prefer routines, and show inconsistent self-control.

- Around age seven, children can typically describe causes and outcomes of emotions and show better regulation of emotions in most situations.

- From ages eight to ten, children have an increased need for independence, want to be viewed as intelligent, experience and better understand emotional subtleties, and may be defiant.

- During adolescence, children begin to master emotional skills to manage stress, increase self-awareness, develop identity, show increased ability for empathy, and learn to manage conflict.

Normal versus abnormal behavior is difficult to distinguish because each person is unique, so creating a standard of normal can be challenging. Though labeling behaviors as normal or abnormal can be problematic, it is important to have some standard by which it is possible to identify those behaviors that are indicative of an underlying psychological condition. Notwithstanding the challenges, it is possible and helpful to have general definitions of normal and abnormal behavior.

Normal behaviors are those that are common to the majority of the population, as related to emotional functioning, social interactions, and mental capacity. **Abnormal behavior** is generally considered that which is maladaptive, dysfunctional, and disruptive to life. These behaviors may be an exaggeration of a normal behavior or even an absence of a typical response. They do not conform to the accepted patterns or common behaviors of society. Sadness over the death of a loved one is considered normal, but disabling depression that interferes with school and work responsibilities is not. The **DSM-5-TR** is the current standard for determining the diagnostic criteria that distinguishes abnormal behavior from normal.

Typical and Atypical Sexual Growth and Development

While not everyone develops sexually on exactly the same timeline, there are certain expectations that define healthy and unhealthy sexual development. These expectations differ based on age. During the early stage of life, from birth until age two, the child is focused on developing a relationship of trust with caregivers. Eventually, children become aware of their genitals and explore these through self-touch. By ages two to five, they begin to develop the ability to name and describe genitalia. They understand that male and female bodies are different. They have little inhibition about nudity.

As children enter middle childhood (ages six to eight or nine), they begin to understand the concept of puberty and what to expect about future body changes. They have a more sophisticated knowledge of reproduction, and may become more inhibited about nudity.

By the age of nine or ten, some children show signs of puberty, although the typical age of onset is eleven for girls and thirteen for boys. During puberty, there is a dramatic development in both primary and secondary sex characteristics. Children at this age show an increased interest in sex and may have questions about sexual orientation, sexual practices, or how the opposite sex behaves. By age twelve or

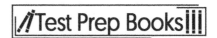

thirteen, they begin to understand the consequences of sexual behavior, such as pregnancy or STDs. As they enter later adolescence, they may form longer relationships with their love interests, but many prefer casual dating. They are beginning to form an identity in terms of sexual orientation, preferences, and values.

It is important to understand red flags that may be signs of unhealthy sexual development. These may be brought on by abuse or by exposure to sexually explicit scenes. Children who are preoccupied with sexuality at an early age and whose behaviors differ from peers their own age may be at risk. Other indicators include attempting adult-like sexual interactions. These behaviors may include oral to genital contact or some form of penetration of another person's body.

These issues should raise concerns:

- A child overly preoccupied with sexual thoughts, language, or behaviors, rather than in more age-appropriate play

- A child engaging in sex play with children who are much older or much younger

- A child using sexual behavior to harm others

- A child involved in sexual play with animals

- A child using explicit sexual language that is not age appropriate

A **sexually-reactive child** refers to one who is exposed to sexual stimuli prior to being sexually mature enough to understand the implications. The child becomes overly preoccupied with sexual matters and often acts out what they witnessed or experienced.

Sexual Development Throughout the Lifespan

Sigmund Freud's Psychosexual Stages of Development

Sigmund Freud was an Austrian neurologist who is considered the father of psychoanalysis. Freud developed important concepts in Western psychology such as the id, ego, and superego. He wrote literature focusing on what he called the unconscious and the repression and expression that stems from it.

Freud also focused on human development, especially relating to sexuality. Freud theorized that each stage of human development is characterized by a sexual focus on a different bodily area (*erogenous zone*), which can serve as a source of either pleasure or frustration. He believed that *libido* (psychosexual energy) is the determinant of behavior during each of five fixed stages, and that if a developing child experiences frustration during one of these stages, a resulting fixation (or lingering focus) on that stage will occur.

Freud's five stages of psychosexual development are as follows:

- **Oral Stage** (Birth to Eighteen Months): The infant satisfies its libido by feeding and by exploring the environment, primarily by putting objects in its mouth. The id dominates the oral stage of development, and every action an infant undertakes is guided by the pleasure principle. The key task of this phase is weaning from the breast, which also results in the infant's first experience of loss. Too much or too little focus on oral gratification at this stage was theorized to lead to an oral fixation and an immature personality. Examples of an oral fixation were believed to be excessive eating, drinking, or smoking.

- **Anal Stage** (Eighteen Months to Three Years): The key task of this stage is toilet training, which causes a conflict between the id (which wants immediate gratification of the urge to eliminate waste) and the ego (which requires delay of gratification necessary to use the toilet). A positive experience with toilet training was believed to lead to a sense of competence that continues into adulthood. Anal-retentive personality results from overly-strict toilet training, characterized by rigid and obsessive thinking. Likewise, anal-expulsive personality results from a lax approach to toilet training, characterized by disorganization and messiness.

- **Phallic Stage** (Three to Six Years): The libidinal focus during this stage is on the genital area, and it is during this stage that children learn to differentiate between males and females. The **Oedipus Complex** develops during this stage; Freud believed that a young boy views his father as a rival for his mother's attention and wants to eliminate his father in order to take his place. Similar to the Oedipus Complex, the **Electra Complex** says that a young girl may view her mother as her rival. Freud also believed that girls experience penis envy. The key task of this stage is identification with the same-sex parent.

- **Latency** (Six years to Puberty): During this period, libidinal energy is still present, but the child is able to direct that energy toward school, friendships, and activities.

- **Genital Stage** (Puberty to Adulthood): The libidinal focus is once again on the genital area (as it is during the phallic stage), but at this point, the psyche is more developed. During the genital stage, an individual achieves sexual maturation, becomes independent of their parents, resolves any remaining conflict from the earlier stages, and is able to function as a responsible adult in terms of both work and relationships.

To understand Freud's developmental stages fully, one must also understand his conceptualization of the human personality.

Freud describes three levels of the mind as follows:

- **Consciousness**: the part of the mind that holds accessible and current thoughts

- **Pre-consciousness**: the area that holds thoughts that can be accessed by memory

- **Unconscious**: where the mind motivates behavior and contains thoughts, feelings, and impulses that are not easily accessible

Freud believed that the personality, or psyche, consists of three parts called the Psychic Apparatus, each of which develops at a different time:

- Id: The **id** is the most basic and primitive part of the human psyche, based on instincts and all of the biological aspects of a person's being. An infant's personality consists only of the id, as the other aspects have not yet developed. The id is entirely unconscious and operates on the pleasure principle, seeking immediate gratification of every urge. It has two instincts:

a death instinct called **thanatos** and a survival instinct called **eros**. The energy from eros is called the **libido**.

- Ego: The **ego** is the second personality component that begins to develop over the first few years of life. The ego is responsible for meeting the needs of the id in a socially acceptable, realistic manner. Unlike the id, the ego operates on the reality principle, which allows it to consider pros and cons, to have awareness that other people have feelings, and to delay gratification when necessary.

- Superego: The **superego** is the final personality component, developed by about age five. The superego is essentially a person's internal moral system or sense of right and wrong. The superego suppresses the instincts and urges of the id, but also attempts to convince the ego to act idealistically, rather than realistically.

In a healthy personality, there is balance between the three personality components. The individual has **ego strength**—the ability to function well in the world despite the conflicting pressures that the id and superego place upon the ego.

Spiritual Development Throughout the Lifespan

Spiritual development refers to the way a person grows and changes spiritually, particularly regarding the purpose for their existence, over the course of their life. This process may have conscious or unconscious origins, and it may be affected by other growth and development factors. Spiritual development is often linked to the stages of cognitive development, but evidence-based research pertaining strictly to spiritual development is limited. Theories often focus on the influence of psychosocial constructs (such as morality), cognitive beliefs, and religious or faith-based influences.

Jean Piaget (1896–1980) is renowned for his work in the field of cognitive development. He examined social, biological, and psychological constructs that influence cognitive development and intellect. He theorized four stages of cognitive development, from birth through adulthood. He believed that a multitude of constructs influences a person's moral beliefs and values, and this leads to their ultimate perspective on themselves and the environment.

Lawrence Kohlberg (1927–1987) studied moral psychology and development, and he developed a theory of the stages of moral reasoning. He theorized that individuals model behavior and behavior patterns around them to develop concepts of right and wrong as they progress through life. The more aware a person becomes of the effects of their thoughts, actions, and decisions, the more capacity they have for moral decision-making. This may be connected to shaping an individual's spiritual beliefs.

James Fowler (1940–2015), a theologian and university professor, contributed his "stages of faith" development, which breaks spiritual evolution down into six stages. He believed in the importance of safety and nurturing in the early years, which leads individuals to feel they are in touch with a greater good. Comparatively, individuals who feel unsafe or do not feel nurtured in their younger years are less likely to focus on spiritual aspects of life. Fowler made connections between his stages of faith and the developmental stages of Piaget and Kohlberg.

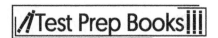

Racial, Ethnic, and Cultural Development Throughout the Lifespan

Racial, ethnic, and cultural identities are developed over the course of a lifespan and influenced by a number of factors. Atkinson, Morten, and Sue's racial and cultural identity development model is accepted as one of the fundamental theories of racial and cultural development. This theory states that most individuals try to conform to the primary culture with which they're surrounded or which they believe is considered superior by peers. However, as the individual develops, they begin to seek out and reflect upon any underlying differences. Ideally, the developed individual ultimately becomes comfortable identifying in the way that feels best to him or her while respecting others' differences. Theorists have also focused on how specific minority groups develop racial, ethnic, and cultural identities.

For example, **Jean Kim's theory of Asian racial identity development** focuses on Eastern populations. Minorities from Asian countries such as India, China, or Japan who grow up in the United States may act in traditional ways at home with their family unit, but they may struggle immensely to identify and assimilate with peers at school. This may be due to the fact that Asian culture is largely rooted in a collective, community identity (as opposed to the more individualistic Western culture). Additionally, Eastern and Western languages, traditions, and foods are different. While younger individuals may try to assimilate, older Asian individuals may tend to group together as they age. **Bernardo Ferdman and Placida Gallegos's model of Latino identity development** states that for Latino groups, ethnicity plays a larger role than race in self-identification. Finally, a number of researchers have theorized constructs and influences of white and black racial identity and culture. Often, these two racial identities are interrelated. Researchers have focused on how the two races co-exist, based on historical interactions and contemporary narratives.

Physical, Mental, and Cognitive Disabilities Throughout the Lifespan

Approximately 7 percent of U.S. children have some type of disability. The most common physical disabilities that impact development are cerebral palsy, hearing issues, and visual issues. Learning disabilities are also common—these could be Down's syndrome or other developmental delays. Common psychiatric disabilities are ADHD and autism spectrum disorders. Others include mood disorders, oppositional disorders, anxiety disorders, and, in rare cases, schizophrenia. The impact upon the child and family corresponds to the family's ability to adapt to the condition and their ability to connect to community resources.

How the individual develops and copes with the disability depends greatly upon the social context and the child's own personal attributes. Raising a disabled child puts tremendous stress on parents and siblings. There are issues of stigma, financial burden, missed days of work for parents, and the time and energy needed to seek useful resources. Siblings may be called upon to take roles of parenting to help out. These siblings may be bullied by peers who make fun of their disabled family member. They may feel neglected by their parents. Additionally, there may be a need for special housing and special schools. Low-income families may face barriers to accessing services such as transportation, medical specialists, or assistance with childcare.

The impact of disabilities on development depends largely on (1) the extent of the disability and (2) whether that disability is experienced across the lifespan or for a limited amount of time. Positive coping skills and sufficient social support may lessen the impact of a disability. Although the tendency is to

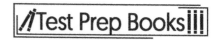

focus on negative impact, disabilities may also leave a positive impact in terms of the strengthening of relationships or the development of skills that an individual may not have otherwise acquired.

Interplay of Biological, Psychological, Social, and Spiritual Factors

The interplay of an individual's biological, psychological, social, and spiritual factors is an indicator of overall health and happiness. If one or more of these factors are imbalanced, the individual is unlikely to feel as though they are at their highest level of well-being or personal fulfillment (even if a clinically diagnosed disease is not present). This framework is often utilized in social-work settings where mental or emotional health appears to be compromised. Practitioners address the issue in the client's life by examining their physical and physiological health, medical history, personal history, moods, reactions to events, environment, family life, home life, cultural beliefs, personal relationships, faith or belief system, spirituality, personal desires, and other factors to provide holistic drivers for any necessary interventions.

A number of these factors strongly influence each other. For example, a client who feels tremendous stress daily at work may find themselves constantly falling sick with colds, as stress negatively affects the immune system's ability to perform. Clients with clinically diagnosed mood disorders may have a more difficult time coping with major stressors, such as a divorce. Clients who report having some level of faith or spiritual belief system often appear to have higher levels of positivity and healthier coping mechanisms in the face of adverse personal events. As practitioners intervene in such scenarios, they must address not only the individual client, but all the systems in which the client exists and interacts. Practitioners may also need to work with the client's families, in communities, or in other group settings in order to effectively create balance between biological, psychological, social, and spiritual factors.

Basic Human Needs

Abraham Maslow is the most notable researcher in the area of basic human needs. Maslow theorized that human needs could be described in the form of a pyramid, with the base of the pyramid representing the most basic needs and the higher layers representing loftier goals and needs. Unless the basic needs are met, a person cannot move on to higher needs. For example, a homeless woman living under a bridge will need food, shelter, and safety before she can consider dealing with her alcoholism.

The foundational layer in Maslow's hierarchy is physiological needs, and the final layer at the pinnacle of the pyramid is self-transcendence.

Maslow's Hierarchy of Needs

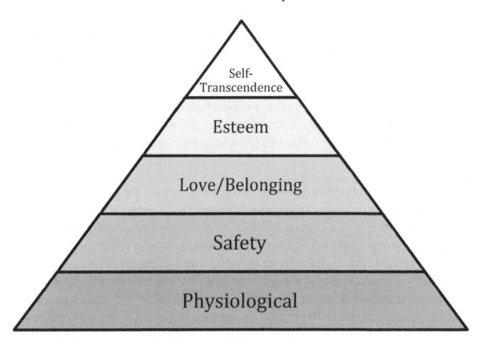

Maslow's Hierarchy of Needs are described in more detail below:

- **Physiological Needs**: These needs, which pertain to what humans need to survive, must be met first. These needs include the basics, such as food, water, clothing, and housing.

- **Safety Needs**: Once primary needs are met, the person may now focus on safety issues. This would include safety from abuse and neglect, natural disaster, or war.

- **Love and Belonging**: Once the first levels of need have been satisfied, people are next driven to find a sense of acceptance and belonging within social groups, such as family, community, or religious organizations. Maslow suggests that humans have a basic need for love, affection, and sexual intimacy. Failure to achieve this level can lead to difficulty in forming and maintaining close relationships with others.

- **Esteem**: The need for esteem is driven by a desire for recognition, respect, and acceptance within a social context.

- **Self-Actualization**: The U.S. Army slogan, "Be All You Can Be," expresses this layer of need. Reaching one's highest potential is the focus. According to Maslow, this cannot be achieved until all the others are mastered.

- **Self-Transcendence**: Devised by Maslow in his later years, he felt self-actualization did not completely satisfy his image of a person reaching their highest potential. To achieve self-

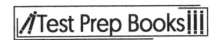

transcendence, one must commit to a goal that is outside of one's self, such as practicing altruism or finding a deeper level of spirituality.

Attachment and Bonding

It has become more important than ever to understand attachment and bonding, especially in relation to changes within the U.S. culture's attitudes about child welfare over the last fifty years. Child Protective Service Teams have become more active in every city. The medical profession, the educational system, and the mental health profession are more informed about children at risk. As a result, more children are being taken from parents, sometimes as early as the day of birth. An older child victim may travel from relative to relative, back to the mother, then into foster or group homes. These children do not have an opportunity to form attachments with their caregivers, nor do caregivers have the opportunity to bond with the children.

Bonding refers to a mother's initial connection to her baby. This generally occurs within the first hours or days of the birth. Mothers who are able and willing to hold their child close to them shortly after birth generally have more positive relationships with the child. When a mother fails to bond, the child is at greater risk for having behavioral problems.

Attachment, on the other hand, refers to a more gradual development of the baby's relationship with their caretaker. A secure attachment naturally grows out of a positive, loving relationship in which there is soothing physical contact, emotional and physical safety, and responsiveness to the child's needs. The baby who has a secure attachment will venture out from their safe base, but immediately seek their mother when fearful or anxious, having learned that mommy will be there to protect him or her. This type of secure relationship becomes impossible if the child is moved from home to home or has experienced abuse or neglect.

A child whose needs have not been met or who has learned through mistreatment that the world is unfriendly and hostile may develop an avoidant attachment or ambivalent attachment. An **avoidant attachment** is characterized by a detached relationship in which the child does not seek out the caregiver when distressed, but acts independently. A child with **ambivalent attachment** shows inconsistency toward the caregiver; sometimes the child clings to him or her, but at other times, the child resists their comfort. Establishing a secure, positive attachment with a caregiver is crucial to a child's life-long emotional and social success. The development of attachment disorder is often present in foster children or those adopted later in life and can create much frustration and heartache as the more stable parents step in and attempt to bond with them.

Effects of Aging on Biopsychosocial Functioning

Biological Aging
Biological aging is based on physical changes that have an impact on the performance of the body's organs and systems.

Psychological Aging
Psychological aging is based on changes in personality, cognitive ability, adaptive ability, and perception. Basic personality traits appear to be relatively stable through the lifespan, as does an individual's self-image. One aspect that does tend to change, however, is the tendency to become more inwardly focused, which may also result in reduced impulsivity and increased caution.

Studies have shown that a pattern of age-related changes in intelligence can typically be observed after age sixty, although changes vary widely across individuals. Furthermore, the somewhat poorer testing results are reflected in fluid intelligence (i.e., reasoning, problem-solving, and abstract thinking unrelated to experience or learned information), but not in crystallized intelligence (i.e., knowledge based on skills, learning, and experience). Normal age-related changes in memory typically involve acquisition of new information and retrieval of information from memory storage. **Sensory decline** is also a common experience for aging individuals.

Social Aging

Social aging is based on changes in one's relationships with family, friends, acquaintances, systems, and organizations. Most older persons experience a narrowing of their social networks. However, they are more likely to have more positive interactions within those networks, and they are more likely to experience more positive feelings about family members than younger persons do.

Disengagement theory states that it is natural and inevitable for older adults to withdraw from their social systems and to reduce interactions with others. This theory has been highly criticized and is incompatible with other well-known psychosocial aging theories. **Activity theory** proposes that social activity serves as a buffer to aging; successful aging occurs among those who maintain their social connections and activity levels. **Continuity theory** proposes that with age, individuals attempt to maintain activities and relationships that were typical for them as younger adults.

Impact of Aging Parents on Adult Children

There are about 10 million Americans over the age of fifty who are caring for aging parents. In the last fifteen years, thanks to modern medicine, the adult population has begun living longer. As a result, the number of adult children between the ages of fifty and seventy who provide care to aging parents has tripled. This amounts to about 25 percent of adult children who provide either personal or economic assistance.

Research indicates that becoming a personal caregiver to a parent increases the rates of depression, substance use, and heart disease. These adult children sometimes take significant financial blows in the form of lost income, earlier than planned retirement, and reduced pension plans, due to leaving the workforce earlier. At the same time, these adult children are assisting their own children as they move towards independence. Those in the youngest generation may still be in college or in the early stages of starting a career and still look to parents for some financial assistance. From a different perspective, the positives of this situation are that children are able to form deeper bonds with grandparents, and the longevity of life in loved ones can have a very positive impact on all involved.

Gerontology

Gerontology is the study of biological, cognitive, and psychological features of the aging process. It includes the study of the impact of an aging population on social and economic trends. Gerontologists practice in the fields of medicine, psychology, physical and occupational therapy, as well as social work. **Geriatric social work practice** refers to a range of services provided to the population of those over age 60. Geriatric social workers are found in nursing homes, counseling programs, advocacy centers, and other programs serving seniors. Aging adults must deal with the very real issues of palliative care, hospice, and other end of life issues. The job of social workers is to support them through difficult

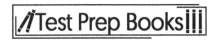

Personality Theories

There are several noted theories as to how personality is formed. In 400 B.C.E., **Hippocrates** attempted to identify personalities based on four temperaments. He called these **humors**, and these were associated with body fluid presence, such as phlegm or bile.

In the 1940s, **William Sheldon** came up with his body type theories that include the **endomorph**, an overweight individual with an easy-going personality; the **mesomorph**, a muscular person with an aggressive personality; and the **ectomorph**, a thin individual with an artistic or intellectual personality.

Gordon Allport developed the trait theory of personality development. He believed that certain personalities were comprised of clusters of traits and that these traits could be categorized into cardinal, central, and secondary traits.

Freud believed the personality was composed of the id, the ego and superego. The **id** refers to a person's unconscious, with its suppressed desires and unresolved conflicts, whereas the **ego** and **superego** are more influenced by the conscious mind. He believed that these three components were often in conflict with one another and that how one resolved these conflicts determined personality. He also stressed the importance of childhood experience in personality development.

Carl Rogers was a proponent of the humanistic theory of personality development. This approach emphasized self-perception and a desire for striving to become the best person one can become. His theory was based on the basic goodness and potential of each person.

The behavioral theories of **B.F. Skinner** and others related to personality development imply that one's persona is developed as a result of classical or operant conditioning. Reinforcement and punishment guide behavioral choices.

Theories of Conflict

Conflict theories center on the premise that all human interactions involve some degree of power struggle, and this struggle may be exacerbated by differences in ideologies, acquisition of resources, culture and class differences, or other variables. Eventually, some groups end up controlling resources and decision-making, therefore limiting opportunities for more submissive or resource-constrained groups. These dynamics eventually shape the culture and interpersonal relationships of a group, whether it is a small team or a country's entire society.

Karl Marx (1818–1883) contributed one of the most widely recognized social conflict theories, **Marxism**, which sees conflict between socio-economic classes as the driver of history. Marx saw capitalist societies as necessarily entangled in conflicts between the working class and the ruling class over resources and opportunities. As privileged groups leave wealth and other resources to their descendants, those descendants have more opportunities, compared to groups who possess lesser quantities and quality of resources. Marx also believed these class conflicts would eventually unseat the ruling class.

Ludwig Gumplowicz (1838–1909) focused on conflicts that arise between different cultures. They arise as one group's desired way of living is threatened by a group with vastly different ideals, especially if

31

one group tries to force its cultural and ethnic norms, beliefs, and systems on another group. These norms may encompass religious views, social views, financial views, family views, and racial views.

C. Wright Mills (1916–1952) developed conflict theories that focus on class structures and political parties. Inspired by Karl Marx, Mills focused his theories on ruling classes in societies and how their behaviors influence the larger group. He states that those in authority shape a society's culture and beliefs; however, the majority of the society does not have the same resources to uphold these behaviors. This is likely to eventually lead to conflict.

Factors Influencing Self-Image

Self-image has to do with how people view themselves. This concept includes **self-esteem**, whether a person has feelings of high or low worth. The concept of self evolves throughout the lifespan, but it always plays a significant role in how a person functions in life.

Impact of Cultural Heritage on Self-Image
Although personal factors play a large role, self-esteem is also based on how closely a person matches the dominant values of their culture. For example, Western society tends to value assertiveness, independence, and individuality. Living up to these values is seen as an important accomplishment, and thus, children receive messages about their personal competence and success based on whether or not they are living up to these ideals.

Children are more likely to develop a positive self-concept when they are able to exhibit behaviors that are valued in their family, home, and culture.

One study suggests that across cultures, self-esteem is based on one's control of life and choices, living up to one's "duties," benefiting others or society, and one's achievements. However, the degree to which one's culture values each of those factors has an impact on how the individual derives their self-esteem.

A widely cited example of the way that a culture can affect a person's self-image is in the portrayal of women's bodies in the media. In the United States, young women are exposed to underweight models and unrealistically drawn cartoon "heroines," which can lead to the development of unachievable expectations and significant negative perceptions about their bodies.

Impact of Race and Ethnicity on Self-Image
Culture, race, and ethnicity can greatly impact one's self-image, whether one is part of a majority population or a minority population. One's ethnic and racial background provides a sense of belonging and identity. Depending on a country's treatment of a particular group, self-image can be negatively impacted through racism and discrimination. Racial jokes and racial slurs are common. Stereotypes abound, and some people judge entire racial groups based on the behavior of a few. Such treatment consistently impacts the self-esteem of minority groups. Non-white Americans who grew up in the fifties or earlier were denied access to restaurants, theaters, high schools, professions, universities, and recreational activities. Even within the last fifty to sixty years, African Americans who had achieved great status in the fields of music, sports, and entertainment were still denied access to certain clubs, hotels, or restaurants.

Every person must explore and come to terms with their own culture, ethnicity, and race. Sometimes, this even means rejecting cultural aspects with which he or she disagrees and embracing new and evolving cultural norms. This is a significant part of self-identity development among teenagers and young adults as they are part of a new generation that may be culturally different from their parents. Those who have more exposure to other cultures and backgrounds will have a more open perspective and are better able to evaluate their own culture and ethnicity objectively.

Effects of Spirituality

Spirituality is sometimes mistaken for religion, but in fact, they are quite different terms. **Religion** is an organized system of beliefs that generally contain a code of conduct and often involve specific devotional or ritual observations. **Spirituality** is more abstract and includes participation in spiritual activities such as meditation, chanting, or prayer. A spiritual person may or may not belong to a religious organization. Spirituality places emphasis on the growth and well-being of the mind, body, and spirit.

Studies have shown that persons who embrace spirituality tend to live both longer and happier lives. Several benefits of being a spiritual person include the following:

- Individuals are encouraged to strive towards being a better person.
- There is an increased likelihood of connections with others.
- It offers hope to the hopeless through strong faith.
- It provides a path to heal from emotional pain.
- It helps reduce anxiety through meditation and other spiritual activities.
- It leads to greater life commitment via the optimism spiritual persons tend to have.

Impact of Age on Self-Image

Aging is an inevitable phase of human development, and the impact is physical, psychological, social, and economic. Self-image is the perception of oneself, but the perception is influenced by societal values. Some cultures revere the elderly and look to them for wisdom and strength. These cultures include the Native Americans, Chinese, Koreans, and Indians. In the United States, there is a different perception of aging. Many elderly Americans feel less valuable or important once they enter retirement. At the same time, they are coping with undesirable body changes and learning to accept that, physically, they can no longer do what they once did. In the U.S., youth and physical attractiveness are highly valued. The elderly are seldom seen as important social figures. They are also less connected with families today, with only 3.7% of homes reporting multigenerational households, per Census Bureau reports. Currently, family support and family contact are less available. However, for some segments of the population, technology has allowed relatives to visit regularly with grandchildren and even participate in family meals or get-togethers.

Self-image throughout the lifespan is explained as follows:

- Infancy: The ego is in charge. The baby thinks primarily of basic needs, such as food or warmth.

- Childhood: In early to middle childhood, children tend to rate themselves higher than peers in terms of talents and intellect. As middle school approaches, there is a decline in self-evaluations. This could be related to feeling unattractive due to physical changes or being teased or bullied by peers in that age group.

- Adolescence: In the early stage of adolescence (ages 9 to 13), another drop in self-esteem occurs. This is thought to be related to the need to let go of childish pleasures, such as a beloved toy or previous interests and step up to the plate of becoming a more responsible person. This can be a painful sacrifice for some youth. The next drop in self-worth occurs at the end of adolescence and beginning of young adulthood (ages 18 to 23). It is during this period that young adults realize that they truly are responsible for their own lives, yet they have not yet achieved a sense of mastery in the academic or vocational world. They are fearful and full of doubt about the ability to be successful as an independent adult.

- Adulthood: Studies indicate a small but steady increase in self-image by mid-twenties. In general, during this period, men tend to have higher self-esteem than women. Persons who live in poor socioeconomic conditions tend to have lower self-esteem than their more financially stable peers. As later adulthood nears (the 70s), women tend to catch up with men in terms of how they evaluate themselves. Women in their eighties tend to have a more positive self-image than male counterparts. As a general rule, for both genders, there is a gradual increase in one's sense of self-worth throughout the life span until late middle age. Research shows that most adults' self-image peaks at around age 60.

Impact of Disability on Self-Image

Disabilities impact self-image regardless of age; however, an individual who is born with a disability tends to fare better than one who acquires one later in life. Responses vary based upon severity of impairments. Some later-life medical conditions cause the individual to give up independence as the person is forced to retire the car keys or move to an institutional setting. Less severe acquired disabilities that still allow the person to maintain much of their previous lifestyle are painful but easier to accept. An individual's personality make-up and resilience to coping with change are also important factors. It is not uncommon for older adults to lapse into depression. This is often generated by a combination of losses. As one enters the later stages of life, loss of friends and family members is common. There may be declines in status, earning capacity, or physical abilities, all of which contribute to depression and negatively impact self-image.

Effects of Trauma on Self-image

Trauma can have a significant impact on self-image as a person's entire identity becomes intertwined with the traumatic event and the subsequent emotions. Some victims of trauma report a sense of isolation from others, feeling that they are not good enough or that they are less competent or less attractive than their peers. This generates feelings of shame and unworthiness, which, in turn, can lead to depression or anxiety. Some trauma survivors—especially victims of child or domestic abuse—feel a deep sense of betrayal and label the world and people as unsafe. They have trouble trusting others, and they may perform poorly in major areas of functioning, such as work or relationships. Some abuse survivors describe themselves as "damaged goods." Some individuals may engage in self-harm behaviors or may feel so depressed that suicide is seen as the only solution. These persons are prone to substance use as a means to numb the emotional pain. Addictive behavior can also negatively impact one's self-esteem. The more resilient will use their painful experiences as a tool for self-growth and may eventually learn to help others who have been through similar experiences.

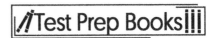

Body Image

Body image refers to the thoughts and feelings about the appearance of one's body as well as thoughts and feelings about how one's body is perceived by others. Body image is shaped by the messages that we receive from the people around us, the culture we live in, and the media.

Persistent negative body image can be associated with these factors:

- Low self-esteem

- Depression and/or anxiety

- Sexual risk-taking

- Impaired relationship satisfaction

- Withdrawal from activities where one's body may be visible to others (e.g., exercise, sexual activity, swimming, seeking medical care)

- Development of eating disorders

Parenting Skills and Capacities

Good parenting practices are essential for raising emotionally healthy children. Child psychologists vary on what types of parenting styles are most effective, but there are four generally recognized styles of parenting:

- **Authoritarian parenting style**: This style of parenting reinforces the role of parent as controller and decision maker. Children are rarely given input into decisions impacting their lives, and the parent takes on a dictatorial role. Children raised by this kind of parent are often obedient and tend to be proficient. The drawback is that they do not rank high on the happiness scale.

- **Authoritative parenting style**: This style of parenting allows for a greater sense of democracy in which children are given some degree of input into issues that impact their lives. There is a healthy balance between firmness and affection. Children raised in this environment tend to be capable, successful, and happy individuals.

- **Permissive parenting style**: This type of parenting allows children to be more expressive and freer with both feelings and actions; they are allowed to behave in whatever manner they please. There are very few rules, and no consequences will be given, even if a rule is violated. These children are more likely to experience problems in school and relationships with others. In the long run, they are often unhappy with their lives.

- **Uninvolved parenting style**: This form of parenting often occurs in dysfunctional families in which parents are emotionally or physically unavailable. They may be remiss in setting clear expectations, yet they may overreact when the child misbehaves or fails to understand what is expected. This is often seen in families where poverty is extreme or addictions or mental illnesses are present.

35

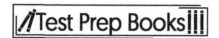

The authoritative style of parenting is considered to be the most effective form of parenting, yet much depends on the individual child or parent and the economic situation or cultural setting. One rule of thumb is that whatever style one chooses, it is helpful to remain consistent. A parent who is permissive one day and authoritarian the next sends mixed and confusing messages to the child. It is also important that the child is completely aware of rules, expectations, and consequences that may follow if the rules are broken. Communicating a sense that children are loved, wanted, and accepted is one of the most important parts of parenting.

Addiction and Substance Use

The repercussions of the addict's behavior can affect many significant aspects of life. The impact of addictions is felt not only by the addict, but also by everyone in that person's family and circle of social support. Those most powerfully affected are the immediate family members—particularly those who live under the same roof as the addict. Friends, extended family, co-workers, and employers also experience fallout from the addict's behaviors.

The spouses or partners of people who struggle with addiction often feel depressed, anxious, and angry. Persons in the throes of addiction often lie and steal to maintain their habit. It is not uncommon for people who struggle with addiction to steal from friends, family, or employers. Families must deal with the anxiety of not knowing when their loved one will come home or what mood or condition the person may demonstrate upon arriving home. Some families must deal with the shame of seeing their loved one arrested or knowing that this person harmed others while under the influence. Others simply become embarrassed by behaviors that loved ones exhibit in public or their failure to show up for an important event, such as a graduation.

Children of parents who struggle with addiction experience embarrassment, fear, anxiety, and sadness. They are more likely to be abused or neglected, especially in single parent homes. Children may suffer when money intended for basic needs is spent on drugs or alcohol instead. When abuse and/or neglect are reported to CPS, these children may be taken from parents and placed in a series of group or foster homes. In some cases, custody is completely severed. Such experiences may lead to deep psychological scars for those closest to the addict.

Feminist Theory

Feminist theory is the study of relations between the sexes, especially in the context of inequality. Discussions often include the topics of gender roles, gender in work-life contexts, societal norms for the genders, and cultural perceptions of gender. Feminist theory also focuses on gender relations and certain power relationships. Feminist pioneers have fought for equal political and social rights for men and women (such as the right to vote or the ability to work outside the home), for making previously male-oriented terms gender neutral (such as using *firefighter* instead of *fireman*), for female body positivity and acceptance, for sexual and reproductive rights and protection, and for encouraging supportive relationships between the genders. Feminist theories also support equality for men in such areas as paternity leave, stay at home parenting for fathers, and a redefined masculinity that includes heightened emotional intelligence, awareness, and expression. Feminist theory researchers have been striving to reinvigorate feminist studies, believing that prior theories formed by primarily male researchers should be reexamined.

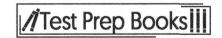

Influential Feminist Theorists

A number of American female psychologists, psychiatrists, and psychoanalysts have been influential in shaping psychological research that pertains to development in women and in serving as leaders in feminist theory:

- **Anna Freud** (1895–1982) made significant contributions to the field of psychoanalysis, especially regarding the ego and child development. She was the youngest daughter of Sigmund Freud. Some of her works include *Introduction to Psychoanalysis: Lectures for Child Analysts and Teachers* and *Ego and the Mechanisms of Defense*.

- **Jean Baker Miller** (1927–2006) is best known for authoring the revered text *Toward a New Psychology of Women* (1976). She is also known for her work with relational-cultural theory, which focuses on how culture affects relationships and how healthy connections with others are an integral part of psychological health and personal growth. These ideas often played a role in diagnosing and treating depression in women.

- **Carol Tavris** (1944–) promotes critical thinking and evidence-based research in psychology, focusing on cognitive dissonance. She believes many of women's so-called psychological issues are actually social beliefs about women's limitations, and that these social beliefs are not backed by science.

- **Nancy Chodorow** (1944–) authored the renowned text *Psychoanalysis and the Sociology of Gender* (1978). Her research focuses on mothering, gender systems, how the family influences female roles in society, and gender identity formation.

- **Harriet Lerner** (1944–) is best known for her work regarding gender roles in marriage, cultural gender norms, and how women can balance self-care with other competing priorities in their lives.

- **Carol Gilligan** (1936–) was a research assistant to Lawrence Kohlberg. She argues that his theories of moral development are male-focused and do not apply to women. Her research focuses on the development of morals and ethics in women. She initially published her findings as *In a Different Voice* in 1982.

- **Gail Sheehy** (1937–2020) was an author and journalist who wrote *Passages* (1976), which supports many of the beliefs and ideas of feminist psychologists. This book covers the different periods of life that women progress through and the emotions they experience in each one. The Library of Congress honored *Passages* as one of the top ten most influential books of its time.

Out-of-Home Placement

Children and elderly or disabled persons are sometimes legally removed from homes when it is determined there is a safety concern such as abuse or neglect. In these situations, the goal of removal is to secure the health, safety, and well-being of the displaced individual. It is likely that many other interventions have been attempted and have not worked, with removal being a last resort. These individuals, particularly children, who have lived in chaotic, dysfunctional environments will already have psychological and behavioral problems, including anxiety, depression, acting out, and displays of aggression. Following removal, these behaviors will likely escalate. Additionally, the parents or other caregivers who have had dependents taken away will also experience anger, confusion, guilt, and an assortment of challenges. Social workers can assume many roles in out-of-home placement, including working with the family of origin, the individual who has been displaced, or the respite caregivers.

Human Genetics

Social workers will begin to see more work done in the area of human genetics in the coming years. Since social workers are often the first individuals to diagnose mental disorders, it's imperative for workers to understand the ethical and legal implications behind a genetic diagnosis. The following is a list of social work *practice skills* related to genetics:

- Biopsychosocial assessment of clients who may have genetic disorders

- Providing assistance to clients with genetic disorders by identifying and/or developing programs for them

- Providing risks-benefits counseling before a client undergoes genetic testing

- Providing post-test counseling following diagnosis of a disorder

- Providing counseling related to family planning

- Providing adoption-related counseling pertaining to implications of an adoptee's genetic information

The following is a list of social work values related to genetics:

- **Accessibility**: availability of genetic screening to those who need it

- **Self-determination**: protection of rights when individuals are asked to take part in population screening

- **Autonomy**: the right and ability for an individual to choose whether or not to undergo genetic testing

- **Confidentiality**: assurance and maintenance of the privacy of genetic testing results

- **Research**: data from screening used for the purpose of developing services that may benefit others

Ethical dilemmas may arise as the result of genetic testing. Social workers should refer to the NASW Code of Ethics (1996) for guidance, paying particular attention to the ethical standards of self-determination, informed consent, and social and political action.

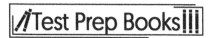

Family Life Cycle

Family life cycle theories assume that, as members of a family unit, individuals pass through different stages of life. Although various theories will break down the stages somewhat differently, the following is a common conceptualization of the stages:

- Unattached Young Adult: The primary tasks for this stage are selecting a lifestyle and a life partner. Focus is on establishing independence as an adult and independence from one's family of origin.

- Newly-Married Couple: The focus in this stage is on establishing the marital system. Two families are joined together, and relationships must be realigned.

- Family with Young Children: The focus in this stage is on accepting new family members and transitioning from a marital system to a family system. The couple takes on a parenting role. Relationships must again be realigned with the extended family (e.g., grandparents).

- Family with Adolescents: The focus here is on accommodating the emerging independence of the adolescents in the family. The parent-child relationship experiences changes, and the parents may also begin to take on caregiving roles with regard to their own parents.

- Launching Family: The focus in this stage is on accepting the new independent role of an adult child and transitioning through the separation. Parents also must face their own transition into middle or older age.

- Family in Later Years: In this stage, spousal roles must be re-examined and re-defined. One focus may be the development of interests and activities outside of work and family. Another focus is on navigation of the aging process and losses that may occur.

The basic family life cycle can vary significantly as a result of cultural influences, expectations, and particular family circumstances (e.g., single-parent family, blended family, multi-generational family).

Family Dynamics and Functioning

Family dynamics are the interactions between family members in a family system. As discussed previously, under "Family Theories," each family is a unique system; however, there are some common patterns of family dynamics.

Common influences on family dynamics:

- The type and quality of relationship that the parents have
- An absent parent
- A parent who is either extremely strict or extremely lenient
- The mix of personalities in the family
- A sick or disabled family member
- External events, particularly traumatic ones that have affected family members
- Family dynamics in previous generations or the current extended family

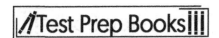

Common roles in the family that may result from particular family dynamics:

- **The problem child**: child with problematic behavior, which may serve as a distraction from other problems that the family, particularly the parents, do not want to face

- **Scapegoat**: the family member to whom others unjustly attribute problems, often viewed as "bad," while other family members are viewed as "good"

- **Peacekeeper**: a family member who serves to mediate relationships and reduce family stress

The Effects of Family Dynamics on Individuals

There are many ways in which the family influences the individual socially, emotionally, and psychologically. All family systems have their own unique characteristics, with both good and bad functional tendencies. The family interactions are among the earliest and most formative relationships that a person has, so they define the relational patterns that the individual develops and utilizes with all subsequent relationships. Parenting styles, conflict resolution methods, beliefs and values, and coping mechanisms are just a few things that a person learns from their family of origin. It is also within the family that a person first develops an image of self and identity, often having to do with the role that they are given within the family system and the messages communicated by parents. If a child has a secure and healthy relationship with the family members, this will likely lead to overall well-being and emotional stability as an adult.

When it comes to physical or mental illness, the role that the family plays is critical in lowering risk factors and minimizing symptoms. A strongly supportive family will help a person function at the highest level possible. Oftentimes, family members can serve as caregivers or play less formal—but still critical—roles in supporting a person's health.

Theories of Couples Development

Social workers who have couples and families as clients should develop an understanding of the theories of couples development as they relate to human growth and development. Multiple existing theoretical perspectives of couples development are helpful in better understanding how couples develop and, more importantly, how they can work with them to promote healthy relationships. One of these is the Developmental Model. The Developmental Model states that couples move through multiple stages of development both as a unit and individually as the relationship progresses. The stages that long-term relationships are likely to move through are as follows:

- Bonding: "Honeymoon" phase, desire for closeness, and discovering similarities

- Differentiation: Starting to acknowledge differences and learning to resolve conflict

- Practicing: Exploring independence and spending time developing separately from the relationship

- Rapprochement: Returning to one another

- Synergy: True intimacy embraced, unifying and learning to be stronger together than individually

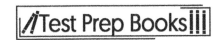

Dr. Susan Campbell proposes another theory of couples development, also marked by five distinct stages. It is important to note that a majority of couples will not develop smoothly through these stages and it is possible to regress into a previous stage of the relationship. Campbell's five stages are listed below.

- Romance: Intense passion and excitement, blinding each other from flaws

- Power Struggle: First experience of conflict, struggling for power and control within the relationship

- Stability: Learning to manage conflict and beginning to establish methods for reaching peace

- Commitment: Reuniting and seeking a balance of love, freedom, and happiness

- Co-Creation: Deciding to move forward as a team, planning for the future together

By using these models, social workers can help couples understand where they currently exist in their development and offer best practices in navigating the challenges that align with that stage.

In addition to the prior theories of couples development, there also exist several theories and models used in couples therapy that social workers may use when working with couples. One commonly referred to theory in social work practice is Attachment Theory, which states that attachment styles developed during childhood shape how individuals relate to others later in life. This, of course, includes (but is not limited to) romantic partners. Social workers can utilize this theory to help partners better understand how their individual attachment styles may be affecting the relationship and eventually learn to develop more secure attachments. The three distinct attachment styles referenced by this theory are anxious, avoidant, and secure.

Another useful theory for working with couples or clients in relationships is the Family Systems Theory, which views the family as a unified system in which each member has a unique role to fulfill that contributes to the smooth functioning of the system as a whole. This theory may be used by social workers to help couples understand how their individual actions, behaviors, and emotions are impacting the relationship, either in a positive or negative fashion. Helping clients to understand their role in the relationship, or family system, should ultimately lead to the promotion of healthy communication and more effective problem-solving skills.

Impact of Physical and Mental Illness on Family Dynamics

In some ways, physical illness is easier for a family to understand and deal with than mental illness because the symptoms and diagnosis are usually more obvious. When a person is diagnosed with a mental illness, the family may have a hard time accepting its reality. They may deny the diagnosis or try to find alternative explanations. There may be feelings of confusion or embarrassment, especially when those outside the family become aware of the illness. Because of the stigma that comes with mental illness, family members may become judgmental toward the individual who has been diagnosed. Since symptoms of mental illness often manifest themselves as emotional or behavioral responses, the family members can be tempted to blame the person with the mental illness and become frustrated with the perceived lack of responsibility and willingness to change.

As with physical illness, mental illness may impact the responsibility structure of the family as well as the financial situation, since all family members must adjust to caring for the mentally ill person. Beyond this, there may be irritation or bitterness toward the person suffering, which may be exacerbated by every episode of anxiety, anger, depression, or psychosis on the part of the mentally ill individual. It may be helpful for the social worker to provide the family with education about the illness, as well as involve them in treatment, when possible. It also helps to engage the family in counseling. Support groups or services for the family are also critical in helping them deal with the stressors they face. While families need to acknowledge the reality and seriousness of the mental illness, they also must recognize that, with their help and support, the ill person can thrive and successfully cope with the illness.

Psychological Defense Mechanisms

Sigmund Freud's **psychoanalytic theory** focused on the conflicts, drives, and unacceptable desires in the unconscious mind and how they affect a person. One method of dealing with unconscious conflicts is through **defense mechanisms**, which are the mind's way of protecting a person from unacceptable thoughts.

Some of the most common defense mechanisms are described below:

- **Repression** is when a person suppresses thoughts or memories that are too difficult to handle. They are pushed out of the conscious mind, and a person may experience memory loss or have psychogenic amnesia related to those memories.

- **Displacement** takes place when someone displaces the feelings that they have toward one person, such as anger, and puts it on another person who may be less threatening. For example, someone may express anger toward a spouse, but the person that they are truly angry at is their boss.

- **Sublimation** is when the socially unacceptable thought is transformed into healthy, acceptable behavior in another direction. Pain may become poetry, for example.

- **Rationalization** is when unacceptable feelings or thoughts are rationally and logically explained and defended.

- **Reaction formation** occurs when the negative feeling is covered up by a false or exaggerated version of its opposite. In such a case, a person may display strong feelings of affection toward someone, though internally and unconsciously hate that person.

- **Denial** is refusing to accept painful facts or situations and instead acting as if they are not true or have not happened.

- **Projection** is putting one's own feelings onto someone else and acting as if they are the one who feels that way instead of oneself.

Addiction Theories and Concepts

Addiction is a complex process involving biological, social, cultural, and genetic factors. There is some disagreement in the addiction treatment community about the causes and best treatments for substance use disorders. There are several models of addiction.

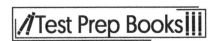

The earliest theory of addiction is called the **Moral Model**. This model implies that the person abuses substances because they are morally weak. The addict is viewed as a sinner or criminal and one who does not have the intestinal fortitude to change negative behaviors, therefore choosing to wallow in the misery of their sins.

The **disease model or medical model of addiction**, upon which the twelve-step program of Alcoholics Anonymous (AA) is based, specifies that the addict suffers from an illness that will never be cured and is progressive in its development. Even if the individual ceases alcohol intake, the disease remains. AA literature indicates that when one relapses, even after years of sobriety, the addict picks up, not where he left off, but where the disease would have taken him if the drinking had continued. It is seen as a medical disorder and, at times, referred to in the Big Book of AA as having an allergy, with alcohol as the identified allergen. This theory is accepted and understood by many successful AA participants who have maintained sobriety throughout this program for years and who have shared their experience of strength and hope to help others struggling with addiction.

The **biopsychosocial model of addiction** focuses on the role of the environment. Cultural and social factors influence one's beliefs and attitudes about substance use. In certain religions, it is unacceptable to use alcohol. In others, it may be encouraged—such as the huge sale and consumption of beer at Catholic picnics and fish fries. An addict's observation of others and their patterns of alcohol ingestion influences their attraction to drug or alcohol use as a means for tension relief or a form of celebration. Exposure to family or community members who use large quantities of intoxicants may serve to normalize dysfunctional patterns of use. Some youth observe their parents drink a quart of vodka each night and believe that their family members are just normal drinkers, whereas other youth are raised in environments where alcohol is unacceptable or served only on rare occasions.

The **learning theory of addiction** is based on concepts related to positive reinforcement. The assumption underpinning this model is that addiction is a behavior learned through operant conditioning, classical conditioning, and social learning. Social learning takes place through observation. Learning theory posits that the interplay between these three factors contribute to the initiation, maintenance, and relapse of addictive behaviors. The intoxicant serves as an immediate reinforcement in the form of increased euphoria or relaxation. In some cases, it also deters withdrawal symptoms. Both of these forms of reinforcement increase the likelihood that the behavior will be repeated in an effort to recreate the sensation of feeling better.

Genetic theory is based on research indicating that biological children of parents who struggle with addiction are more prone to addiction than children of non-addicts. According to genetic therapy, this genetic predisposition towards addiction accounts for about half of one's susceptibility to becoming an addict. Theorists of this model agree that other factors, such as social experiences, have an impact upon the formation of an addiction.

Systems and Ecological Perspectives and Theories

Systems Theory in social work refers to the view that human behavior is explained by the influences of the various systems to which individuals belong. When evaluating and conceptualizing an individual's behavior, that behavior must be considered in the context of the individual's family, society, and other systems.

All systems are seen as possessing interrelated parts and exerting influence on each other. There are many iterations of the premise of the basic systems theory. In practice, systems theory allows a social worker to better understand the dynamics of a client's systems while also creating an appropriate intervention approach. The originator of systems theory in social work was **Ludwig von Bertalanffy**, a biologist who was influenced by sociologists Max Weber and Emile Durkheim.

Talcott Parsons expanded on earlier work with his framework of structural functionalism, which proposes that a system is defined by its function in its social environment.

The **four states of social systems** are adaptation to the social environment, goal attainment, integration with other systems, and latency or homeostasis (social patterns and norms are maintained). It's also important to note the designations of social systems in social work. **Microsystems** are small systems, like an individual or a couple. **Mezzosystems** are medium-sized systems made up of extended families or groups to which the individual belongs. **Macrosystems** are large systems made up of organizations or communities.

The **ecological systems perspective** is concerned with the transactions between systems. It says that people and families must be considered within cultural and societal contexts, which also necessitates examining the events that have occurred in an individual's life. Changes made by the individual that cause the entire system to shift must also be considered.

The following are common interventions based on systems theory:

- Strengthening a part of the system in order to improve the whole system

- Creating a genogram: a family tree constructed with a client in order to improve understanding of the familial relationships and to identify recurring patterns

- Connecting clients to organizations or individuals who can help them to function better within and between their systems

- Developing an ecomap: an illustration of client's systems, such as family and community and how it changes over time

Role Theories

Different role theories have culminated in the social role theory, which emphasizes that people's behaviors are motivated by the roles they are given within society. These roles can include aspects of race, gender, employment, position in the family, etc. When a person assumes a particular role, they tend to adopt the expectations of that role as governed by social norms and conventions. Some roles, such as gender, may affect many domains of life, while others—like being a student—may be confined to a particular situation or environment. The roles that a person adopts can strongly impact self-image and behaviors.

Social roles can both negatively and positively impact the individual. While the smooth functioning of society is dependent on different people fulfilling different roles and responsibilities, certain role expectations can limit a person's individuality and self-determination. For example, typical gender roles may cause a woman to feel that her role in society is restricted by the expectations placed upon her.

Theories of Group Development and Functioning

Some aspects of planning interventions for a group will be similar to planning for an individual. Other aspects are unique to groups. Methods for planning interventions with a group may include:

- Conducting a needs assessment for the group to determine issues

- Ensuring that key stakeholders are involved in data collection and planning

- Continuously involving and updating all stakeholders

- Delegating components of the intervention appropriately by individuals' strengths and resources

- Establishing SMART objectives for changes (specific, measurable, achievable, relevant, time-based)

- Setting goals

- Developing an evaluation plan to assess progress

Techniques for Managing Group Process and Maintaining Group Functioning

Before working on issues, the **process of group therapy** begins with members becoming familiar with each other. There should be group rules that the entire group agrees upon before entering therapy. The social worker acts as a guide and mediator, and sometimes an instructor, for the group. There are phases of group therapy process and functioning that include forming, norming, and storming elements. Groups may be open and allow members in at any time, or they may be closed, which means that a group is specifically formed and only select participants are allowed entrance. Both the social worker and the group members are responsible for managing group dynamics.

The group and the social worker are involved in managing group process and maintaining group functioning. Group participants may be invested in maintaining group coherence and functioning, and someone may take the role of gatekeeper in maintaining the group. The social worker may assume the role of leader concerning group process and functioning and may be responsible for group growth and termination. Sometimes group members take specific roles within the group, such as helper, peacemaker, or gatekeeper. At times, group members may also assume negative roles within the group setting. The social worker should recognize when negative roles are assumed and facilitate the members in changing their tendency to take on those negative roles.

Theories of Social Change and Community Development

Community development theory focuses on oppressed people who are in the process of overcoming social problems that were imposed upon them by external forces. In the process of community development, members of a community learn how to improve that community and gain control of their local environment. **Community-level change** brings people together and demonstrates the power of solidarity. This theory also acknowledges the reality that many problems are at the social, rather than individual, level. An implication of the theory is that therapy addresses only the symptoms of a problem and not the underlying causes.

Interpersonal Relationships

Interpersonal relationships refer to interactions (often of a close, friendly, romantic, or intimate nature) between people. They can form due to shared personal, professional, social, charitable, or political interests. Strong interpersonal relationships are built over time as participants are willing to honestly communicate on a regular basis, support one another's well-being, and develop a shared history. Psychological, evolutionary, and anthropological contexts suggest that humans are an inherently altruistic, community-oriented species that relies on interpersonal relationships to survive and thrive. These types of relationships (when healthy) provide security, a sense of belonging, an exchange of benefits and rewards, and a sense of self-esteem. Healthy interpersonal relationships are characterized by mutual respect, care, and consideration between members. Almost all groups assemble into a power structure of some kind, with natural leaders taking over decision-making, resource sharing, and other tasks that affect the group as a whole. Dysfunctional interpersonal relationships may be characterized by an extreme power imbalance and dominance by one or more involved members, often leading to submissiveness, learned helplessness, and feelings of low self-esteem in the relationship's less powerful members. Submissive members of a group may find themselves without material resources or respect from the rest of the group.

Family Life Education in Social Work Practice

Family life education is an important aspect of social work practice in the psychoeducational realm of treatment. Families sometimes need to be educated concerning their biopsychosocial structure and other kinds of family structures. Family life models have changed in recent years and continue to change at a rapid pace with the advent of the legalization of gay marriage and the increase in extended and blended families. Family life has become very diverse, and social workers need to be educated on these models so they can further educate clients.

Strengths-Based and Resilience Theories

Rather than focusing on problems and pathology, the **strengths perspective** (or *strengths-based approach*) in social work encourages social workers to focus on a client's strengths or assets and to build upon the client's inherent resiliency and positive characteristics. Outcome studies regarding use of the strengths perspective are limited; however, it is posited that a strengths-based approach could help to remove some of the stigma attached to groups or conditions (e.g., mental illness, poverty).

Resilience theories account for risk factors that may threaten an individual's ability to cope with adverse events. Risk factors include lack of support, diagnosis of mental health disorders, and resource constraints. Protective factors support high levels of resiliency and can include the ability to think positively about situations, the ability to feel hope, strong confidence in one's self-reliance, problem-solving abilities, and competence. Developing resilience should be treated as a preventative approach, rather than a reactive approach.

Strengths- and resilience-based approaches allow individuals to feel empowered and maintain a sense of self-efficacy, both of which are crucial components for lasting behavior change and resolution. Additionally, they minimize the client's self-identification with a problem or issue, which can cause the client to fall into a self-fulfilling prophecy. It is important to note that clients can build the capacity to be resilient as a healthy method of coping. This type of skill building can often serve as a crucial component of an intervention. Exercises may include reframing perspectives, journaling, learning new abilities (such

46

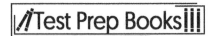

as problem-solving skills), practicing flexibility when unexpected changes arise, and examining public stories of strength and resiliency with the client. Finally, practitioners can support clients by providing positive reinforcement and feedback when the client displays strong and resilient behaviors.

Impact of Stress, Trauma, and Violence

Trauma affects everyone differently. The reaction depends on the person's emotional resiliency, history of past trauma, and other factors. Some trauma survivors exhibit symptoms that clearly meet the criteria for PTSD, while others exhibit smaller clusters of symptoms, such as anxiety or depression. Others show little or no symptoms. Below is an overview of common responses:

- **Foreshortened future**: This refers to the sense that one's life is shortened or forever altered and that a normal life may never be experienced again.

- **Emotional responses**: These may be fear, sadness, shame, anger, guilt, and/or anxiety.

- **Physical reactions**: Survivors of trauma often have multiple somatic issues, including gastrointestinal complaints, neurological problems, poor sleep, and muscle pain.

- **Hyperarousal**: Trauma survivors often become hypervigilant. They are frightened by neutral stimuli, such as a dog barking or a child screaming. They may experience a continual feeling that something terrible is going to happen.

- **Intrusive thoughts**: Survivors can become flooded with unwanted thoughts and memories about the trauma.

- **Trigger/flashbacks**: Triggers are stimuli that set off memories and provide a sensory reminder of the traumatic event.

- **Dissociation**: This coping mechanism allows the person to "check out" temporarily. This process severs connections to the painful memories.

- **Self-harm**: Some survivors use self-harm as a means of distraction from emotional pain. This could transition into more serious self-harm and can result in suicidal behaviors if not treated.

- **Substance use**: Many survivors use substances to medicate unpleasant emotions, such as fear or shame.

Common Effects of Stress, Trauma, and Violence

Many people equate stress with an emotional experience, but stress can actually have a profound effect on the body, cognition, and behavior as well.

Common Effects of Stress

Body	Mood	Behavior
Headache	Anxiety	Overeating or undereating
Muscle tension or pain	Restlessness	Angry outbursts
Chest pain	Lack of motivation or focus	Drug or alcohol abuse
Fatigue	Irritability or anger	Tobacco use
Change in sex drive	Sadness or depression	Social withdrawal
Stomach upset		
Sleep problems		

Although everyone experiences some degree of stress, stress becomes trauma when the intensity of the stress causes a person to feel helpless and seriously threatened, either physically or psychologically. Unfortunately, trauma and violence are common experiences for both adults and children, and the risk for traumatic and/or violent events is particularly high for individuals suffering from mental illness. Some people will experience a trauma with little to no lasting impact, while others may struggle with the aftermath of the trauma for the rest of their lives.

Many variables can either exacerbate or ameliorate the impact of trauma:

- Whether the event occurred once or was ongoing
- Whether the event occurred during childhood or adulthood
- Intensity of the traumatic event
- Personal experience vs. observation
- Ability to access supportive resources
- The way in which people and systems respond to the individual who has been traumatized

Potential effects of trauma and violence include the following:

- Substance use and abuse
- Mental health problems
- Risk-taking behavior
- Self-injurious behavior
- Increased likelihood or exacerbation of chronic illnesses, including cardiovascular disease
- Difficulties with daily functioning, including navigating careers and relationships

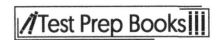

Post-Traumatic Stress Disorder (PTSD)

Some people who have experienced trauma or violence will experience an impact significant enough to be diagnosed with PTSD. Symptoms must last for more than one month before the diagnosis of PTSD is considered and must include the following:

- One or more **re-experiencing symptoms** (flashbacks, disturbing dreams, frightening thoughts)

- One or more **avoidance symptoms** (avoiding reminders of the trauma, experiencing emotional "numbing," losing interest in activities that one previously enjoyed)

- Two or more **arousal and reactivity symptoms** (startling easily, experiencing tension, hypervigilance, difficulty falling or staying asleep, eruptions of anger)

- Two or more **cognition and mood symptoms** (difficulty remembering the traumatic event, persistent negative thoughts, excessive feelings of blame or guilt)

Crisis Intervention Theories

Crisis intervention is typically a short-term treatment usually lasting four to six weeks and is implemented when a client enters treatment following some type of traumatic event that causes significant distress. This event causes a state of disequilibrium when a client is out of balance and can no longer function effectively. Social workers can either use generic crisis intervention models for varied types of crises or can create an individualized plan for assisting the client. The main goal of crisis intervention should be to help clients develop and use adaptive coping skills to return to the level of functioning prior to the crisis.

Gerald Caplan's Stages of Crises

Caplan theorized that individuals need to maintain homeostasis or remain in balance with their environment. A crisis is caused by an individual's reaction to a situation, not by an actual incident. Following a crisis event, an individual experiences the following stages:

- Stage 1: Increase in feelings of stress immediately following the event. Client may experience denial and typically tries to resolve the stressful reactions using past problem-solving and coping skills.

- Stage 2: Client experiences higher levels of stress as the usual coping mechanisms fail. Client may employ higher-level coping skills to alleviate the increasing stress levels.

- Stage 3: As stressful feelings continue to escalate, client experiences major emotional turmoil, possible feelings of hopelessness, depression, and anxiety.

- Stage 4: The final stage is marked by complete psychological and emotional collapse, or the individual finds a method to resolve the situation; however, there may be remaining emotional and psychological dysfunction or impairment if the coping mechanisms used were maladaptive.

The Crisis Intervention Process

Engage and Assess

Social workers participate in client engagement by helping to de-escalate volatile emotional states through establishing rapport, using empathy, employing emotional management techniques, and accessing outside systems (family, friends, and support groups). Additionally, the social worker assesses the crisis situation to determine the level of care required (general triage may include intensities ranging from one to three) and how the client has been impacted.

Set Goals and Implement Treatment

Goal setting should occur in collaboration with a client's treatment plan. Intervention strategies, tasks, and timeframes should correspond with the desired goal and objectives. The primary goal should be to assist clients in returning to pre-crisis functioning. However, there will likely be additional and related goals and tasks as the plan of action is implemented.

Evaluate and Terminate

At the end of the process, the worker concludes treatment and evaluates the completion of goals. It is important to discuss with the client the coping skills that they have developed, including how they might be able to use those skills for future crises and challenges.

Theories of Trauma-Informed Care

Trauma-informed care refers to providing interventions in a way that accounts for the possibility that a client has had traumatic experiences. The definition of trauma will be relative to the client, but common experiences include major loss, assault, abuse, manipulation, neglect, major injury or accident, and major life change. If these events occur during vulnerable periods in a client's life (such as early childhood), symptoms associated with trauma may be more pervasive or exacerbated. Personal trauma often drives mental health and behavioral conditions, so understanding a client's history and the influence of any experienced trauma is a critical component of providing effective care. Experiences of multiple or repeated trauma are associated with higher rates of substance use and other health problems. These can present with additional coinciding and related risk factors, such as poverty, infectious disease, homelessness, or lack of personal support.

The trauma-informed model of care encourages all practitioners who work with clients experiencing mental or physical health issues to recognize the influence of traumatic experiences. This model helps practitioners assess the level of risk assumed by clients and provides preventative interventions to help mitigate risks at different trauma levels. The client's perspective of how the traumatic event occurred (e.g., unexpectedly or expectedly, from a stranger or loved one); the time during the lifespan in which the event occurred; and other cultural, social, or personal factors determine the level of risk faced by the client. Reactions to traumatic events may manifest less subtly than obvious problems such as substance use. They can present as anxiety, pain, muscular tension, elevated heart rates or cortisol levels, depression, headaches, and so on. Therefore, allowing room for the consideration of prior trauma when working with all clients broadens the scope of interventions that practitioners choose to employ.

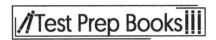

Impact of the Environment

Impact of Physical Environment

The ecological perspective focuses on the *person in environment,* or the interaction between the individual and the environment around them (including physical environment and family). Privilege, or lack thereof, may also have a large impact on the development of individuals.

As mentioned, the **person-in-environment (PIE) theory** emphasizes the importance of viewing and treating a person within the context of their environment, rather than as a completely independent entity. In order to understand and effectively treat a person, it is critical to evaluate the environment they are in and the physical, emotional, and psychological impact that it has had regarding individual strengths and needs. The environment includes the dynamics of family, school, work place, culture, and social relationships. Rather than being exclusively person-focused or environment-focused, the PIE theory looks at the interplay between the two. If a person is displaying anxiety or depression, for example, the goal would be to determine what cultural, social, or familial factors may be playing a role. PIE seeks to have a holistic view, which then leads to broader and more comprehensive treatment options.

The importance of the PIE theory can be seen when working with children. Often children with behavioral or emotional issues are identified as the primary problem. However, when the situation is explored more closely, there are almost always other factors that are contributing to the child's behaviors, including parental conflict, abuse and neglect, or some traumatic experience. If the child's environment is not evaluated and their behaviors are the only focus, it is impossible to determine the root cause of the presenting problem or the most appropriate steps to take. Similarly, it would be futile to merely change or address the child's environment without also dealing directly with the child's emotional and behavioral needs. The person, their emotions and behaviors, and their environment and the circumstances in which they live are all significant when it comes to planning treatment.

Impact of Political Environment

The political environment shapes the laws and policies that govern social programs and services and thus impacts individuals, families, groups, organizations, and communities. Examples are as follows:

- Individuals: Under the Obama administration, the Affordable Care Act, also known as the ACA, was implemented. This expanded access to healthcare for millions of Americans who were previously uninsured.

- Families: Changes in immigration policies have a significant effect on families who have been separated due to detention or deportation. Additionally, any change to social welfare programs such as the Temporary Assistance for Needy Families (TANF) or Supplemental Nutrition Assistance Program (SNAP) will impact families who rely on these programs to help fulfill their basic needs.

- Groups and organizations: Groups and organizations that rely on government funding will feel the impact of a changing political environment. Non-profits may find themselves struggling if funding is cut due to changes in political priorities. Advocacy groups will, similarly, encounter greater difficulties in attempts to advance their cause if the current political climate is hesitant to support them.

51

- Communities: Day-to-day lives of communities are affected by the political environment. Policies related to environmental regulation affect the health and well-being of communities that are exposed to pollutants, while changes in policies related to education can impact the quality of education within a community.

Impact of Social Environment on Client Systems

Social institutions exist to meet the needs of individuals, promote prosocial behavior, define social norms, and create order. There are five major social institutions:

- Family:
    - Regulates sexual behavior (monogamy)
    - Creates and provides for new society members
    - Socializes new society members
- Religion:
    - Provides explanations for the unexplainable
    - Supports societal norms and values
    - Provides a means of coping with life situations
- Government:
    - Institutionalizes norms (by creating laws)
    - Enforces laws
    - Protects members of society
    - Provides a means of resolving conflict
- Education:
    - Prepares society members to contribute to the society in specified roles
    - Teaches skills necessary to function within the society
- Economics:
    - Produces and distributes goods needed by society members
    - Provides services necessary to the society

Impact of Economic Changes

Economic changes, particularly negative ones, can have a substantial impact on client systems:

- In times of economic turmoil, people tend to cut back on spending and stop seeking services in order to conserve money. Over time, this can lead to a backlog of individuals with major problems that need to be addressed, burdening many components of society.

- A poor economic climate can also exacerbate pre-existing problems, such as depression or substance use, and can create significantly more stress on the family unit, which may spill over into work or school.

- Unemployment has been linked to a withdrawal from social activity, low self-esteem, an increased sense of hopelessness, poorer mental health, and an increase in substance use.

- Such change has an impact within a family, and when enough families are affected, entire communities can experience shifts in attitude and behaviors.

- The experience of living in poverty for many years or at crucial points in time is linked to certain individual outcomes. Children living at the poverty level during preschool and

52

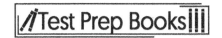

elementary school years are less likely to finish their schooling than are those who experience poverty during later childhood or adolescence only.

- When economic factors are at play with regard to a client's well-being, social workers must be prepared to assist with the development of appropriate coping skills and identification of resources for the client and family system.

Impact of Cultural Environment

As mentioned, it is important not to use information about culture, race, and ethnicity in a stereotypical or overgeneralized manner. There are vast differences within groups. For example, group members holding a traditional viewpoint are likely to identify very strongly with their group and to reject the practices of other groups. In contrast, other individuals may be acculturated into a dominant group culture and may not identify with their culture of origin.

Race refers to biologically distinct populations within the human species. *Ethnicity* is a cultural term referring to the common customs, language, and heritage of a category of people. **Ethnic identity** is the identification with a particular group of people who share one's culture and heritage.

William Cross's Stages of Identity Development

William Cross is a theorist and researcher in the field of ethnicity identity development. He is known for his **Nigrescence model** and for his novel *Shades of Black*. The following depicts **William Cross's Stages of Identity Development** for people of color:

- **Pre-encounter**: Unless prompted to do so, children do not critically evaluate the race-related messages that they receive from the world around them.

- **Encounter**: Often experienced in early adolescence, the individual has one or more experiences that are related to race. Though it is possible for the experiences to be positive, this is often when an individual first experiences racism or discrimination and begins to understand the personal impact of their race.

- **Immersion-Emersion**: After experiencing a race-related incident, the individual strongly identifies with their racial group and may seek out information about history and culture.

- **Internalization**: Racial identity is solidified, and the individual experiences a sense of security in identifying with their race.

- **Internalization-Commitment**: Racial identity is taken one step further into activism pertaining to issues related to the experiences of the individual's racial group.

Sue & Sue's Stages of Racial/Cultural Identity Development

Derald Sue and David Sue developed **Stages of Racial/Cultural Identity Development**. **Derald Sue** is a professor of counseling psychology at Columbia University. **David Sue** is a professor emeritus of psychology at Western Washington University. Their works revolve around multicultural issues in counseling and multicultural therapy. The following are the stages of racial-cultural identity development:

- **Conformity**: The individual displays a distinct preference for the dominant culture and holds negative views of their own racial and/or cultural groups. They may also experience shame or embarrassment.

- **Dissonance**: The individual undergoes a period of re-thinking or challenging their beliefs. For the first time, the individual examines and appreciates positive aspects of their own racial/cultural group.

- **Resistance and Immersion**: The individual shows preference for minority views and actively rejects the views of the dominant culture, experiencing pride about and connection to their racial or cultural group.

- **Introspection**: The individual becomes aware of the negative impact of the resistance and immersion stage and may realize that they do not actually disagree with all majority views or endorse all minority views.

- **Integrative Awareness**: The individual is able to appreciate both their own culture and differing cultures.

Life Events, Stressors, and Crises on Individuals, Families, Groups, Organizations, and Communities

Life events are experienced by all families and can be both positive and negative—everything from marriage or childbirth to death or divorce. If the life event is more negative and sudden, it may be considered a crisis, such as the unexpected loss of a family member, diagnosis of a major illness, a car crash, financial trouble, or something even more intense like a natural disaster or terrorist attack. Even positive life events can become crises for families if they have difficulty adjusting to the changes. Crises often involve both hard decisions and emotional turmoil.

The **ABCX Model**, introduced by **Reuben Hill**, seeks to explain how families deal with stressful situations that arise. A is the event that occurs, B is the family resources, C is the family perception, and X stands for a crisis. It claims that the event, plus the family resources and plus the family's perception, all combine to determine whether the event is viewed as a crisis and whether the family is able to cope with it. Depending on the family's ability to adapt their normal functioning patterns, a life event or crisis can either strengthen their relationships and the family unit or tear them apart. A family can effectively deal with the crisis if they utilize **positive coping mechanisms**, such as pursuing practical solutions to deal with the issues that arise, seeking counseling from a therapist or clergy, engaging social supports, and communicating openly with each other. **Negative coping strategies** could involve drug or alcohol use, isolation, or displacement of anger and frustration onto family members. Though all families will face a period of disordered chaos in trying to deal with a crisis, the families that are successful are those that can engage in new and positive coping methods.

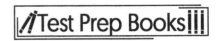

Person-In-Environment (PIE) Theory

Carel Germain described person-in-environment interaction based upon earlier work in systems theory. This perspective takes into consideration an individual's environmental and systemic influences. It is specific to social work, which differentiates it from other like professions.

- **Life stress**: the normal tension that occurs as the result of both external demands and internal experiences

  - What is experienced as stressful varies across people and their perceptions. For example, two people placed in the same environment may have completely different experiences due to the ways in which they experience and perceive the situation.

- **Adaptation**: when the environment and the individual change in response to the interaction with each other

- **Coping**: individual use of one's own strengths and problem-solving abilities to navigate life stress and develop self-esteem and hope

- **Power**: can be a source of stress to individuals as well as the larger system when misused by certain groups

- **Human Relatedness**: the ability of individuals to cultivate relationships

Three related concepts are **self-direction**, **competence**, and **self-esteem**. These attributes are interdependent and occur cross-culturally.

Communication Theories and Styles

One of the main names associated with communication theory is **Niklas Luhmann**, a sociologist and systems theorist. In **Luhmann's theory**, it is the communication *between* people and not the people themselves that makes up a social system.

Luhmann used the term **autopoiesis** to define social systems as self-creating, meaning that a social system has the ability to produce itself and maintain itself. Luhmann believed that communications make up the system as well as create other communications. The meaning of a communication is the response it generates.

The **Shannon and Weaver model of communication**, though its origins are mathematical and technical, is cited as one of the primary communication models. This model was the first to conceptualize the activity of the sender and the receiver. For communication to occur in this model, the sending entity has to prepare and actively deliver information, and the receiver has to wait and actively accept information. The **Berlo model of communication** added that all communication also needed a channel over which to travel.

There are four primary communication styles. **Passive communication** refers to senders who avoid full, direct, and clear verbal or written expression to send a message. Rather, their body language and behaviors may provide a large chunk of the intended message. **Passive communicators** tend to avoid

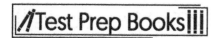

direct communication; they are unassertive, quiet, and anxious. **Aggressive communicators** are overly direct senders, so much so that their communications may harm those who are listening to them. Aggressive communicators are characterized as dominating, impulsive, and critical. **Passive-aggressive communication** refers to senders who outwardly show mildly expressive communication but inwardly feel aggression that is manifested in body language or behavior. **Passive-aggressive communicators** often have a difficult time with confrontation, expressing powerful feelings, and understanding anger. **Assertive communication** refers to senders who are clear and firm yet considerate when stating their message. **Assertive communicators** tend to speak clearly, feel in control, and respect themselves and others.

Psychoanalytic and Psychodynamic Approaches

Psychodynamic approaches engage clients in discovering how their unconscious drives affect their conscious lives. Unconscious drives include sexual and aggression drives that may be unknown to the client on a conscious level. Clients engage in stream of consciousness discussion with the therapist, and the therapist acts mostly as a listener. There is also a focus on dream interpretation in psychodynamic approaches, in which clients are encouraged to discuss their dream states with the social worker. Psychodynamic approaches originate with Freud's "talking cure," in which Freud encouraged clients to attend sessions several times a week.

There are several psychoanalytic organizations in the United States devoted to psychodynamic training. These schools usually have multiyear programs to train new psychoanalysts. While psychodynamic approaches may not encompass the entirety of a client's experience, they are useful for certain clients and may be integrated into psychotherapeutic treatment along with other approaches.

Carl Jung's Psychoanalytic Theory
Jung's theory is similar to Freud's psychoanalytic theory, with differences related to the purpose of the libido, the unconscious, and behavioral motives. Libido is a psychic energy that motivates individuals.

Jung theorized two parts to the unconscious:

- **Personal unconscious**: contains information not accessible to the conscious mind

- **Collective unconscious (transpersonal)**: the memories from a person's ancestors that the individual has from birth

Jung identified this collective unconscious into four main archetypes.

- **Persona**: the artificial self that an individual shows to the world to hide who they really are

- **Anima/Animas**: the masculine qualities that women express to society and the feminine qualities that men express to society

- **Shadow**: similar to Freud's id, signifies raw needs and desires

- **Self**: the unconscious and conscious mind come together to form a unified whole, occurs as a consequence of individuation

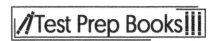

Loss, Separation, and Grief

The **concept of loss** is at the root of many depressive episodes. Losses can include anything one holds dearly. Losing a loved one, a pet, a job, housing, or financial or social status can all bring emotional pain. Other losses include the loss of physical or mental health. **Separation** is a form of loss that can occur in many forms, including divorce, military deployment, a job that requires one to move far away, or the loss of custody of a child. **Grief** is the emotional response to loss. Grief includes the main emotion of sadness, but other strong emotions may be present as well. Other feelings include confusion, anger, frustration, anxiety, or guilt.

The **five stages of grief** is a concept developed by **Elisabeth Kubler-Ross** in her book *On Death and Dying* in 1969. The five stages model originally pertained to those experiencing the dying process as the result of a terminal illness, but the model has been widely used to understand the grief reactions that people have in response to a number of situations, including loss of a loved one. The stages were first posited to be linear, but Kubler-Ross later stated that they are five common experiences that may or may not be experienced during grieving.

- **Denial**: This is the first stage. It occurs when a person becomes aware that they have lost someone or something dear but refuses to accept the truth. This stage is generally brief as the person begins to process irrefutable evidence.

- **Anger**: This is a period of venting anger at anyone who the person feels contributed to the loss occurring. It may be towards God, the drunk driver who caused an accident, or the CPS worker who takes a child from the home. In the case of a suicide, there could be anger at the deceased for choosing to leave.

- **Bargaining**: This stage is almost a form of magical thinking. A person may think that if they promise to do better, work harder, or pray harder, the loss process can be reversed. This is generally a short-lived phase as one realizes that promises made will still not bring back that which has been lost.

- **Depression**: During the fourth stage, a person allows themself to feel the sadness, and they may experience an even deeper emotional pain while learning to accept the loss and move forward. It may be a time of crying, despondency, and anguish. It must be experienced in order to move to the next stage.

- **Acceptance**: The last stage is the point at which the grieving person recognizes that, while the pain is tremendous, they will be able to handle it. Those at this stage understand that time will ease some of the suffering. They are learning to make peace with the experience and move forward with their lives.

Concepts of Abuse and Neglect

Physical abuse is the intentional act of physical force that may result in pain, injury, or impairment to a child or other dependent. Physical abuse is typically thought of as violent acts such as hitting, kicking, burning, etc., but it may also include extreme physical discipline, force-feeding, and some uses of drugs or restraints. Physical indicators of physical abuse are multiple physical injuries in various stages of healing; physical injuries that are inconsistent with an individual's account of how the injuries occurred;

multiple injuries, accidents, or unexplained illnesses occurring over a period of time; and injuries reflecting the object used to inflict the injury (e.g., cigarette burns, tooth marks, bruising in the shape of finger/hand marks). Behavioral indicators of physical abuse are flinching; offering inconsistent explanations of injuries or being unable to remember how injuries occurred; exhibiting wariness around adults or authority figures; aggression or abusive behavior toward others; and withdrawn, sad, depressed, or even suicidal behavior.

Neglect is failure by a parent or other responsible party to provide basic needs for a child or other dependent, resulting in endangerment of the dependent. Basic needs of a dependent are food, adequate supervision, medical care, shelter, or clothing. Some indicators of neglect are not registering for school or not attending school (if a school-aged child), abandonment, inappropriately dressing for the weather or season, poor hygiene, lack of shelter, ingestion of dangerous substances, recurrent hunger and/or malnourishment, and untreated medical conditions.

Abuse and Neglect Throughout the Lifespan

Indicators and Dynamics of Sexual Abuse

Sexual abuse is forced or coerced sexual contact or exposure, usually by someone older or in a position of authority over the victim. Sexual abuse can also include forcing someone to watch sexual acts or receive messages involving unwanted sexual content. The impact of sexual abuse is complex, and the emotional and psychological response to the trauma may evolve as the victim gets older and understands more fully what happened to them. Children who suffer sexual abuse may struggle from confusion about the abuse, especially if they are told by the perpetrator that it is right and good and if that person is someone with whom they have a relationship of trust. They may be blamed by the perpetrator for the abuse, which leads to further feelings of confusion and guilt. If they report the abuse to someone who does not believe it, the long-term effects of the abuse may be even greater, as well as the guilt, self-doubt, and shame. A history of sexual abuse will normally impact a person's relationships with others throughout life, and there may be issues of trust as well as confused feelings toward sex.

The following are indicators of sexual abuse (child):

- The statement that one has been sexually assaulted

- Mistrust or fear of those who bear resemblance to the abuser, potentially due to gender or size (children may be mistrustful of all adults)

- Changes in behavior

- Depression

- Anxiety with presenting symptoms (hair loss, fluctuations in weight)

- Increased fearfulness (possible night terrors and enuresis/bed wetting from children)

- Withdrawal from preferred activities/social isolation

- Compulsive masturbation

- Substance use

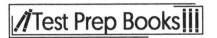

- Overly-sexualized behavior

- Parent, spouse, or caregiver demonstrating inappropriate behaviors

- Role confusion, distortion of child's role in the family

- Jealousness or over-protection of the victim

- Excessive, abnormal alone time with the child

- Lack of appropriate social and emotional contacts outside the home

- Substance and/or alcohol abuse

- Parent or caregiver reports being sexually abused previously (possible normalization or continuation of the cyclic behavior)

Indicators and Dynamics of Psychological Abuse and Neglect

Psychological abuse—or emotional abuse—is more difficult to define than sexual or physical abuse, but it can be just as damaging to the victim. Psychological neglect, especially as a child, involves withholding the love, affection, and emotional security that a child needs in order to grow and thrive. Psychological abuse involves emotional manipulation that uses strategies of shame, fear, and guilt to control someone's behaviors. Another aspect of psychological abuse can be verbal abuse which takes the form of yelling, constant criticisms or belittling, threats, or name-calling.

Alternatively, the child may be ignored, be made the witness of violence, or isolated as a punishment. These are all forms of psychological abuse and neglect. Because of the often vague or indefinable aspects of psychological abuse, it may be difficult for victims to understand or believe that they are being mistreated. Even if they do, they may be convinced that no one will believe them because of the manipulation of the perpetrator, who may either threaten or undermine the victim to such an extent that they are unwilling to take any action. Long term, a victim of psychological abuse is more likely to be fearful and withdrawn as a result of the many insecurities that have developed because of the abuse.

Indicators and Dynamics of Physical Abuse and Neglect

Physical abuse can be defined as bodily mistreatment, including hitting, slapping, kicking, burning, unnecessary constraints, strangling, or other acts of physical violence. Physical abuse is often perpetrated out of anger or frustration, as is the case with parents who use physical abuse to inappropriately discipline their children. In cases where there is a higher level of family stress or conflict or when parents have not received adequate training in parenting strategies, the levels of physical abuse may be higher. Physical abuse can also take place in adult relationships, most usually in an intimate relationship where one person struggles with anger management. Victims of physical abuse may show obvious signs of the abuse, such as injuries or multiple trips to the emergency room. However, there are other less obvious signs of physical abuse, such as fearful withdrawal, aggression, or other forms of misbehavior.

Physical neglect is withholding anything that is necessary for physical health and safety, as well as educational and medical needs. If a parent, for example, does not provide a child with enough food or with warm clothes in the winter, this would be considered neglect. This type of neglect can sometimes be deliberate, but may also be the result of ignorance or a lack of resources.

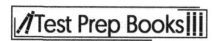

Effects of Physical, Sexual, and Psychological Abuse

People may experience abuse at the hands of strangers, caretakers, or close friends and family. The effects of abuse are traumatic, pervasive, and long lasting. Beyond affecting the abused parties, abuse often impacts those who are close to the victims. Physical, sexual, and psychological child abuse can lead to impaired intellect, learning disabilities, deficits in trust and language skills, long-term inappropriate behaviors, or lack of coping mechanisms. As abused children grow, they may be unable to make healthy friendships or lack the ability to desire or maintain intimate relationships. They may have failed marriages, or they may perpetuate the cycle of abuse when they become parents. They may often feel unworthy or that they did something to cause the abuse. This often has an impact on their attachment styles and how they relate to others.

In adults, abuse may cause permanent or temporary physical damage, low self-esteem, shame, despair, or feelings of helplessness. Victims of abuse as an adult may experience mental health disorders such anxiety and depression. If children witness their loved ones experiencing abuse, it may be traumatic for them, or they may normalize the behavior and perpetuate abuse themselves. Elder abuse, especially in nursing homes, often goes undetected as victims may be weak or losing mental faculties. Elders are especially vulnerable to physical and financial abuse. Effects may include rapid physical or mental deterioration, submissiveness, bedsores, increased rate of illness, or premature death.

In traumatic cases, both children and adults may become severely depressed or anxious. They may abuse substances or commit suicide.

Exploitation Across the Lifespan

Exploitation is taking advantage of someone in a vulnerable position for personal gain.

Financial exploitation of older adults occurs when caretakers, family members, or other individuals take advantage of the elderly member's finances. Indicators of financial exploitation are missing identification, money, credit cards, documents, or valuable possessions; large or frequent checks made out to cash; frequent or expensive gifts for caregiver; older adult's unawareness of income or bills; and blank checks, cash withdrawals, or money wires/transfers.

Sexual exploitation of children occurs when an individual takes advantage of a minor by trading sexual acts or pornography for basic needs. Indications of sexual exploitation are spending time with older individuals or an older "boyfriend" or "girlfriend"; spending time in inappropriate locations such as hotels or bars; signs of emotional or physical abuse or neglect; uncertainty of where oneself is (as they have moved around to various geographic locations); being missing from home or not attending school; acting fearful or anxious around others; and signs of being groomed (someone building a connection with the child, either online or in-person, in order to gain trust and ultimately abuse and/or exploit the child). Individuals who are being groomed might be secretive about their behavior, might possess unexplained money or items, and may have access to alcohol and/or drugs.

Girls are disproportionately affected by sexual exploitation and trafficking. The majority of children and adolescents are exploited by someone they know.

Perpetrators of Abuse, Neglect and Exploitation

Abuse perpetrators are individuals who cause or allow mistreatment of a child or other dependent. Common characteristics of abuse perpetrators are having experienced or witnessed abuse during childhood; lack of coping skills to manage anger and frustration; isolation or lack of a substantial support system; immaturity with poor regulation of emotions; abuse of alcohol or other substances; inappropriate expectations for the behavior of others; and poor social skills.

Diversity, Social/Economic Justice, and Oppression

Effects of Disability on Biopsychosocial Functioning Throughout the Lifespan

Disability can be a difficult adjustment, especially when it comes on acutely. People may experience disability from a traumatic incident, or it may come on gradually from a chronic disease. Some individuals are born with disabilities; they and their families and caregivers must adjust traditional ways of living. The **biopsychosocial model** is a view that accounts for biological factors, psychological factors, social factors, and their interplay within certain contexts. With regard to disability, an individual who experiences a disability is likely to go through biological changes, psychological adjustments, and social issues. From a biological perspective, an individual with a disability may have a body part that does not function typically. This in turn may affect adjacent body parts or other biological functions. For example, a patient with a heart disability is also likely to have certain vascular dysfunctions. From a psychological standpoint, an individual with a disability may have trouble adjusting if the disability is sudden (e.g., an unanticipated amputation).

This individual may struggle with feelings of depression or low self-worth, or they may simply feel a general sense of limitation. Socially, people with disabilities may feel it is more difficult for them to do things that other people can do easily. They may worry about making friends or finding romantic partners, or they may worry that they will be unfairly discriminated against in public or in the workplace. Children, especially, may experience teasing or exclusion from peers who are not developmentally mature enough to regularly exhibit sensitivity and compassion. Adults and elders with disabilities may mourn losses of freedom or changes in their lifestyles more than children who were born with disabilities and therefore have not experienced any other way of living. Practitioners who work with individuals experiencing disability should use strengths-based approaches to empower the client to live as well as they can with a disability. Acceptance, positive reinforcement, positive perspective and mindsets, and fostering a sense of community among individuals who are facing similar struggles are ways to support individuals with disabilities.

Effects of Culture, Race, and Ethnicity on Behaviors, Attitudes, and Identity

Societally, culture, race, and ethnicity appear to be distinguished by certain behaviors, attitudes, and identities. These may be misinterpreted, rejected, or stereotyped by other groups. Data show that minority groups tend to have less access to and receive fewer health care services; minority groups also tend to have higher rates of chronic disease. Additionally, these groups are more likely to be punished or incarcerated than are majority groups for the same crimes. This may lead to a sense of learned helplessness, in which minority groups believe they cannot eliminate these risks and tendencies from their lives and that these patterns of societal activity are normal. The **theory of learned helplessness** also states that those who experience the phenomenon are also more likely to suffer from mental

61

illness, such as depression and anxiety. These individuals may also become more defensive and aggressive as a result.

Additionally, the misunderstanding of certain cultural beliefs may promote rejection or outward hatred of some groups. This can lead to behaviors of microaggression, which are daily, relatively ingrained acts performed by society to marginalize some groups. It can also lead to large-scale instances of violence and rejection, including bullying and homicide of minority group members due to their perceived differences.

Effects of Discrimination and Stereotypes on Behaviors, Attitudes, and Identity

Discrimination is the unfair or unequal treatment of a person or group that is based on a characteristic, such as race, ethnicity, religion, age, sex, or sexual orientation.

Direct discrimination refers to unfair treatment based on someone's characteristics. An example would be refusing to hire someone because of their ethnicity.

Indirect discrimination refers to situations in which a policy applies the same to everyone, but a person or group of people are negatively impacted due to certain characteristics. For example, a company might require that everyone help unload shipments that come to the office. The policy is the same for everyone, but it's discriminatory towards any disabled employees. In a workplace environment, indirect discrimination can sometimes be allowed if there's a compelling reason for the requirement. For example, firefighters have to meet certain physical criteria due to the nature of their work.

Another form of discrimination is **harassment**. This involves unwanted bullying or humiliation intentionally directed to another person. **Secondary victimization** refers to the unfair treatment received when a person reports discrimination and is not supported by authorities.

Effects of discrimination on an individual may include depression, anxiety, and other mental health issues as well as medical/health-related problems caused by lack of access to health resources. Effects of discrimination on society include diminished resources (e.g., employment, educational opportunities, healthcare) and a culture characterized by fear, anger, or apathy.

Influence of Sexual Orientation on Behaviors, Attitudes, and Identity

Even with today's advances in technology, medicine, and genetics, scientists have not clearly established how sexual orientation develops. It is believed that sexual orientation is a complex interplay of environmental, hormonal, and genetic influences. According to the American Psychological Association, **sexual orientation** refers to an innate attraction to either or both sexes, as well as the person's identity in relation to their attraction. As such, the Association opposes psychiatric treatments such as **conversion therapy**—a form of treatment designed to help homosexuals become heterosexuals through therapy and, sometimes, medical interventions.

Research indicates that family composition may play a role in sexual orientation. For example, homosexual males are more likely to have older male siblings than homosexual women. For men, other factors include being the youngest child or having older mothers, absent fathers, or divorced parents. In women, examples include being an only child, being the youngest child, being the only girl in the sibling group, or experiencing the death of a mother during adolescence. Setting and culture also influence homosexual behavior, e.g., urban areas vs. rural areas.

62

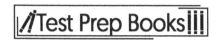

Impact of Transgender and Transitioning Process on Behaviors, Attitudes, Identity, and Relationships

Being **transgender** can be defined as identifying as a gender other than the gender one was born with. Publicly sharing that one is transgender can be difficult for some individuals. Transgender individuals may live in a community where their identity is not positively accepted or is misunderstood, and they may feel shamed or ridiculed. It may be a difficult experience for close family members to understand the perspective of a transgender individual, which can affect the cohesiveness of family relationships and the family unit. Transgender individuals may also feel a lack of acknowledgement when others fail to use the correct pronouns or respect other identity wishes.

Some transgender individuals choose to medically transition to the gender they identify as. This is a procedure that requires physical, emotional, and psychological support. Individuals not receiving support during their transition can experience extreme feelings of sadness, isolation, and lack of belonging. Medically transitioning individuals also undergo hormonal changes in addition to surgical procedures, and these can cause unexpected feelings and reactions in the individual. There are also medical risks that go along with both the surgical and hormonal procedures of transitioning that the individual has to be aware of and manage. Finally, after the transition is complete, individuals may struggle with living as someone who is relatively unfamiliar to their friends, family members, and colleagues. The transgender person may or may not experience support and acceptance in these groups and relationships, and some group members may even act aggressively toward the transgender person. If this is the case, it may be helpful to find support groups where transgender individuals can find not only friendship and community, but also guidance on how to navigate their new life, society, friends and relationships, and medical recovery.

Systemic Discrimination

Systemic (institutionalized) discrimination refers to discrimination taking place within a society or other institution (e.g., a religion or educational system). Such discrimination can be either intentional or unintentional and results from the majority of people within the institution holding stereotypical beliefs and engaging in discriminatory practices.

Systemic discrimination is often reflected in the laws, policies, or practices of the institution. Systemic discrimination creates or maintains a disadvantage to a group of people by way of patterns of behavior; it can have wide-reaching effects within a region, profession, or specific institution.

The following are example of systemic discrimination:

- Hiring practices that create barriers or result in lower wages for certain groups

- U.S. Supreme Court case, *Plessy vs. Ferguson* (1896) – "separate but equal" public facilities for African-Americans

- Oppression of women in certain countries (e.g., being unable to vote, obtain education, or hold jobs)

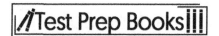

Culturally Competent Social Work Practice

Social workers must be culturally competent to meet the needs of all clients. One way to do this is to have the staff demographics reflective of the community served. Workers must also recognize the differences in individuals of the same culture and not use a cookie-cutter approach to deal with people of the same demographic group. Social workers must also work to create agency policies that encourage culturally sensitive treatment and do not allow discriminatory practices. When choosing interventions, treatment methods, and evaluation techniques, workers must also consider the appropriateness of the selection for the client's cultural background. According to the NASW Code of Ethics, social workers must:

- Understand and be knowledgeable of their clients' culture and demonstrate sensitivity in providing services.

- Become educated as it relates to oppression and diversity regarding race, ethnicity, nationality, gender, disability, sexual orientation, age, and religion.

- Be aware of their own biases and prejudices and use culturally sensitive language in communications with clients.

Gender, Gender Identity, and Sexual Orientation Concepts

The term **gender** refers to a range of physical, behavioral, psychological, or cultural characteristics that create the difference between masculinity and femininity. **Gender identity** is a person's understanding of their own gender, especially as it relates to being male or female. **Sexual orientation** is a more complex concept as it refers to the type of sexual attraction one feels for others and how they identify sexually. This is not to be confused with **sexual preference**, which refers to the specific types of sexual stimulation one most enjoys.

Types of sexual orientation are as follows:

- **Heterosexual**: An individual who is sexually and emotionally attracted to members of the opposite gender, also known as "straight"

- **Homosexual**: An individual who is sexually and emotionally attracted to members of the same gender, sometimes referred to as "gay" or "lesbian"

- **Bisexual**: A male or female who is sexually attracted to both same and opposite gender sex partners

- **Asexual**: An individual who has a low level of interest in sexual interactions with others

Types of gender identity are as follows:

- **Bi-gender**: An individual who fluctuates between the self-image of traditionally male and female stereotypes and identifies with both genders

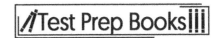

- **Transgender:** A generalized term referring to a variety of sexual identities that do not fit under more traditional categories, a person who feels to be of a different gender than the one he or she is born with

- **Transsexual:** A person who identifies emotionally and psychologically with the gender other than that assigned at birth, lives as a person of the opposite gender

Those who are transgender or transsexual may be homosexual, heterosexual, or asexual.

Social and Economic Justice

Professional Commitment to Promoting Social Justice

Social justice is defined as equal rights, opportunities, and privileges for all members of society. The Code of Ethics of the National Association of Social Workers (revised 2008) specifically lists social justice as a core value. The **NASW Code of Ethics** states, "Social workers pursue social change, particularly with and on behalf of vulnerable and oppressed individuals and groups of people. Social workers' social change efforts are focused primarily on issues of poverty, unemployment, discrimination, and other forms of social injustice. These activities seek to promote sensitivity to and knowledge about oppression and cultural and ethnic diversity. Social workers strive to ensure access to needed information, services, and resources; equality of opportunity; and meaningful participation in decision-making for all people."

Effects of Poverty

Poverty is often the foundation of a number of other socioeconomic and health problems faced by individuals, families, and communities. Without resources such as money, transportation, or housing, it becomes difficult to buy healthy food, access medical care, drive to work, have quality childcare, or live in a safe area. For adults in poverty, the extreme level of stress that arises from trying to pay bills, provide basic necessities for themselves and their families, and manage multiple jobs often leads to a number of mental, physical, and emotional problems. These can include substance use, domestic violence, inability to maintain family units and romantic relationships, hopelessness, depression, and desperation.

Children who live and grow up in poverty are prone to traumatic and catastrophic health risk factors, such as experiencing or witnessing violence, chronic malnutrition, higher rates of illness, and mood disorders. Experiencing such adverse events in childhood is associated with high levels of stress, impaired functioning, and impaired cognitive ability that can be irreparable. Individuals experiencing poverty are more likely to visit the emergency room for health problems (and often be unable to pay), require government assistance, and commit crimes (often in order to obtain necessary resources). These outcomes create a financial burden on the community and local economy.

Criminal Justice Systems

Social workers can have an important role in the criminal justice system. Prison and jail systems are full, and less than a third of incarcerated individuals who are released remain free. Most end up back in the criminal justice system. Additionally, a number of incarcerated individuals have mental and emotional disorders that often contribute to unlawful behavior. These can include substance use problems or high levels of personal stress. Social workers are trained to understand these contexts, and therefore they can provide valuable insight and counsel before, during, and after legal cases. Therefore, social workers

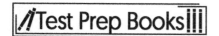

can intervene and offer support during all phases of the justice system. Social workers can work with individuals who were the victims of criminal activities. They are also able to work with perpetrators who have been released, thereby helping to prevent re-incarceration. Social workers can also provide support to the families of both victims and perpetrators, assist with the transition of having a family member in jail, assist with the transition of having a family member released, and support in educational and professional activities after release.

Finally, social workers can have a meaningful impact in the lives of children who may be at risk of ending up in the criminal justice system. By focusing interventions on vulnerable youth, such as education, positive recreational activities, mentoring programs, support for parents, and so on, social workers potentially have the ability to prevent youth and families from ever entering the criminal justice system. This is a much more powerful approach for positive behavior and social change, rather than addressing individual, family, and community issues after crimes have already been committed. Social workers will need to remember to show compassion and withhold judgment when working with criminal offenders; however, they must also be mindful to protect their personal safety in these situations.

Impact of Globalization on Clients

Globalization, or the process of working and operating in a hyper-connected, international capacity, has affected nearly every industry, including social work. Social workers are no longer limited to working with clients who are in close geographical proximity. They now have the ability to connect with audiences and clients all over the world through social media, email, virtual consultation, and web platforms. This expanded level of outreach can be positive, in that mental health and behavioral interventions, support, and awareness are more easily accessible. However, connecting online with clients can sometimes hinder the quality of personal interaction that practitioners cultivate with their clients. Additionally, it can be tricky to navigate the financial, legal, and security aspects of working with clients online, as these standards vary by geographical location.

Globalization has also opened new topics of interest for social workers. Globalization has led to increased working time, increased use of technology, and increased interactions across cultural, socioeconomic, and gender lines. In many ways, these changes have been associated with higher levels of work-related stress, health problems such as poor sleep, increased rates of mood disorders such as depression and anxiety, and higher awareness of harassment against women and subordinate employees. These are all issues that social workers may not have typically handled with clients in previous decades. They must now become skilled in addressing these issues. Finally, the use of technology, screens, and social media in children has been potentially linked with addictive behaviors, cyberbullying, and increased depression and anxiety rates. This is yet another avenue in which social workers must develop interventions that work in a relatively new context with variables about which research is still emerging.

Practice Quiz

1. What is the last stage of Freud's model of the five stages of human development?
   a. Latent stage
   b. Adult stage
   c. Genital stage
   d. Self-actualization stage

2. In Erikson's eight stages of development, identity vs. role confusion begins at age twelve and contains all but which of the following challenges?
   a. Working through and understanding multiple changes and demands placed upon the child as he or she moves toward adulthood
   b. Increasing understanding of sexual, hormonal, and other physical changes that are occurring
   c. Finding a long-term partner and starting a family
   d. Assessing one's talents, sexual preferences, and vocational interests

3. According to Piaget, what is the process by which old ideas or beliefs must be replaced with new ones due to obtaining new and more factual information?
   a. Schemas
   b. Assimilation
   c. Object permanence
   d. Accommodation

4. Ivan Pavlov is best known in the field of psychology for his concepts regarding which of the following?
   a. Classical conditioning
   b. Training dogs to behave obediently
   c. Development of sexual identity and orientation
   d. How positive reinforcement affects behavior in children

5. According to B.F. Skinner, providing positive reinforcement increases the likelihood that a desired behavior will be repeated. Which of the following is NOT a form of positive reinforcement when working with children?
   a. A trip to the park with Mom following a week of good behavior
   b. Praise in response to a task well done
   c. Taking away TV and computer privileges for a week
   d. Putting a colorful sticker on a poster each time the child goes to bed on time

See answers on next page.

Answer Explanations

1. C: The Genital stage starts in adolescence and lays the groundwork for future life relationships. As one enters adolescence, sexual identity and orientation begin to develop. Values regarding sexuality, views about the opposite sex, and the process of interacting with others on a more intimate level occur. These more mature elements of relationship-building lay the foundation for future relationships, but not only from a sexual standpoint. Choice A, the Latent stage, occurs from age 6 to puberty, and it is a time when the child's sexual energy becomes somewhat dormant. Choices B and D are not included in Freud's model of human development.

2. C: Developing a long-term relationship and starting a family are concepts more closely associated with stage six of Erikson's Model. This is intimacy vs. isolation, occurring from age eighteen through age forty. During this period, one is faced with the challenge of coming to terms with sexual preference; choosing a career path; and determining where, with whom, and how one plans to live. Long-term, future-oriented thinking is required. This phase is important because if it is not successfully mastered, the following phases—generativity vs. stagnation and ego integrity vs. despair—could lead to emotional pain and anxiety in later life.

3. D: Accommodation occurs when one recognizes that previous beliefs were incorrect or no longer beneficial, based upon learning and integrating new information. Accommodation should occur throughout one's life as new information enters the consciousness and the process of assimilation occurs. If one is unable to accommodate new ideas, then it is difficult to grow emotionally and intellectually. If an individual continues to insist that a yellow legal pad and an encyclopedia are just as efficient as using a computer to complete a complex research project, accommodation has failed to occur. This forces the person to work at a snail's pace in comparison to using technology to more quickly and accurately complete the task. Choice A is incorrect in that schemas are a set of thoughts and ideas that fit together and present the person with a belief, or even a script, for life. Choice B is incorrect because assimilation refers to the process of integrating the new information gained through accommodation. Choice C refers to object permanence, a process in which an infant learns that even though a person or object leaves the room, that person still exists, and this understanding reduces anxiety and fear of abandonment.

4. A: Pavlov developed the theory of classical conditioning in which it has been demonstrated that pairing one stimulus with another produces specific responses in animals and humans. In his famous experiment, he noted that when feeding a dog and simultaneously pairing that feeding with the sound of a bell, the ringing of the bell eventually became associated with feeding time. Soon, a behavioral change was noted. The dog salivated to the sound of the bell, even when no food was provided. This demonstrated that people and animals can learn things through pairing one stimulus with another. Although dog training was part of his research, Choice B is wrong as it was not the focus of his research. Choice C reflects one of Erikson's stages of development, and D relates more to the function of behavioral theory devised by B.F. Skinner.

5. C: Taking privileges for a week is a form of punishment for negative behavior, versus a reward for positive behavior. While punishment can be an effective means for changing behavior, research indicates it is less desirable than positive reinforcement. Choices A, B, and D are all forms of positive reinforcement in which a person is rewarded for performing a specific behavior.

Assessment and Intervention Planning

Biopsychosocial History and Collateral Data

Biopsychosocial Assessment

In order for an assessment to be comprehensive, the practitioner must gather information and assess the individual **holistically**, which includes examining systems related to the biological, psychological, and social or sociocultural factors of functioning. In some cases, a spiritual component may be included. This process is based on the **biopsychosocial framework** that describes the interaction between biological, psychological, and social factors. The key components of the biopsychosocial assessment can be broken down into five parts: Identification, Chief Complaint, Social/Environmental Issues, History, and Mental Status Exam.

Identification

Identification consists of the details or demographic information about the client that can be seen with the eye and documented accordingly. Some examples of identification information are age, gender, height, weight, and clothing.

Chief Complaint

The **chief complaint** is the client's version of what the overarching problem is, in their own words. The client's description of the chief complaint may include factors from the past that the client views as an obstacle to optimal functioning. It could also be an issue that was previously resolved but reoccurs, thus requiring the client to develop additional coping skills.

Social/Environmental Issues

The social and environmental issue component evaluates social development and physical settings. **Social development** is critical to understanding the types of support systems the client has and includes information about the client's primary family group, including parents, siblings, and extended family members.

The client's peers and social networks should also be examined. There should be a clear distinction between peers available *online* (such as through online social networks) and peers the client interacts with *face-to-face,* as online systems may provide different forms of support than in-person systems.

The client's work environment and school or vocational settings should also be noted in this portion of the assessment. The client's current housing situation and view of financial status are also included to determine the type of resources the client has. Legal issues may also be included.

History

History includes all of the events in the client's past. Clients may need to be interviewed several times in order to get a thorough picture of their history. Some information in a client's history, such as events that occurred during the stages of infancy and early childhood, may need to be gathered from collateral sources. Obtaining the client's historical information is usually a multi-stage process and can involve the following methods of data collection:

Presenting Problem

Clients should be asked to describe what brings them in for treatment. Although a client may attempt to delve into information that is well in the past, the practitioner should redirect the client to emphasize the past week or two. Emphasis is placed on the client's current situation when assessing the presenting problem.

Past Personal

When reviewing a client's history, noting biological development, may determine whether or not the client hit milestones and the ensuing impact it had on their health. In reviewing biological development, other physical factors should also be assessed for impact on current emotional well-being, including those that may no longer persist, like a childhood illness. As much information as possible regarding the client's entire lifespan (birth to present) should be gathered, with attention paid to sexual development.

Medical

During the medical component of the assessment process, information should be obtained on the client's previous or current physiological diagnosis. These diagnoses can contribute to the client's current situation.

For example, a client with frequent headaches and back pain may be unable to sleep well and therefore be experiencing the physical and psychosocial effects of sleep deprivation. Additional information on other conditions, such as pregnancy, surgeries, or disabilities, should also be explored during this time.

Mental Health

Previous mental health diagnoses, symptoms, and/or evaluations should be discussed. If a client discloses prior diagnoses or evaluations, the practitioner should determine the following:

- Whether the client has been hospitalized (inpatient)

- Whether the client has received supervised treatment in an outpatient setting (to include psychotherapeutic intervention)

- Whether the client has been prescribed medications

- Whether the client has undertaken other treatments related to mental health diagnoses

The client's psychological development should also be reviewed. It is important to gather details on how clients view their emotional development, including their general affect.

The client's cognitive development, in relation to information previously obtained regarding the biological development, should also be reviewed.

Substance Use

Without demonstrating judgment, practitioners should encourage clients to disclose whether or not they have used controlled substances. It is important that thorough information is gathered and symptoms related to substance use are assessed BEFORE rendering a primary mental health disorder diagnosis.

Should a client disclose that he or she has engaged in the use of substances, information as to the type of substance, frequency of use, and duration of exposure to the lifestyle, should be gathered.

Additionally, information on what the client perceives as the positive and negative aspects of substance use should be gathered, noting whether or not the client perceives any consequences of substance use, such as job loss, decreased contact with family and friends, and effects on physical appearance.

Mental Status Examination

A **mental status exam** is a concise, complete evaluation of the client's current mental functioning level regarding cognitive and behavioral aspects (rapport-building, mood, thought content, hygiene). There are mini-mental status examinations available that allow practitioners to provide a snapshot of the client's overall level of functioning with limited resources and time available. Mental status examinations are usually conducted regularly and discreetly through questioning and noting non-verbal indicators (such as appearance) in order for the practitioner to best guide the session.

Practitioners should document a mental status examination as part of the individual's personal file in order to complete an accurate assessment with all client information. This examination also serves as a baseline for the development and implementation of ensuing therapies, treatments, and interventions. The mental status typically includes details about the individual, such as appearance, grooming, facial expressions and general body language, cognition, orientation, manner of speech, indicators of the influence of any controlled substances, mood, impulse control, judgment, thinking style, memory, intellectual functioning, perception of reality, presence of hallucinations or delusions, and interest in the session.

Biopsychosocial Responses to Illness and Disability

Receiving a diagnosis of a serious physical illness is life changing in many ways. Along with the many physiological impacts of the illness, such as pain and tiredness, there are many psychological and social factors that influence a person's ability to cope with the new diagnosis. Parenting, careers, and intimate relationships are just a few areas that may be impacted.

One's lifelong aspirations are challenged and may have to be adjusted with the reality of a foreshortened future. Some illnesses may bring feelings of guilt or shame, if related to unsafe sexual behaviors, drug use, smoking, overeating, or other unhealthy behaviors. Depression is a common response to a diagnosis of illness, which may reduce motivation to comply with treatment. It could also cause the person to withdraw at a time when support is important or reduce one's confidence in asking others for needed assistance.

Many illnesses have an emotional component, and symptoms can be triggered or exacerbated by stress. In addition to counseling or the use of antidepressant medication, taking an active role in treatment and finding a support group of others dealing with the same illness has been proven helpful. Marriage and family therapy may be useful as well since serious illness impacts all the people who are close to the patient.

Biopsychosocial Factors Related to Mental Health

The **biopsychosocial model** proposes multiple causes from three main groups (biological, psychological, and social/environmental) that can contribute to mental health disorders. **Biological factors** are related to the body's physiological responses and may present in the form of fluctuations in heartbeat, sweating, shortness of breath, digestive issues, or issues with brain function.

Biological factors are also linked to genetics. One may have predisposed vulnerabilities to mental health disorders due to inherited traits or a history of mental health disorders within one's family. Although biological factors may heighten one's vulnerability to mental health issues such as stress and anxiety, they are not enough to substantiate a mental health diagnosis.

Psychological factors refer to cognitive processes, such as thoughts, beliefs, one's view of an experience, and one's view of self. Thought process can shape the view of self, which, in turn, shapes the sense of stability and control across environments and has a direct impact on how a person functions. Specifically, cognitive processes or psychological factors determine whether a person perceives a situation as threatening or non-threatening and reacts accordingly.

Social or environmental factors are present in one's immediate physical surroundings and social systems such as work, school, home, and peer group. A person's social environment is significantly influenced by the aforementioned biological and psychological environments. For example, their level of stress may be directly and simultaneously affected by conditions in the workplace and by a peer group. The stress may present with physiological symptoms (such as muscle pain), negatively contributing to one's overall health and wellness.

Psychosocial Stress

Psychosocial stress occurs when an individual perceives a real or imagined threat and feels unable to cope with it. Unchecked, stress can lead to physiological and mental health problems such as heart disease, depression, and anxiety. Indicators of psychosocial stress include:

- High blood pressure
- Regular feelings of sadness, irritability, or anxiousness
- Withdrawal from social events
- Sweating
- Feeling faint or dizzy
- Feeling jittery or antsy
- Muscle and joint pain and stiffness
- Teeth clenching and grinding; chronic jaw pain
- Headaches
- Feeling constantly overwhelmed or unable to complete routine tasks
- Chronic fatigue or sleep problems
- Inability to concentrate

Basic Medical Terminology

Basic medical terminology can help the practitioner determine the relationship between an individual's physiological and psychological health. It can also help practitioners work seamlessly in multidisciplinary teams with health care professionals such as psychiatrists and nurses. There are ten primary biological systems in the human body, and learning certain prefixes and suffixes can help one understand which systems are related to common medical conditions and terminology.

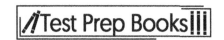
Cardiovascular System

The **cardiovascular system** circulates blood through the body via the heart. It uses arteries to bring oxygen and nutrients to the organs of the body and veins to take away waste from the organs. Related terms include:

- **Cardi-/Cardio-**: heart
- **Angi-**: vessel
- **Veno-**: vein
- **Hem-/Hemo-**: blood
- **Thromb-**: clot
- **Atherosclerosis**: hardening of the blood vessels
- **Angina pectoris**: chest pain
- **Arrhythmia/dysrhythmia**: abnormal heart rhythms (e.g., too fast or too slow)
- **Ischemia**: insufficient blood flow, which can lead to angina or heart attack

Digestive System

The **digestive system** removes nutrients from consumable energy sources through the mouth, esophagus, stomach, and intestines. It removes wastes from the body through the intestines and bladder. Related terms include:

- **Gastr-/Gastro**: stomach

- **Hep-/Hepato-**: liver

- **Chol-**: gall

- **Cyst-/Cysto-**: bladder, sac

- **Emes-**: vomit

- **Gastroesophageal Reflux Disease (GERD)**: a condition where stomach acid reverses into the esophagus and causes severe burning and inflammation

- **Cirrhosis**: progressive liver disease, often caused by alcoholism

- **Crohn's Disease**: a chronic, painful bowel or intestinal disease marked by constant inflammation

- Peritonitis: inflammation of the abdomen

Endocrine System

The **endocrine system** uses hormones to regulate complex functions like growth, reproduction, and metabolism. Related terms include:

- **Thyro-**: thyroid

- **Aden-**: gland

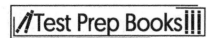

- **Hypo/hyperthyroidism**: a condition where the thyroid makes too little or too much thyroid hormone, resulting in metabolic and energy issues

Integumentary System

The **integumentary system** consists of skin, hair, and nails to protect the internal organs from external damage. Related terms include:

- **Adip-**: fat

- **Lip-**: fat

- **Cutaneo-**: skin

- **Derm-**: skin

- **Melan-**: black, dark

- **Seb-**: sebum, oily

- **Melanoma**: a type of skin cancer

- **Dermatitis**: inflammation of the skin

- **Kaposi Sarcoma**: usually fatal skin tumor

Lymphatic System

The **lymphatic system** is a network of vessels that promote the body's ability to fight infection and disease. Related terms include:

- **Blast-/-blast**: bud or germ
- **Lymph-**: clear fluid
- **Phag-**: eat
- **Lymphoma**: a malignant condition of lymph tissue
- **Metastasis**: the spreading of cancerous cells, usually through lymph

Musculoskeletal System

The **musculoskeletal system** enables the body to physically function and provides support for it. Related terms include:

- **Oste-**: bone
- **Chondr-**: cartilage
- **Arth-**: joint
- **Myel-**: bone marrow
- **Ten-**: tendon
- **Burs-**: bursa
- **Myo-**: muscle
- **Arthritis**: loss of mobility and cartilage in joints
- **Osteoporosis**: loss of calcium in bones resulting in structural weakness

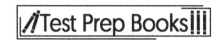

Nervous System

The **nervous system** is responsible for communication between the brain and the muscles, resulting in physiological action and tangible sensation. Related terms include:

- **Ceph-**: head

- **Myel-/Myelo-**: spinal cord

- **Neur-/Neuro-**: nerve

- **Multiple Sclerosis**: a disease where nerve fibers lose their insulation and ability to communicate with muscles, often leading to paralysis or other sensory problems

- **Epilepsy**: recurring seizures or convulsions

- **Aphasia**: loss of speech

Renal System

The **renal system** comprises primarily the kidneys, which filter waste from the blood. Related terms include:

- **Neph-**: kidney
- **Ren-**: kidney
- **Ur-/-uria**: urine
- **Pyel-**: renal ducts
- **Nephrosis**: diseased kidneys
- **Nephrolith**: kidney stone
- **Urethritis**: inflamed urethra, which affects the expulsion of urine
- **Enuresis**: uncontrollable bladder and urine expulsion

Reproductive System

The **reproductive system** includes sexual organs responsible for conception and maturation of a fetus. Related terms include:

- **Orchid-**: testes

- **Test-**: testes

- **Andr-**: male

- **Hyst-**: uterus

- **Colp-**: vagina

- **Men-**: menstruation

- **Mammo-**: breast

- **Masto-**: breast

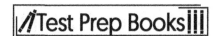

- **-pareunia**: intercourse

- **Prostate-Specific Antigen**: a protein which, in high levels, may indicate prostate cancer in males

- **Endometriosis**: excessive, hardened uterine tissue that can cause abdominal bleeding and painful menstruation in females

- **Pelvic inflammatory disease**: inflamed uterine tubes in females

- **Dyspareunia**: painful sexual intercourse

Respiratory System

The **respiratory system** brings oxygen into the body and releases carbon dioxide out of the body through the lungs. Related terms include:

- **Rhin-/Rhino-**: nose

- **Laryn-**: larynx

- **Trach-**: trachea

- **Bronch-**: lung

- **Pne-/Pneu-**: breathing, lungs

- **Pulmo-**: lung

- **Emphysema/Chronic Obstructive Pulmonary Disease (COPD)**: a lung condition where the progressive deterioration of the membranes results in the inability to exchange oxygen

- **Cystic fibrosis**: a genetic disease resulting in abnormal mucous production, lung infections, and lung scarring

- **Pneumoconiosis**: any lung disease in which pollutants become trapped or lodged in the lungs

Mental and Emotional Illness Throughout the Lifespan

Mental and emotional illness can present in a number of ways and vary depending on the illness, the person, and the circumstances. Some symptoms of mental and emotional illness include:

- Chronic feelings of sadness

- Inability to focus

- Extreme mood variation

- Loss of interest in activities one used to enjoy

- Lack of sexual interest or desire

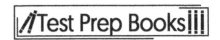

- Intense, and sometimes unexplainable, feelings of guilt, shame, regret, fear, or worry

- Chronic fatigue

- Sleep problems, such as insomnia or sleeping too much

- Feeling overwhelmed by daily routines or tasks

- Substance use

- Compulsive or obsessive thoughts or behaviors

- Hallucinations

- Thoughts of suicide

- Thoughts of harming oneself or others

- Excessive weight gain or weight loss

- Unexplained anger or irritability

- Detachment from loved ones

- Medically unexplained physical symptoms (psychosomatic) such as headaches, jaw pain, stomach pain, or joint stiffness.

Information Available from Other Sources

When working with clients, social workers need to compile a complete and accurate assessment of the client's background. Assessments may include information from a variety of sources. **Primary sources of information** are those provided directly by the client. This may include the intake form they complete, direct responses to questions asked by the social worker (such as during an interview or counseling session), documented medical history provided straight from the client, journal entries or other personal communications of the client, or body language exhibited in person. **Secondary sources of information** are taken from a source other than the client.

A medical history provided by the client's doctor, rather than by the client, is considered a secondary source. Records from the client's place of employment, schools, and public data such as home ownership or jail information are also examples of secondary sources of information. Social workers may choose to interview or provide group services to a client's family and friends. Any information that is shared about the client by people close to him or her is considered secondary information. Additionally, if the social worker chooses to conduct literature reviews or searches of evidence-based research to shape an intervention, they are seeking secondary sources.

When requesting or seeking secondary information, such as from employment records or from interviews with family members, social workers must carefully consider the legal, ethical, and moral consequences of their actions. Whenever applicable, consent to seek and use secondary source information should be provided by the client. When this is not possible, such as with a client who is physically or mentally unable to provide valid consent, social workers should use empathy, compassion,

77

a high standard of ethics, and discretion when searching for information about the client. The client should be treated with dignity and respect during this process. All information should be gathered with the sole intention of providing help and support in the client's best interest.

Obtaining Sensitive Information

Interviews are a critical component of social work practice wherein clients provide verbal reports, accounts, or narratives that serve as the main source of information and data collected during the assessment process.

The basis of the interview is a verbal report that involves introductions between the practitioner and client. In some practice settings, the verbal report may be supplemented by an **information sheet** that provides client demographics and a brief overview of the *presenting problem*. **Presenting problems** are prevailing circumstances, symptoms, or difficulties that the client believes is a problem requiring psychotherapeutic assistance.

Principle: Practitioners Need to Establish Rapport with the Client

Providing a description of the services provided and what the client can expect during sessions is the practitioner's first opportunity to build rapport with the client. Rapport development impacts the thoroughness of the information provided from the client. If the level of rapport is limited, the client may not feel comfortable enough to provide sufficient information. The level of rapport also affects the type of impression the client wishes to make on the practitioner. Consequently, it is linked to the client's perception of self-awareness. Some key points to remember are as follows:

- The social worker's own personal characteristics (gender, race, age, etc.) may affect the level of client interaction, based on the client's cultural background.

- Clients may adjust their responses to questions based on how they perceive the social worker's characteristics.

- The social worker's demographics may also have an impact on how the client feels about disclosing sensitive information, such as domestic violence, sexual conduct, or child abuse.

Principle: The Basics of Social Work Practice Should be Used When an Interview is Conducted

Once the introductions have been made and an overview of services and interview processes provided, the client should be asked to explain why they came in for treatment.

Empowering clients to share their concerns and emphasizing the point of hearing things from their perspective provides the practitioner with an opportunity to gauge a client and start "where the client is" in the initial phases of the assessment process.

Technique

The use of encouraging, neutral phrases will help move the conversation forward and encourage the client to share, e.g., "What brings you in to see me today?"

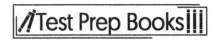

While being encouraging to the client, it is important that practitioners are genuine and not phony. Practitioners should avoid overly complimentary statements, such as "I'm so glad you came in today!" If the client senses the interest is insincere, they may not wish to share.

Principle: The Practitioner Should Start Where the Client is

After engaging the client, they should be allowed to open up, "vent," or speak freely for approximately fifteen minutes.

Technique

While the client is delving into any emotions, the practitioner should utilize active listening to keep the client engaged. Additionally, it is important to observe the client's **non-verbal cues** (posture, gestures, voice tone and pitch, and facial expressions) that lend to the emotional state. Once the client shares primary concerns, the practitioner can focus on what is important to the client.

The practitioner should observe the client's emotional state, allowing them to feel those emotions freely while providing the account of the problem. Demonstrating empathy is important when responding to the client's emotions. The emotion observed should be acknowledged. For example, if a client is crying, the practitioner can state, "You seem saddened about this," to demonstrate empathy. This practice can also hone in on an important area of the client's life that may be addressed later.

Once the client has been allowed to speak freely, the practitioner should utilize exploratory interviewing skills to delve into the specifics of topics that seemed particularly troubling for the client during the disclosure of the presenting problem.

After the client has revealed the presenting problem and the emotional state has been observed, the client should be asked to delve further into details about current life circumstances. This will provide an opportunity for the practitioner to gain additional information related to the context of the client's problem. It also allows the practitioner to uncover particularly troubling areas that can be explored later. Moreover, it may reveal certain boundaries for the client who is unwilling or unready to discuss certain details of their life.

Principle: It is Important to Engage the Client Verbally While Simultaneously Observing Non-Verbal Cues

The practitioner should ask questions to provide clarification and deeper insight into the client's problems and level of functioning.

Question Techniques

Open-ended questions may provide more detail and allow the client to expand into other areas that can be explored later.

Closed-ended questions are ideal for fact-finding from a client.

Clarification questions should be asked whenever necessary. This may be done through active listening and reflective sharing on the social worker's part to foster comprehensive communication and further build rapport.

Note Taking Techniques

If the client has questions as to why notes are taken, the reasoning behind it should be explained, and a copy should be offered to the client to make them feel more comfortable and involved in the interview process.

Observation of client behaviors during the interview may be indicative of how the client behaves or reacts in settings outside of the session. Conversely, clients may act outside of their norm, due to the perceived pressure from the interview process. The aforementioned questions and non-verbal observations are essential to determine factors of the client's personality and the context of presenting issues.

Practitioners should also be aware that their interactions affect client behaviors and responses during the interview process. For example, the client may mimic rigid body language (folded arms, crossed legs, minimal eye contact) from the practitioner and become defensive in speech pattern, pitch, or tone.

Indicators of Addiction and Substance use

Substance use and addiction problems come in many forms. These problems are often undetected or incorrectly attributed to other causes. Indicators include:

- Problems at work or school

- Friction with romantic partners, friends, or colleagues

- Neglect of household responsibilities, self-care, or hygiene

- Reckless behavior leading to legal trouble or financial problems

- Violence

- Tolerance of the substance/behavior over time

- Inability to stop using the substance/engaging in the behavior

- No longer engaging in normal activities in order to spend time/resources on the substance or behavior

Indicators of Somatization

Somatization refers to physical and physiological manifestations of mental, emotional, and psychological conditions. Somatization most commonly occurs when a client does not have the coping tools or capacity to manage mental, emotional, or psychological stressors. There may or may not be physical or physiological indicators of the symptoms that the client says they feel; however, the symptoms feel extremely real to the client. If a client visits a medical doctor reporting physical or physiological symptoms for which the doctor can find no tangible cause, this may be an indicator that the client is experiencing a somatoform disorder.

Common somatoform symptoms include pain, muscle stiffness, nausea, fatigue, gastrointestinal disorders and discomfort, the experience of losing a function or sense, and hypochondriasis. When investigated from a biopsychosocial perspective, these symptoms often correspond with anxiety, stress,

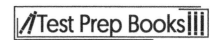

or trauma. Pediatric patients often report somatoform symptoms if they feel neglected, scared, or in need of attention. Therapeutic interventions often involve cognitive behavioral therapy, including introspective practices, the development of healthy coping mechanisms, and the development of problem-solving skills. Therapy may extend to the family unit in pediatric cases, as a shift in parenting style or the provision of parenting support can often help alleviate the pediatric patient's symptoms.

Co-Occurring Disorders and Conditions

Co-occurring disorders may also be known as **dual disorders or dual diagnoses**. Co-occurring disorders are more prevalent in clients who have substance use history or presently use substances. Substance use is diagnosed when the use of the substance interferes with normal functioning at work, school, home, in relationships, or exacerbates a medical condition. A substance use diagnosis is often made in conjunction with a mood or anxiety related disorder, resulting in a dual diagnosis.

Co-occurring disorders or dual diagnoses may be difficult to diagnose due to the nature of symptom presentation. Some symptoms of addiction or substance use may appear to be related to another mental health disorder; conversely, some symptoms of mental health disorders may appear to be related to substance use. On the contrary, there are some signs that a co-occurring disorder is present:

- *Mental health symptoms worsening while undergoing treatment*: For example, a client suffering from depression may be prescribed antidepressants to address depressive symptoms. However, if the client is using substances, he or she may mix other medications with antidepressants. This can be dangerous in itself, but it may also create a prolonged false sense of well-being while under the influence. Once this feeling fades, it can be confusing for the client to realize whether the prescribed medications are working. Even worse, the client may increase recreational substance use, leading to worse overall mental health symptoms over time.

- *Persistent substance use problems with treatment*: There are some substance use treatment centers that transition clients off of one medication and place them on another, for example, methadone. This may result in a transfer of dependence and ongoing substance use while the client is receiving treatment for mental health disorders.

Another scenario is that a client may seek treatment from a substance use treatment center with clinicians that are not equipped to provide adequate mental health treatment for the client. As the mental health problems persist or worsen while undergoing withdrawal, the client may continue to engage in substance use as a coping skill, therefore making the substance use problem appear resistant to treatment.

It is important for co-occurring disorders or dual diagnoses to be treated together because they occur simultaneously. This may be done utilizing a multidisciplinary team approach in an outpatient or inpatient setting. Treatment of dual diagnoses or co-occurring disorders at the same time in the same setting by the same treatment team is also known as an *integrated treatment* approach.

Symptoms of Neurologic and Organic Disorders

Neurological and organic processes control the nervous system, and, consequently, all of the physical sensations, muscle contractions, perceptions, sensory experiences, and other biological mechanisms.

81

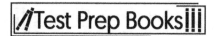
Therefore, if something goes wrong in these processes, the symptoms that present can vary vastly. These symptoms include:

- **Pain**: muscle pain, joint pain, nerve pain, tingling or burning in an area

- **Physical dysfunction**: muscle paralysis, muscle tremors, muscle spasms, involuntary muscle tics, imbalance, fainting, vertigo, slurred speech, loss of tongue control

- **Abnormal sensations**: tingling, burning, hot or cold bursts on the skin, inability to feel cold or heat, incorrect indicators for cold and heat (e.g., touching something warm only to have it feel cool), numbness, "creepy-crawly" feelings on the skin

- **Sensory dysfunction**: sudden partial or complete blindness, abnormal smell and taste perception, hallucination, ringing in the ears

- **Cognitive changes**: loss of memory, difficulty in comprehending language or speech, inability to form sentences, difficulty recognizing familiar objects or faces

Indicators of Sexual Dysfunction

Sexual dysfunction can be related to physical or psychological causes and symptoms—or both. A medical examination can determine if the cause is physical and can usually provide treatment options that include medication or lifestyle changes. If the cause is psychological, such as a result of abuse, depression, or stress, then psychotherapeutic intervention may also be needed. Indicators of sexual dysfunction include:

- Erectile dysfunction in men
- Vaginal dryness or pain in women
- Pain during intercourse or arousal
- Lack of interest in sexual behavior (physically, mentally, or emotionally)
- Fear of sexual interaction
- Inability or difficulty reaching orgasm
- Inability to become aroused or difficulty maintaining arousal
- Negative emotions associated with sexual behavior (e.g., guilt, fear, shame, regret)

Methods Used to Assess Trauma

Trauma occurs when a client experiences a deeply disturbing experience that yields an intense emotional response. Traumatic events may interfere with a client's baseline level of functioning. It is important for the social work practitioner to have an understanding of the detrimental effects, both visible and invisible, that traumatization can have on a client.

The practitioner should have an understanding of the client's baseline level of functioning. This information may be gathered first-hand from the client or through collateral sources if the client is unable or unwilling to provide that information.

The practitioner should have an understanding of how to guide the client gently through describing the traumatic experience and the emotions related to it. In doing so, the practitioner should have an

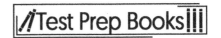
understanding of the widespread, lasting effects that trauma can have, as well as the multiple recovery and treatment options. This knowledge also helps prevent re-traumatizing the client.

An adult client may present with traumatic stressors due to one or more events that occurred during childhood. Symptoms of anxiety, depression, or other mood disorders that are actually related to the traumatic event(s) may present in session and daily functioning. A practitioner should be aware that symptoms of trauma could manifest in places and interactions outside of the client, such as within the family system, with peers, and at work.

Traumatic Stress and Violence

In normal circumstances, an individual is typically able to return to a calm state after a stressor passes. Traumatic stress and violence, however, cause long-term effects, and the patient may not be able to recover to a normal state.

Indicators of traumatic stress and violence include:

- Unexplained anger or outbursts

- Substance use and abuse

- Uncontrolled behaviors such as binge eating, compulsive shopping, gambling, hoarding, or sex addiction

- Attachment issues

- Chronic and intense feelings of shame, regret, guilt, and/or fear

- Obsessive thoughts or behaviors related to the traumatic event

- Eating disorders

- Self-harm, self-injury, or other self-destructive behaviors

- Sleep problems such as insomnia or sleeping too much

- Intense anxiety, especially in social or crowded situations

- Fear, clinginess, aggression, withdrawal, or regression in developmental behavior in children

Psychotropic and Non-Psychotropic Prescriptions and Over-the-Counter Medications

Psychotropic prescription medications are used to treat disorders such as schizophrenia, psychosis, depression, anxiety, bipolar disorder, attention deficit disorder, and a variety of mood disorders. Common antipsychotics include the brand names Abilify, Risperdal, and Seroquel. Possible side effects of antipsychotic medications include fatigue, weight gain, nausea, vomiting, anxiety, and gastrointestinal discomfort. Common mood stabilizers include the brand name Depakote and a variety of lithium-based medications. Possible side effects of mood stabilizers include gastrointestinal discomfort, weight gain, and fatigue. Common antidepressants include brand names Celexa, Lexapro, Zoloft, Prozac, Elavil,

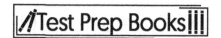
Tofranil, and Parnate. Possible side effects of antidepressants include nausea, weight gain, sexual dysfunction, sleep disorders, and gastrointestinal discomfort. Common anti-anxiety medications include brand names Ativan, Xanax, Valium, Lexapro, and Buspar. Possible side effects of antianxiety medications include fatigue, nausea, and gastrointestinal discomfort. Other psychotropic prescription medications include Vyvanse, which manages attention deficit disorders and hyperactivity, and Lyrica, which prevents seizures.

Non-psychotropic prescription medications are used to treat non-psychological disorders, such as hormonal disorders. The most common non-psychotropic prescription medications include the brand names Lipitor and Crestor (which lower cholesterol levels), Synthroid (which manages hypothyroidism), Ventolin (which manages asthma), and Nexium (which manages acid reflux). The side effects of these medications vary based on pre-existing conditions but can include appetite dysfunction, nausea and vomiting, gastrointestinal discomfort, sleep problems, jitters, dry mouth, and fatigue.

The most commonly used over-the-counter medications include cough, cold, pain relief, and fever-reducing medications. These include the brand names Tylenol, Motrin, Aleve, Advil, Mucinex, Sudafed, and Claritin. Major side effects are typically only associated with over-the-counter cough and cold medications and can include extreme drowsiness. Other commonly used over-the-counter medications include those that treat acid reflux, constipation, and diarrhea.

Assessment Methods and Techniques

Problem Formulation

The **problem system** refers to factors that are relevant to the client's presenting problem, which may include other people or environmental elements the client deems relevant to the situation. It is important that questions be asked to determine what the client's perception of the presenting problem is.

Additionally, the practitioner should determine if there are other legal, medical, or physical issues related to the problem. For a comprehensive assessment, the client should also be asked how long the problem has been present and if there are any triggers that he/she believes contribute to the problem. Identification of external supports and access to resources is also key when examining and discussing the problem system.

The presenting problem is generally revealed in the client's statement about why he or she has come in for treatment. If collateral sources are used, information can also be gathered from one or more of the collateral sources who have insight as to why the client is in need of assistance.

Disclosure of the presenting problem allows the social worker to determine the prevailing concerns deemed important by the client.

Social workers can gain a sense of how distressed the client is about the problem or situation and what client expectations are for treatment.

The manner in which the client describes the presenting problem can also provide insight as to how emotionally tied the client is to the problem and whether or not the client came in under their own volition.

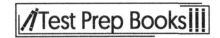

It is important to determine the true root causes of the presenting problem. Although a client may come in and voice a concern, it may not be the root cause of the issue. Rather, this concern may simply be an item the client feels comfortable discussing. For example, a client who is experiencing sexual issues may initially speak about anxiety before disclosing the actual problem. This may require an investment of time to allow the client to become comfortable trusting the practitioner.

The history of the problem is important to address because it clarifies any factors contributing to the presenting problem, as well as any deeper underlying issues. Gathering background information on the problem history is also helpful for developing interventions. There are three key areas to address when reviewing the problem history: onset, progression, and severity:

- Onset: Problem onset addresses when the problem started. It usually includes triggers or events that led up to the start of the problem; these events may also be contributing factors.

- Progression: Assessment of the progression of the problem requires determining the frequency of the problem. The practitioner should ask questions to determine if the problem is intermittent (how often and for how long), if it is acute or chronic, and if there are multiple problems that may or may not appear in a pattern or recurring cluster.

- Severity: Practitioners should determine how severe the client feels the problem is, what factors contribute to making the problem more severe, and how the situation impacts the client's adaptive functioning. This may be determined by addressing the following questions:

    o Does the problem affect the client at work?

    o Is there difficulty performing personal care because of the problem?

    o The practitioner should ascertain whether or not the client has access to resources that can provide adequate care (running water, shelter, and clothing).

    o The client's living situation should be explored if there are difficulties with personal care activities.

    o The practitioner should also ask if there are others for whom the client is responsible, like children or elderly parents/relatives.

    o Has the problem caused the client to withdraw from preferred activities?

    o Has the client used alcohol or other controlled substances to alleviate or escape the problem? If so, for how long and to what degree?

Psychosocial Stressors

Psychosocial stressors related to the problem should also be addressed by examining what the stressors are and addressing how they may influence the presenting problem.

A **Likert Scale** can be designed to assess the client's perception of how certain stressors are influential.

A **Life Events Scale** can also be utilized to assess the impact of psychosocial stressors. This scale has more than 40 life changes including divorce, death of immediate family members, marriage, work

85

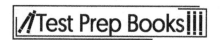

termination, and retirement, and it provides a quantitative level of stress associated with such major events.

<u>Problem ABCs</u>

The **ABCs of a problem** refer to the Antecedent, Behavior, and Consequences linked to a client's perceived problem. The discovery of these items allows the client to define the problem specifically and examine factors affecting emotional well-being.

Antecedents to a problem may be prefaced by the involvement of certain individuals in the client's life. It is important to gather understanding on how the client was involved with these individuals and how the client felt affected. Environmental antecedents may also be present.

The client may disclose interactions that lead to problematic **behaviors**, based on the aforementioned information in the evaluation of the antecedent. When addressing the behavior, it is important that practitioners gather information on what is said before, during, and after the maladaptive behavior takes place.

The **consequences** to a presenting problem are comprised of both cognitive—or personal (internal)—and environmental (external) interactions or reactions to the behavior. The client and other identified participants linked to the problem will reveal their belief sets and values based on the role played in either sustaining the behavior or attempting to decrease it.

The client's coping skills should be evaluated to determine the type of mechanism that he or she implements when the problem is present and whether or not it is an appropriate coping mechanism for the situation.

If the client presents with a heightened emotional reaction as a consequence to the problem, it could progress into another problem and create more complex issues for the client.

At this juncture, the information previously gathered on the client's legal and medical history should be incorporated into the assessment process as it may have a significant impact on the factors shaping the client's problem and the resulting consequences.

Involving Clients/Client Systems in Problem Identification

Accurately identifying an individual's problem helps the practitioner tailor an appropriate intervention. This process includes defining the issue and why it's an issue in the individual's life. It's important to note that the problem is separate from the individual in order to allow the individual to look at the issue objectively without directing blame or shame. Problem identification can be accomplished by administering written or verbal assessments, interviewing the individual's social system or support, and holistically examining the individual's personal situation.

Techniques and Instruments used to Assess Clients/Client Systems

Many psychometric instruments exist to assess and diagnose psychological functioning. Some of the most common tests include:

- Beck Depression Inventory-II (BDI-II): **BDI-II** is a twenty-one-question inventory used to measure presence and severity of depression symptoms in individuals aged thirteen years and older.

- Bricklin Perceptual Scales (BPS): **BPS** is a thirty-two-question inventory designed for children who are at least six years old. It examines the perception the child has of each parent or caregiver and is often used in custody cases.

- Millon Instruments:

    o **Millon Clinical Multiaxial Inventory III (MCMI-III)**: This 175-question inventory is used to determine indicators of specific psychiatric disorders in adults aged eighteen years and older.

    o **Millon Adolescent Clinical Inventory (MACI)**: This 160-question inventory is used to determine indicators of specific psychiatric disorders in adolescents aged thirteen to nineteen years.

    o **Millon Adolescent Personality Inventory (MAPI)**: This 150-question inventory is used to determine specific personality indicators in adolescents aged thirteen to eighteen years.

    o **Millon Behavioral Health Inventory (MBHI)**: This 165-question inventory is used to determine psychosocial factors that may help or hinder medical intervention in adults aged eighteen years and older.

- Minnesota Multiphasic Personality Inventory (MMPI-2): **MMPI-2** is a 567-item inventory. It is one of the most widely administered objective personality tests. It is used to determine indicators of psychopathology in adults aged eighteen years and older.

- Myers-Briggs Type Indicator: **Myers-Briggs** is a 93-question inventory widely used to help people aged fourteen years or older determine what personality traits influence their perception of the world and decision-making processes. A preference is identified within each of four different dimensions: extraverted (E) or introverted (I); sensing (S) or intuitive (I); thinking (T) or feeling (F); and judging (J) or perceiving (P).

- Quality of Life Inventory (QOLI): **QOLI** is a 32-question inventory that determines the perception of personal happiness and satisfaction in individuals aged seventeen years and older.

- Thematic Apperception Test (TAT): **TAT** is a narrative and visual test that typically requires the individual to create a story and allows the practitioner insight into the individual's underlying emotional state, desires, behavioral motives, and needs. It's used for individuals aged five years and older.

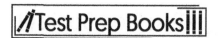

- Rorschach Test: **Rorschach test** is a visual test that records an individual's perception and description of various inkblots. It's used to determine underlying personality or thought disorders in individuals aged five years and older.

- Wechsler Adult Intelligence Scale – Fourth Edition (WAIS-IV): **WAIS-IV** is a series of subtests that assesses cognitive ability in individuals aged sixteen years and older.

Incorporating Psychological and Educational Tests into Assessment

Psychological and educational tests play a critical role in understanding client backgrounds, belief systems, and perspectives as part of the overall assessment. They also indicate any current or potential psychological, social, or physical needs that the client may have. These pieces of information shape the way social workers develop and tailor interventions for a specific client; they also allow social workers to maintain the highest level of safety for the patient as well as themselves. Psychological testing usually includes an interview component, in which the social worker may conduct the initial intake assessment, ask the client personal and family-related questions, and notice body language and other physical behaviors.

Answers to interview questions and body language observations are incorporated into assessments by indicating potential risk or protective factors, individual capacity to accept and receive services, and strengths and challenges that the social worker can incorporate into the client's treatment plan. Clients are also often tested for their communication, comprehension, reasoning, and logic skills in order to determine which methods of intervention will be best received. For example, a client who is unable to communicate verbally may not benefit from simply listening to the social worker providing counseling; a non-verbal, interactive approach will need to be developed for such a client. Clients may also take personality and behavior tests, which allow the social worker to incorporate aspects of the client's beliefs, attitudes, perspectives, and reactions into the assessment.

Risk Assessment Methods

The practitioner conducts a **risk assessment** to determine any influence that could result in harm or increased risk of harm to the individual. Assessing risk can be an ongoing process, as it's important to always have updated, accurate information. Risk-assessment methods will also vary depending on the circumstance (e.g., criminal justice, child abuse or neglect, community care). Some common methodology themes in risk assessment include the following:

- Universal risk screening: This is a general screening for certain risky behaviors (e.g., violent behavior, substance use problems, self-harm) that may result in additional screenings, referral for treatment, or stronger outcomes such as institutionalization (in the instance of high suicide risk, for example). This screening often takes place in initial consultations or as part of the individual's intake forms and may be administered on an ongoing basis (e.g., at every session) to remain current.

- Unstructured methods: These typically include clinical assessments without any specific, prepared structure. While high-level professionals often make judgments during this process, outcomes can sometimes be considered biased and unreliable.

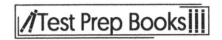

- Actuarial methods: These include highly logical, regimented tests and scales used to predict the likelihood of certain behavior patterns in a specified time frame. While scientific and evaluative in nature, some argue that these methods may place undue blame on individuals or be too inflexible to allow for the likely interplay of many influencing factors in an individual's presenting issue.

- Structured professional judgment: This combination of the previous two methods is generally the most accepted. It uses structured tools appropriate for the scope of the case but allows for the judgment and flexibility of the practitioner to decide what information is useful and to note any external information that may not be caught by standardized assessments.

Client's Danger to Self and Others

Practitioners should always be alert to indicators that individuals may pose a threat to themselves or others. These indicators may be obvious or discreet and may include:

- Substance use and abuse

- Sudden apathy towards others or society

- Sudden lack of personal care or grooming

- Isolation

- Apparent personality change

- Drastic mood shifts

- Marked change in mood. Both depressed mood and a positive change in mood can be associated with suicidal thoughts or plans. A sudden positive change may indicate that the individual has made a decision and is no longer experiencing personal turmoil.

- Verbalization of feelings such as extreme self-loathing, desire to be dead, being a burden to others, or volatility toward others.

Risk Factors for Danger to Self and Others

A client who presents as a danger to self or others should be assessed through a biopsychosocial lens. In addition, tailoring crisis management techniques to the immediate problem can help de-escalate the situation. Open-ended questions should be used to gather as much information from the client as possible. It is also important to consult collateral information from any nearby family members to document other pertinent information about the client.

- The client should be asked if there are plans to harm anyone. If the client states yes, the practitioner should determine what the plan entails.

- Any and all threats made should be taken seriously and reported to the proper authorities. Colleagues may be consulted to determine the validity of a threat if the practitioner is unclear on the client's intent.

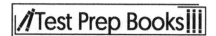

- Identifying the critical event and antecedent that preceded it is important. The client should be asked to provide as much information on this as they are willing in order for the practitioner to gain a better perspective of the client's point of view.

- Determining whether or not the client has engaged in self-injurious behaviors (SIB) is also important. Here are a few examples of SIB:

    o Excessive use of alcohol or other substances

    o Cutting

    o Banging one's head against a hard object

    o Ignoring necessary medical advice (not taking prescribed pills, leaving a hospital against medical advice)

- The practitioner should also evaluate the social and cultural factors that contribute to how the client reacts to stressful situations, including the following:

    o History of violence

    o Stability of relationships (school, work, and home)

    o Social isolation or withdrawal from others

    o Limited access to social resources

- Any recent life stressors that would lead to the client carrying through with a plan to harm self or others

- Assessing the client's current thought process is important. Do they present with confusion, clarity of the situation, or irrational thinking?

- If the client has a clear, concrete plan of action, then the risk for harm to self or others should be considered high.

Risk Factors Related to Suicide

- Previous attempts at committing suicide

- History of cutting

- Multiple hospitalizations related to self-injurious or reckless behavior, such as those noted below:

    o Drug overdose

    o Alcohol poisoning

    o Inhalation of carbon monoxide

90

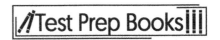
- Statement of a plan to commit suicide/suicidal ideations and access to the means to complete it

- Ownership or access to a lethal firearm

- Stated plan to cut one's wrists "the right way"

- Warnings or statements that suicide is planned

- Other factors related to suicide risk

- Age—middle-aged adults present highest suicide risk over other age groups

- Gender—males more likely to commit suicide than females

- Adolescents—high suicide risk, especially those heavily-entrenched in social media groups as a means of support and socialization

- Presence of a mental health disorder

- Life stressors from work or school

- Family history of suicide

- Family discord or other relationship trauma (divorce, break-up, widowed)

- Excessive drug or alcohol use

- Chronic illness

- Job loss

Assessing the Client's/Client System's Strengths, Resources, and Challenges

Once the client has identified the existing problem and systems, the client's **internal support systems** should be assessed, which includes examining the client's strengths and coping abilities. As with other facets of the assessment process, the client can provide a verbal report answering an open-ended question about what they view as current strengths and weaknesses.

Additionally, the social work practitioner can ask the client to provide a narrative related to a recent experience (it does not necessarily have to be linked to the presenting problem), in order to showcase strengths and weaknesses. Using finding questions can guide the client to describe their reaction to events comprehensively, to identify what favorable actions were taken, and to research what alternative actions could be taken. The social work practitioner may then summarize back to the client the strengths they heard in the narrative. This ensures that the client feels heard and understood.

The social work practitioner may also use scales to assess the client's strengths and weaknesses. A **dual perspective worksheet** may be utilized to identify the supports and obstacles perceived by the client in current social interactions. The worksheet helps create a visual map of the areas of strength the client can rely on as a means of improving areas of functioning, while simultaneously allowing the client to see areas that could use additional improvement. The social work practitioner can create a treatment plan with the client to develop or enhance coping skills, focusing on strengthening weaker areas and utilizing stronger ones.

Assessing Motivation, Resistance, and Readiness to Change

Motivation and resistance pertain to the individual's readiness to acknowledge and change behaviors. Motivation is higher and resistance is lower when an individual feels ready to make a change. Some indicators of high motivation and low resistance include:

- Awareness and open acknowledgment of the presenting issue
- Willingness to list pros and cons of behavior change
- Willingness to make small steps toward and document outcomes of behavior change
- Acknowledgment that changing behavior is in the individual's best interest

Some indicators of low motivation and high resistance include:

- Lack of recognition of a present problem
- Hostility or apathy towards the practitioner (which may be revealed by skipping sessions)
- Discussion of a presenting issue without openness to changing associated behaviors

Practitioners can increase the client's motivation by discussing changes positively in terms that demonstrate benefit to the client's life, allowing the client to set their own goals and providing assistance only for those specific goals, highlighting the tools the client possesses to make changes, and acknowledging and respecting the client's fears about change.

Assessing the Client's/Client System's Communication Skills

An individual can communicate verbally and non-verbally through body language or silence. Interviews, two-way casual conversations, and written or verbal standardized assessments can help the practitioner determine the individual's communication skills. Role-playing a specific situation can help the practitioner determine how an individual communicates in certain contexts. Assessing the individual's personal, family, social, or cultural context can also provide valuable insight to communication skills and help validate an assessment.

Assessing the Client's/Client System's Coping Abilities

It is essential that a social worker be able to accurately assess a **client system** when addressing one's coping abilities. The client system can either be the individual or their support system, such as family, guardian, spouse, etc. There are different coping mechanisms that a client or client system may use in response to their situation or trauma. Some of these mechanisms include: **avoidance pattern**–the individual manipulates their behaviors in a way that allows them to avoid thinking about, feeling, or dealing with their difficult situation; some individuals become dependent in that they begin to rely on their family members or friends (their support system) to manage the situation for them; and some individuals cope by turning to aggression or acting out. By accurately assessing the client or client's system, a social worker can identify the client's coping skills and develop a stronger plan for helping them in their situation.

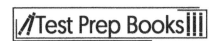

Strengths and Challenges of the Client

A client's personal and system strengths are aspects that support and promote an effective intervention and recovery. **Individual client strengths** may include a desire for positive change, willingness to collaborate with the social worker in developing an intervention, an interest in personal growth, resiliency, the presence of positive coping mechanisms, reliable transportation to and from counseling sessions, a way to pay for services, and any other physical, psychological, emotional, or financial behavior that promotes a continuous journey toward a positive resolution for the client. The **client's system** refers to their personal support system (such as family, friends, and professional colleagues) and the environment in which the client lives and works. Strengths in the client's system include aspects like close friends and family who support intervention procedures, employers that allow time off or sponsored insurance for receiving care, and colleagues that support the client's goals during the work day.

Client challenges include any personal aspect that may be a barrier to an effective intervention. Challenges may include a client who does not desire to change, who is not willingly attending social services, who feels their situation is hopeless, or who does not have the means to reliably attend intervention services (whether due to financial reasons, lack of child care, lack of transportation, and so on). Challenges in the client's system may include a non-supportive family unit (one that does not support receiving social services or that is unwilling to examine the family's role in the client's issues), a lack of close friendships or relationships, the inability to leave work for sessions, or cultural norms or beliefs that stigmatize receiving counseling services.

Assessing Ego Strengths

Ego strength is the ability of the individual to be resilient in the face of stressors. Generally, individuals with high ego strength will be able to return to a normal emotional state after experiencing crisis. They will be able to appropriately process it and cope with the demand of doing so. Positive or high ego strength is marked by:

- The ability to acknowledge mood shifts without getting overwhelmed
- The ability to cope positively with loss and setbacks
- Realizing painful or sad feelings will decrease in intensity over time
- Taking personal responsibility for actions and reactions
- Self-discipline in the face of temptation or addictive urges
- Setting and respecting firm limits and boundaries
- Avoiding people who are negative influences
- Learning from mistakes rather than blaming oneself or someone else

Consequently, the absence of these indicators may reveal areas around which to tailor intervention or treatment. These indicators may be determined through verbal discussion or standardized assessments.

Placement Options Based on Assessed Level of Care

A client's need for care can fall on a wide spectrum. Some clients may comfortably live in their own residence but attend regularly scheduled meetings with a social worker to receive care. Other clients, after being appropriately assessed, may require institutional care where they can receive medical and

93

therapeutic support as often as needed. Institutional care may be a long-term or short-term solution for a client.

The level of care required for a client is assessed by examining a number of self-sufficiency factors, such as the presence of any formally diagnosed developmental disabilities, physical disabilities, or mental disorders. Additionally, the client's ability to communicate needs, IQ level, ability to complete self-care tasks (such as dressing, toileting, grooming, etc.) alone or with assistance, and risk of voluntary or involuntary harm to self or others will also be taken into consideration. Based on the client's health and caretaking needs, they may receive outpatient services (such as regular therapeutic appointments), inpatient services (such as a behavioral program that lasts for a predetermined period of time), assisted living in a facility such as a nursing home, or in-home support (such as a home health nurse). Regardless of where a client falls on the care spectrum, services for mental wellness and adjusting to this new context of life will likely be beneficial to care.

Diagnostic and Statistical Manual of the American Psychiatric Association

The current American Psychiatric Association manual for the classification of mental disorders is the *Diagnostic and Statistical Manual of Mental Disorders, Fifth Edition, Text Revision*, or the **DSM-5-TR**. It is an updated and revised version of the APA's previous classification and diagnostic tool from 2013, the **DSM-5**. The **DSM-5-TR** serves as an authority for mental health diagnosis and functions as a tool for counselors to make treatment recommendations. The *DSM-5-TR* is organized in accordance with the developmental lifespan. In addition to guiding diagnosis, the updated framework of the *DSM-5-TR* is designed to help researchers and clinicians better understand how disorders relate to one another and ultimately improve treatment outcomes for patients.

There are several notable changes to the *DSM-5-TR* as of 2022:

- the addition of scientific knowledge accumulated since the 2013 update

- the recognition of the role of culture in psychiatric diagnosis

- the revision of language used regarding race, gender, and gender identity

- the description of a Cultural Formulation Interview for use in the counseling intake process

- the correction of ICD codes for mental health disorders

- the addition of more precise criteria for childhood conditions

- the addition of a new mental disorder, Prolonged Grief Disorder, to the category of Trauma- and Stressor-Related Disorders

- the addition of new conditions of clinical attention

- the updated names of two disorders, Functional Neurological Symptom Disorder and Intellectual Development Disorder

- the addition and removal of diagnosis specifiers, including those for Bipolar I, Bipolar II, Obsessive-Compulsive Related Disorder, Persistent Depressive Disorder, and Gender Dysphoria

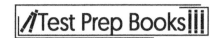

The following is a complete listing of *DSM-5-TR* diagnostic criteria chapters:

- Neurodevelopmental Disorders
- Schizophrenia Spectrum and other Psychotic Disorders
- Bipolar and Related Disorders
- Depressive Disorders
- Anxiety Disorders
- Elimination Disorders
- Other Mental Disorders and Additional Codes
- Obsessive-Compulsive and Related Disorders
- Trauma- and Stressor-Related Disorders
- Dissociative Disorders
- Somatic Symptom and Related Disorders
- Feeding and Eating Disorders
- Sleep-Wake Disorders
- Sexual Dysfunctions
- Gender Dysphoria
- Disruptive, Impulse-Control and Conduct Disorders
- Substance-Related and Addictive Disorders
- Neurocognitive Disorders
- Personality Disorders
- Paraphilic Disorders
- Medication-Induced Movement Disorders and Other Adverse Effects of Medication
- Other Conditions That May Be a Focus of Clinical Attention

Indicators of Behavioral Dysfunction

Ideas about what is normal versus what is abnormal with regard to behavior are society-dependent. People tend to equate *normal* with "good" and *abnormal* with "bad," which means that any behavior labeled as abnormal can potentially be stigmatizing. Use of person-centered language is one way to reduce stigma attached to abnormal behavior or behavior health issues (e.g., saying "a person with schizophrenia," rather than "a schizophrenic.")

The **"Four Ds" of Abnormality** assist health practitioners when trying to identify a psychiatric condition in their clients. Deviance marks a withdrawal from society's concept of appropriate behavior. **Deviant behavior** is a departure from the "norm." The *DSM-5-TR* contains some criteria for diagnosing deviance. The second "D" is dysfunction. **Dysfunction** is behavior that interferes with daily living. Dysfunction is a type of problem that may be serious enough to be considered a disorder. The third "D" is distress. **Distress** is related to a client's dysfunction. That is, to what degree does the dysfunction cause the client distress? A client can experience minor dysfunction and major distress, or major dysfunction and minor distress. The fourth "D" is danger. **Danger** is characterized by danger to self or to others. There are different degrees of danger specific to various types of disorders. **Duration** is sometimes considered a fifth "D," as it may be important to note whether the symptoms of a disorder are fleeting or permanent.

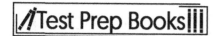

Crisis Plans

Any client who visits a social worker may experience a personal crisis at any time. A **crisis** is defined as any instance where the client is unable to cope with an event in a healthy, resolution-seeking manner. While all social workers should have a general plan developed for unexpected client crises (such as calling for backup support or an emergency contact), a tailored plan should be developed during the initial sessions with the client based on what the client's needs are. To promote a sense of responsibility, accountability, empowerment, and engagement, the client should be invited to collaborate in developing this plan. Developing a crisis plan may include discussing the client's possible stress and crisis triggers as well as determining the client's best solution for diffusing a crisis situation (such as employing trusted family members, utilizing a security item, managing therapeutic medications, and so on). This plan should be reviewed at regular intervals with the client to ensure it is still valid and does not need revisions to account for new triggers or resolved behaviors.

Finally, should a crisis arise, social workers should be as transparent as possible about implementing the crisis plan. They should clearly communicate the steps they are taking as they take them, and invite the client to engage in the plan as well (if it is possible). Social workers should be mindful to note the context and present situation of the crisis, so that they can provide the best support in that moment. If the social worker tries to push the client too far in taking responsibility during a crisis or is too overbearing when the client would like to practice self-sufficiency, the crisis intervention may backfire and create a long-term barrier between the client and the social worker.

Objective and Subjective Data

Both objective and subjective data are used during the assessment and treatment processes. The client provides their perspective on what happened and the correlated feelings and experiences felt, which is the **subjective data**. Subsequently, the social work practitioner uses the information and may ask finding questions to better understand where the client is emotionally, while teasing out facts related to the client's situation. These facts are **objective data**.

The information from both the subjective and objective data is combined to formulate a concise, yet comprehensive, assessment for the client. In some note-taking practices, the identification of the subjective and objective data along with assessment formation is required. This style of documentation is known as the **SOAP method**, an acronym that stands for Subjective, Objective, Assessment, and Plan. Another note-taking style that focuses on the subjective and objective data is the **BIRP documentation method**. *BIRP* stands for Behavior, Intervention, Response, and Plan. It is not as commonly used as SOAP.

Methods to Interpret and Communicate Policies and Procedures

Social workers have direct contact with clients and are in strategically critical positions to develop, implement, evaluate, and communicate policies and procedures. Policies and procedures allow clients and employees to be aware of treatment and agency goals, objectives, resources, and limitations. Policies can sometimes be a barrier to client services, so social workers must be aware of this possibility and point out these barriers when necessary.

96

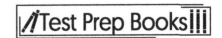

Factors in policy and procedure development:

- Front line workers should be involved in policy and procedure development since they are in the best position to determine and evaluate how clients are affected.

- Policies should be clearly written and communicated to clients/workers with copies available for distribution. Workers should receive periodic training on current policies and procedures.

- Policies should be in the best interest of clients, but they should also protect the agency and staff.

Factors to consider when evaluating the effectiveness of policies and procedures:

- The origins of the policy and/or procedure, including values and the related ideology

- Client reactions, thoughts, and feelings about the policy

- Alignment with social work ethics and values

- Intentional and unintentional consequences and benefits

- Regular re-evaluation to ensure policies and procedures are still relevant and in the best interests of clients, workers, and the agency

Research Designs and Methods

Basic and applied research are two separate categories of systematic investigation. **Basic research** aims to expand knowledge, although the new knowledge may not have any immediate application in the real world. Basic research can often lead to new ideas and theories. Basic research can explore, explain, or describe existing or potential ideas, with the end goal of simply understanding or creating new information. **Applied research** is conducted with the specific aim of answering a question or solving a problem. It is often used by business entities, scholars, and non-profit organizations to gather and analyze data relating to a very specific inquiry.

Basic and applied research designs can be qualitative (where qualities of interest are examined) or quantitative (where measurements of data are examined to statistically explain relationships between variables). **Qualitative data methods** include performing case studies on a specific entity, observation, interviews, and developing and confirming narratives about a phenomenon.

These techniques are commonly employed in social work cases and interventions, where human behavior, family history, relationship history, environmental interactions, and other subjective variables are examined and manipulated to support a client's health outcome. **Quantitative methods** measure two or more variables and concretely examine the relationship between them. **Correlational design** is a quantitative method that examines two or more variables to determine the influence one variable has on other variables (such as the relationship between age and IQ). **Causal comparative design** examines groups with similar features and differences to understand factors that may influence the similarities and differences. **Experimental design** establishes one control group as a baseline and conducts an experiment on another group to quantify the influence of the experimental factor. Control and

97

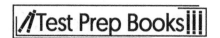

experimental groups may be randomly assigned or assigned with a purpose (such as employing a sample of 21-year-olds in order to examine a specific behavior in this age range). Some designs use both quantitative and qualitative methods; these are called **mixed research designs**.

Data Collection and Analysis Methods

Qualitative data can be collected through interviews, observations, anecdotes, and surveys, and by reviewing literature and other relevant documents. Qualitative data collection methods are often subjective and cannot be generalized to larger samples or populations. Quantitative data can be collected from experiments, recordings of certain events and timed intervals, surveys in which an answer choice must be selected for each question, data management systems, and numerical reports. **Quantitative data** methods are often objective and abstract, and they can be generalized to explain relationships between variables in large populations.

To analyze data, researchers must ensure all collected data are relevant to the questions being posed; are accurate; come from a credible, unbiased source; and are complete. Often, all "cleaned" data sets are entered into a computer-based data management system software from which analyses and inferences can be calculated. Clean data sets can be accurately described for relationships between variables and to make simple observations. They can also be used to answer related hypotheses or propose new ideas and inferences based on visible relationships. Often, these can be applied to explain behaviors, phenomena, or other questions related to a large population.

Reliability and Validity in Social Work Research

Reliability is used to describe whether a measurement method produces the same results over a long period of time and across different users. The reliability of a measurement method is analyzed through **inter-rater reliability** (if multiple researchers can use the method the same way), **test-retest reliability** (when measurements stay the same even when the method is used multiple times by the same person), **parallel forms reliability** (measuring the same results even when slight variations in the method exist), and **internal consistency reliability** (how consistent responses to the measure are). A strong measurement method performs well across all four of these reliability techniques.

Validity is used to describe how well a measurement method works to collect the data it is designed to collect. **Face validity** is used to describe how well a measurement method appears to be collecting desired information to the participant who is using the method. This is believed to influence participants into responding accurately. **Construct validity** is used to describe how well a specific variable is measured (as opposed to other measures that may be present). **Criterion validity** is used to infer performance. **Formative validity** is used to study outcomes and determine how to improve a measure or program. **Sampling validity** is used to describe how complete a sample is in order to eliminate bias.

Measurement methods can have high reliability and low validity, and vice versa. A strong research metric will be high in both reliability and validity.

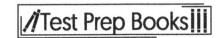

Intervention Planning

Methods to Involve Clients in Intervention Planning

Practitioners should always treat the individual as the expert on the individual's life, and while practitioners should gather relevant external and collateral information, they should make all efforts not to allow these sources to supersede information provided by the individual. Practitioners should involve the individual as much as possible in problem identification and resolution planning by asking about details about the individual's life, any presenting issues and what might be causing them, what kinds of changes the individual would like to make, how these changes might enrich quality of life, and real and perceived fears.

All of these details should be acknowledged, respected, valued, and referred to when planning and implementing interventions. Practitioners should also tailor interventions to highlight and utilize established strengths and resources of the individual.

Indicators of Motivation, Resistance, and Readiness to Change

Motivation and resistance impact a client's readiness to change behavior. These are two crucial components to examine when developing an intervention plan. High motivation is indicated by self-confidence and self-efficacy, as the client believes they are capable of change. High motivation is also characterized by a client's desire to correct an identified problem, work toward a goal, and reliably show up for sessions. High motivation also shows in the client's belief that implementing a change will improve their overall quality of life.

Resistance can refer to any behavior that indicates the client does not want to work with the social worker or improve their personal situation. Resistance may be indicated by a client's refusal to show up on time, or at all, for sessions. A client involuntarily coming to sessions (such as by a court order) may state that there is no tangible problem to work on, or the client may state they feel no changes are occurring. Social workers should examine resistance holistically to ensure they are not contributing to it. For example, clients may exhibit resistance to counseling sessions if they do not feel comfortable with the social worker, if they do not understand the social worker, or if they are expected to work on issues that they do not yet feel ready to address.

Readiness to change occurs in six stages: **pre-contemplation** (where an individual does not believe a need for change exists or is not self-aware), **contemplation** (where an individual recognizes a problem but is not ready to address it), **preparation** (where an individual recognizes a problem and sets the stage for change), **action** (where an individual takes active, involved steps to stop a problem), **maintenance** (where the individual commits to the desired behaviors), and **termination** (where the individual is able to regularly sustain the desired behaviors without relapse).

Cultural Considerations in the Creation of an Intervention Plan

An intervention's success depends in part on whether the intervention plan is aligned with the individual's cultural experience. All individuals are part of cultures with specific traditions, habits, and norms. These can vary by race, ethnicity, immigration status, income level, geographical location, or social status. It's important to take culture into context in order to show respect for the individual's way of life, tailor interventions to be easily understood, create trust and cooperation, and avoid wasting time

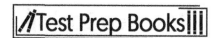

or resources. Cultural contexts can be understood through researching the community, reading literature or periodicals from the area, and networking with people in the setting.

Intervention/Treatment Modalities

When utilizing a holistic approach for client assessment and treatment planning, practitioners should utilize evidence-based research to support the selected interventions and treatment modalities. The interventions and treatment modalities selected will be based on a number of things, including the client's current level of functioning (based on the biopsychosocial assessment), level of care needed, presenting symptoms, and the practitioner's background. Here are some things a practitioner will want to consider when constructing interventions or treatment modalities:

- Are the selected interventions evidence-based?

- Do the selected interventions arise from a strengths-based perspective specifically tailored around the client's strengths, interests, and needs?

- Do the associated risks with the selected interventions outweigh the possible positive outcomes?

- Is the selected intervention culturally-sensitive and culturally-appropriate?

- Did the client participate in the construction of the intervention selection and/or consent to it?

- Does the practitioner feel comfortable and well-versed in the selected intervention to increase the levels of intensity as needed and provide a continuity of care for the selected modalities?

- Does the selected intervention coincide with the client's financial ability to pay?

Intervention, Treatment, and Service Plans

Creating SMART objectives allows for data-driven and measurable intervention plans. When creating objectives, practitioners should be able to measure the desired behavior that is exhibited, the number of times the desired behavior is exhibited over a period of time, the conditions in which the desired behavior must be exhibited, and progress from the undesired behavior to the desired behavior through baseline evaluation and evaluation at predetermined intervals.

Psychotherapies

Social workers need skills in a broad spectrum of areas, including case management, advocacy, and political change. Social workers also need to be versed in psychotherapy modalities so as to enhance client engagement in the change process. Psychotherapy modalities originated with the "talk therapy" based on Sigmund Freud's work and include, but are not limited to, cognitive behavioral, narrative, psychodynamic, solution focused, and behavioral therapies. It is up to social workers to decide which psychotherapies are most effective for their clients and should be pursued. Agencies may favor a particular type of psychotherapy that the social worker should learn. Insurers may favor psychotherapy modalities and social workers need to consider this in their work with clients.

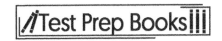

Impact of Immigration, Refugee, or Undocumented Status on Service Delivery

Immigrants, refugees, and undocumented individuals often have the highest need for social services but also have the most barriers to effectively receiving support. Immigrants often face the stress of leaving their home country and assimilating into a completely new culture, economy, and lifestyle. While a social worker can help navigate these changes to set the foundation for a new life, immigrants often experience language barriers or simply may not realize such services exist for their use. Social workers may need to actively advertise their assistance and understand the background and culture of the immigrant in order to help.

Refugees often have the same stresses and barriers that immigrants have, but often they have also left violent or destructive situations in their home country. They may be happy to be safe, but they may also have deep feelings of sadness, especially if their families were affected (such as through death of a loved one or the necessity of leaving family members behind). While many immigrants come on work visas, refugees may have no means to make money and may need help navigating welfare benefits. There may also be feelings of discomfort in receiving these benefits. Social workers should be especially sympathetic to the diverse reasons behind an individual's refugee status.

Undocumented individuals may feel scared to seek out social services, fearing reprisal or deportation, even though social services can be an avenue to help undocumented families change their status to documented. Social workers who hope to help these groups should focus on building trust and creating spaces of security and safety.

Discharge, Aftercare, and Follow-Up Planning

An important part of treatment planning is discharge planning. There are numerous reasons that services for a client may end. Clients may feel that they no longer need the services, that they are not compatible with the social work practitioner providing the services, that an increased level of care is needed that is beyond the scope of the practitioner, or they may have successfully met goals for treatment.

Discharge planning should begin with the onset of the initial assessment for the client. The practitioner should not delay discharge planning, as discharge may occur at any time. Making the client aware of the choices for discharge and the discharge planning process empowers the client during treatment. It also provides continuity of care for the client.

The main purpose of **discharge planning** is to develop a plan of care that goes beyond the current treatment sessions to promote success once services have concluded. In the event that the client is going to a higher level of care or to a different professional, effective discharge planning is useful in disseminating pertinent information about the client to assist in continuity of care and effective treatment. In this sense, the current practitioner should prepare to become a collateral source linked to the client's level of care for the next professional.

In addition to benefiting the other practitioners the client may meet with, effective discharge planning benefits the client as well. If services have been completed successfully and the client has met the stated goals, then discharge planning ensures that the client has a plan to sustain a stable level of function and maintain the successes achieved. This is particularly useful with clients who suffer from substance use or other addictive behaviors, as effective discharge planning can prevent relapse.

Upon the conclusion of the client discharging from services, a discharge summary should be created and placed in the client's file. The *discharge summary* should include the following information:

- Reason for discharge
- Description of treatment goals and the degree to which they were met
- Client's response to the interventions
- Description of the client's levels of functioning
- Baseline
- Progress during treatment
- Functioning at discharge
- Recommendations for follow-up care
- Links to community resources
- Appointment dates for other providers (if available)
- Provision of additional contacts, client supports
- Description of potential risks post-discharge
- Contact information for post-discharge support and crisis intervention

Follow-Up Techniques in Social Work

At the final session, the social worker and client can schedule a follow-up session at a predetermined time to evaluate the client's continued progress after termination. Another option is to propose a time to meet and alert the client that the worker will contact the client to schedule a follow up. The follow-up session enables the social worker the opportunity to determine how well the client has progressed and to determine the effectiveness of the intervention(s) used during sessions.

Practice Quiz

1. Which of the following is NOT a critical part of a client interview?
   a. Building rapport
   b. Verifying payment
   c. Starting where the client is
   d. Use of encouraging, neutral questions

2. How many main sections make up the *DSM-5-TR*?
   a. One
   b. Two
   c. Three
   d. Four

3. Jane wakes up every morning with a headache, jaw pain, and neck pain. She struggles to get out of bed, and even basic household tasks seem to take all of her energy. She has trouble getting to work on time, and even when she has an important deadline, she doesn't seem to care or be able to concentrate. She always feels cranky and sometimes finds herself crying over things that never used to bother her. At her office health fair, a vendor took Jane's blood pressure and found it to be 150/90. What might Jane's symptoms indicate?
   a. Psychosocial stress
   b. Gout
   c. Alzheimer's disease
   d. Generalized Anxiety Disorder

4. An individual with schizophrenia may be prescribed which of the following medications?
   a. Vyvanse
   b. Ritalin
   c. Nexium
   d. Abilify

5. What does a genogram visually depict?
   a. History of all prescribed medications and dosages
   b. Social interactions over a specific period of time
   c. Risk of carrying certain genetic diseases
   d. Stress triggers

See answers on next page.

Answer Explanations

1. B: Verifying payment is not a critical part of the client interview. Payment may occur before the interview process or may be pre-determined based on the work setting. Choice *A*, building rapport, happens at all stages of the client interview and is an important characteristic of interviews. Choice *C*, starting where the client is, is another important feature of the interview and is part of empowering the client by hearing things from their perspective. Choice D, the use of encouraging, neutral questions, is also part of empowering the client and moves the conversation forward, encouraging the client to share.

2. C: The *DSM-5-TR* has three sections—one that explains an overview of the changes, one that lists the classes of and criteria for disorders, and one that covers areas for future research.

3. A: Psychosocial stress. Gout is a kind of arthritis characterized by joint pain and inflammation. Alzheimer's disease is a neurological condition characterized by memory loss and confusion. Generalized anxiety disorder is characterized by persistent and excessive worrying and fear.

4. D: Abilify. Abilify is an atypical antipsychotic used to treat symptoms of schizophrenia. Vyvanse and Ritalin are stimulants typically used to treat attention-deficit/hyperactivity disorders. Nexium is a proton-pump inhibitor used to treat reflux diseases.

5. B: Social interactions over a specific period of time. The other three answers do not fit the function or purpose of a genogram, which is used to show how a person's social (often familial) relationships affect attachment, behavioral patterns, and relationship dynamics.

Interventions with Clients/Client Systems

Intervention Processes and Techniques for Use Across Systems

Interviewing Techniques

Interviewing is common in social work. An interview should always be focused and have a purpose—this is often to gather data, make a diagnosis, and provide therapy. An interview can be used to discuss behavior patterns, ensure the practitioner and the individual are discussing the same presenting issues, bring attention to presenting issues, or provide new perspectives on presenting issues. Interviews are generally verbal, although the practitioner should be mindful of observing non-verbal communication. While the questions of the interview should be planned, the practitioner should be able to tailor the questions based on the individual's needs.

There are several communication techniques beneficial to the social work practice other than the basic interview process used to gather general demographic and presenting problem information:

- Furthering: A technique that reinforces the idea that the worker is listening to the client and encourages further information to be gathered. This technique includes nodding of the head, facial expressions, or encouraging responses such as "yes" or "I understand." It also includes accent responses, whereby workers repeat or parrot back a few words of a client's last response.

- Close/Open-Ended Questions: Depending on the timing or information the worker is seeking to elicit from the client, one of these types of questions may be used. Close-ended questions, such as "How old are you?" will typically elicit a short answer. Conversely, open-ended questions, such as "What are your feelings about school?", allow for longer, more-involved responses.

- Clarifying and Paraphrasing: This is when social workers ask a client for clarification to ensure they understand the client's message. Clarifying also includes encouraging clients to speak more concretely and in less abstract terms to provide clearer messages. When paraphrasing, workers should convey a message back to the client to ensure an understanding of the client's meaning.

- Summarizing: This is similar to paraphrasing, but summarizing includes more information. It's frequently used to help focus the session and allow the worker to summarize the overall messages, problems, or goals of the client.

- Active Listening: Active listening involves using facial expressions, body language, and postures to show that the worker is engaged to the client. Workers should display eye contact and natural but engaged body movements and gestures. An example would be sitting slightly forward with a non-rigid posture. As with all communication techniques, social workers should be aware of cultural differences in what is appropriate, especially related to direct eye contact and posturing.

105

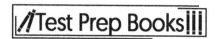

Methods of Summarizing Communication

Social workers may paraphrase and echo clients' verbal statements to acknowledge their feelings. Summarizing may involve reflecting back the statements made by the client to clarify what the client has said. Social workers also must summarize communication in order to provide sufficient records of the session. Further, during the end of the session, the social worker may wish to clarify goals and homework assigned for the next week so that the client is clear on the changes that need to take place.

Methods of Facilitating Communication

Social workers may facilitate communication with the client by verbally encouraging communication or by addressing the client with constructive information concerning the case. Social workers need to recall information concerning the client from session to session in order to facilitate communication and move forward with the client. Clarifying what the client has said and the client's feelings helps not only to ensure the social worker clearly understands what is being communicated, but also lets the client know that the social worker is engaged and actively listening. Development of trust with the client may facilitate additional communication, and social workers should be sensitive to the trust-building process because it is the cornerstone of the helping relationship. Social workers may provide clients with homework outside of a session that facilitates communication during the next session.

Mandated clients, including court ordered clients or clients ordered to counseling from child protective services, may face challenges in communicating with the social worker because they do not choose to be in treatment. Developing trust with these clients to facilitate communication is especially important for progress to be made. It's helpful to acknowledge the client's feelings and possible frustration about the mandated treatment. Clients who require out-of-home placement need clear communication with the social worker to clarify what is happening and make appropriate psychological adjustments to their circumstances.

Using Bias-Free Language in Interviewing

When interviewing a client, a social worker must be careful to eliminate all personal bias from their language. This relates to all subtle negative phrasing related to race, ethnicity, socioeconomic status, gender, gender identity, life choices, disability, or psychological disorders. The job of the social worker is to support the client without bias, always promoting the client's self-identity. Phrases or expressions that demean or stereotype a particular group of people should never be used. Similarly, labeling someone can be hurtful, especially in cases where that label has a negative connotation or stigma attached to it. Sometimes it may even be appropriate for the social worker to ask the client how they wish to be identified or addressed. Inclusive and affirming language should be used when talking about all groups of people and especially when talking to or about the client. Terms that are known to be offensive or degrading should always be avoided.

Phases of Intervention and Treatment

The **treatment intervention process** consists of four stages. There is some crossover between stages, and the activities of each stage may occur at other times during the process. For instance, the

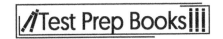

assessment and evaluation phases of intervention are ongoing throughout treatment. Here are the four stages:

- Engagement and Assessment: During this stage, the worker focuses on relationship and rapport building with the client. The worker gathers data, assesses the client's history and systems, and identifies problems and challenges.

- Goal Identification and Intervention Planning: This stage consists of the client and worker collaborating to identify goals to be accomplished. Plan of care/treatment is developed and the contract is implemented.

- Implementation: The caseworker implements selected interventions and tasks. The client works toward identified goals. During this stage, the plan is frequently reviewed by the worker in collaboration with the client to assess progress toward goals. Adjustments are made by either party if necessary.

- Termination and Evaluation: The social worker should begin the termination phase at the onset of services, since the client may abruptly terminate services for various reasons. It is within best practice guidelines and the best interest of both social worker and client to be prepared for service termination. The social worker should inform the client about the termination guidelines once services begin. Moreover, goal attainment is assessed and evaluation of interventions occurs. The social worker should also review the plan for maintenance of acquired skills while follow-up procedures are discussed and implemented.

Problem-Solving Models and Approaches

When working with clients to develop problem-solving skills, workers must first engage and prepare clients by discussing the benefits of improving such skills and encouraging clients to commit to the problem-solving process during the goal setting/contracting phase.

Steps in the problem-solving process are as follows:

- Assess, Define, and Clarify the Problem: As with goal setting, social workers should assist clients in clearly determining and defining the specific problem. Workers should focus on the current problem and ensure that clients do not become distracted by other past or current difficulties. Examine specific aspects of the problem, including behaviors and the needs of those involved.

- Determine Possible Solutions: Social workers should lead the discussion among participants to determine possible solutions and encourage client(s) to refrain from limiting options at this point. The purpose is for clients to gain practice in solution development. In the case of family work, all capable members should be allowed to offer solutions and should feel safe to do so without fear or criticism from other members.

- Examine Options and Select/Implement a Solution: Workers should assist clients in examining the benefits and drawbacks of each possible solution and choose an option that best meets the needs of those involved.

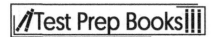
- Evaluate and Adjust: Social workers should help clients to determine the success of the solution. Client(s) can use a practical form of tracking solution effectiveness (charts, logs, etc.). If it is determined that the solution is not working, the client can return to the solution-generating stage.

Engaging and Motivating Clients/Client Systems

When determining a client's motivation, the engagement and assessment stage is crucial. When clients voluntarily seek services and/or are facing a crisis, the commitment and motivation will likely be high. **Non-voluntary clients** are identified as those who are seeking assistance based on pressure outside of the legal system (e.g., a woman gives her spouse an ultimatum to get help or she will leave). When working with non-voluntary or involuntary clients who are mandated legally to seek treatment, the social worker must help determine client-identified problems. This should be in addition or complementary to the presenting problem. The worker and client collaboratively should create a treatment plan that addresses both types of issues.

Additionally, the worker must help the client overcome any negative feelings of anger or mistrust about treatment. With all clients, appropriate relationship-building between the worker and client is a necessary part of engagement and motivation. Clients must feel they are in a safe, empathetic environment. They also should experience a sufficient level of trust for the social worker in order for treatment to be effective. To create an effective treatment relationship, the social worker must project an attitude free of judgment; recognize the client's individual attributes, strengths, and abilities; and encourage the client's right to be an active participant in their own treatment.

Engaging and Working with Involuntary Clients/Client Systems

When working with involuntary clients, motivation levels can be improved by helping the client realize they have options. Even if services are mandated by a government agency, the client can choose to accept the consequences of not participating. Therefore, agreeing to adhere to the mandate is still a choice. When setting goals and treatment planning, ensure that the client's identified problems are included along with the mandated goals. Attempts to protect a client's right to self-determination should be practiced as much as possible (e.g., encouraging a client's participation in goal setting, problem identification, and priority setting, etc.).

Obtaining and Providing Feedback

There are several ways social workers can receive feedback. It can come in the form of evaluation by another social worker during supervision, or from a client during treatment. Obtaining feedback is an important means to improve a social worker's skill and ensure effective treatment for clients. Feedback from clients may be formal or informal. Clients may offer unsolicited feedback verbally or non-verbally during treatment, using words, body language, or tone of voice. Social workers must be sensitive to the messages clients are expressing to decipher how to interpret feedback that may not be clear.

When seeking feedback from a client, the social worker should ensure the method is appropriate to the skills, resources, and abilities of the client (e.g., in writing, by mail, text, in person, etc.).

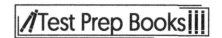

The following are factors to consider when obtaining feedback from clients:

- Social workers may consider a client's progress toward a goal or lack thereof as a type of feedback. If treatment is not progressing as expected, the worker should evaluate and make adjustments as necessary.

- Always be clear why the information is needed and ensure client confidentiality to the fullest extent possible.

- Feedback can be sought at different times throughout the treatment process to ensure reliability and consistency.

- Workers should seek feedback regardless of whether it is expected to be negative or positive. All feedback should be viewed as a learning tool to enhance treatment and worker skill.

The following are factors to consider when receiving feedback during supervision/consultation:

- Social workers can benefit from feedback during supervision or consultation, especially with difficult clients/cases or at significant times in treatment, such as termination.

- When discussing cases, client confidentiality should be protected as much as possible, and client consent to release information should be acquired.

Active Listening and Observation

Active listening is crucial to the relationship and rapport building stage with clients. Social workers must be fully engaged in the listening process and not be distracted by thoughts of what will come next or intervention planning. The worker must not only hear the audible language the client is offering but must also look at the non-verbal behaviors and the underlying meaning in the words and expressions of the client. **Nonverbal behaviors** include body language, facial expressions, voice quality, and physical reactions of the client. Other aspects of active listening include head nodding, eye contact, and using phrases that show understanding and provide clarity (e.g., "What I hear you saying is..." and "You (may) wish to..."). Workers may verify that they understand the client's message by paraphrasing and asking for validation that it is correct (e.g., "What I hear you saying is...").

Verbal and Nonverbal Communication Techniques

Social workers use verbal and nonverbal communication techniques to engage clients in completing treatment goals. Verbal communication is vital to the social worker/client relationship, and social workers should be skilled at greetings, summarization, reflection, and the conveyance of new information to the client. The client may misconstrue a social worker's body language if it does not represent openness and trust. Likewise, the social worker needs to be adept at analyzing the client's body language in order to move forward. Clients use both verbal and nonverbal communication to convey their story to the social worker, and communication techniques used by the social worker can be modeled to teach the client improved communication. Clients should be instructed to recognize their own communication techniques in the context of the relationship with the social worker. Clients who are withdrawn or isolated may need especially sensitive communication with the social worker in order to better communicate verbally and nonverbally.

In order to build a strong helping relationship with the client, the worker must learn to use effective verbal and nonverbal techniques. These skills are necessary throughout the treatment process and especially during assessment and engagement.

Congruence in Communication

Social workers need to be congruent—in agreement and harmony—with client feedback and encourage clients' self-direction. Social workers and clients begin treatment by enhancing congruence in communication so that mutually agreed upon goals may be developed for the client. The social worker should be invested in the therapeutic relationship and able to participate in a way that assists the client in becoming more self-aware. If a social worker is not congruent with the client, then treatment progress may be hindered and the client should be referred to another worker who is a more appropriate fit.

Limit-Setting Techniques

Although it may be difficult for social workers to develop the ability to set limits with clients, it is necessary for treatment to be effective. Many clients struggle with the ability to follow rules and maintain healthy boundaries. In addition to ensuring the treatment process progresses smoothly, when workers set limits, clients also learn to develop helpful life skills. This is especially important with involuntary clients receiving legally mandated services that cannot be modified or negotiated. Other ways to set limits include ensuring the maintenance of an appropriate client-worker relationship, refusing a client request to give misinformation to a legal institution/employer, and saying no if a client asks for monetary loans.

Role-Play Techniques

Role-play is a type of modeling and is also called behavior reversal. This technique enables clients to view the different ways a person may handle a challenging situation. It also allows a client to view a non-tangible behavior in a more tangible way. When clients practice skills and develop new and more productive methods of coping, they are able to take an active role in treatment, increasing their sense of empowerment and self-determination.

Role Modeling Techniques

Role modeling, which offers the client a real-life view of desired target behaviors, can be an important tool to learn new skills. The social worker can request that clients demonstrate the behavior before modeling it, thereby allowing the worker to assess a client's current skills and abilities. Social workers can demonstrate a coping model showing the skill or desired behaviors, including difficulties, anxieties, or challenges. The worker can also demonstrate a mastery model, which shows confidence and competence with the desired behaviors. Each method has benefits and drawbacks. In coping mode, the client and worker can process the interaction and identify improvements or changes that can be made to the desired behaviors or actions.

There are several types of modeling:

- **Symbolic Modeling**: client watches a visual representation of the modeled behavior (i.e., video, TV, images)

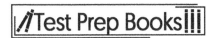

- **Live Modeling**: client watches while a person performs the behavior

- **Participant Modeling or Guided Participation**: client observes the model performing the behavior and then performs the behavior and/or interacts with the model

- **Covert Modeling**: client visualizes the desired behavior

Harm Reduction for Self and Others

Clients who are in immediate danger of self-harm should be referred to a local emergency room or hospital immediately. Clients who are a danger for self-harm may develop a no-harm contract with the social worker, even though this may not be legally binding. Clients who engage in self-harm may find relief in applying ice to the area of harm, snapping a rubber band, or using colored markers instead of sharp objects. Social workers also need to engage clients in changing distorted thinking related to harm reduction. Clients who are at risk for harm to others may need to be hospitalized or placed in protective custody. Social workers who are aware that the client is at risk of harming a specific victim have a duty to warn the potential victim and report this threat to the appropriate authorities. This mandate originated with the Tarasoff case involving a client who was not reported to the prospective victim and then proceeded to kill her. This is a mandatory legal requirement when a client threatens a specific victim.

Teaching Coping and Other Self-Care Skills to Clients

Social workers may act in the role of teacher to instruct clients about coping and other skills. Coping skills may include relaxation techniques, deep breathing, time out, and improved communication skills. Common diagnoses that often require the instruction of coping skills include stress reduction, anxiety, and major depression. Clients may be able to utilize coping and acceptance skills for these diagnoses because they are frequently chronic, and clients will need to cope with them on an almost daily basis. Clients often need to learn a plethora of new skills to manage their issues and complex problems, and they and the social worker should collaborate on coping and other skills to manage these circumstances. Social workers can partialize and brainstorm with clients concerning coping and other treatment skills. Clients sometimes need detailed instructions in order to succeed with treatment goals. Clients need to be engaged in therapy outside of sessions and learn how to cope when the social worker is not present, so assigning clients homework between sessions is a method for building skills. While the social worker may offer suggestions to the client for coping and other skills, the client is ultimately the most effective arbiter of their own treatment.

Client Self-Monitoring Techniques

Client self-monitoring can be a useful technique for turning subjective qualitative information into more quantifiable data. Clients may engage in self-assessment techniques and practices that include journaling, questionnaires, and evaluations. Clients collect data about goals, objectives, and the targeted behavior. This technique collects important information about client progress, but it also adds to clients' feelings of empowerment and self-determination as they become collaborators in treatment. Clients can either track information related to thoughts or behaviors or can use more formal charting techniques. Social workers should assist clients with defining and identifying which type of information to track and then demonstrate how to use the selected tracking technique. Self-monitoring methods serve several purposes. As clients become more invested in treatment, their awareness of strengths and areas in need

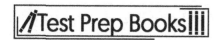

of improvement may also increase. This will enable the client to monitor behaviors as they occur, allowing for the development of insight related to behavioral change.

Methods of Conflict Resolution

Social workers may engage in conflict resolution with clients by acting as a mediator or advocate. Mediators work with clients to intervene in the conflict and develop helpful solutions that reflect all parties involved. For example, the social worker may act as a mediator in family or couples therapy conflicts. Social workers may also work with clients on developing their own conflict resolution skills through methods such as reflection, role-playing, and empty chair techniques. Social workers may also encourage clients to practice the use of **metacommunication**, which is communication about the behaviors and reactions of their regular and possibly dysfunctional method of interactions or communication. Sometimes the client is in conflict with the social worker and transference issues must be resolved before progress can be made. Social workers and clients need to be in collaboration concerning treatment goals and modalities so that conflict is reduced.

In some cases, agencies contract with mediation services outside the agency to assist clients in resolving conflicts. Professional mediators are trained in mediation techniques and are paid by the agency for their services. They can be the final step of resolution when the agency cannot resolve client conflict. Child protective services agencies sometimes use professional mediators to reduce or eliminate conflict in cases involving juveniles.

Crisis Intervention and Treatment Approaches

A **crisis** can occur whenever a client is in physical danger or has an extreme emotional need that goes unmet. For example, suicidal threats or ideation qualify as a crisis situation. When a crisis arises, the very first concern is always safety. It is important to get the client into a safe situation, protected from themselves or others. After safety is established, it is then possible to assess the level of need and what should happen next in order to best assist the client.

Another important strategy is **de-escalation**. When there is a crisis, extreme emotions are usually involved. If possible, a client should be guided through relaxation techniques to help calm them down. Oftentimes, a calm and neutral party who can facilitate a conversation or listen to the client empathetically, but without feeding the emotion, will automatically de-escalate the situation. **Confrontation** or matching the client's emotions will escalate the situation. Allowing the client to communicate the situation fully may help them to become less emotional and more focused on the facts. At this point the client may be able to focus on the next steps and specific tasks that need to be done. If possible, help the client to regain emotional control so that extreme options such as restraints are unnecessary.

In cases where a client is suicidal, it is important to establish if there is a suicide plan or means of committing suicide in place. These two things will determine the severity of suicidal ideation and how at-risk the client is. If it is determined that a client is at imminent risk of suicide, they should be admitted to the hospital or a mental health facility for their own protection.

Creating crisis plans ahead of time, in collaboration with clients, may assist them in preventing crisis situations or more quickly regaining control when the crisis arises. If clients have been part of the planning process, they may feel empowered, even when their emotions are overwhelming them. Part of the plan should be to identify the potential triggers or warning signs and have immediate steps that can be taken to avoid a crisis. This could be engaging in relaxation strategies or calling a supportive friend, family member, or clinician.

Trauma-Informed Care

Trauma-informed care systems ensure that trauma and its effects are understood by health services providers and that signs and symptoms of trauma are recognized even when not explicitly stated by the client. Trauma-informed care means that trauma-informed practices are integrated into all procedures of the care system. Incorporating these aspects into care involves ensuring a sense of safety and security for the client and the client's family. Trauma-informed care also ensures that the client feels they can trust the social worker and that all procedures are communicated and transparent. It provides a network of support, empowers the client to collaborate with their health care providers to develop a suitable intervention, and encourages the client to ask questions and voice concerns at any time. Trauma-informed care also accounts for each client's specific personal history, cultural and social norms, and other unique factors. Interventions encourage respect, self-efficacy, and hope for future outcomes, and they can identify various behaviors that are used as coping mechanisms for specific instances of trauma. Trauma-informed care is a model that is encouraged with any social services client, but it is especially beneficial for survivors of abuse, those experiencing eating disorders or addiction, or those who grew up in poverty or violence.

Anger Management Techniques

Anger management is a fairly common treatment goal for clients, so social workers need to be familiar with anger management techniques. Clients may manage anger by counting to ten before responding to a situation, taking a time out from the situation to reduce intensity, or practicing deep breathing techniques. Clients may also benefit from vigorous physical exercise to reduce anger. If clients are involved in vigorous exercise, they may need to consult with a physician for approval. Clients may also engage in thought stopping techniques to alleviate anger. Thought stopping sometimes involves the use of guided imagery, such as a stop sign, to reduce moments of intense emotion or thinking.

Stress Management Techniques

Social workers will often encounter clients with stress related problems and should be well versed in stress management techniques to offer clients suggestions for this issue. Social workers may engage clients to practice relaxation techniques in order to manage stressors. Clients may engage in physical exercise at their physician's discretion to relieve stress. Deep breathing exercises are also beneficial for relieving stress. To reduce stress, clients may use treatments such as cognitive behavior therapy or rational emotive therapy to change fallacious thinking patterns and distorted perceptions. Clients may be stressed concerning basic living needs and social workers can link clients to services in the community to assist them with these issues. If clients are at the safety and physical stages of the hierarchy of needs, these stressors should be addressed before other issues are included in the therapeutic process.

Cognitive and Behavioral Interventions

Cognitive Approaches
Cognitive approaches to the social work process involve changing the way the client thinks in order to facilitate progress and problem-solving skills. Cognitive approaches tend to be evidence based and

113

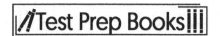
favored by insurance carriers, as they are efficacious for a variety of client issues, including substance use and personality disorders. Cognitive approaches focus on changing maladaptive thinking and cognitive distortions, and thus may help clients engage in behavior change. **Cognitive distortions** involve fallacious thinking patterns engaged in by the client, such as black-and-white thinking. Types of cognitive approaches may include cognitive behavior therapy, rational emotive behavior therapy, and solution focused brief therapy. There are many modalities of cognitive therapies and social workers should become familiar with—and implement—them when necessary.

Behavioral Approaches

Behavioral approaches, which originated with Skinner and Pavlov, include methods of changing and motivating client behaviors toward reaching constructive goals. The underlying concept is that if clients can change behavior, they may also alter the way they think. Skinner and Pavlov believed that all behavior is learned, and they believed in conditioning. Tokens may be awarded for positive behavioral changes in the client; this occurs in what is called a token economy. **Cognitive behavioral therapies**, which focus on both the cognition and the behavior of the client, are considered evidence-based and are favored by managed care insurers.

Strengths-Based and Empowerment Strategies and Interventions

Empowerment is a strengths-based modality, and the goal is that all clients should feel empowered based on their personal identities. Clients need to feel in control of most of their lives and circumstances, and this is what empowerment permits. Working from a strengths-based perspective empowers clients to facilitate change in their own lives. Social workers may seek to empower clients by focusing on strengths and bolstering clients' social constructs. Clients may need to be empowered from a racial, ethnic, religious, gender, or age perspective because they have suffered discrimination in these areas. Social workers may act as political advocates in these realms to combat social oppression affecting clients. The social worker should take into account the differences each client possesses due to their personal race, religion or circumstance and use these differences as strengths.

Client Contracting and Goal-Setting Techniques

Goal setting is a necessary factor in both the treatment and evaluation of direct practice. Social workers should work collaboratively with clients to determine goals. To be effective, goals need to be specific, measurable, achievable, realistic, and timely. They also should be directly related to the target problem. During the assessment process, begin identifying possible goals for treatment. Depending on the identified issues, goals may focus on desired behavioral, cognitive, or emotional changes.

Reciprocal goals are complementary goals agreed upon by members of a system related to the same target problem (e.g., a father's goal is to offer more compliments to his son, while the son agrees to increase verbal acknowledgement of his father's positive feedback).

Shared goals are when members of a system choose the same goal that addresses an identified problem (e.g., spouses each agree to communicate needs more frequently).

Contracts

Once goals are determined, a contract is the next step to engage the client in services. Contracts can be formal or informal, and written or verbal depending on the policies of the agency and the nature of treatment. A **contract** between client and worker provides a set of expectations and guidelines for

114

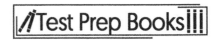

treatment. Clients should be made aware that the contract is a commitment by both parties but not a legal document. **Components of the contract** include goals, assignments of tasks, timeframes, frequency of sessions, methods for determining progress, and how updates or revisions of the contract can occur. Other items that can be included are lengths of sessions, financial arrangements, and procedures for cancelling appointments.

Partializing Techniques

Partializing means to break down into smaller steps. Clients sometimes need partializing techniques to address complex problems such as trauma, grief, or even personality disorders. A social worker can partialize with the client by encouraging the client's suggestions about solving the problem or making a written list. Partializing assists the client in reaching treatment goals in a more organized and efficient fashion. Case management of the client's goals may also include partializing techniques so that the client does not encounter stressors in addition to the problem-solving process. Clients with complex cases may benefit from partializing techniques because they can focus on one step at a time and avoid becoming overwhelmed with treatment goals. Clients may learn partializing techniques from the social worker and then learn to implement them in their own lives so that they can partialize issues that they encounter at home.

Assertiveness Training

Assertiveness training is an intervention that can be used in multiple settings with an assortment of interpersonal difficulties. This type of training helps individuals learn to express their emotions, thoughts, and desires, even when difficult, while not infringing on the rights of others. There are ways in which individuals can assert themselves, including saying no to a request, having a difference of opinion with another person, asking others to change their behavior, and starting conversations. Social workers must respect cultural differences when working with clients to develop assertiveness skills. For example, some cultures feel it is inappropriate for women or children to assert themselves. Role-play is an effective technique to help clients develop assertiveness skills.

Task-Centered Approaches

Task Centered Practice consists of a practical, evidence-based intervention that lasts for six to twelve sessions (short term). Task Centered Practice can help resolve problems related to daily living tasks, e.g., lack of basic needs, interpersonal/social relationships, role performance, and decision-making skills. This method is client-driven, with the social worker acting as a guide or collaborator. A specific problem is identified with an associated goal to be accomplished. Afterward, the social worker assists the client in identifying and conquering smaller tasks to resolve the problem. Subsequently, the assessment phase is vital to this process as both client and social worker identify issues, strengths, and resources, and work together to define goals/tasks. The Task Centered Practice model also places emphasis on contracting, carefully planned task implementation, evaluation, and termination.

Psychoeducation Methods

Psychoeducation refers to any form of training or instruction that is provided to clients and the client system as a part of understanding mental health or psychological issues and treatments. Its goal is to support clients experiencing mental illnesses, their families, and their networks while eliminating the stigma that has been associated with mental health issues for decades. Psychoeducation methods

115

include explaining potential causes for specific mental health issues, understanding the challenges of specific mental health issues, explaining how support systems can acknowledge and cope with not only a client's mental health condition but also their own caregiving stress, teaching coping skills, building resiliency, and overcoming obstacles in ways that are accessible.

This form of education can occur in group settings, seminars or webinars, and in individual or family sessions. It can also be found through newsletters, other media, and formal courses. It may be offered in home, online, in hospitals or other healthcare facilities, in community centers, or at conference venues. It is not considered treatment, but it is a beneficial complement to clinical care. It promotes positive and inclusive language, eliminates shame and fear around mental illnesses, creates educational value, fosters network support and understanding, and acknowledges a variety of feelings and responses to mental health conditions. Psychoeducation techniques are associated with reduced inpatient and hospitalization rates for clients with mental health conditions. Psychoeducation is correlated with clients' self-reported feelings of acceptance and increased family support. Family and friends self-report a better understanding of their loved one who may have a mental health condition, a better understanding of their role in providing positive support and care, the ability to draw healthy boundaries for themselves, and relief from learning and utilizing self-care techniques that reduce caregiver stress.

Group Work Techniques and Approaches

Group work can be defined as a goal-directed intervention with small groups of people. The intention of this work is to improve the socioemotional and psychoeducation needs of the individual members of the group through the group process. There are two types of groups in social work: therapeutic and task groups. Task groups are created to perform a specific task or purpose. These groups differ in the amount and type of self-disclosure, confidentiality, and communication patterns. There are several types of treatment groups, including support, educational, and therapy groups. Groups can also be long-term or short-term, depending on the type and purpose.

Groups can be open or closed. **Open groups** are ongoing and allow for new members to enter at any time. Open groups are typically used for support and life transitions. There are challenges to this type of group, since the members are at different stages in the group process. The frequently changing membership can be disruptive to the group process because members may not feel as emotionally safe to share with others. **Closed groups** are time-limited, and new members can only join during the beginning stage. The advantages to this type of group are more engagement and better trust by the members, since the group process is more stable. A disadvantage is that if several members leave the group, the group process may not be as effective. There are several variations by theorists that describe the stages of group development. A general method of categorizing the group process uses stages—the beginning, middle, and end. Each stage is classified by different activities, processes, and tasks:

- Beginning Stage: Social workers determine the group's purpose, members, objectives, and other logistical tasks (time, location, etc.). Group formation occurs at this stage as new members come together. The social worker fosters a safe and trusting environment by establishing acceptable group norms. As group members become more comfortable, conflicts arise as power and control behaviors emerge. Group roles and alliances begin to form. The worker's role is to help guide the group through these challenges and process any conflicts that arise within the group.

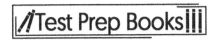

- Middle Stage: This stage is where most group work is done. Members share information, openly address issues, and work through conflicts. Some groups do not make it to this stage for several reasons, including member dynamics and a lack of investment by the group members. Group cohesion or the connectedness of the members is extremely important at this stage. The role of the worker is to help members focus on methods and the meaning of communication, working through group differences and confronting members when necessary. Workers should also help develop more intensive levels of cohesiveness while building on member individuality.

- End Stage: Group members come to resolutions on the issues addressed during the group process. Members may have strong reactions to termination, especially if there was a high level of cohesion developed during the group process. The social worker should lead the group in discussing feelings about termination and be aware of negative reactions that may surface. When these types of emotions occur, social workers should address any challenges that arise with members. The social worker should also help group members identify and reflect on the skills learned in the group process and how those skills can benefit the members with future challenges.

Working with Individuals in the Group Context

It is the role of the social worker to encourage all members to participate in the group process. The worker can solicit feedback from each member of the group throughout the group process. Clients typically take on various roles during group treatment. Roles can be defined as functions that the individual members of the group are fulfilling or performing that facilitate the group process. Some roles include that of a clown, scapegoat, mediator, etc. The worker must be aware of the roles of each individual and how those roles are affecting the group so interventions can be made when necessary.

Family Therapy Models, Interventions, and Approaches

One of the main goals of family therapy is to allow each family member to function at their best while maintaining the functionality of the family unit. When working with families, the social worker must do the following:

- Examine and consider all systems affecting a family and each individual member to determine problems, solutions, and strengths and also consider the functionality of the family subsystems.

- Respect cultural, socio-economic, and non-traditional family systems and not automatically define those systems as dysfunctional if they are not the norm. The overall and individual family functioning should be accounted for.

- Work to engage the family in the treatment while considering the specific traits of the family (i.e., culture, history, family structure, race, dynamics, etc.).

- Assist in identifying and changing dysfunctional patterns, boundaries, and family problems.

Important Concepts

Boundaries: Healthy boundaries around and within the family must exist for families to function effectively. The boundaries must be clear and appropriate.

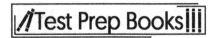

Emotional Proximity and Distance: This refers to the amount of emotional and physical space that each family member needs to effectively function.

Enmeshed: Boundaries are unclear and pliable. Families that have very open boundaries within the family unit may have very fixed boundaries between outside forces and the family.

Disengaged: Boundaries are rigid with little interaction and emotional engagement. Families that are disengaged within the family system tend to have very open boundaries around the family unit.

Family Hierarchy: The power structure within the family. For families to function effectively, there must be a clear delineation of authority. There must be an individual or individuals who hold the power and authority in a family system. In a traditional family, this should ideally be located within the parental system.

Homeostasis: Family systems should maintain homeostasis or remain regular and stable. When life events become too stressful and the family can no longer function as it normally would, the state of homeostasis is threatened. This is usually when many families seek help.

Alliances: Partnerships or collaborations between certain members of a family. When alliances exist between some members of a family, it can lead to dysfunction (e.g., parent and child have an alliance that undermines the parental subsystem).

Couples Interventions and Treatment Approaches

Many couples enter treatment after experiencing long-standing problems and may seek help because all other options have failed. One of the goals of couple's therapy is to help clients develop effective communication and problem-solving skills so they can solve problems throughout and after treatment. Other goals include helping the couple form a more objective view of their relationship, modifying dysfunctional behavior/patterns, increasing emotional expression, and recognizing strengths. Workers should create an environment to help the couple understand treatment goals, feel safe in expressing their feelings, and reconnect by developing trust in each other. Interventions for couples are often centered on goals geared toward preventing conflicting verbal communication and improving empathy, respect, and intimacy in a relationship. Therapeutic interventions, along with exercises, are designed to help couples learn to treat each other as partners and not rivals. Cognitive Behavioral Therapy is also used when working with couples. It uses cognitive restructuring techniques to help change distorted thinking and modify behavior.

Out-of-Home Displacement

Out-of-home displacement is considered one of the most stressful adjustments a person can experience in their lifetime. It often leads to homelessness, an inability to work, and permanent loss of meaningful personal items. Out-of-home displacement also usually results from a distressing event to begin with (such as a natural disaster, a divorce, immigration from a poor situation in another country, flight from a war zone or other humanitarian crisis, job loss, and so on). Alongside the long-term consequences, individuals can face considerable internal and external struggle as a result of out-of-home displacement.

The intensity of struggle is correlated with four distinct factors: how far the individual is displaced, the type of housing (or lack thereof) to which they are displaced, how many times the individual has to move, and how long the individual has to stay in displacement housing. Another important variable is

118

whether or not separation from family members, close friends, or other important community members occurs. Clients may deal with general psychological distress, post-traumatic stress disorder, acute or long-term poverty, adjustment stress disorder, and unhealthy coping mechanisms, such as substance use. Children are more profoundly affected and become vulnerable to future risks of obesity, substance use, and chronic disease. It is also important to note, however, that while many clients who experience home loss or displacement experience health and wellness issues that impact them in the long term, a fair number also self-report feeling an increased sense of resiliency and self-efficacy, a strong sense of community and gratitude for receiving aid from others, and hope for the future as their situation begins to improve.

Permanency Planning

Juvenile clients who are in danger within their families of origin and/or in foster care may benefit from permanency planning. Clients whose parents have terminated parental rights may be adopted into their foster home or put up for adoption by the state. While the first goal of social workers is to reunite juveniles with their family of origin, this is not always possible due to harmful circumstances in the home. Native American juvenile clients, for instance, are bound by the Indian Child Welfare Act (ICWA) when making considerations for permanency planning. ICWA regulations favor the placement of the child with Native families so that the child does not lose contact with their heritage.

Adults who are at risk of abuse and neglect may require permanency planning. Vulnerable adults may be reported to Adult Protective Services agencies. Adult foster care has become more popular in the last few decades and may be an option for at-risk adults. Group homes are another form of permanency planning for vulnerable adults, but the quality of these homes varies. The social worker should make careful screening of these facilities.

Mindfulness and Complementary Therapeutic Approaches

Complementary therapeutic approaches, such as mindfulness, meditation, yoga, exercise, spending time in nature, music therapy, and art therapy can provide emotional, physical, and mental relief for clients who are struggling to cope with adverse events. **Mindfulness** is the act of paying purposeful attention to specific or general events without attaching feelings, judgment, or reason to the events. It can be practiced during a specific time set aside for it, it can be incorporated in increments, or it can be an ongoing behavior throughout one's day. This practice allows clients a way of introspecting and reducing external stimuli, and it is an evidence-based method of stress reduction.

Meditation, another evidence-based method of stress reduction, can include mindfulness as a component. Meditation encourages the practitioner to focus on thoughts and repetitive mental patterns in order to clear them, relax the mind, and improve physiological indicators of stress (such as deeper and slower breathing rates, lowered heart rates, and reduced muscular tension).

Yoga incorporates meditation, focused breathing exercises, and movements to promote mental clarity and strength, improve circulation and respiration, reduce muscular tension, and connect with one's mind and body. Under the guidance of well-trained instructors or a certified yoga therapist, clients can take group or private sessions that are tailored to and address common counseling issues, such as trauma, grief, post-traumatic stress disorder, aging, physical changes, and so on.

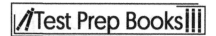

Different forms of exercise can have a therapeutic effect, including strength and resiliency building (both mentally and physically), stress reduction, and the management of chronic disease indicators (such as excess weight or blood lipid levels). Group exercise can also be a way to build community and support through a shared, wellness-oriented interest. Finally, exercise programs often support clients in the practice of setting and achieving goals. While this may start off as a primarily physical practice, a number of mental and emotional benefits (such as improved moods and higher self-esteem), introspection, and behavior change often follow suit. Other types of recreational activity, such as creating art, listening to musical sounds and vibrations, and spending time in nature are associated with positive changes at the cellular level.

Case Management

Clients frequently experience difficulty navigating everyday life problems and systems. One of the roles of a social worker is to help link clients with needed services and resources. To perform this role effectively, social workers must have a thorough knowledge of available local resources to aid the client.

When acting in the case manager role, social workers help clients define, locate, and access needed services and resources. Additionally, social workers must often interact with other professionals, including external resources to ensure the client's needs are met. In the case management role, social workers also make referrals directing the client to the appropriate resource for needed services. The worker acts as a manager, following up with the client on a regular basis to ensure the client is following through with their case plan. Workers may also serve as an advocate in this role, working on behalf of the client if any barriers to resources are met.

Process of case management:

- Assessing needs and client engagement
- Creating an intervention plan of care that includes goals, needed services, and timelines
- Administering the plan
- Monitoring progress and reassessing the plan at fixed intervals
- Termination of services
- Evaluation and follow-up

Follow-Up Techniques

At the final session, the social worker and client can schedule a follow-up session at a predetermined time to evaluate the client's continued progress after termination. Another option is to propose a time to meet and alert the client that the worker will contact the client to schedule a follow up. The **follow-up session** enables the social worker the opportunity to determine how well the client has progressed and to determine the effectiveness of the intervention(s) used during sessions.

Case Presentation

Elements of a social work case presentation may include identifying data, the presenting problem, history of the presenting problem, medical/psychiatric information, significant personal and/or social information, impressions and summary, and recommendations. This format is only one model to choose from. There are many formats for a case presentation, and the social worker needs to make sure that they are following their agency's or organization's case presentation format.

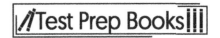
Measurable Objectives for Client System Intervention, Treatment, and Service Plans

Goals in intervention plans should be **SMART**—Specific, Measurable, Achievable, Relevant, and Time-bound. Devoting specific attention to the measurability of a goal requires mutual agreement between the client and practitioner.

Key recommendations are as follows:

- Measurable terms used in writing the goals should be based on the criteria of the type of desired behavior or action to be demonstrated (and how often), in order to achieve the proposed solution(s).

- Positive, action-oriented language should be utilized when describing the methods that an objective will be measured by. For example, the client should "plan" or "attend" a social gathering. Success of the stated objective will be "demonstrated" or "evidenced" by actually attending or planning a social gathering of some kind. The use of action-oriented language with specific targets assists the practitioner in more effective data collection.

- Objectives should be both short and long-term.

- Short-term objectives should only be a few weeks in length.

- Long-term objectives should be broken down into incremental, small chunks so as not to overwhelm the client and make progress towards success readily visible. The time-frame for completion should align with the nature of the objective. Often, many short-term objectives can make up one long-term objective or goal (for example, the short-term objective of developing a twice-weekly exercise habit leads to a long-term objective of losing five pounds).

Evaluating a Client's Progress

Treatment evaluation is a necessary part of direct practice. Social workers should strive to exercise best practice techniques by using evidence-based practice evaluation. It is beneficial for clients to see the progress they have made, while simultaneously providing information to funders and insurance companies that typically require documentation and outcome measures for reimbursement of services. Other benefits include providing indicators that interventions should be modified or that treatment is complete and termination is warranted. Several factors are important in the evaluation of a client's progress, including identifying specific issues to be addressed; creating appropriate goals, objectives, and tasks; using effective and relevant techniques and tools to measure success; and routinely documenting progress.

Client progress may be measured using a quantitative or qualitative approach used in research. **Quantitative measures** relate to the rate of occurrence or severity of a behavior or problem. When performing quantitative evaluation, first establish a baseline, which is a measurement of the target problem, prior to intervention. **Qualitative measures** are more subjective and reflective of the client's experience (information is gathered largely from observation and different forms of interviewing) and provide a view of whether progress is being made.

Primary, Secondary, and Tertiary Prevention Strategies

Emphasis on Prevention in Social Work

During the past few decades, the social work profession has increasingly moved toward a prevention-focused service distribution model. This movement has resulted in the development of a **three-stage model of prevention** in social work practice. These three stages are primary prevention, secondary prevention, and tertiary prevention. Each stage assesses the severity of the problem impacting individuals or groups and provides appropriate and evidence-based social work interventions:

- Primary Prevention: The **primary prevention stage** includes actions that practitioners take to address the potential causes of a problem before the problem occurs for the client. These actions are specifically aimed at getting rid of a problem's root cause, such as advocating against unfair policies or laws before they are voted upon or take effect. This type of prevention focuses on meeting the needs of the population at an almost universal level.

- Secondary Prevention: The **secondary prevention stage** occurs when a problem has already started to impact a person or group. Actions to be taken involve attempts to stop specific social problems before they spread and cause further harm. These actions are designed to help any individuals or groups that are beginning to show symptoms of increased problem severity.

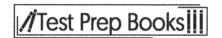
- Tertiary Prevention: The **tertiary prevention stage** occurs when both previous stages have failed to address the problem. These actions are designed to decrease a problem's severity through remedial service provision that will decrease its lasting effects and duration. This stage is more intense than the previous stages and focuses on individuals that are most impacted by the problem.

Visualizing the Three Stages of Prevention

These stages can be visualized as three parts of a pyramid. The wide base of the pyramid represents primary prevention, as these are more universal services that reach the broadest portion of the population. The middle of the pyramid represents secondary prevention, in which more prevention services are applied to a smaller portion of the population. The top of the pyramid represents tertiary prevention, with the highest degree of prevention services for the smallest percentage of the population.

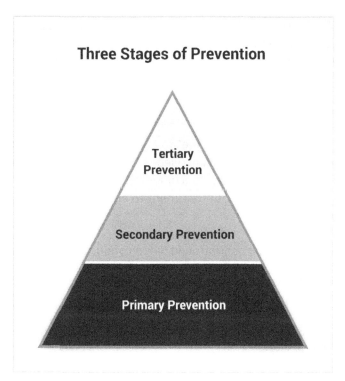

Client Readiness for Termination

When clients have made significant progress on the treatment plan, goals, and objectives, the worker can begin planning for termination. Depending on the identified goals and objectives, a standardized assessment can be used to determine how much progress has been made. Social worker practices vary depending on what level of goal attainment should be completed before termination (i.e., some, most, all). Other options such as groups, workshops, and reading materials can be offered to the client for continued work and learning. In many instances, services are terminated due to limitations by insurance or other funding sources. It is extremely important in these circumstances that the worker assists the client in locating additional resources that can be used following service termination.

When preparing clients for termination, workers should discuss the following topics with the client:

- Initial reasons for requesting help

- What skills the client initially lacked that led to initiating services

- Skills developed as a result of treatment and how those new skills will help the client with future challenges

- Ways the client will continue to build on the newly developed skills

- Social worker and client feelings about termination

Methods, Techniques, and Instruments Used to Evaluate Social Work Practice

Evaluation is an important component of any field of study, as it allows practitioners to understand which processes are working well and providing results. Evaluation also allows one to identify areas of opportunity and areas for improvement. The process often utilizes data and consumer feedback, and it focuses on processes that are in place and specific desired outcomes of the practice.

Evidence-Based Practice

Social workers can use **Evidence-Based Practice methods** to ensure effective treatment for clients. This type of practice uses both research and clinical knowledge. Social workers using evidence-based practice will choose interventions that have scientifically documented effectiveness. With this method, workers also evaluate chosen interventions throughout treatment to ensure a successful outcome.

Research Terms

Independent variable: a factor changed or controlled when conducting an experiment or research

Dependent variable: a factor that is dependent on the independent variable and that is observed for changes as the independent variable is manipulated

Randomized controlled trial (RCT): a quantitative study that uses participants or subjects who are chosen randomly to participate

Reliability: the consistency of a measure, or the likelihood the same result will be achieved each time a measure is used

Validity: reflects whether a test, tool, or study is measuring what it intends to measure

External validity: the ability of a study to be generalized to other people or circumstances

Internal validity: refers to cause and effect; one question that can be posed: Are the effects of the study caused by the intervention?

Case Recording for Practice Evaluation or Supervision

Social workers must document their practice with the client. Social workers document sessions with clients as well as client legal mandates, such as visitation with minors in state custody. Documentation may be a combination of narrative and quantitative descriptions, depending on agency requirements. Records should be kept confidential either electronically or in a physical location. New laws require that all records be electronic, and they are called electronic health records. These records must be confidential as stated in the **Health Insurance Portability and Accountability Act of 1996 (HIPAA)**. It is crucial for the social worker to maintain accurate documentation.

Consultation Approaches

Although it may lead to possible conflict due to differing perspectives, opinions, and approaches to treatment, the use of consultation assistance from an expert in a related field can be extremely beneficial to an individual's treatment. The **NASW Code of Ethics (2.05)** specifically addresses consultation with other disciplines. Accordingly, workers should seek consultations with other areas when it benefits clients. When seeking consultation, social workers should maintain client confidentiality to the greatest extent possible, only releasing necessary information. When seeking consultation, the worker should seek competent colleagues and only consult with those who are appropriately qualified. Additionally, the worker should ensure the guidelines are clear for the consultation process by defining goals, the presenting problem, and the role of the consultant(s). In line with the code of ethics, social workers also may provide consultation or supervision. When providing consultation, workers must also be knowledgeable in the focus area and always maintain appropriate and culturally sensitive boundaries.

Interdisciplinary and Intradisciplinary Team Collaboration

Interdisciplinary collaboration is a frequent part of social work practice. This process can be beneficial to the client, offering the availability of different views and a varied knowledge base. While collaborations are advantageous, they may lead to conflicts due to differences in approaches, treatment preferences, and codes of ethics. The social worker should attempt to resolve these issues within the group, seeking alternative methods to address conflict when necessary. Collaborations can be completed by phone or in person, and can be ongoing or limited to a single occurrence. As with any group, the social worker should lead the effort to ensure all members' opinions and contributions are valued and validated. Social workers should identify and define roles and responsibilities for all members of the team, acknowledge the differences between disciplines and perspectives, and help to resolve any conflicts.

Basic Terminology of Other Professions

Social workers may need to work with professionals in a number of other fields to support their clients. Therefore, it is important to have a basic understanding of some of the terminology that is used in the professions with which social workers most commonly collaborate. These include the criminal and legal fields, since social workers may often support legal cases such as those of abuse, negligence, divorce, and child custody. Social workers should understand basic legal terms so that they can provide relevant support to the clients as well as to the other professionals involved in the case.

Social workers often collaborate with educators in the school setting, and they work with children who may be in a vulnerable position. In these contexts, social workers should understand the values of the school system and the laws that school systems must follow when working with children, and they should ensure that social work does not detract from the child's educational experience.

Social workers may commonly collaborate with or refer patients to professionals in the medical field. They may need to understand basic medical and health terminology associated with their client's conditions. They may need to understand the impact that clinical issues may have on both the client's current behavior and desired outcomes. For example, a social worker may see a client who has severe depression linked with alcoholism. A physician may diagnose the client with stage 4 cirrhosis; the social worker will need to understand the severity of this diagnosis and how it will impact the client's depression and future sessions with the social worker. When in doubt, the social worker should ensure that their working relationships allow clarifying questions to be asked. Asking questions as needed will allow the social worker to fully understand any unfamiliar contexts and to serve the client.

Case Recording, Documentation, and Management of Practice Records

Accurate case recording is an integral part of social work practice. It is necessary to accurately document clients' information for effective treatment and protection of confidentiality. It is also required to protect the agency from possible legal ramifications and to ensure reimbursement from funders. Client records should be kept up-to-date, objective, and completed as soon as possible to ensure accuracy of information. Social workers should assume it is always possible that records may be requested as part of legal proceedings. Treatment notes should always be clearly written and only include information necessary to the client's treatment to protect confidentiality as much as possible. Social workers must also adhere to any state or federal legal requirements related to storage, disclosure of information, release of client records, and confidential information.

Intervention Processes and Techniques for Use with Larger Systems

Methods to Establish Program Objectives and Outcomes

When developing a social work program, objectives should be developed for each process that is used or evaluated and for each outcome that is desired or evaluated. Often, a funding source will require that certain process and outcome objectives are evaluated in order for the organization to receive funds; this often provides a practice with some objectives to manage. When objectives are not tied to a funding source, programs may decide to develop them based on a needs assessment or the program's service interest and capacity. These may be inspired by evidence-based research, successful outcomes in other programs, or data collected from focus groups. They may also be tailored to a specific case. A **logic model** is a useful tool to map out what the program hopes to achieve, the inputs it requires, and the expected outputs. It can also be used at the end of a program to map out the actual intervention and analyze how it compared to the expected plan.

Process objectives set standards for procedures, activities, and other implementation constructs of the social work program. Outcome objectives set standards for what exactly the program hopes to achieve. All objectives should follow SMART criteria. This means that any objective that is set forth should be Specific (the action to be taken and the person to perform the action are clearly stated), Measurable (changes can be measured and analyzed), Achievable (the objective is realistic for the client, the social worker, and the available resources), Relevant (the objective relates to the desired overall goal), and Time-bound (the objective can be achieved in a specified time period).

Availability of Community Resources

There is a wide range of community resources available, making it confusing for some clients to navigate the system and identify what would be most helpful for them. Therefore, a case manager plays a critical role in helping the client to find and utilize the community resources that would be most beneficial. When seeking resources, it is useful to look at the different domains of life—physical, psychological, emotional, spiritual, and educational—and then compile a collection of resources that may be useful for the client in each of these domains.

Physical needs can include food, shelter, clothing, or medical care, and there are many government programs available for these needs, such as free health care, affordable housing, and food stamps. For the elderly or disabled, their greatest need may be related to the accessibility of physical resources. In that case, the delivery of meals through Meals on Wheels or transportation services may be the most appropriate recommendation. Another help would be prescription assistance programs offered by some pharmaceutical companies to those with low income, which provide medications for free or at reduced cost. Other resources for the elderly can be accessed through the Administration on Aging and other local departments for elder care.

Ensuring the provision of adequate emotional and psychological services would first involve making sure the client is receiving emotional support from family and friends, or getting involved in support groups with others who have similar struggles. For the elderly, there may be community centers with programs to help seniors connect with each other and stay active. When it comes to finding the right psychological resources, both therapeutic and psychiatric, there are many options, so the client must be involved in the process of deciding what type and format of therapy would be best.

An often overlooked area of whole-person care is the spiritual needs of the client. In addition to providing spiritual support, religious organizations are often nonprofits that can assist the client in physical or emotional ways as well. Fraternal organizations may provide similar benefits to a person, offering emotional, social, and spiritual components.

Educational resources should not be disregarded, especially in the case of someone who has mental or physical health needs. Whether formal training or informal learning through the library or online, there are many resources for gaining knowledge in almost any area. As discussed, education related to the individual's specific health needs is a crucial element of self-management care, client activation, and empowerment.

Calling United Way's helpline at 211, checking the U.S. government website, or conducting an internet search are easy and effective means of identifying the relevant community resources in the client's locality. Collaborating with other service providers can also make use of those who already know the client and can also prevent overlap in the provision of services. Finally, and perhaps most importantly, help the client to find resources through the people and organizations with whom they are already connected. Not only does this encourage self-determination and empowerment by helping the client see how many resources they already have in their life, but many clients will be most comfortable with places and people they already know.

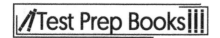

Methods of Service Delivery

Social workers use a variety of methods of service delivery to provide interventions to clients and client systems. The method should be determined through a combination of the client's needs, the type of problem being addressed, and the resources available. Several methods are as follows:

- Individual: Counseling, therapy, and individual case management. Individual delivery occurs when working directly with the client to address their specific needs. Social workers engaging in this method of service delivery often focus on building a trusting relationship with the client to facilitate change.

- Group: Working with a group of clients who share a common problem, often manifesting in support, therapy, and educational groups, which serve as a supportive environment in which clients can share their experiences and learn from one another.

- Family: Working with families as a unit to address issues impacting the family as a whole through family therapy, parent education, and family advocacy. Social workers engaging in this method may do so to help the family members better understand healthy family dynamics, productive communication, and problem-solving skills.

- Community: Community organizing, advocacy, and policy development can help address social issues that impact the community as a whole and empower community members to become active participants in creating positive change.

Methods of Advocacy for Policies, Services, and Resources to Meet Client Needs

Social workers must help clients understand their needs versus the services and resources available to them. Workers must be knowledgeable of the services available at their agency and in the communities in which their clients live. It is the role of the worker to assist clients in obtaining resources, but also to help clients understand their options and their right to choose or refuse which resources to access. Clients should receive assistance in identifying the pros and cons of each resource. They should also be involved in identifying and seeking resources as much as possible to foster the development of self-determination and empowerment.

Policies and Procedures that Minimize Risk for Individuals, Families, Groups, Organizations, and Communities

Often, the clients and client systems that require the services of a social worker are already in a vulnerable place. Therefore, minimizing additional risk to individuals, families, groups, and their associated organizations and communities (such as places of employment and recreation) is an important component of providing care. To ensure that policies and procedures minimize additional stress, burden, discomfort, or suffering on the part of the client and client systems, practices should employ the constructs of the **National Association of Social Work's Code of Ethics** in their policies and procedures. Practices should utilize a sense of transparency, empowerment, and respect in all service procedures. These factors support clients and their systems in playing an active role, when possible, in the services they receive. Policies and procedure should ensure that all services offered have the overarching goal of benefiting clients or client systems, maintain the dignity and self-respect of the

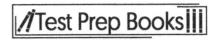
client and client systems, and emphasize the importance of cultivating healthy human relationships and the effects those have on recovery.

As social workers implement interventions and treatment, they should always keep lines of communication open with their clients, foster and nurture trust, and continue their educational efforts to ensure they are delivering the highest quality of care at each session. All client intake work should include an informed consent process, and it should engage the client in developing portions of the intervention plan. Social workers should treat all clients of all backgrounds with open-mindedness, without judgment, and with the client's desired intervention outcomes at the center of all interactions. Social workers may work with clients of different cultures, and social workers should respect the opinions and boundaries that these differences bring to treatment. If a social worker runs into a situation that falls outside the scope of the practice, such as the requirement of clinical intervention for a client, there should be policies in place to address such a situation, and social workers should feel comfortable referring to avenues of care outside of their scope.

Social Policy Development and Analysis

Social policy analysis is a process of systematically and strategically examining policies to determine overall effectiveness. When analyzing policies, social workers must determine both the intentional and unintentional effects of the policy, examine whether the policy is cost-effective and feasible, identify potential problems with the policy, determine how the policy is viewed by those affected, and identify possible policy alternatives.

Organizational and Social Policy

Social workers may act in a macro capacity for the common public good and serve as policy advocates or provide leadership in the policy change process. There are many types of societal influences that can affect social policy:

- Cultural: Societal perceptions or beliefs can shape policy. For instance, a general belief that children should have access to health care can aid in the development of child health care laws. Additionally, the media can bring problems/issues to the forefront and have a huge impact on public opinion, which can then influence policy development.

- Economic: Lack of or an availability of resources has a significant impact on policy development. Additionally, those who control the resources also impact how policy is shaped.

- Institutional: The capabilities, resources, and structure of government offices affect policy development. The institutions that create and implement policies have to be able to do so in an effective manner for those policies to be successful.

- Social: The social environment, including events or situations such as recessions, wars, or poverty, all affect how policies are developed.

- Legal: Existing laws and policies can influence future trends in policy development. New policies may or may not be adopted, depending on how they complement those already in existence and the current social climate. Legal events may also influence new policies.

- Political: The political climate directly influences social policy, since the parties in control of governing bodies directly affect which policies and laws are implemented and repealed.

Formal Documents

Social workers may need to develop formal documents that are used for a broad range of functions; therefore, it is important to develop writing and communication skills that can be employed in a variety of professional contexts.

Social workers may be expected to write grant and research proposals for securing external funding for practical and applied work. They may need to write brochures or pamphlets that advertise their practice (especially if they are running their own business), explain types of interventions, or promote community initiatives. Social workers may need to communicate through letter or email correspondence regarding a client's progress. In these instances, they must be careful to explain clinical concepts in ways the client can understand from simply reading the correspondence without the social worker there to answer any potential questions. Additionally, written correspondence with the client must always remain appropriate and in compliance with HIPAA and other privacy concerns. Social workers may be required to provide their superiors with weekly, monthly, or annual reports about the work they performed. They may also need to maintain regular reports of individual client progress updates or milestones. Social workers can be expected to provide evaluation reports on processes and outcomes utilized in their cases. Depending on the field of work (such as government agency, private institution, medical setting, etc.), the requirements for reporting and evaluation may vary significantly.

Finally, today's social workers can expect to maintain some degree of technological capability and have the ability to leverage web platforms and social media. Web platforms can provide an avenue for blogging or other information sharing that makes people aware of the work of social institutions. Social media posts can provide this avenue as well, and they can also serve as another point of connection for clients and colleagues. Social media can be an important tool in business-building and networking. It is imperative that social workers maintain a respectful, professional online presence that maintains both the trust and privacy of their potential clients.

Service Networks or Community Resources

Due to limited funding and resources and a rapidly growing demand for services, establishing service networks to maximize community resources has become a necessary part of social work practice. Social workers and social service agencies frequently create partnerships, collaborations, or networks to bridge gaps in service and provide a comprehensive system of care for clients. These collaborations can be formal with the use of a comprehensive intake process and service or memorandums of agreements between programs. Partnerships can also be informal, in which workers routinely refer clients to specific providers. When establishing new community resources, social workers must first perform a community assessment, which involves examining existing resources, community needs, and demographics.

Community Organizing and Social Planning Methods

The **social change process** is one in which interested groups (i.e., community members, lawmakers, businesses, government agencies, community organizations) can work together to create change or solve an identified community or societal problem. Collaborative social planning increases the chances of positive change and allows community members to take ownership of the change and resulting

130

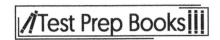

policies. It also encourages the community to become more energized and more likely to make positive changes in the future. The role of the social worker as a leader in this process includes the following:

- Community engagement
- Problem identification
- Organization and engagement of community members
- Identification of resources, challenges, and solutions
- Creation and implementation of a plan
- Evaluation and follow-up

Methods of Networking

Networking in social work can be defined in different ways. One type of networking occurs when social workers connect with colleagues and other professionals to improve services and skills. External collaboration with community resources and colleagues with similar goals enables social workers to learn about available resources and to provide opportunities for developing relationships with others who have a similar purpose.

Additionally, social workers may also help develop connections between clients, organizations, or other groups. This networking assists with the acquisition of support, skill development, and the facilitation of ongoing learning related to resources. Networks are typically more informal than official organizations and can therefore sometimes be more easily accessed by individuals.

Mobilizing Community Participation

Limited resources in communities make community member participation in social change movements vital to the success of the community. Mobilizing community members is an important part of creating macro-level change. The community develops a sense of self-determination when it takes an active role in removing barriers, creating needed services and resources and advocating for the rights of its members. Members are encouraged to participate in problem identification, goal setting, and resource mobilization to create change. When community members become engaged in the change process, the overall sense of community empowerment increases. There are some challenges with community participation in which social workers can assist. Community members may lack necessary skills, or there may be barriers created by institutions that operate in the community. Social workers can serve the role of educator to help community members develop needed social organizational skills. The worker may also serve as an advocate to overcome barriers created by larger systems and institutions. Workers must engage a community and mobilize its strengths, resources, and support systems to create positive changes.

Governance Structures

The **National Association of Social Workers (NASW)** is considered the most reputable association for the field of social work. NASW sets the tone for the field's standards, competency requirements, and public and legislative initiatives. It also provides social workers with resources to stay current on emerging research and news and with which to continue their social work education.

Other important governance structures in the United States that social workers may deal with depend on their field of practice. Social workers who work in a small, private setting may only have a single office manager to whom they report. If a social worker owns their own practice, they may choose how they establish the organization's reporting hierarchy. Social workers who work as part of a large government agency, such as a case worker for a state's Department of Child and Family Services, may work with a more bureaucratic structure that involves a supervisor, manager, division director, agency director, and the state governor. Social workers who work as part of a national non-profit may have a large, hierarchical governing structure similar to that of a state or federal agency, whereas social workers who work in local non-profits may be part of a lateral leadership system.

Often, nonprofit and government groups will collaborate with one another or with private companies to lead social work initiatives. Therefore, social workers may need to be flexible in how they adapt to the governance structures of the organization they are serving while still maintaining the standards established by the NASW.

Organizational Development and Structure

One aspect of mezzo-level social work is intervening with organizations. Social work organizations often begin with the admirable desire to help vulnerable populations. However, developing and sustaining such an organization can be an overwhelming challenge. Organizational policy development can improve the efficiency and effectiveness of the organization by providing assessments and identifying the strengths and weaknesses. This type of policy development is also important to ensure that the goals and objectives of the organization are being met and that they are in compliance with legal and ethical standards. Another aspect of organizational development has to do with the leadership hierarchy, or the formal power structure. This outlines the various positions of authority and leadership in relation to one another, and is necessary for the smooth functioning and decision-making of the organization. However, in addition to the formal power structure, there is also informal power, which has more to do with the influence of relationships and skills than with structured influence. Organizational intervention in this area may address issues of team building, skills enhancement, and interpersonal skills. Intervention and development in both informal and formal power structures are necessary for a successful and sustainable organization.

Effects of Policies, Procedures, Regulations, and Legislation on Social Work Practice and Service Delivery

Social workers may be employed in a variety of agencies. Some organizations, such as hospitals or government entities, employ diverse professionals. Other types of organizations, such as direct service non-profits or private practice agencies, maintain predominantly social services staff. Agency policies directly and significantly impact the working environment, the services provided, and as a result, the effectiveness of the care clients receive. All agencies should have a mission statement that gives the agency purpose and serves as an umbrella for the agency's smaller goals and objectives. Agency policies must be in the best interest of the client and must support the ethical guidelines to which social workers adhere. They must also be clearly written and available to workers and clients where appropriate. Social workers and all those providing care to clients should be able to help shape policy development to ensure consistency with client and worker needs and protection. Policies must address:

- Appropriate confidentiality, consent, and information protection
- Case management and supervision
- Cultural competency guidelines

- Professional development and ongoing trainings
- Anti-discriminatory/diversity practices

Policies and procedures are typically established by an organization to define its operational standards. These are normally managed by the organization's human resource department. Regulations and legislation are typically established by external entities, such as independent or government-run regulatory agencies. Organizations should tailor their policies and procedures to ensure they align and comply with established regulations and standards.

Policies and procedures establish the flow of operations within an organization that provides social work services. They integrate business needs and employee needs while also accounting for legal implications and risk mitigation. Policies and procedures related to service delivery often guide how clients should be treated, what (if any) conditions exclude a client from treatment, what to do in emergency cases or crises, payment and reimbursement requirements, privacy and security practices, hours of operation, and organizational map of staff members. Employee code of conduct and other information related to the workplace are often part of an employee handbook or human resources manual. These documents often cover workplace culture, workplace expectations, leadership roles and responsibilities, employee benefits programs, payroll questions, examples of inappropriate workplace conduct, grounds for termination, and licensure (when applicable). They also contain an outline of required ethics, other forms of workplace training, useful phone numbers and emails for employees, and other information that may be pertinent to a specific role.

Social work regulations and legislation set standards to which all social work organizations and employees should adhere. These may include documentation processes, licensure rules, payment rules, continuing education requirements, and patient privacy and security rules. Groups such as the NASW often compile research and promote initiatives to serve the field and its clients, for which they advocate to lawmakers.

Quality Assurance

In social work, **quality assurance** is the practice of ensuring that services rendered meet established criteria and deliver intended, beneficial outcomes. Quality assurance practices review procedures in place to ensure they lead to high caliber service delivery, to identify gaps that need to be addressed, and to prevent errors before they are made.

Methods of quality assurance include program assessments, benchmarking, social worker evaluations, and internal and external audits. **Program assessments** and **social worker evaluations** often utilize a list of standardized best practices; actual processes are compared to the standardized best practices to determine compliance. **Benchmarks** are clear, quantitative indicators of performance that serve as a standard for outcomes. Program evaluations may compare program outcomes to benchmark metrics to determine how well the program is performing. If there is a large gap, the program may undergo quality improvement procedures (such as a gap analysis or root cause analysis) to determine what is causing the discrepancy. Once this has been determined, a plan-do-study-act cycle (PDSA, a quality-oriented test of change) can be implemented to see whether benchmark indicators improve.

Auditing is a regular practice in the social work field. **Auditing** is conducted both on processes performed, as well as on the actions of the social worker to ensure ethical conduct and high levels of competence. For example, during licensure application and renewals, social workers' educational histories are audited to ensure they meet licensure and continuing education requirements. Audits may be conducted internally by the organization in which the social worker is employed or externally by regulatory bodies. The NASW performs comprehensive audits nationally, while state or local appointed boards and associations may audit for other requirements.

Impact of the Political Environment on Policy-Making

Social welfare legislation can have a dramatic effect on social work practice. Some legislation may help solve social problems that social workers encounter and other legislation may create more problems, challenges, and barriers through which social workers must help clients navigate. To be effective, social workers must be knowledgeable about legislative measures that affect clients. Social workers can also take on the role of legislative advocate by working to change, modify, or create legislation that can benefit groups of people.

Significant Social Welfare Legislation:

- Civil Rights Act of 1964
- Older Americans Act of 1965
- The Child Abuse and Prevention Act of 1974
- Adoption Assistance and Child Welfare Act of 1980
- Americans with Disabilities Act of 1990
- The Family Medical Leave Act of 1993
- The Health Insurance Portability and Accountability Act of 1996 (HIPAA)
- The Patient Protection and Affordable Care Act of 2010

Leadership and Management Techniques

Leading and managing teams requires a range of organizational and interpersonal skills. An effective leader can clearly develop a vision for a preferred future state as well as develop strategies to make the vision a reality. An effective leader must also be able to identify key stakeholders who are necessary to reach the vision and keep them actively engaged throughout the operational process. These tactics require that the leader is self-motivated, is able to think uniquely to solve problems, and has a desire to develop and attain a feasible end result. However, a single leader cannot accomplish a vision alone. Therefore, leaders must be able to communicate the vision and motivate their team to take the actions that are necessary to reach the desired goal.

Leaders should be individuals who the team can trust and feel comfortable supporting. The most effective team will be one where leadership vision and team motivation align; however, this arrangement may not always be the case in a work setting. Therefore, a leader must know how to make projects seem of value to the employee, know which tasks are a good fit with an employee's personality type, and understand what motivates a team member's work. When managing a team, leaders may fall on a spectrum of laissez-faire (hands-off and relatively unstructured) to autocratic (which involves a high-level of micromanaging). Most successful leaders manage their teams by falling somewhere in the middle—establishing clearly defined goals and strategies and hand-selecting appropriate workers to execute tasks, but allowing their team members to have a sense of autonomy and creativity over their delegated responsibilities.

Fiscal Management Techniques

Social workers should be well-versed in basic fiscal management techniques for a number of reasons. First, they may be involved in running a practice or owning a practice, in which case they must have a foundational understanding of business finances. Next, social workers should have personal financial health and know how to manage their own money. As financial issues are considered one of the leading causes of stress, social workers who are dealing with these kinds of issues will be unable to fully serve their clients. Finally, since many clients who come through social work organizations are likely to be dealing directly or indirectly with financial issues, social workers must know how to serve clients in various situations (such as in poverty, having relationship issues due to money management, etc.).

A lack of money and resources, or improper management of money and resources, can lead to stress, anxiety, malnutrition, unmet basic needs, and other health issues. Fiscal management techniques that social workers may need to utilize in client sessions may include providing resources to earn more money or spend less, education focused on social support and benefit programs, debt counseling, practical and impractical methods of debt relief (such as credit counseling programs versus pawn shop schemes), working through emotional states related to money (such as feelings of lack, shame, or control), and teaching parents fiscal management skills to teach their children.

Educational Components, Techniques, and Methods of Supervision

Social workers should expect to continuously learn. Educational components include staying abreast of new and emerging research and methodology in the field, brushing up on less-used skills, learning from mentors and more experienced social workers, and ensuring that one's practical expertise is up to the most recent standards. Supervisors or managers may choose to ensure that social workers who report to them have the time and resources to continuously learn, that they can learn materials for their needs, and that they feel comfortable addressing any gaps in their education with their superiors in order to resolve the discrepancies.

Techniques for learning may include **visual techniques** (such as books, videos, newspaper articles, and journal articles), **listening techniques** (such as lectures, seminars, podcasts, and audiobooks), or **hands-on techniques** (such as field work or practicums with a mentor). Some learning opportunities include tactics from all three learning techniques.

Supervisors may choose to be more involved in their approach to their team's education, or they may be more distant and allow their team members to pursue their educational goals and requirements independently. An effective supervisor will allow their team members to introspect as to what may be the best educational route for them and provide space coupled with guidance and support to support their team members in achieving their goals. Effective supervisors will also ensure that the professional goals individual team members are seeking serve the goals of the group as well.

Learning Needs and Learning Objectives for Supervisees

Supervisors must ensure that their team members are competent and ethical, that they deliver service effectively, and that they are satisfied with their performance and work environment. Supervisors may audit or review performance with their team members to ensure that standard competency and operational requirements are met. If gaps exist, supervisors may choose to develop training that addresses them. Speaking directly with team members individually or as a group can also help supervisors to find out where personal learning concerns or interests lie. In general, supervisors should ensure that their team is knowledgeable about current literature and able to deliver social service to the highest acceptable quality, that their team understands the legalities and risks of their work, and that all team members perform professionally and ethically in any given situation.

When choosing to develop learning objectives that are not based on any existing gaps, supervisors may focus on new and emerging research, skill sets, or modalities that their team may want to use in their practical work. They may also choose to focus on improving current processes to enhance the client experience; often, this practice may focus on areas that are important but may not regularly get attention in the day-to-day routine tasks (such as writing competence, leadership skills, business skills, and so on). Supervisors may choose to teach learning objectives in a workshop or other interactive format, conduct online trainings, or engage in field work as a learning modality.

Effect of Program Evaluation Findings on Services

Often the urgency of immediate client services takes precedence over program evaluation, but evaluation is a necessary step in ensuring that an organization provides effective and affordable services for clients. Program evaluation can be conducted during the formative stage of a program in order to establish the best objectives and methods, but it can also be summative, evaluating outcomes of the program at a later stage. Summative evaluations can be used to determine what changes should be made or even if the program should continue.

Needs assessments, which explore the needs of constituents or clients, play a pivotal role in program development. Needs assessments can measure program usefulness as well as provide evidence that funding is necessary for a program. **Cost-effectiveness** looks at whether programs are being conducted in a way that makes the best use of the available money. **Cost-benefit analysis** is a process of comparing the beneficial outcomes of a program to the amount of money spent on them to see if the benefits are worth the cost. Both of these cost-related aspects of program evaluation are important, especially for grant proposals. Ultimately, program evaluation seeks to do outcomes assessments, something frequently requested by funding agencies. **Outcomes assessments** look at the program's effectiveness at meeting its objectives and in making the expected changes.

Techniques Used to Evaluate a Client's Progress

There are several techniques to evaluate client progress, including self-reporting by the client, quantitative measures that are collaboratively discussed by the social worker and the client, and narrative approaches that utilize a textual basis for describing progress. Social workers may ask the client scaling questions to measure client mood and/or progress. Client progress should be measured at regular intervals in order to assist with treatment planning and intervention efficacy. Clients should be informed of progress, and social workers should develop progress notes to reflect client progress. Social workers need to be aware of client progress and compliance in order to accurately measure the steps the client is taking to move forward.

Practice Quiz

1. Which of the following best describes Contingency Theory?
   a. Based on the notion that systems within an organization are dependent on each other
   b. Emphasizes the protection of women from gender-based discrimination
   c. Places emphasis on organizations and employees obtaining maximum profits
   d. Describes organizations in terms of the complexity of all the forces affecting them and their ability to function

2. Which role of a social worker can be defined as working to change, modify, or create legislation for the benefit of a group of people?
   a. Legislative advocate
   b. Broker
   c. Case manager
   d. Cause advocate

3. What is a task performed by community members during the mobilization process?
   a. Participating in problem identification and goal-setting
   b. Creating comprehensive intake processes
   c. Performing a community assessment
   d. Establishing service networks

4. Which choice is NOT a benefit of collaborative social planning?
   a. Changes are more likely to occur
   b. It is cost-effective, easy to use, and efficient
   c. Community members take ownership of the change and related policies
   d. Participants become energized and more likely to continue to make positive changes in the future

5. Which choice is NOT a topic that should be addressed by agency policies?
   a. Professional development
   b. Inducements
   c. Case management
   d. Cultural competency

See answers on next page.

Answer Explanations

1. A: Contingency Theory is based on the notion that systems within an organization are dependent on each other. Feminist Theory emphasizes the protection of women from gender-based discrimination. Economics Theory places emphasis on organizations and employees obtaining maximum profits. Chaos Theory describes organizations in terms of the complexity of all the forces affecting them and their ability to function.

2. A: A social worker working to change, modify, or create legislation for the benefit of a group of people is fulfilling the role of a legislative advocate. The broker role is a part of case management that includes identifying and linking clients to resources. Case management also includes service planning and managing client care throughout the service process. Cause advocacy is working to assist individuals or groups and to affect change on a larger level to allow significant systemic shifts.

3. A: During the community mobilization process, community members participate in problem identification, goal setting, and resource mobilization to create change. The other choices include creating comprehensive intake processes, performing a community assessment, and establishing service networks – all roles of the social worker in establishing service networks or community resources.

4. B: The benefits of collaborative social planning are increased chances of change, community members taking ownership of the process, and members becoming more energized to create change in the future. Cost-effectiveness, ease of use, and efficiency are advantages of single subject designs.

5. B: Agency policies should address a social worker's professional development, cultural competency, and case management and treatment guidelines. Inducements mean salary and benefits and is a term introduced by neoclassical theories.

Professional Relationships, Values, and Ethics

Professional Values and Ethical Issues

Professional relationships with clients develop in six stages. In the first stage, social workers focus their efforts on building rapport and trust with clients. This involves the development of a comfortable and trusting working relationship using listening skills, empathic understanding, cultural sensitivity, and good social skills. In the second stage, the practitioner identifies the problem(s) that led the client to seek the assistance of a social worker. Together, the practitioner and client identify the initial problems that will be addressed, check the understanding of each issue through a conversation, and make appropriate changes as necessary. The third stage involves the social worker using skills that allow him or her to understand the client in deeper ways. The practitioner begins to make inferences based on their theoretical orientation about the underlying themes in the client's history. Once these inferences are made, then goals can be established based on these overarching themes.

The fourth stage of professional relationship development involves working on the issues that were identified and agreed upon between the practitioner and client. The client takes responsibility for and actively works on the identified issues and themes during and between sessions. As the client successfully works through issues, it becomes increasingly clear that there is little reason for the meetings to continue. Therefore, in stage five, the end of sessions is discussed, and both the client and the social worker work through feelings of loss. The sixth stage occurs after the relationship has ended if the client returns with new issues, if they want to revisit old ones, or if they want to delve deeper into their self-understanding. This stage is the post-interview stage and occurs with many but not all clients.

Legal and Ethical Issues Related to the Practice of Social Work

Social workers are, by nature, helping professionals. In theory, they are much like other helping professionals such as counselors or family therapists. The goal of the field of social work is not only social justice but also improving the lives of individuals through empowerment and advocacy. Social work maintains a person-focused perspective that stipulates that the profession strives to "meet people where they are," not forcing ideals and decisions onto those in need, but instead using their own values to empower them to make changes.

The social work profession has a set of values that governs how social workers do their jobs. These values are the root of the social work profession and lay the groundwork for everything that social workers do. These six values are: service, social justice, dignity and worth of the person, importance of human relationships, integrity, and competence.

In order to meet the needs of the various populations served by social workers, there are certain rules and regulations regarding ethics that social workers must follow. The National Association of Social Workers (NASW) has a Code of Ethics that serves to educate social workers on how they should conduct themselves.

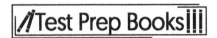

The NASW Code of Ethics has six core purposes. These purposes are:

- To establish the core values on which the mission of social work is based

- To provide a set of ethical standards for social workers, as well as specific information regarding different ethical dilemmas

- To help identify information that social workers should take under advisement when ethical conflicts may exist or when an ethical dilemma presents itself

- To provide standards that can be used by others to ensure accountability and responsibility by those in the profession

- To inform new social workers about core issues relating to the mission of social work and to the ethical standards of the field

- To provide the rules and standards that social workers can use to evaluate the conduct of others in the profession

Professional Values and Principles

Values are ideas or beliefs that guide an individual's thoughts and actions. The values that a person holds have their basis in the moral foundation to which they were exposed in childhood and adolescence. **Moral foundations** can include anything from family-specific beliefs and religious moral codes to the ethics and laws of society. As an individual gets older, they are increasingly exposed to new value systems that coincide or challenge their existing values. When someone must consider adopting one value system over another, this is called a **value conflict**. Value conflicts may occur when someone makes new friends, engages in romantic relationships, joins a new community, attends a new school, and accepts a new job.

The process of acquiring values is important for social workers to keep in mind when working to understand where their own values and their clients' values originated. Social workers should be aware of their own moral codes, values, biases, and prejudices to avoid conflict with the treatment they are providing to clients. The process of acknowledging and controlling personal values in social work practice is called **value suspension**. Self-awareness is a vital part of ensuring that one's personal values and beliefs do not intrude on the social worker/client relationship. It may be necessary to seek consultation from a supervisor or colleague in situations where one's personal values or beliefs conflict with those of the client and when those feelings cannot be resolved. In extreme cases where consultation and self-reflection cannot remedy the conflict, termination of the social worker/client relationship and referral to another therapist may be necessary.

All professions are built upon a foundation of values and guided by ethical codes. At times, these values trump that profession's empirical knowledge base. The focus of the social work profession is providing care and improving society rather than simply defining and explaining existing problems. To these ends, social workers must apply the knowledge and skills in other fields, including sociology, philosophy, law, and psychology.

Social workers must distinguish between and cater to social and individual morality. **Individual morality** describes the behavior of one person in private or specific people in public roles. Social morality is the

140

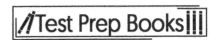

wide range of behaviors that create and contribute to public life and impact greater society. Social workers must recognize the interplay between these types of morality and advocate when their absence creates social injustice.

Below are the three main values in social work:

- **Preserving human rights**: Social workers are charged with preserving the rights of all people. This means taking a compassionate, holistic view of the individuals that social workers serve and advocating for them when society cannot meet their needs. Still, it's important that clients retain the power to make decisions about the direction their lives will take. The social worker can guide clients, but the clients maintain the ultimate decision. Only when clients pose a risk to the well-being of others should social workers intervene on their behalf. Social workers should take a strengths-based approach in their practice and help their clients develop and use their personal strengths to achieve their goals and compensate for weaknesses. The ultimate goal of social work is to provide clients with the tools they need to empower themselves to make their own decisions and enhance their personal health and the well-being of their family, community, and the greater society.

- **Advocating for social justice**: Social workers advocate for justice and fair treatment for those they serve. Practitioners should challenge prejudice and discrimination against their clients to model good moral judgment and to uphold anti-discrimination laws. Practitioners must also inform those in power when they become aware of policies that violate anti-discrimination laws or unethical practices. In this role, social workers are agents of social change who help improve society for future citizens.

  Social workers should celebrate the diversity of their clients and the communities where they work. This includes identifying differences and similarities between cultures and maintaining an "open door" policy to all individuals in need of assistance. These practices are intended to promote a society inclusive to all individuals and groups, regardless of their personal characteristics, values, or beliefs. Practitioners must identify resources in their community and their own organization that best serve their clients. Social workers should use good moral judgment to make sure that these resources are given equally to their clients and are tailored to the specific needs of those they serve.

- **Following the ethics and morality of the profession**: Practitioners must follow the profession's code of ethics and act with honesty, compassion, and dignity. Social workers should be familiar with the most recent version of the social work code of ethics, which contains the values and principles endorsed by the practitioners and researchers in the field. They should apply these principles in practice and evaluate how they can be tailored to their specific communities. Practitioners should also be respectful of clients and colleagues by acting with sincerity and good moral judgment. This includes setting and following professional boundaries with clients and coworkers, following the profession's ethical code, and taking responsibility for their actions.

Ethical Dilemmas

Ethical dilemmas occur when three different conditions are met in a situation. The first is that the practitioner must make a decision. If the situation does not require that a decision be made, then there

141

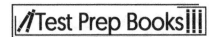

isn't an ethical dilemma. The second is that there are different decisions that could be made or different actions one could take. The third condition is that an ethical ideal will be conceded no matter what decision is made.

One type of ethical dilemma occurs when you have a situation in which two ethical principles are conflicting. This is a pure ethical dilemma because either choice of action involves conceding one of these principles, and there is no way to keep both principles intact. Another type of ethical dilemma occurs when ethical principles conflict with values and/or laws. In these types of situations, a social worker's values may conflict with an ethical principle, and a decision must be made.

Once you have determined which kind of ethical dilemma you are facing, there are steps to take in order to reach a conclusion and, ultimately, the resolution of the dilemma. The NASW lays out steps that should be taken when attempting to resolve an ethical dilemma.

Client Competence and Self-Determination

Social workers realize that clients have a right to lead their lives as they see fit, making their own decisions based on their values. Issues may arise when the values of clients do not align with how others believe clients should behave or live. Social workers must advocate on the behalf of clients with other professionals to ensure that their values are at the core of any plan. It is the job of the social worker to work with the client to aid in goal creation and identification that is congruent to the client's values.

There are situations in which promoting client self-determination may cause conflict between the client, social worker, and other professionals. For example, if a client has entered a hospital due to medical issues arising from alcohol abuse, healthcare professionals may recommend that the client attend an alcohol and drug rehabilitation facility for treatment. However, if the client does not wish to seek treatment, then the social worker should advocate on their behalf and help to devise a plan that honors the client's wishes. Exceptions to this value would be when a client needs protection from self-harm or harming others. In this situation, the social worker must act in accordance with legal and ethical standards to do no harm versus promoting the self-determination of the client.

Protecting and Enhancing Client Self-Determination

One of the core values of social work is to not only respect, but also promote the self-determination of clients and client systems. Self-determination refers to an individual's ability to make their own decisions and maintain control over their own lives. Social workers can use a variety of techniques to protect and enhance client self-determination.

One of these techniques is to include clients in the decision-making process as often as possible, which includes providing options and information in addition to asking the client for their input and preferences when there are decisions to be made. Social workers should look to develop a collaborative relationship with their clients, creating a process where the client is consistently an active participant. Social workers can also utilize a strengths-based approach to self-determination. This focuses on identifying and building upon the client's resources and strengths to empower them, and helping promote self-determination by emphasizing their ability to make positive changes in their lives and overcome challenges. Education and advocacy can also be used to promote self-determination. This means educating the client about all options and resources available to them while advocating for their rights and needs. Providing information, as well as support, will help clients make educated decisions and maintain control of their own lives.

To actively avoid imposing their own beliefs on the client, social workers should always be aware of their own biases and values. Social workers have to respect the client's autonomy and support their right to make personal decisions, especially when those decisions do not fall in line with the social worker's own thoughts or beliefs.

Client's Right to Refuse Services

As per the NASW Code of Ethics, the client has the right to refuse all or a portion of social work services and utilize self-direction at any point. During the intake process, social workers should address this possibility with the client and also inform the client fully about the possible ramifications of refusing services. Clients may need outside service linkages from the social worker during the termination process; they may also choose to continue service but decide to work with a different social worker or in an entirely different social or health field.

Social workers should be respectful of clients who terminate services before completing the problem-solving process, and they should remain detached and objective during the termination without taking any critical feedback too personally. Rather, this can be viewed as a learning opportunity to understand different types of clients better. It is important to note that not all clients can voluntarily cease services. For example, court-appointed social work sessions often cannot be terminated by the client. In these cases, the social worker may have difficult interactions with the client and face resistance, especially if the client truly does not want to be in the session. Additionally, clients who are unable to make decisions due to a medical reason (such as a mental condition that inhibits decision-making) may voice opposition to the treatment, but they cannot be the actual person who terminates treatment. This is usually left to a proxy, such as a legal representative or family member.

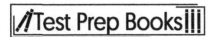
Professional Boundaries

Difficulties in Setting and Maintaining Professional Boundaries in Social Work

Professional boundaries in social work are clearly defined limits on the practitioner-client relationship that provide a space for the creation of safe connections. Some helpful things to keep in mind include: the line between being friendly and being friends; being with the client versus becoming the client; and understanding the limits and responsibilities of the social worker role.

Conflicting values occur when the social worker's values and knowledge about best practices are at odds with the client's values, history, relationships, or lifestyle. **Vicarious trauma** may happen when a social worker experiences symptoms of trauma after listening to a client's experience. These symptoms may arise due to the practitioner sharing a similar history of trauma. Boundaries may be difficult to maintain if the social worker feels that they need to rescue the client due to an unhealthy attachment to positive results in practice. This is termed the **rescuer role**. Professional boundaries may also be difficult to set and maintain if there is poor teamwork between colleagues in the social work organization. This is evident when social workers assume the roles of other team members because they believe they are not fulfilling their responsibilities to the client.

Professional boundary issues occur when social workers have multiple types of relationships with a client. This may include a professional, business, or personal relationship. For example, it is permissible to see a client out in public at a restaurant, but not to invite a client to dinner for business or personal reasons. When encountering a client in public, the relationship with the client must be kept confidential. However, if the client chooses to say hello, saying hello in return and quickly ending the encounter would be acceptable.

There are several boundary issues that come with working with clients. These issues are:

- **Intimate contact**: This refers to things such as hugging a client at the end of a working relationship, or patting a client on the hand during a crying session. Sexual contact also falls into this category.

- **Personal gain**: This refers to instances in which a social worker engages in activity with a client that results in a monetary (or otherwise valuable) benefit to the social worker. This could involve situations such as referring a client to a business owned by the social worker or a friend/family member of the social worker, selling something to a client, or even asking a client for professional suggestions.

- **Emotional and dependency issues**: This refers to instances in which a social worker's own personal issues cause the social worker to have impaired judgment, possibly resulting in other boundary issues, such as a dual relationship with the client.

- **Altruistic instincts**: In some instances, a social worker's own good intentions and concerns for a client can result in boundary violations and confusion about the relationship between the social worker and the client. An example of this would be going to a client's bridal shower or retirement party.

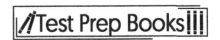

Strategies for Setting and Maintaining Professional Boundaries in Social Work

Despite these difficulties, social workers must set and maintain boundaries with their clients and colleagues to ensure an effective practice. Practitioners should consistently monitor how their professional boundaries enhance or harm relationships with clients, colleagues, supervisors, and administrators. They must also gauge the impact of their boundaries on the amount of time they devote to work, their ability to cope with stress at work, and the amount of time and energy that they spend on extraneous activities and relationships.

There are several strategies for building and maintaining appropriate professional boundaries and relationships. First, practitioners should examine their motivations for giving extra time and attention to a client. If a social worker treats one client differently, this indicates that the boundary may be overextended. Social workers can manage this situation by determining whether the services provided are in line with the client's care plan, the organization's mission, the job description, and scope of practice.

Social workers should also avoid encouraging clients to contact them through personal channels. Clients should use the channels of communication set in place by the organization, such as work email, voicemail, cell phones, pagers, receptionists, and on-call staff, and procedures for after-hours referrals to 911, emergency rooms, or mental health crisis centers. Extending the professional boundaries of the social worker role puts colleagues and the organization at risk for failure. It also sets an unfair expectation that other colleagues will extend their professional boundaries. If boundaries are inconsistent between colleagues and within the organization, then clients may become confused and distrust the entire organization.

A third strategy for building appropriate professional boundaries is establishing clear agreements with clients during the initial sessions about the role of a social worker and the dynamics of a client-practitioner relationship. When warning signs indicate that healthy boundaries may be in jeopardy, social workers must address the issues with the client clearly, quickly, and sensitively. This involves clarifying the roles and boundaries with the client and asking the client to restate these boundaries to ensure understanding.

A fourth strategy is limiting self-disclosure about the social worker's personal life to information directly related to the client's goals. If there is a dual relationship between the social worker and client, the practitioner must preserve the client's confidentiality, physical security, and emotional well-being in social situations.

A fifth strategy is avoiding social media within professional practice. Practitioners should not connect with clients on social media. This includes adding clients as friends on Facebook or following clients on Twitter. To prevent conflicts of interest, social workers should use discretion and limit the amount of online information that is made available to the public or to social network connections. Social workers also shouldn't attempt to access online information about clients without prior informed consent. Finally, practitioners shouldn't post negative information about colleagues or the organization online.

A sixth strategy is for social workers to foster strong work relationships with their colleagues at the organization. These connections will help practitioners cope with stresses, think through questions of ethics and professional relationships, and help maintain a sense of humor. Practitioners should be sensitive to signs of bullying in the workplace, as each practitioner deserves respect and dignity to ensure social justice for others. It's important that social workers use appropriate channels of

145

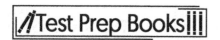
supervision and consultation to determine appropriate boundaries in difficult situations. Supervision can also be useful when trying to remedy concerns with existing organization procedures that address or inhibit client needs.

A final strategy for maintaining professional boundaries is ensuring appropriate self-care. This includes taking time for nurturing oneself throughout the workday, maintaining a regular work schedule, and taking time away from the office each day to refocus. Practitioners should limit communication when they are away from work to ensure time for rejuvenation, especially during vacations or personal time. They must also be aware of how they handle work stress and monitor how often they take work home. This includes physical work, emotional strain, or hyper-vigilance about work situations. If a practitioner consistently struggles to maintain professional relationships and work boundaries, they should seek supervision or outside mental health counseling.

Self-Disclosure

Self-disclosure is a tool used by social workers to build rapport and trust with their clients, while also providing insight and modeling behavior. It is crucial to approach self-disclosure with caution to maintain healthy boundaries and avoid ethical concerns. It is recommended that social workers limit self-disclosure about their personal lives to information directly related to the client's goals. In rare cases, it may be appropriate for social workers to self-disclose to clients. It is important to remember that the therapeutic process is to help clients, not indirectly benefit social workers.

The principles of self-disclosure are being intentional, selective, and appropriate when sharing personal information with clients. Social workers should always be conscious of the potential impact of disclosing personal information on the client's well-being and therapeutic relationship. It is not appropriate for clients to be burdened with social workers' emotions, as it could shift the atmosphere and power dynamic. Generally, social workers should only engage in self-disclosure when it is in the client's best interest and never to satisfy their own needs.

There are a variety of reasons to utilize self-disclosure. One example is to help clients feel understood and validated, while simultaneously helping the client see the social worker as a real individual, further enhancing the therapeutic relationship. It is important, however, to ensure that any self-disclosure is relevant and maintains the focus on the client.

As a general rule, self-disclosure should never include intimate or personal details that are irrelevant to the client's treatment. Social workers should also be cautious of ethical considerations surrounding self-disclosure, such as the potential for boundary violations and the risk of exploitation or harm to the client. Social workers should be cognizant of their clients' level of functioning and issues prior to any purposeful self-disclosure to ensure professional boundaries are maintained.

Documentation

Keeping accurate client records has many purposes, such as documenting the history and treatment of a client, getting insurance reimbursement, and providing social workers a historical account of client sessions. The information contained in a client record can also be used to evaluate the effectiveness of services. Client records, when combined with other evaluation tools (e.g., client satisfaction surveys, reactions to treatments, accomplishments of goals), can be an effective method of evaluating treatment progress. Supervisors may review client records to evaluate the effectiveness of the treatment process, social worker performance, and client progress, or to ensure documentation is being completed accurately and on time. When reviewing client records for evaluation, ethical standards must always be upheld.

The NASW Code of Ethics specifically addresses guidelines for using client information for evaluation, including:

- Protecting confidentiality to the fullest extent possible

- Accurately reporting information

- Protecting clients from harm

- Obtaining required client consent for all uses of their information (e.g., supervisory review, reimbursement)

- Making clients aware that the consent can be withdrawn without punishment

Termination

Termination of the relationship occurs when the client and the social worker have reached treatment goals. Even though the relationship is terminated, the client may feel warmly toward the social worker, and congruence and empathy may still be part of the relationship. Some clients may require maintenance sessions to continue stability, but when termination is the next clear stage in the relationship, psychotherapy sessions should end.

In the case of a client choosing to prematurely terminate services, the social worker should clearly explain the risks to the client and also carefully document all meetings and interactions to protect against legal ramifications. **Abandonment**, which refers to the social worker terminating services prematurely without adequate reason or in an improper manner, is considered malpractice and can lead to lawsuits. When the social worker decides to end the working relationship, they must ensure that the client is adequately prepared and warned about the end of services and that the client is emotionally equipped to deal with the termination. Social workers can refer clients to other types of providers, who can continue working with the client after their own services have ceased. If a social worker needs to terminate services early, such as in the case of leaving a job, they should connect the client to a new social worker who can continue to provide the same level of services.

Death and Dying

Some clients have documented clear wishes about their death and dying (advance directives), while others do not. In these cases, social workers may be called upon to provide information and counsel to the client and client system. This can be an emotional process, and social workers should show compassion, sympathy, and respect as the client and the client system adjust to the news. Terminal clients are allowed to take comfort measures, such as hospice services, but are not allowed to take any external measures that would intensify or speed up the dying process (such as requesting a lethal medication dose).

Terminal clients may choose to refuse treatment and pass away naturally; while this process may hasten death, it is considered a natural and acceptable alternative to prolonging the dying experience with intervention, and it is also considered the client's choice. Terminal clients may choose this route if they have made peace with the decision and with their family and friends, if they want to remove a physical and financial burden from loved ones, and if they are ready for the process. Still, in such a case a social worker could provide guidance to ensure the client truly understands the process and consequences of their decision. With a do not resuscitate (DNR) order, a client chooses to refuse services if their cardiopulmonary system ceases to work.

In clients who are unable to make decisions (such as those who are in a permanent vegetative state), the next of kin or a legal appointee may make medical decisions on the client's behalf. This may include taking the client off life support, if applicable. This can be a highly contentious situation if family members or legal proxies do not agree on the best course of action. This situation can be avoided by preparing advanced directives, which document the client's wishes in such contexts.

Research Ethics

Research performed on living creatures, especially humans, is always scrutinized for ethical concerns. Such research often uses experiments for which the outcomes are unknown. Therefore, it is possible that any research performed on a person may have unintended, unwanted, or otherwise harmful psychological, physiological, emotional, or social effects. Research ethics are intended to protect participants, ensure that research is being conducted for some public benefits, and ensure that participants who are involved have been provided with informed consent. Informed consent involves explaining to an individual, in as much detail as possible, the processes of the experiment or study and all potential side effects or outcomes and giving an individual the opportunity to make an educated decision independently about participation in such a study. Informed consent also documents the fact that the participant may leave the study at any time. Informed consent paperwork is usually signed by the participants, the researcher, and an independent third party. Some controversy still exists over research that affects vulnerable populations, such as those with psychological disorders, the elderly, children, the poor, and others who cannot easily make objective decisions or could be persuaded by experiment incentives (such as gift cards or the like).

An **Institutional Review Board (IRB)** is any independent group that reviews research and clinical trial designs that have human participants to ensure there are no potential ethical violations. IRBs are accredited by the US Food and Drug Administration. These groups can request changes, additions, and eliminations to any study proposal; they can also completely deny a proposal for approval. Without IRB approval, research designs cannot come to the experiment phase. While research is in session, IRB committees conduct regular audits to ensure compliance is still intact. Noncompliance can result in heavy fines, penalties, criminal investigation, and termination of a study.

Supervision and Consultation

In social work, supervision takes place when a more experienced professional mentors or coaches an emerging professional in fieldwork, practical application, or other service delivery settings. This requires strong interpersonal skills, a sense of respect, and open communication between both parties. The supervisor should be able to provide supportive instruction and guidance without arrogance and condescension; the supervisee should be receptive to instruction and have an honest desire for professional growth and learning. Some commonly used models of supervision in the social work setting include individual-oriented types of supervision, in which the supervisor may ask the supervisee to reflect upon their interactions with different clients or their personal judgments and biases that may

148

have arisen during a session. The supervisor may also present the supervisee with different forms of research and data and ask the supervisee to utilize the evidence to structure interventions. Finally, the supervisor may provide coaching related to the supervisee's development, by establishing small objectives that lead to larger professional goals.

In peer-oriented and group-oriented approaches, lateral-level colleagues (perhaps with the aid of one or two supervisors) learn from one another by sharing clinical experiences and lessons, new research and literature, or other professional development opportunities. This may take the form of team meetings at the beginning or end of the day, social events where work can be discussed, or conference settings. In some workplaces, individual, peer, and group models may be integrated to provide a more holistic sense of supervision.

Consultation can take place in any interaction that a social worker has with a client, regardless of setting or context. Consultation can primarily be divided into organizational, program, educational, mental health, and clinical cases. These can take place one-on-one with an individual or in group therapy settings.

Supervision and Management

Supervisors and managers should always be aware of the hierarchical power they wield over subordinates, and they should ensure that their leadership does not take advantage of this dynamic. Behaviors that would be unsuitable in a lateral colleague may be ignored in a supervisor if a subordinate feels their job or work environment would be in jeopardy should a complaint be filed.

Interpersonal work dynamics between supervisors and subordinates should ensure that the supervisor treats subordinates with professional respect and support, even when they are challenging them to grow professionally or learn more. It is critical to not become domineering in this regard. Additionally, if a supervisor needs to coach a subordinate on performance, this should be done privately rather than in front of other colleagues. On the other hand, supervisors also need to make sure that their relationships with subordinates do not become overly friendly or intimate. Supervisors should avoid confiding overly personal details to subordinates or pursuing romantic relationships in the workplace. Not only could this cause extreme discomfort for colleagues, it could also be reported for harassment. When in doubt, supervisors can refer to the NASW Code of Ethics to drive not only their service delivery, but also their interactions in the workplace.

Social Worker Safety

Social workers are often in high-risk situations, working with high-risk populations. The threat of violence or other personal safety issues is relatively high compared to other fields of work. Implementing policies and procedures that help protect social workers during their workday can help mitigate some of this risk. This includes the provision of an avenue to report unsafe settings or clients, and if necessary, to terminate working relationships in which the social worker does not feel safe without fear of workplace reprisal. Reviewing the daily processes of service delivery can help identify areas where risk management techniques may be necessary.

Since social workers work in a number of different places—office settings, jails, courtrooms, family homes, community centers, hospitals, and so on—they should treat each session individually and assess safety risks each time. This assessment may include an overview of the location, the ability to receive

149

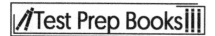
emergency services quickly, other available workers who may be able to help in an emergency, and the state of the client at each visit (even if it is someone the social worker has treated for some time). Social workers should also protect their personal boundaries, such as not allowing clients to call or visit them at home, not sharing personal information in person or online, and maintaining protocols to address client emotions that could lead to violence. (Examples include shouting at or threatening the social worker. While these are not physical assaults, they are still verbal and emotional violence toward the social worker, and they could escalate.)

Supervisee's Role in Supervision

Although the focus is often on the supervisor's role of ensuring that clients are provided with ethical services by training and evaluating the supervisee, the supervisee's role in supervision is not passive. The social worker should fully engage in the process of supervision and use this relationship to grow and improve. In order to do that, the supervisee must be willing to discuss areas of ethical or legal concern that have arisen in their interactions with clients. They must also be ready to honestly address their own struggles and identify their learning needs, and seek the help and advice of the supervisor. This can only happen effectively through genuine self-assessment, which flows from a real desire to become a better social worker. The process of self-assessment in supervision can help them see any biases or weaknesses that may be holding them back from fully meeting their clients' needs. If the social worker is defensive or resistant to the supervisory relationship, then they will make little progress.

Factors to consider when receiving feedback during supervision/consultation:

- Social workers can benefit from feedback during supervision or consultation, especially with difficult clients/cases or at significant times in treatment, such as termination.

- When discussing cases, client confidentiality should be protected as much as possible, and client consent to release information should be acquired.

Accreditation and Licensing Requirements

In the United States, social work accreditation and licensure requirements vary by state. Therefore, aspiring social workers should ensure they follow standards set forth in the state in which they hope to practice.

The **Council on Social Work Education (CSWE)** is the main accrediting body for higher education programs in social work, and the majority of states require that social workers receive undergraduate or graduate degrees from universities whose social work curriculum is CSWE-accredited in order to become a licensed professional. CSWE-accredited programs ensure that coursework includes not only information related to competencies established by the NASW, but that an emphasis is placed on ethics, professionalism, and practical application. Most states do not allow aspiring social workers to take board examinations without proof of a CSWE-accredited degree.

Other licensing information pertains to the type of social work a person hopes to do and the education they have received. Clinical social workers have different licensing requirements. Some states require post-graduate education in social work before licensure can be obtained. Other levels of licensure require practical and field work for a designated period of time. While board scores may be transferred across state lines, licensure is a separate process in each state that reviews both the worker's education and working experience comprehensively.

150

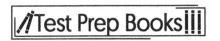

Professional Development Activities

Professional development activities are a vital component of continuing education and ensuring social workers remain competent over the course of their careers, especially as public needs and norms shift. Social workers can find a plethora of continuing education courses, seminars, and trainings at the college or university from which they received their degree. Often, these are free or discounted for alumni. The NASW provides various free to for-cost opportunities on their website, including a portal which allows the user to filter opportunities by date, topic, location, and cost. The web site also provides online courses that can be done at home, free teleconferences in which to learn from peers, online articles, and links to new scholarly literature.

The NASW also invites professionals to write and advocate for issues on behalf of the organization, which allows social workers to hone research and writing skills while also promoting themselves professionally and serving causes about which they are personally passionate. Networking and conferences are another way to meet and learn from peers and develop professionally. Additionally, employers may provide free or discounted opportunities for social workers to pursue professional development activities. This may include providing activities such as in-house workshops or sponsoring employees to attend conferences or trainings.

In order to maintain licensure, social workers must pursue a certain number of continuing education hours per designated time cycle. Therefore, all social workers can inherently expect to continuously develop as professionals as long as they are continuing to renew their licenses. The specifics of continuing education are determined by the state issuing the license and the type of license that is held. Certain licenses may also require that all or a portion of the continuing education credits cover specific topics.

Confidentiality

Elements of Client Reports

Elements of client reports may include developmental history, family history, substance use information, medical history, the presenting problem, and recommendations. There are a variety of elements of client reports that may be required by the agency. With the advent of electronic records, client reports are often built into the software that the agency uses. Client reports may also be in **DAP** (data, assessment, plan) format or in the model of **SOAP** notes (subjective, objective, assessment, and plan). Reports are at the agency's discretion, and the social worker should use the format that is required by the agency to develop client reports.

Obtaining Informed Consent

Social workers must obtain informed consent from clients prior to providing services. An **informed consent form** is a document signed by both parties agreeing to provide or receive a service. Some of the main topics included on an informed consent form are the qualifications and credentials of the social worker and the risks and benefits of receiving the service. The right to terminate the service by either party and transfer service to another provider, if applicable, should also be discussed. Confidentiality is a prominent legal aspect of informed consent. The consent form should clearly outline situations in which confidentiality cannot be honored, such as in cases of neglect, intent to harm, and abuse of vulnerable

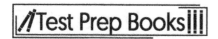
populations. Additionally, informed consent documents should include clear expectations of fees, payment methods, and cancellation policies.

Because of legal and ethical issues surrounding privacy and informed consent, which are a means of maintaining a client's self-determination and dignity, it is critical that social workers always complete the appropriate forms when information is being shared about the client or decisions are being made on their behalf. Foundational to service provision is to first get written informed consent from the client to participate in services. Clients must fully understand the services being offered and agree to participate before services begin. Because it is often valuable for social workers to collaborate with other providers and professionals, it is important to obtain the Consent for Release of Information form before sharing any information with other providers. Clients must also be made fully aware of the reasons for this collaboration and information sharing and be told what information will be shared. Even if the client consents to having information released, the social worker should share only the relevant information with other providers, being careful to still maintain the client's confidentiality and privacy.

When providing services, it is important to ensure that clients understand all aspects of the services they will receive. In addition to a plan of treatment or plan for services, it is also necessary to ensure that clients understand the possible risks involved, the costs associated, the length of treatment or services, and any limitations to confidentiality that might exist due to both mandated reporting laws and third-party payers. Alternatives to the plan may also be discussed with clients before beginning services or treatment. Clients need to be given the opportunity to ask questions and receive answers to ensure they completely comprehend what the services will entail. Informed consent should require that the client sign legal documentation stating that they fully understand what will be involved—including all the risks, limitations, and alternatives—prior to beginning treatment. This documentation should become a part of the client's chart.

There will be circumstances in which a person may be receiving treatment on an involuntary basis. In these situations, the social worker should fully explain the terms of the treatment as it pertains to the individual's situation, as well as any rights the person does have in regard to refusal. An example of this type of situation would be someone who is court mandated to receive treatment, such as drug and alcohol counseling, anger management, or other therapies. Sometimes client information needs to be shared with other individuals such as the client's family or other professionals for referrals. In these situations, the client must agree to these disclosures, and consent for disclosure of information must be obtained. Confidentiality also becomes more complicated when a social worker is working with two or more people, either in a family or group session. All participants must agree that any information shared within the context of treatment will be kept confidential and not shared with others. However, the social worker should stress with clients that they cannot force other members to abide by the confidentiality agreement and that breach of confidentiality is a risk.

Client Records

Issues relating to confidentiality include the storage and maintenance of records and charts. All confidential material should be kept in a secure location and locked at all times. For example, if a social worker takes a clipboard into client rooms to make notes for later documentation, that clipboard should be locked in a drawer when not in use so that no one can turn it over and see confidential information when the social worker is away from their desk. With the use of electronics and computers, there should be policies in place to lock computers when away to avoid anyone seeing notes or other confidential information. Collaboration between colleagues in which clients may be discussed should be done behind closed doors to avoid anyone else hearing the conversation.

Social workers are to provide clients with reasonable access to records. Social workers are permitted, however, by the Code of Ethics to withhold all or part of the client record from the client if the social worker determines there is a great risk of harm in releasing the information. In these cases, it is important to fully document the request, whether the records were released, and the rationale for either releasing or not releasing them.

There may be instances in which a social worker is sued for malpractice. In these cases, the Code of Ethics states that it is permissible for the social worker to share confidential client information to aid in self-defense, but only so far as is necessary to adequately defend oneself.

Throughout the development of a professional relationship in social work, it is important to keep case notes and records for several reasons. Case notes are important in the process of conceptualizing the case and the client's needs. They can help the practitioner pull together their thoughts when making a diagnosis. Case records also serve as a measure of the standard of care and subsequently can be used in court to show adequate client care. They help social workers determine whether clients have made progress and remember what the client said from visit to visit, and they can be used when a practitioner seeks supervision about the case. In addition, case notes are needed by insurance companies, agencies, and schools to support the treatment that is provided to clients.

Legal and Ethical Issues Regarding Confidentiality

Social workers have a duty to protect confidential information of clients. Ethically, client information should not be discussed with anyone other than the client. Legally, a client has a right to keep their medical and therapeutic information confidential. The **Health Insurance Portability and Accountability Act of 1996 (HIPAA)** requires that medical information (including therapeutic and mental health information) be protected and kept confidential. However, there are certain limitations to confidentiality. These generally involve risk of harm to the individual being served as well as to others.

Social workers are not as protected as some other professionals when it comes to confidentiality and often find themselves being called to testify in court cases related to their clients. There are also certain situations in which social workers may have to release confidential information to protect the client or satisfy the duty to warn.

Providing services to minors can be challenging when it comes to confidentiality issues, especially since the legal rules and regulations vary from state to state. At times, there can be a conflict between the social worker's feeling of ethical responsibility to maintain the privacy of the minor and the legal right of parents to be informed of issues discussed. Adolescents in particular may discuss concerns with a social worker that they do not want their parents to be aware of, and it can be a violation of trust if these issues are subsequently revealed to parents.

It is imperative that at the start of treatment, the expectations of the social worker's relationship with each person as well as the benefits and limits of confidentiality are discussed with the parents and minors. Minors should never be promised confidentiality when the social worker cannot keep that promise, but the privacy and individuality of the minor should be maintained as much as possible. In cases where private information about the minor is going to be revealed, social workers should always inform the minor. This holds true whether it is with the client's consent, mandated reporting, or due to the parent utilizing their right to information.

With technology being utilized extensively by helping professionals, confidentiality of electronic information is another important issue. Counseling sessions are now being provided by telephone, video chat, and online simulation, and these media open new possibilities for information abuse. If a practitioner provides a video therapy session, they should be aware that it is possible for the client to have someone else in the room, off-camera, without informing the clinician or other participants. The same could be true with electronic communication such as texting or email. There is no way to know if a client is forwarding electronic information to third parties without the clinician's knowledge.

Mandatory Reporting

Some clients may disclose intent to harm themselves. It is necessary in these situations to fully assess suicidal intent and determine if the client is serious about carrying out a plan for self-harm. It might be sufficient, in cases where a client has considered self-harm but has no clear plan, to complete a safety plan with the client. The safety plan will outline what the client agrees to do should they begin to experience the desire to engage in self-harm. However, if the client has a clear plan of action and access to items necessary to carry out the plan, then confidentiality should be broken to protect the client. This would involve notifying police and having the client committed for observation for their own protection.

In addition to protecting clients from themselves, social workers also have a duty to warn third-party individuals if there is threat of harm. Duty to warn was established by the 1976 case Tarasoff vs. Regents of the University of California. In this case, a graduate student at the University of California-Berkeley had become obsessed with Tatiana Tarasoff. After significant distress, he sought psychological treatment and disclosed to his therapist that he had a plan to kill Tarasoff. Although the psychologist did have the student temporarily committed, he was ultimately released. He eventually stopped seeking treatment and attacked and killed Tarasoff. Tarasoff's family sued the psychologist and various other individuals involved with the university. This case evolved into the duty to warn third parties of potential risk of harm. Satisfying the duty to warn can be done by notifying police or the individual who is the intended victim.

Because ethical dilemmas can involve legal situations, they may also have legal consequences for a social worker or necessitate involving the legal system. For example, a client may disclose that he frequently drinks large amounts of alcohol and then drives his children to school. Ethically, there is an obligation to keep what the client has said in confidence. However, the client's children are being placed in a situation in which they are in great danger of being injured or harmed. Due to laws protecting the welfare of children, the social worker would need to make a report to Child Protective Services. In some states, if someone has a good faith reason to believe that a child is being neglected or abused and does not report the situation, that person may face a civil lawsuit and even criminal charges.

It's important to note as well that social workers are considered mandated reporters in all states. This means there is a legal and ethical obligation to break confidentiality to report any signs and symptoms of child and elder abuse. In some cases, it will be impossible to know for sure if abuse or neglect is happening. Often the social worker will have only a small amount of information that may raise concerns but must make a report so that an investigation can occur. A social worker cannot be held liable for reports made in good faith to Child Protective Services or Adult Protective Services.

154

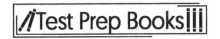

Liability is another legal issue that social workers may sometimes face. Clients can sue a social worker for malpractice. When a social worker is sued, the liability does not stop with the social worker. In lawsuits, a social worker's supervisor can be named as a defendant, and liability can extend as far as the head of the agency that employs the social worker. Agencies that provide social services carry malpractice insurance for this very reason. It is good practice, however, for individual social workers to also carry malpractice insurance for extra protection.

Ethical and Legal Issues Regarding Mandatory Reporting of Abuse

Mandatory reporting laws require social workers, and other professionals, to report any suspected abuse or neglect. This means that any professional who has a suspicion of abuse or neglect of a child or a vulnerable adult must legally make a report to either Child Protective Services or Adult Protective Services. Note that some states, such as Tennessee, have laws that require all citizens to report suspected abuse or neglect, making everyone a mandated reporter.

Often when abuse or neglect is suspected, the concern about breaking confidentiality is at the forefront of the mind of the social worker. During informed consent, this requirement to report any signs of abuse or neglect should have been disclosed to the client. When such breaks in confidentiality occur, they can damage the relationship. In some cases, it may be necessary or appropriate to disclose to the client that a report is being made. For example, if a new mother has tested positive for cocaine and the infant has tested positive for cocaine while in the hospital, the infant will remain in the Neonatal Intensive Care Unit due to withdrawal. Disclosing to the mother that a report is being made, and why it's being made, could prepare her and create an opportunity to speak further with her about treatment options and other important considerations. It's important to note that social workers who fail to report suspected abuse or neglect can be subject to civil penalties and/or prosecution.

When disclosing information due to legal requirements, it is always important to discuss the situation with the client. It should be noted that the social worker should evaluate their own safety when discussing disclosure of confidential information with the client. If the social worker believes the situation to be unsafe if/when the client learns of the disclosure, then it is not necessary to alert the client prior to disclosing the confidential information. This is something that should be discussed in detail with clients during the informed consent process and throughout the relationship.

One of the difficulties associated with breaking confidentiality to protect a third party is that the threat isn't always clearly established. If a client discloses during treatment that he is going to go home and stab his neighbor, this is clearly a plan of intended harm. However, what about an HIV-positive client who fails to warn sexual partners of her HIV status? What if the client fully understands the risk to her partners and has no intention of disclosing her status? This is a situation that would require thorough documentation, thoughtful debate, and possibly conferencing with colleagues to decide upon the best course of action.

Impairment

Impairment is a professional issue that should be addressed swiftly. Impairment occurs when a social worker's personal problems (e.g., mental health conditions, difficult life circumstances, or alcohol/drug use) have an impact upon their practice. The Code of Ethics states that social workers should seek to rectify their impairment by consulting with colleagues or supervisors, seeking their own treatment, limiting work, and/or terminating client relationships until the impairment has been fully addressed. In the event that a colleague is suffering from some sort of impairment, a social worker should address the concern with the colleague and encourage the colleague to rectify the issue. If the issue continues without proper attention, the social worker should go through appropriate channels to seek additional help for the colleague and to prevent consequences to clients. The same is true if the social worker feels there has been unethical behavior by a colleague. The social worker should discuss the behavior with the colleague and possibly with a supervisor. If a colleague is unfairly accused of unethical behavior, assisting the colleague in rectifying the situation is the best course of action.

Professional Development and Use of Self

Components of the Social Worker-Client Relationship

The relationship between the social worker and the client or client system is influenced by a number of components. These include the type of emotion that is shown by the parties during sessions, the general attitude toward the working relationship (e.g., positive, supportive), and the value each party places on the working relationship. The social worker should ensure that empathy, sympathy, and acceptance of the client and client system are shown during sessions to help foster a positive relationship. These aspects can be further supported by the social worker's initiative to build rapport with the client, such as through allowing the client to openly express feelings, work at a pace that feels comfortable, and encouraging them to shape and make decisions related to the intervention.

Additionally, a number of external tools may be a vital part of the social worker/client relationship. These include tools and documents that provide information related to the client's personality and behavior and items such as assessments, medical history, family history, current living situation, socioeconomic situation, and personal goals for the intervention. All of these items can help the social worker shape the intervention for the client.

Client's Role in the Problem-Solving Process

Whenever possible, social workers should invite their clients to take a collaborative perspective in designing interventions, establishing objectives, and developing program goals. This allows the client to feel empowered and engaged as an active member of the problem-solving process. These factors are associated with higher incidences of positive outcomes, as they encourage clients to feel accountable for their behaviors, actions, and personal changes.

Collaboration should begin at the intake process. This is a period in which the social worker can make assessments, but they can also get information directly from clients about why they are in the session and what they hope to achieve. The social worker can also ask clients the steps they believe they need to take to reach their desired outcomes. While clients may or may not provide useful or feasible answers, this process still sets the tone that allows clients to feel acknowledged and involved in their own care.

In the intake session or in the sessions that immediately follow, the social worker can invite the client to develop SMART objectives to reach their goals. This may also include establishing accountability tools, documenting plans of action to address potential barriers and how to overcome them, and identifying any other support protocols that clients may need for their individual situations. Depending on the client's specific case, this process may take one session or may take much longer. Social workers should continuously show patience, compassion, and a welcoming desire to engage the client in the process.

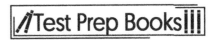

Social Worker's Role in the Problem-Solving Process

The **problem-solving therapeutic model** serves to teach clients how to manage stressors that come in life. Often, clients do not possess skills that allow them to effectively navigate negative events or emotions without increasing personal harm. The goal of the problem-solving model is to teach clients the skills necessary to deal with negative life events, negative emotions, and stressful situations. In particular, goals of this model should be to assist clients in identifying which particular situations may trigger unpleasant emotions, understanding the range of emotions one might feel, planning how to effectively deal with situations when they arise, and even recognizing and accepting that some situations are not able to be solved.

The social worker, however, may be an instructional guide to facilitate problem solving for the client. Because problem-solving skills are one of the primary methods of resolving issues and often are skills that clients lack, the social worker may need to model them for the client so that the client can then develop their own skills. Social workers need to maintain empathy and congruence with the client during the problem-solving process, and even though they may have verbally instructed or modeled problem-solving methods, they need to maintain rapport in the relationship.

Roles and Responsibilities of the Social Worker and Client in the Intervention Process

Clarifying the roles and responsibilities of the social worker, the client, and the client system in the intervention process can reduce the chance of miscommunication, misunderstanding, and interventions not working as intended. This clarification process can be developed during the intake process and initial sessions by actively listening to what the client hopes to achieve, and working together to develop a step-by-step intervention methodology. When possible, the stages, objectives, and milestones of the intervention should be documented in order to have an available reference point, drive accountability, and reduce any confusion around the expectations of all involved parties.

The **problem-solving approach to interventions** is a commonly used framework to cover these points. This is a seven-stage model that includes:

- active listening and engagement techniques (such as eye contact and other receptive body language)

- fostering trust and collaboration with the client (such as by showing genuine interest in the client as a person, rather than just in the context of the issues at hand)

- working together to identify the problem to be addressed and possible solutions, introducing allies in the resolution processes (such as clinical providers, a yoga or meditation teacher, or other experts that could help the client)

- developing a documented resolution plan and actively engaging all parties to follow it (such as through accountability cues, positive reinforcement, and celebrating small victories)

- providing support for sustaining the desired behaviors until the client is capable of terminating the intervention

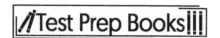

While one can be hopeful that the client and client systems will be cooperative and willing in this framework, that is not always the case. Clients may show distrust, anxiety, fear, or apathy, especially in the beginning. Often, the most important role of the social worker is building trust with the client and the client system. The social worker should continue to encourage a trusting, collaborative relationship until the time of service termination.

Building and Maintaining a Helping Relationship

As the principal conduit for client change and acceptance, the social worker/client relationship is primary to the problem solving and therapy process. If the social worker cannot develop a positive relationship with the client, the change process is hindered. The worker/client relationship should be based on trust, empathy, and acceptance by both parties in order to facilitate growth. Some clients may have difficulty building trust with the social worker, and the social worker may need to be patient with the client in order to make treatment goal progress. If the social worker cannot develop an appropriate trusting, empathetic, and accepting relationship with the client, the social worker should seek supervision. In some cases, the social worker will need to transfer the client because it will be very challenging for the client to make progress if trust does not exist. Social workers should be alert for countertransference issues in the relationship with the client and address these issues promptly if they occur.

Principles of Relationship Building

Rapport building begins during the initial contact the social worker has with the client, a crucial time for establishing trust and harmony. After building rapport, the client and the social worker can begin working on client issues and continue developing the relationship on deeper levels. The relationship that the client has with the social worker is representative of the relationships the client has in other areas of life; the social worker needs to engage with the client within this framework to effect the greatest change.

Acceptance and Empathy in the Social Worker-Client Relationship

Empathy is being able to relate to client circumstances and direction without the social worker actually experiencing it themselves. Sympathy differs from empathy in that sympathy is compassion for the client without having experienced the client's state of being. Empathy involves "being with" the client in their time and frame of mind. It involves connecting to the client on a visceral level while still maintaining some objectivity. Because empathy is the framework on which social work practice is built, it is imperative that social workers be empathetic with their clients. Those who cannot be empathetic should seek additional supervision or counsel in order to do their work effectively or refer the client to another worker.

Power and Transparency in the Social Worker-Client Relationship

Throughout their careers and in specific interventions, social workers should always remain aware of the power differential that is likely to exist between themselves and their clients. As the main person guiding the intervention, social workers inherently have more power in the relationship. Additionally, social workers may have more education, more independence, a clean legal record, better finances, or some other privilege that may make the client feel uncomfortable, ashamed, or defensive (especially when the client is involuntarily in the session, such as court-ordered cases). Awareness is one fundamental component of ensuring that this power dynamic doesn't have a negative effect.

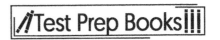

Transparency is another fundamental component, as it allows the client to feel like an equal who is involved in the problem-solving process. Social workers can foster transparency in the working relationship by openly discussing areas of privilege they may have, sharing as much information as they can about the problem-solving process and how it may be of benefit to the client, and empowering the client to take as much of the process as possible into their own control (such as through independent decision-making). When possible, the social worker should avoid hiding information or being unclear about why certain processes of interventions are being pursued.

Dual Relationships

Dual relationships are clearly outlined in the NASW Code of Ethics. The Code of Ethics states that social workers should not engage in dual relationships with clients or former clients in which exploitation of the client may occur. The Code of Ethics does recognize that there might be situations where dual relationships are unavoidable. For example, a social worker might have two jobs, one of which involves providing group therapy to survivors of sexual abuse. It is possible that a member of the aforementioned therapy group could become an employee or client at the social worker's second place of work. In these types of situations, the Code of Ethics suggests that the social worker establish clear boundaries that are sensitive to the client/former client.

Under no circumstances should a social worker ever become involved in a sexual relationship with a client. In addition, the Code of Ethics establishes that social workers must avoid sexual relationships with anyone who is related to or has a close personal relationship with a client or former client. The Code of Ethics also states that social workers should not become involved in sexual relationships with former clients because of the high risk of harm that may occur with such relationships. If, however, a social worker does become involved in a sexual relationship with a former client, the social worker is responsible for demonstrating that the former client entered into the relationship without manipulation or exploitation. The Code of Ethics also specifies that, due to the obvious risk of harm, a social worker should not provide professional services to anyone with whom the social worker has had a previous sexual relationship.

Situations called "**boundary crossings**" are when a social worker does not intend to create a dual relationship but inadvertently does so, as would be the case were a clinician to self-disclose personal information during a therapy session. This is distinguished from a **boundary violation**, which occurs when a dual relationship is established that is inherently coercive or manipulative and therefore harmful to the client. What are some clues about whether a boundary crossing is unethical?

- It hinders the social worker's care.
- It prevents the social worker from being impartial.
- It exploits or manipulates the client or another person.
- It harms clients or colleagues.

Dual relationships are sometimes unavoidable in practice, particularly in small communities. However, it is possible to avoid dual relationships that involve boundary violations and ethical violations.

Transference and Countertransference in the Social Worker-Client Relationship

Transference occurs when the client consciously or unconsciously relates feelings, thoughts, or emotions to the social worker because the social worker reminds the client, in some way, of a person from a past relationship. Transference by clients toward the social worker often occurs during the course of treatment and the client needs to be made aware of transference issues and how to reduce them. If clients are experiencing transference with the social worker, they may also be experiencing transference in other relationships in their lives, and this needs to be addressed. Transference is a common occurrence for many clients and can be a useful tool in therapeutic treatment to develop both healthier relationships and a productive relationship with the social worker.

Countertransference occurs when the social worker identifies the client with someone from the social worker's past. Social workers must work through countertransference issues while assisting the client in recognizing and coping with transference situations. If social workers recognize countertransference, they may want to seek the assistance of a supervisor to work through countertransference issues. Transference and countertransference may be useful for the social worker and client to experience because they may impact other areas in the relationships of both.

Impact of Domestic, Intimate Partner, and Other Violence on the Helping Relationship

Any type of abuse in a client's life can impart symptoms of trauma to the client. These symptoms may be subtle in nature, or they may be relatively obvious to the social worker. Obvious indicators of abuse include physical marks; chronic muscular or stomach pain (as a result of trauma or stress); consistently dressing in high-coverage clothing, even in cases where it seems abnormal (such as a hot day); or particular body language when the abuser is in the room or attending a session. Most abusive relationships occur as a manifestation of dysfunctional power and control tactics. If the client is an abuser, it may be difficult for him or her to be guided by a social worker, as there may be an experience of a loss of control or power. Abuse victims may feel distrustful or fearful of the social worker and the helping relationship; they also may be uncomfortable discussing their abuser in a negative light. This can be a setback to the intervention process, and social workers may need to spend extra time fostering rapport and building a trusting relationship with these types of clients.

Diversity in the Social Worker-Client Relationship

Attitudes and Beliefs
Social workers should be culturally aware of their attitudes and beliefs. This requires a keen awareness of their own cultural background and gaining awareness of any personal biases, stereotypes, and values that they hold. Practitioners should also accept different worldviews, be sensitive to differences, and refer minority clients to a practitioner from the client's culture when it would benefit the client.

Knowledge
Practitioners should have the appropriate knowledge of different cultures. Specifically, practitioners must understand the client's culture and should not jump to conclusions about the client's way of being. Throughout their careers, social workers should be willing to gain a greater depth of knowledge of various cultural groups and update this knowledge as necessary. This includes understanding how issues like racism, sexism, and homophobia can negatively affect minority clients. Practitioners should understand how different therapeutic theories carry values that may be detrimental for some clients. Social workers should also understand how institutional barriers can affect the willingness of minority clients to use mental health services.

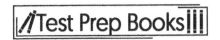

Cultural Skills

Social workers should be well-versed in cultural skills. They must be able to apply interviewing and counseling techniques with clients and should be able to employ specialized skills and interventions that might be effective with specific minority populations. Practitioners should be able to communicate effectively and understand the verbal and nonverbal language of a client. They also should take a systematic perspective in their practice, work collaboratively with community leaders, and advocate for clients when it's in their best interests.

When working with clients from diverse backgrounds, practitioners should be able to shift their professional strategies.

The following are important techniques and strategies for working with various cultural and racial backgrounds:

- Have appropriate attitudes and beliefs, gain knowledge about the client's background, and learn new skills as needed.

- Encourage the client to speak in their native language and arrange for an interpreter when necessary.

- Assess the client's cultural identity and how important it is to the client.

- Check accuracy of any interpretations of the client's nonverbal cues.

- Make use of alternate modes of communication, such as writing, typing, translation services, and the use of art.

- Assess the impact of sociopolitical issues on the client.

- Encourage the client to bring culturally significant and personally relevant items.

- Vary the helping environment to make it conducive to effective work with the client.

The following are important techniques and strategies for working with various religious backgrounds:

- Determine the client's religious background in the beginning sessions.
- Check personal biases and gain information about the client's religion.
- Ask the client how important religion is in their life.
- Assess the client's level of faith development.
- Avoid making assumptions about the religion.
- Become familiar with the client's religious beliefs, important holidays, and faith traditions.
- Understand that religion can deeply affect the client unconsciously.

Effect of Client's Developmental Level on the Social Worker-Client Relationship

A client's development level will vary from client to client, and it may even vary for the same client over the full course of an intervention. Therefore, the social worker should make no assumptions about the client's ability to cope, the way the intervention will be accepted and utilized, or any other aspect of the working relationship. These factors should be assessed upon intake and at regular intervals thereafter, the frequency of which may vary on a case-by-case basis. Assessments should holistically take into account the client's development, including age, psychological factors, emotional factors, social factors, acute personal conditions (such as an impending divorce or recent refugee status) that may temporarily impact the client's functioning, and any other scope of development that may be appropriate for the client's need. For example, a client who has a history of violent behavior and a history of playing physical sports with extreme contact may find it beneficial to undergo neurological development assessments. By viewing the client through a holistic perspective, social workers can ensure interventions are appropriate across all domains of development; if so, the interventions are more likely to be effective and received positively by the client.

Social Worker Self-Care Principles and Techniques

Self-care practices may include establishing boundaries between one's work and personal life, having a regular meditation practice or other mental exercises that are shown to soothe the nervous system, eating a healthy diet and engaging in regular physical exercise (as these behaviors decrease inflammation in the body and reduce stress hormones), and having a trustworthy support system of friends and colleagues.

Introspective exercises, such as daily journaling, can provide the social worker with a better understanding of which activities bring stress to their lives and which activities bring peace. By knowing these, the social worker can bridge the gap to reduce stress in areas they can control, such as setting a clear cut-off time for answering emails or scheduling personal activities that bring them joy. They can adopt healthy coping mechanisms for the areas in which they are unable to control factors that might contribute to their stress, such as an emotional case or external funding issues.

Burnout, Secondary Trauma, and Compassion Fatigue

Due to the highly emotional, interpersonal, and empathic demands of the social work field, social workers must employ and sustain self-care practices to protect their personal health. Without self-care, social workers are highly susceptible to burnout and compassion fatigue—two risks that occur when working in a field that often provides exposure to disheartening humanitarian situations, abusive intrapersonal relationships, and cases that, for bureaucratic or personal reasons, take a long time to resolve. Unchecked, these experiences can lead the social worker to feel detached from work and hopeless toward cases or to consistently experience the ill effects of chronic stress. Sometimes it may be necessary to seek supervision if the social worker experiences burnout, secondary trauma, compassion fatigue, countertransference or the inability to develop a trusting relationship with the client.

Burnout Symptoms

At times, social workers may experience a sense of disinterest or disengagement from their work, which may signal burnout. Symptoms of burnout can include physical symptoms, such as fatigue, headaches, insomnia, and decreased resistance to illness. Emotional symptoms can include depression, anxiety, boredom, lack of empathy, cynicism, and anger. **Burnout** may be a result of overworking and/or providing service to clients who are not progressing, thus causing social workers to feel incompetent and ineffective. It is important to know the warning signs of burnout and engage in self-care, which may involve taking a vacation; getting increased supervision or therapy; making changes to one's hours, fees, or practice; or seeking continuing education options.

162

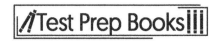
Secondary Trauma and Compassion Fatigue

Social work often involves working with individuals and communities who have experienced intense trauma. Secondary trauma and compassion fatigue can occur as a result of consistently being exposed to the trauma of others. In order to maintain their own well-being and continue to provide effective services, social workers should be aware of these potential issues and take steps to address them.

Secondary trauma refers to the emotional and psychological impact that social workers may experience due to working with individuals who have experienced trauma. Anxiety, depression, and avoidance behavior are some of the symptoms that can arise due to secondary trauma. It is crucial for social workers to not only recognize these symptoms and signs, but also be proactive in taking steps to address them by, for example, seeking support from colleagues or engaging in self-care activities.

Compassion fatigue is another issue common among social workers due to the nature of the job. Compassion fatigue refers to emotional exhaustion and decreased ability to empathize with clients. Social workers may become desensitized to their clients suffering, resulting in feelings of burnout and detachment. Once again, it is important for social workers to seek support and spend time and energy on themselves to avoid compassion fatigue and its symptoms.

In addition to self-care activities, social workers can also take steps to prevent secondary trauma and compassion fatigue through professional development. This includes, but is not limited to, continuous education and training on trauma-informed care and strategies of self-care. Additionally, social workers should maintain a support network of colleagues and mentors who can provide comfort, support, and guidance in times of need. It is important to note that, while it is the duty of social workers to care for others, it will become increasingly difficult to do so without effective methods for maintaining their own mental health.

Safe and Positive Work Environment

Social workers have an emotionally and physically taxing job; therefore, a safe and positive work environment is crucial in supporting social workers in their jobs and in doing their best work. A safe and positive work environment is characterized by processes that foster work-life balance; good boundaries between work and personal life; a culture of respect and ethical behavior toward colleagues and subordinates; just compensation for tasks performed; support for the social worker's personal and professional development; and a zero-tolerance policy for threats, violence, harassment, or bullying in the workplace. Additionally, a documented process that allows social workers to express feelings of unsafety (whether with coworkers or with clients) and established avenues for resolution are other ways to ensure a positive and safe work environment. Social workers should feel comfortable employing these avenues without fear of consequences from colleagues or supervisors. Finally, leadership should ensure their workers feel comfortable communicating their professional goals, successes, and obstacles; leadership should also provide opportunities that support professional goal achievement or resolution to overcome obstacles.

Professional Objectivity in the Social Worker-Client Relationship

While social workers should show empathy toward a client, it is also important that they remain objective and do not become enmeshed in the social worker/client relationship. Enmeshment occurs when the social worker is overly involved with the client's emotional life, and it may harm the client. Social workers must demonstrate professional objectivity with the client to avoid countertransference,

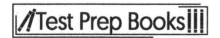
which occurs when a social worker redirects their emotions onto the client. In addition, social workers can engage in professional objectivity by recognizing that the client is the party who needs to do the majority of the work in the relationship. It is difficult to maintain professional objectivity when enmeshment occurs, and social workers should seek supervision if they cannot maintain professional objectivity with the client.

Social workers must also ensure that they're competent to fulfill any job that they are assigned before practicing with clients. This includes being a life-long learner and reviewing relevant research literature related to their therapeutic approaches and the clients they serve. Practitioners should also use evidence-based practices in their work with clients whenever possible. Practitioners should behave in morally responsible ways, advocate for their clients when they are faced with discriminatory practices or policies, practice self-care to ensure that they are effective in their work, and should only work within the scope of their practice.

Influence of Social Worker's Own Values and Beliefs on the Social Worker-Client Relationship

Social work as a profession prides itself on practitioners putting personal values aside, even when those values conflict with client values. Social workers must not engage in discriminatory practices or condone the discriminatory practices of others. For example, if a social worker is personally uncomfortable with same-sex relationships, but has a gay or lesbian client, the social worker will need to take steps to evaluate their own values and beliefs. The social worker must ensure that personal feelings are put aside in order to appropriately meet the client's needs. Self-awareness is a vital part of ensuring that one's personal values and beliefs do not intrude on the social worker/client relationship. It may be necessary to seek consultation from a supervisor or colleague in situations where one's personal values or beliefs are in conflict with the client and when those feelings cannot be resolved. In extreme cases where consultation and self-reflection cannot remedy the conflict, termination of the social worker/client relationship and referral to another therapist may be necessary.

Time Management Approaches

Social workers can effectively manage their time through a number of organizational methods. These may include daily prioritization of tasks for the day (such as urgent tasks versus tasks that can wait until the next day), ensuring that all meeting and phone calls with colleagues are scheduled with objectives in mind (such as with the use of a meeting agenda), breaking more tedious tasks into chunks, and planning in a way that works best for one's personality. For example, one person may enjoy making weekly color-coded schedules of tasks with gaps available throughout the week for unexpected assignments that come up; another may prefer to manage tasks daily in a simple list style, with flexible room built in per day. While no schedule can be absolutely rigid, as unforeseen circumstances are guaranteed to arise from time to time, a schedule that is guarded and respected by the social worker fosters effective time management. It is important to decline non-urgent tasks or responsibilities if one's schedule is booked, while ensuring there is space in one's schedule to assist with unanticipated emergencies.

Transference and Countertransference Within Supervisory Relationships

Transference and countertransference are used to describe how projections occur in an interactive relationship. **Transference** occurs when supervisees project certain attitudes, values, beliefs, or feelings onto their supervisors; **countertransference** occurs when supervisors project certain attitudes, values,

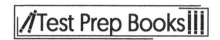
beliefs, or feelings onto their supervisees. Depending on the intensity or type of projections that take place, transference and countertransference experiences may impact the boundaries, mentoring relationship, or professional collaboration that takes place between supervisors and supervisees. Transference and countertransference experiences may also occur as a result of temporary situations the supervisor or supervisee find themselves in, and interactions that occur afterward may have a long-lasting impact.

For example, a supervisee may have heard from a colleague a long, emotional story about harassment from another supervisor. Upon meeting with their personal supervisor, the supervisee may project irrational feelings of anger, fear, or resentment on the supervisor for the rest of their working relationship. Additionally, supervisors must take care to examine supervisees when they are working with clients. Transference and countertransference can take place unexpectedly between social workers and their clients, and it can have similar impacts on the intervention process. Finally, overly positive transference and countertransference experiences can be somewhat problematic as well. They may unwittingly place one person on a pedestal, result in an insincere mentoring relationship, or cause feelings of disillusionment in supervisees when they see their supervisors make an error.

Transference and countertransference experiences can be minimized by openly discussing their potential in the beginning of a professional relationship. By discussing the fact that both parties are vulnerable to this experience, both parties can become more self-aware and reflective about occurrences and how to handle them. This sets the stage for professional and collaborative growth, transparency, and effective communication.

Impact of Social Worker's Own Values and Beliefs on Interdisciplinary Collaboration

Reflecting on one's personal values and beliefs in order to maintain objectivity and reduce biases when providing treatment for clients is a fundamental component of the NASW's Code of Ethics. Providing treatment as part of an **interdisciplinary collaboration** (such as part of a team consisting of medical professionals, allied health workers, financial experts, legal experts, and other professionals that support a client) is becoming more common in the field of social work. It can be difficult to manage all competing interests, as each professional on a collaborative team will bring a different perspective with different ideas for the most effective treatment. While a social worker may focus primarily on psychosocial factors that influence a client's life, a doctor may focus more on the client's physical health, and a financial expert may focus on providing the client with better financial resources.

Therefore, working in collaborative groups requires keeping the client's desired outcomes for the intervention as the primary goal of the interdisciplinary team. Documenting the client's goals and mapping out each professional's objectives can help mitigate the effects of professional and personal biases. Additionally, a documented plan can help establish clear job roles for each professional so that a single set of values does not take over the full scope of the intervention. When interdisciplinary collaboration accounts for these factors, the benefits of providing the client with multiple skill sets and perspectives can be tremendous.

Practice Quiz

1. Which of the following terms is used to describe the way in which a client aligns their ego for the therapeutic relationship and how much the ego is or is not joined with the social worker's ego?
    a. Empathy
    b. Cognitive complexity
    c. Psychological adjustment
    d. Therapeutic alliance

2. Which of the following is NOT a factor in the RESPECTFUL Counseling Model?
    I. Family history
    II. Sexual orientation and identity
    III. Career or vocation
    IV. Ethnic and racial identity

    a. Family history
    b. Sexual orientation and identity
    c. Career or vocation
    d. Ethnic and racial identity

3. Bioethical issues in social work practice may include all but which of the following?
    a. Sustainable farming and recycling practices
    b. Pregnancy and fetal rights
    c. Juvenile rights to medical treatment
    d. End-of-life issues

4. When working in an interdisciplinary collaboration, what should be kept in mind to ensure a seamless working relationship?
    a. Educate, Communicate, Experience, Skill levels, Conflict
    b. Advocate, Understanding, Common Ground, Differences, Conflict
    c. Advocate, Communicate, Experience, Skill levels, Closure
    d. Educate, Understanding, Common Ground, Differences, Closure

5. Interdisciplinary collaboration is commonplace in social work. To avoid conflict, there are steps that can be taken to promote a smooth working relationship. The first step is to advocate. What does this mean within the context of interdisciplinary collaboration?
    a. Educating team members about the role of the social worker
    b. Standing up for the social workers when other team members try to keep them from being heard
    c. Making sure everyone on the team hears what the social workers have to say
    d. Asking team members to remember that everyone has strengths they bring to the table

See answers on next page.

Answer Explanations

1. D: The therapeutic alliance, like the other choices listed, is a strategy that social workers can employ to maintain effectiveness in practice. Therapeutic alliance refers to how the client aligns their ego for the therapeutic relationship and the degree to which their ego is—or is not—joined with social worker's ego or self. Choice *A*, empathy, refers to the therapist's ability to sense the client's feelings and communicate acceptance and understanding to the client. Choice *B*, cognitive complexity, refers to the social worker's ability to view an individual within both an individualistic and systemic framework, to understand that knowledge is not fixed, and to remain open to feedback and different points of view. Psychological adjustment enables the social worker to identify and empathize with the client's own experience.

2. C: The RESPECTFUL Counseling Model suggests that practitioners pay careful attention to the following aspects of their clients because they may affect the client personally and the approach to working with the client: Religious and spiritual identity, Economic background, Sexual orientation and identity, Psychological development, Ethnic and racial identity, Chronological disposition, Trauma and other threats to personal well-being, Family history, Unique physical characteristics, and Language and location of residence. Career and vocation are not explicitly mentioned, although they can be factors that social workers should consider for certain clients. The "C" stands for chronological disposition or development.

3. A: Bioethical issues relate to areas regarding the society's responsibility for protecting the rights and values of human health and life. Social worker should familiarize themselves with bioethical issues through continuing education practices and reviewing relevant literature. Issues of sustainability, conservation, and the environment are not bioethical issues, but those regarding prenatal and fetal rights, juvenile rights to healthcare, and end-of-life rights are some of the important topics that social workers may encounter.

4. B: The things to remember when working with an interdisciplinary collaboration are Advocate (educating team members about the role of the social worker), Understanding (striving to understand the other disciplines by asking questions about their roles, functions, and goals), Common Ground (attempting to find things in common that would contribute to better collaboration), Differences (recognizing that differences exist between disciplines and their goals and approaches), and Conflict (striving to approach conflict directly and with sensitivity and respect).

5. A: In this context, *advocate* means that the social worker will educate the rest of the team about the role of the social worker. Often the professional goals and vision of social work differs from that of other disciplines. The social worker should educate team members about this and attempt to gain understanding.

Practice Test #1

1. As an elementary school social worker, you are interacting with an eight-year-old child who is unable to speak clearly or coherently, who sometimes has issues with bladder control, and who cannot yet tie his own shoes. The child should receive further assessment for which of the following?
    a. Developmental delays
    b. Conduct disorder
    c. Genetic deficiencies
    d. Oppositional defiant disorder

2. Most researchers divide adult development into three sections of life following the end of adolescence. What are these three sections called?
    a. Early adulthood (ages eighteen to forty), middle adulthood (ages forty to sixty-five), and late adulthood (age sixty-five until death)
    b. Post adolescence (ages eighteen to twenty-four), middle adulthood (ages twenty-five to forty), and mature adulthood (age forty until death)
    c. Initial adulthood (ages eighteen to thirty-five), middle adulthood (ages thirty-six to sixty) and later life stage (age sixty until death)
    d. Stage one adulthood (ages eighteen to twenty-eight), stage two adulthood (ages twenty-nine to fifty-eight), and stage three adulthood (age fifty-nine until death)

3. Biological, psychological, and social factors all interact together as an individual transitions through various life stages. As a clinician evaluating biological factors that may contribute to the person's current psychological issues, the areas to review should include which of the following?
    a. A parental history of psychiatric illness and/or addiction
    b. Family income and social status
    c. Years of education completed
    d. Employment history

4. Which of the examples listed depicts obtaining information from a collateral source?
    a. An initial verbal consultation conducted with a potential client
    b. A self-report assessment filled out by the client
    c. An official medical report brought by the client to their first session
    d. The client draws a picture illustrating their current mental state during a session

5. Which of these is NOT a commonly used psychometric in social work?
    a. Myers-Briggs Type Indicator
    b. Beck Depression Inventory
    c. Wechsler Adult Intelligence Scale – Fourth Edition
    d. Miller Analogies Test

6. Social workers typically examine a client's personal history holistically through what kind of lens?
    a. Clinical
    b. Biopsychosocial
    c. Psychosomatic
    d. Environmental

7. What are the components of a SMART objective?
   a. Sensitive, Makeshift, Attainable, Reliable, Time-Specific
   b. Sensitive, Measurable, Attentive, Retainable, Tolerable
   c. Specific, Measurable, Ability, Retention, Timing
   d. Specific, Measurable, Achievable, Relevant, Time-Specific

8. The NASW Code of Ethics has six core purposes. Which of the following choices are included in those core purposes?

   I. To provide the rules and standards that social workers can use to evaluate the conduct of others in the profession
   II. To help identify information that social workers should take under advisement when ethical conflicts may exist or when an ethical dilemma presents itself
   III. To inform new social workers about core issues relating to the mission of social work and to the ethical standards of the field
   IV. To relate the vision of social work in a standard way throughout the profession
   V. To establish the consequences of violating the ethical standards of social work
   VI. To ensure that collaborating professions are aware of the expectations to which social workers are held

   a. Choices I, II, and III
   b. Choices I, IV, and V
   c. Choices II, III, and VI
   d. Choices III, IV, and VI

9. Claudia is coming to therapy for the first time. She meets her therapist, Susan, a licensed clinical social worker, and Susan tells her what she can expect from treatment. Claudia says that she understands the process of therapy, as well as the risks, and that she is excited to begin. Susan makes a note of their discussion and begins her assessment. Has Susan satisfied the informed consent requirement, and why or why not?
   a. Yes. Susan discussed the process and risks of therapy, and the client agreed.
   b. No. Susan didn't ask Claudia if she understood everything fully.
   c. No. Susan did not have Claudia sign a consent form.
   d. Yes. Susan made a note that Claudia agreed as part of her documentation.

10. Susan's husband is employed in the IT sector and is looking for a new job. Susan's client, Claudia, mentions during their therapy session that her husband is an IT recruiter. At the end of their session, Susan asks Claudia for her husband's contact information. She says she would like her husband to reach out to Claudia's husband to find a better IT job. What boundary issue does this represent?
   a. Dependency
   b. Personal gain
   c. Dual relationship
   d. Altruism

169

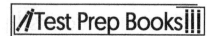

11. Joe is a fifteen-year-old white male. He and his family immigrated to the United States from Israel when Joe was five years old. His family celebrates traditional Jewish holidays like Hanukkah, Rosh Hashanah, and Yom Kippur with neighbors in their subdivision who are also of the Jewish faith. All of these qualities are examples of Joe's what?
   a. Upbringing
   b. Class
   c. Culture
   d. Friendships

12. Ella comes to her therapy session and is openly hostile towards her social worker. She remains quiet whenever a question is asked, and only speaks to say things like "This is a stupid idea"; "I don't need to change, they need to change"; "I hate doing this, and it's pointless." Ella is showing _____ motivation and _____ resistance.
   a. high, high
   b. low, low
   c. high, low
   d. low, high

13. For therapists working primarily with adolescents, it is helpful to share which of the following with clients?
   a. Sexual Identity and preferences will probably never change throughout one's lifetime.
   b. It is important to offer a diagnosis to the adolescent of their sexual orientation so that they can be reassured of where they stand.
   c. Disclosure of oneself or others' sexual orientation to help the client feel empowered to share their own experience.
   d. Sexual development is a unique and individual process, and not everyone reaches sexual milestones at the same time.

14. Gerontology is the study of what?
   a. The biological aspects of aging, economic trends of the aging, population, and the impact of aging on social trends
   b. Economic trends of youth, consumer spending as it pertains to children, and the focus on youth in the media
   c. The impact of social trends on schools, how schools function in the technology age, and the evolution of administration within schools
   d. The biological aspects of mental illness and how substance use is viewed within social trends

15. Which best describes a definition of client advocacy?
   a. Helping clients recognize and then use their strengths, resources, and systems to obtain goals
   b. Working on behalf of clients to remove barriers and obtain needed resources and/or services
   c. A short-term treatment usually lasting four to six weeks that is implemented when a client enters treatment following some type of traumatic event that causes significant distress
   d. Helping to link clients with needed services and resources

16. Which is NOT a method of working with involuntary clients?
    a. Helping clients to recognize participation is still a choice
    b. Including a client's goals in a service plan along with mandated goals
    c. Protecting a client's right to self-determination
    d. Refraining from getting a client's consent in treatment, since participation is mandatory

17. Which of the following is an aspect of the psychosocial approach to treatment?
    a. Unique to the field of social work, allowing it to stand out from other professions
    b. Used when clients experience a state of disequilibrium, are out of balance, and can no longer function effectively
    c. Emphasizes the concept of problems of living
    d. Short-term, practical, and evidence-based intervention

18. An autopoietic social system has which of the following qualities?
    a. A clear hierarchy within itself
    b. The ability to produce and maintain itself
    c. The ability to expand and regrow itself
    d. A definitive start and end point innate in the design

19. For many years, Abraham Maslow, who developed the hierarchy of human needs, described self-actualization as the highest level of achievement. In later years, he adjusted the model in order to add another level, which is referred to as what?
    a. Peace and serenity
    b. Spiritual attainment
    c. Self-determination
    d. Self-transcendence

20. Those who research self-image throughout the life cycle report which of the following?
    a. Most people's self-image tends to peak around the age of sixty.
    b. Adolescents have the highest likelihood of a positive self-image when compared with other age groups.
    c. There is very little change in self-image once middle school is completed.
    d. Young adults who are completing high school and entering the work force or college show an increase in self-image.

21. According to Elizabeth Kubler-Ross, there are five stages of grief. They occur in what order?
    a. Denial, anger, bargaining, acceptance, depression
    b. Anger, depression, denial, isolation, and bargaining
    c. Refusal, denial, isolation, anger, acceptance
    d. Denial, anger, bargaining, depression, acceptance

171

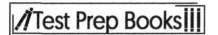
22. Which of the following statements regarding the three stages of the prevention-focused service distribution model of social work is NOT correct?
   a. The primary prevention stage involves addressing potential causes and getting rid of the problem's root cause.
   b. The problem occurs prior to the primary prevention stage.
   c. The secondary prevention stage involves actions that attempt to stop the problem before they spread and cause further harm.
   d. Actions in the tertiary stage are designed to decrease the problem's severity through remedial service provisions, which decrease the problem's lasting effects and duration.

23. What are the components of an ethical dilemma?
   a. Conflicting values; the social worker must decide between different courses of action; the social worker may have to terminate with the client.
   b. Ethical principles are at odds; the social worker can either make a decision or not; the situation is troubling to the social worker.
   c. Different courses of action exist; ethical principles are at odds; the social worker can either make a decision or not.
   d. The social worker must make a decision; different courses of action exist; no matter what choice of action is made, an ethical ideal will be compromised.

24. There are steps to resolving an ethical dilemma that have been outlined by the NASW Code of Ethics. What is the correct order of these steps?
   a. Consider, Specify, Rank, Establish, Implement, and Enforce
   b. Consider, Specify, Rank, Establish, Implement, and Reflect
   c. Determine, Identify, Rank, Develop, Implement, and Reflect
   d. Determine, Identify, Rank, Develop, Implement, and Enforce

25. Wellbutrin, Zoloft, and Prozac are all prescription medications classified as what?
   a. Atypical antipsychotics
   b. Typical antipsychotics
   c. Antidepressants
   d. Anti-inflammatory

26. In the *DSM-5-TR*, which term is defined as "a sudden, rapid, recurrent, nonrhythmic motor movement or vocalization?"
   a. Motor stereotypy
   b. Compulsion
   c. Spasm
   d. Tic

27. According to the *DSM-5-TR*, selective mutism is categorized with which type of disorders?
   a. Anxiety disorders
   b. Neurodevelopmental disorders
   c. Depressive disorders
   d. Trauma and stressor related disorders

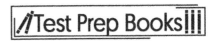

28. An intervention plan should be which of the following?
    a. Data-driven
    b. Short, with details that can be expanded later as needed
    c. Cumbersome
    d. Mostly observational

29. Which of the following statements regarding the focus of the social work profession is FALSE?
    a. It is to provide care and improve society.
    b. It is to define and explain existing problems in individuals and society at large.
    c. It involves incorporating knowledge and skills in other fields such as sociology, philosophy, law, and psychology.
    d. It involves distinguishing between and catering to social and individual morality and advocating when the absence of morality creates social injustice.

30. Janelle is a therapist at a nonprofit agency, and she is supervised by Susan, who meets with the executive director each month to alert her of any issues. Janelle has been seeing Brad for over a year for individual therapy. Brad wanted to focus on marital issues, but his wife refused to join him, telling him the issues in their marriage were because of his own personal problems. Brad told Janelle he wanted to improve himself to be a better husband. Last week, Brad's wife moved out and filed for divorce. She told him he had not improved himself during the last year of therapy. Brad believes this is Janelle's fault and has filed a malpractice lawsuit against Janelle. Legally, could Brad do anything else regarding malpractice?
    a. No. You can't sue someone because your wife left you.
    b. Yes. Brad could also file suit against Janelle's supervisor and go up the chain of command, naming even the executive director in the lawsuit.
    c. Yes. Brad can also file suit against Janelle's direct supervisor.
    d. No. Brad can only sue Janelle, because she was his therapist.

31. Brad has filed a malpractice lawsuit against his therapist, Janelle. The agency for which Janelle works has liability insurance. What options are available to social workers like Janelle, to protect them from malpractice lawsuits such as this one?
    a. If a social worker's agency has liability insurance, the social worker is covered by the agency insurance.
    b. A social worker needs their own liability insurance, because the agency insurance will only cover supervisors and the director.
    c. If the informed consent document states that the client holds the therapist harmless, then the therapist is protected from claims of malpractice.
    d. It is good practice to have personal liability insurance even if the agency one works for also has liability insurance.

32. Which component of the problem-solving process is left out of these steps?
1. Assess, define, and clarify the problem.
2. Examine options and select/implement a solution.
3. Evaluate and adjust.

a. Emphasize contracting and carefully planned task implementation.
b. Determine possible solutions.
c. Function as a collaborator to assist the client in identifying smaller tasks.
d. Identify issues, strengths, and resources.

33. Due to the brief nature of short-term therapy, what should begin early in the treatment process?
a. Assessment
b. Termination planning
c. Educational services
d. Metacommunication

34. What is NOT a typical role of a social worker?
a. Advocate
b. Case manager
c. Educator
d. Scapegoat

35. Receiving a diagnosis of a serious pulmonary illness can have many biopsychosocial impacts. Some things a therapist will want to address with a client who has just received a diagnosis of this nature may include which of the following?
a. Asking why he or she continued to smoke, even after being told by a doctor it was affecting the respiratory system
b. Insisting that the client discuss the diagnosis with all immediate family members within twenty-four hours
c. Providing support and encouraging ventilation of emotions, especially grief and anger
d. Accompanying the client to his next medical appointment to make sure the information is accurate

36. Changes that occur in a normal family life cycle tend to cause a re-alignment of relationships and roles within the family unit. This is because of what?
a. At some point, the adult child is expected to provide more care and support to the parent than the parent can provide to the adult child.
b. Families often split apart due to disagreements over money and relationships.
c. Most parents view their adult children as being incapable of properly raising children and feel they must intervene.
d. Some elderly people are constantly critical when their adult children are having a more successful career than the parents had.

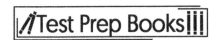
37. Hypervigilance, disturbing dreams, and eruptions of anger are symptoms of what psychiatric disorder?
    a. Claustrophobia
    b. PTSD
    c. Borderline personality disorder
    d. Severe anxiety with panic attacks

38. Sigmund Freud and his daughter Anna developed a lengthy list of defense mechanisms, including denial, projection, rationalization, and sublimation. They proposed that the need for people to employ defense mechanisms was for which of the following reasons?
    a. Because they were dishonest and did not want others to see the real person.
    b. Because if they admitted the truth about themselves others would no longer accept them.
    c. Because the defense mechanism allows one to avoid perceiving or accepting something very unacceptable about themselves, which they are not yet ready to address.
    d. Because using defense mechanisms gives one an emotional advantage over others and makes it easier to exploit them.

39. Which is NOT associated with the provision of educational services to clients?
    a. It may be done in individual, family, small group, classes, or large group forums.
    b. Workers may recommend resources such as books, articles, or websites.
    c. Workers must have a thorough knowledge of available local resources.
    d. The social worker must determine what skills, information, or knowledge needs to be acquired by clients.

40. Which factor is NOT part of evaluating a client's progress?
    a. Identifying specific issues to be addressed
    b. Creating appropriate goals, objectives, and tasks
    c. Administering the intervention plan
    d. Using effective and relevant techniques and tools to measure success

41. What is the definition of reciprocal goals?
    a. Complementary goals agreed upon by members of a system and related to the same target problem
    b. When members of a system choose the same goal that addresses an identified problem
    c. Social worker's goals related to ending treatment
    d. The plan to rate the occurrence or severity of a behavior or problem

42. Which choice is NOT a frequently used term in family therapy?
    a. Disengaged
    b. Boundaries
    c. Alliances
    d. Cohesion

43. To meet the client's needs and produce successful outcomes, intervention plans should be what?
    a. Tightly structured
    b. Flexible
    c. Typed
    d. Five-dimensional

175

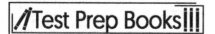

44. During a mental status exam (MSE), assessing how well the client pays attention is an example of what main element of the MSE?
    a. Psychomotor behavior
    b. Mood and affect
    c. Cognition
    d. Thought patterns

45. It's essential that client information is always stored in what way?
    a. In a filing cabinet
    b. In an online database
    c. Securely
    d. At the end of the session

46. In the *DSM-5-TR*, attention-deficit/hyperactivity disorder is classified as which of the following?
    a. Neurocognitive disorders
    b. Neurodevelopmental disorders
    c. Neurological disorders
    d. Section III

47. Professional values for social workers focus on all but which of the following main values?
    a. Employing a scientifically sound solution-based model for clients' problems
    b. Preserving the general human rights of those they serve
    c. Preserving and advocating for social justice
    d. Maintaining the strong moral base of the profession

48. Client information is protected by confidentiality. However, in the instance where a client makes a threat against another individual during treatment, the social worker is required to warn the individual, thus breaking confidentiality. What court case established the duty to warn?
    a. *Tarasoff vs. Regents of University of California*
    b. *Regents of University of California vs. Bakke*
    c. *Blonder-Tongue vs. University of Illinois*
    d. *Fisher vs. University of Texas*

49. When required by law to disclose confidential information about a client, the social worker should always discuss the disclosure with the client before the disclosure occurs. Is this true or false? Why?
    a. False. At the time of the informed consent, the client should have been told about legal requirements that cause the social worker to break confidentiality, and therefore, the social worker never needs to discuss a specific disclosure with the client.
    b. True. The social worker must get the client to sign a new informed consent form stating that the client understands the disclosure will be made.
    c. False. The social worker should assess any threat to their personal safety, or the safety of others, and should only discuss the disclosure with the client if no one appears to be at risk of harm.
    d. True. The social worker has a duty to tell the client that a disclosure is being made and that confidentiality is being broken.

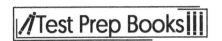

50. Which of the following is true regarding the difference between the Ethical Theory and Decision-Making Period and the Ethical Standards and Risk Management Period of the social work ethics evolution?
    a. The Ethical Standards and Risk Management Period preceded the Ethical Theory and Decision-Making Period.
    b. The Ethical Standards and Risk Management Period focused on the potential for abuse in the profession and how to avoid such abuse, malpractice, and litigation issues.
    c. The Ethical Theory and Decision-Making Period focused on the relationship between applying the Code of Ethics and managing the risk of malpractice and legal liability.
    d. During the Ethical Standards and Risk Management Period, the National Association of Social Workers updated the Code of Ethics to include a summary of the core values and mission of social work.

51. Which choice is NOT a stage of the group process?
    a. Pre-beginning
    b. Beginning
    c. Middle
    d. End

52. Which of the following is NOT a type of coordination that social workers can provide?
    a. Case management
    b. Wraparound services
    c. Service integration
    d. Prescribing medication

53. Which choice is NOT a reason to accurately record case information?
    a. Contribute to effective treatment.
    b. Protect the agency from possible legal ramifications.
    c. Protect confidentiality.
    d. Engage clients in the treatment process.

54. What are two components of empathic communication?
    a. A social worker perceives client's feelings and communicates understanding of those emotions back to client.
    b. A social worker nods and displays genuineness.
    c. A social worker engages client in treatment and creates an environment of trust.
    d. A social worker shares common feelings with the client and is affected by those feelings in the same way.

55. Which of the following is NOT true?
    a. Social context refers to one's environment and how this influences behavior.
    b. What appears normal in one culture may appear bizarre or disgusting in another.
    c. The neighborhood where one resides has no bearing on behavior.
    d. Certain behaviors are acceptable in some social contexts, but the exact same behavior in a different social context might cause a person to be shunned or excluded from certain circles.

56. According to Erikson's stages of development, what is the dichotomy experienced during maturity (sixty-five years or older)?
    a. Intimacy vs. isolation
    b. Industry vs. inferiority
    c. Ego integrity vs. despair
    d. Generativity vs. stagnation

57. According to Sue & Sue's Stages of Racial/Cultural Identity Development, which stage is characterized by a period of re-thinking or challenging one's beliefs where the individual examines and appreciates positive aspects of their own racial/cultural group for the first time?
    a. Dissonance
    b. Conformity
    c. Introspection
    d. Resistance and immersion

58. Studies have shown that those who embrace spirituality tend to live longer and happier lives. The benefits of being a spiritual person include all of the following EXCEPT?
    a. It increases the likelihood of connection with others.
    b. It increases the likelihood of being artistic.
    c. It increases the likelihood that the client will find purpose in their lives.
    d. It increases the likelihood of self-actualization.

59. Jane works in an agency providing individual therapy. She has an office that she shares with another social worker. Their office door has a lock on it, and they both have a key to the office. Jane keeps her records in a filing cabinet under her desk and does not lock it because her office door is always locked, even if she is in the building. Is Jane providing enough security for her records?
    a. No. Even though Jane keeps her office locked, she should still lock her filing cabinet.
    b. Yes. If Jane's office is locked, she is doing her part to keep her records secure.
    c. Yes. Because Jane and her office mate work for the same agency, the office mate is not a risk.
    d. No. Jane should advocate for records to be kept in a single location in the agency with a separate locked door.

60. Due to legal requirements, which of the following is the most important element when a social worker is dealing with record requests and disclosures of confidential information?
    a. Follow through
    b. Documentation
    c. Consultation with colleagues and supervisors
    d. Informed consent

61. Thomas is a social worker that has been working with client Karen for the past year. He has been implementing strengths-based assessments, life and vocational skills coaching, and connecting Karen with various community social groups such as the adult local softball team. The strategies that Tom is employing relate to which of the following core values of the social work field?
    a. Competence
    b. Service
    c. Human dignity
    d. Human relationships

62. What is the goal of cognitive restructuring?
    a. Use of self-monitoring to keep track of situations that occur and accompanying thoughts or feelings
    b. To help clients change irrational or unrealistic thoughts that result in a change in behaviors
    c. To identify situations that evoke reoccurring themes in dysfunctional thoughts and beliefs
    d. Rewarding oneself for using functional coping skills

63. Which of the following is NOT a way that social workers receive feedback from clients?
    a. Verbally or nonverbally
    b. Intentionally or unintentionally
    c. By the amount of progress toward goals
    d. The client's expression of negative feelings about termination

64. What is the first stage a client experiences after a crisis event?
    a. Higher levels of stress as the usual coping mechanisms fail; clients may employ higher-level coping skills to alleviate the increasing stress levels.
    b. Increase in feelings of stress; clients may experience denial and typically try to resolve the stressful reactions using past problem-solving and coping skills.
    c. Client experiences complete psychological and emotional collapse, or the individual finds a method to resolve the situation; however, there may be remaining emotional and psychological problems.
    d. Client experiences major emotional turmoil, possible feelings of hopelessness, depression, and anxiety.

65. When the client provides their perspective on what happened and the correlated feelings and experiences felt, it is known as what?
    a. Measurable data
    b. Objective data
    c. Subjective data
    d. Planning data

66. What is the first step in designing a community-level intervention?
    a. Touring the community's dining establishments
    b. Conducting a needs assessment for the community
    c. Holding a press conference with a community leader
    d. Working with policymakers to create a new law for the community

67. The prefix *cardi-* generally indicates what?
    a. Skin
    b. Stomach
    c. Liver
    d. Heart

68. The prefix *gastro-* generally indicates what body area?
    a. Skin
    b. Stomach
    c. Liver
    d. Heart

69. Angina pectoris is marked by which of the following?
    a. Sharp chest pain
    b. Bone fractures
    c. Hair loss
    d. Allergies

70. When people experience a major life-changing crisis, such as an earthquake or a terrorist attack, which of the following is NOT true?
    a. Children are more resilient and, therefore, less likely to experience the negative impact as severely as adults.
    b. Some immediate reactions may include disorientation, disbelief, or a sense of helplessness.
    c. As the event and its aftermath are processed, more symptoms, such as insomnia or withdrawal, may begin to surface.
    d. Most events of this nature are sudden and unexpected, and there is no way to prepare for them emotionally.

71. One's cultural background is based primarily upon all of the following EXCEPT?
    a. Where one was born
    b. At what point in time one was born
    c. Sociological practices and standards in which one was raised
    d. Genetic predispositions inherited at birth

72. You are running a therapy group for teenage girls who have been sexually abused by a family member, and one common thread you have noted is that most of the girls experience feelings of shame and unworthiness, as well as a sense that they are different from most of their peers. Which of the following is NOT a learning goal of therapy within this group?
    a. They have been deeply betrayed by someone who was supposed to love and protect them.
    b. These feelings are normal and are experienced by most people who have been sexual assault victims.
    c. Most people who engage in therapy eventually feel better about themselves and can learn to make peace with what happened.
    d. Assess why self-defense did not come into play so that next time they will be better prepared to fight back.

73. Amy is a social worker for a home health company. She has been visiting her seventy-five-year-old client, Sofia, for about six months. Lately, Sofia's daughter has seemed on edge when Amy is visiting. As Amy approached the house for her most recent visit, she could hear Sofia's daughter yelling at her, along with what she believed to be sounds of Sofia being hit. Amy then observed Sofia holding her arm and saw red marks when Sofia moved her hand. Amy attempted to speak to Sofia about her home life, but Sofia simply shook her head "no." Amy also noticed that Sofia has lost some weight over the last couple of months. Amy has concerns about Sofia's well-being. What should Amy's course of action be?
    a. Amy should continue to observe Sofia and make notes regarding what she sees.
    b. Amy should make a report to Adult Protective Services.
    c. Amy should look at the nursing notes to find out what other health care professionals have observed.
    d. Amy should drop in more often to see if she can catch Sofia's daughter in the act.

74. Which of the following is NOT one of the six core values of the social work profession?
    a. Independence
    b. Dignity and worth of the person
    c. Importance of human relationships
    d. Competence

75. Ethically, social workers are required to maintain confidentiality when working with clients. Legally, HIPAA requires that social workers keep psychotherapy notes confidential. What does HIPAA stand for?
    a. Health Information Personal Acceptability Act
    b. Health Insurance Personal Acceptability Act
    c. Health Information Perpetuating Accountability Act
    d. Health Insurance Portability and Accountability Act

76. What factor influences the crisis intervention approach?
    a. The situation itself
    b. Homeostasis
    c. Environmental balance and social circumstances
    d. Client reaction to the situation

77. What is the furthering communication technique?
    a. Allows clients to know that the worker is listening and encourages more information
    b. Using questions that elicit short answers
    c. Using facial expressions, body language, and postures to show that the worker is engaged and listening
    d. When the social worker asks for clarification to ensure the client's message is understood

78. Which is NOT a factor in policy and procedure development?
    a. Front line workers should be involved in policy and procedure development, since they are in the best position to determine and evaluate how clients are affected.
    b. Policies should be clearly written and communicated to clients/workers, with copies available for distribution.
    c. Policies should be in the best interest of clients, but also protect the agency and staff.
    d. Examine the origins of the policy and/or procedure, including values and the related ideology.

79. Which of the following is an example of indirect discrimination?
    a. An employer who tosses a resume in the trash because the name on it is commonly held by persons of the Muslim religion
    b. A school requiring all students to come to school on Saturday for a make-up day despite having Jewish students who observe Saturday as a day of rest
    c. A restaurant owner who refuses to serve a customer because the customer is black
    d. A landlord who tells an interracial couple seeking an apartment that there are no vacancies, even though there are several empty units ready to be rented

181

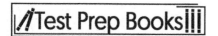
80. You are a psychiatric social worker completing a psychosocial history on a new patient admitted to the psych unit. As part of the assessment, you ask sexual health questions. This person indicates that they tend to fluctuate between a self-image of traditional male and female stereotypes and indicates feeling comfortable as both genders. This would be an example of which of the following?
    a. Sexual identity confusion
    b. Bi-gender gender identity
    c. Bi-sexual sexual orientation
    d. Transvestite sexual behavior

81. Risk-taking behavior often increases in adolescence. Which of the following is NOT a common theory to explain the prevalence of risk-taking behaviors among adolescents?
    a. The need for excitement and thrill outweighs any potential consequences or dangers.
    b. Risk-taking often occurs within groups to gain status and acceptance among peers.
    c. Adolescents are modeling adult behavior that has been romanticized.
    d. Adolescents engage in risk-taking behavior as a healthy outlet to channel their talents.

82. Due to mandated reporting laws, social workers must report any suspected abuse or neglect. Those who fail to report can be held to both civil and criminal lawsuits. Social workers can NOT be held responsible for reports made in which of the following?
    a. Earnest
    b. Good faith
    c. Concern
    d. Private

83. Jane is working with a client whose goals are based on his personal values. Jane finds her own values in direct conflict with the client's values. Jane has tried to self-reflect and work through this issue, but she finds herself having a harder time putting her own values aside each session. What should Jane's next step be?
    a. Termination
    b. Consultation
    c. Speaking to the client about the conflict she is having
    d. Personal exploration

84. Social workers strive to consider cultural impact on individual values. How should cultural differences and values be addressed?
    a. Cultural values and differences should be pointed out so that the client knows the social worker is aware of them.
    b. Cultural values and differences should be learned by the social worker and worked around when issues arise.
    c. Cultural values and differences should be learned by the social worker and used as strengths and to empower change.
    d. Cultural values and differences should be compared to the greater society to find similarities.

85. In your job as a social worker at a community senior center, you are facilitating a group on wellness in later life. One area of group focus is on spirituality. You introduce this topic because of which of the following reasons?
    a. It is important that older people all have a religious community for a sense of support and belonging.
    b. You believe that persons who go to church are more likely to enter the kingdom of heaven.
    c. Spiritual persons tend to be more optimistic, which leads to a greater quality of life.
    d. Persons who prefer not to attend church regularly tend to be angry and egocentric.

86. The learning theory of addictions is based on the premise that addictions are developed due to which of the following?
    a. A need to reduce feelings of shame and poor self-esteem
    b. Operant conditioning, classical conditioning, and social learning
    c. An inability to be morally strong or to use willpower to overcome the addiction
    d. The interplay of social and cultural factors and one's genetic makeup

87. What defense mechanism occurs when a negative feeling is covered up by a false or exaggerated version of its opposite?
    a. Reaction formation
    b. Displacement
    c. Projection
    d. Denial

88. Which of the following may be a dysfunctional family pattern?
    a. Scapegoating a child
    b. Affirming a child
    c. Undermining a child
    d. Disavowing a child

89. What is the definition of external validity?
    a. Uses participants or subjects chosen randomly to participate
    b. The consistency of a measure; the likelihood that the same result will be achieved each time it's used
    c. The ability of a study to be generalized to other people or circumstances
    d. Refers to cause and effect

90. Which significant social welfare legislation was enacted first?
    a. The Child Abuse and Prevention Act
    b. The Family Medical Leave Act
    c. The Civil Rights Act
    d. The Patient Protection and Affordable Care Act

91. All of these are factors that must be considered in client empowerment EXCEPT which choice?
    a. Self-perception, including strengths and knowledge
    b. Interactions and experiences with others that affect the client's present situation
    c. Interactions with relevant institutions or groups
    d. A client's feelings of anger or mistrust about treatment

92. Osteopenia is a disease marked by which of the following?
    a. Decline in cognitive function
    b. Decrease in bone density
    c. Decrease in red blood cells
    d. Decrease in liver function

93. Danny wakes up every morning and drinks three beers. Then he goes to work, where he's a senior manager. Lately, his subordinates have said that he never answers their emails or questions, and often they are unable to find him for important client meetings. Danny recently went to court for a driving under the influence charge, but he was released after paying a fine. Danny feels that because he's employed and isn't in jail, the charge isn't really a big deal. Before sleeping, he always drinks half a bottle of wine and two shots of whiskey. Danny is exhibiting signs of what?
    a. An eating disorder
    b. A liver disorder
    c. A gambling addiction
    d. A substance use disorder

94. Approximately what percentage of Americans take at least one prescription medication?
    a. 90
    b. 80
    c. 70
    d. 60

95. Social workers have a set of core values that shape the profession. One of these values is service. What does this mean for a social worker?
    a. Service means that the social worker will address social problems and help those in need. Service also means that social workers will provide pro bono or volunteer work when not at a paid position.
    b. Service means that the social worker will provide the best client service possible and always look for ways to improve.
    c. Service means that the social worker will try to help as many people as possible, often working in more than one position.
    d. Service means having pride in how social workers serve their clientele.

96. The field of social work has a set of core goals for the profession. What are these core goals?
    a. Consult with colleagues, put the client first, challenge wrongs, and make a difference
    b. Improve social function, consult with colleagues, put the client first, and challenge wrongs
    c. Resolve problems, put the client first, meet self-defined goals, and challenge wrongs
    d. Improve social function, resolve problems, achieve desired change, and meet self-defined goals

97. What is it called when a social worker's own mental health issues, such as anxiety or depression, begin to interfere with their ability to serve their clients?
    a. Self-awareness
    b. Interference
    c. Impairment
    d. Transference

98. Which type of abuse involves the use of shame and manipulation to control a person, such as yelling, constant criticizing, or belittling, threatening, or name-calling?
   a. Physical Abuse
   b. Vocal Abuse
   c. Psychological Abuse
   d. Critical Abuse

99. What factor can cause family members or those outside the family to be judgmental toward a person suffering from mental illness?
   a. Ease
   b. Confusion
   c. Ambiguity
   d. Stigma

100. Which of the following is NOT a common characteristic of a perpetrator of abuse?
   a. Uses/abuses drugs or alcohol
   b. Has a learning disorder
   c. Tends to be controlling toward others
   d. Has a history of mental illness

101. Which item is NOT something social workers should discuss with clients when preparing for termination?
   a. What skills the client initially lacked that led to initiating services
   b. Initial reasons for requesting help
   c. Assisting the client in identifying and changing dysfunctional patterns
   d. Ways the client will continue to build on new skill development

102. What is the second phase of treatment intervention?
   a. Termination and Evaluation
   b. Engagement and Assessment
   c. Implementation
   d. Goal Identification and Intervention Planning

103. Which choice is NOT an advantage of single subject designs?
   a. Cost-effective
   b. Easy to use, efficient
   c. Results can easily be generalized to other clients
   d. Provides immediate data

104. Excessive sleepiness, untreated medical problems, excessive hunger, and reports that no one is around to provide care are indicators of what?
   a. Physical neglect
   b. Biological assessment flaws
   c. Sexual neglect
   d. Starvation

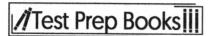
105. Interventions matched to client problems are based on _____ and empirical data gathered by the social worker.
    a. biopsychosocial assessment information
    b. behavioral approach
    c. problem causation
    d. solution identification

106. When does resistance from a client appear?
    a. Usually at the beginning of an intervention plan
    b. Usually at the end of an intervention plan
    c. At any time during the intervention
    d. Rarely; once a client has started seeing the practitioner, they are unlikely to resist

107. In the *DSM-5-TR*, which of the following is classified as an addictive disorder?
    a. Internet gaming disorder
    b. Sex addiction
    c. Kleptomania
    d. Gambling disorder

108. A client's right to live life per their own values and beliefs is supported by social workers in a way that it is not by other professions. What is this right called?
    a. Personal responsibility
    b. Self-determination
    c. Self-guided
    d. Self-rule

109. Which of the following is true regarding sexual relationships between social workers and colleagues or co-workers?
    a. They are not permissible under any circumstance.
    b. They are permissible if the colleague is not at the same agency.
    c. They are not permissible unless the social worker was in the relationship prior to employment.
    d. They are permissible except when one person is in a position of authority over the other.

110. Which of the following statements are FALSE regarding the Morality Period of social work?
    a. It occurred during the late 19th to early 20th century.
    b. It focused on the morality of clients rather than the ethics of social workers.
    c. The goal was to build the ethics of individuals in poverty.
    d. Controversial issues like economic hardship, substance use, and race relations were at the forefront.

111. At every level of professional development, it is important to continually participate in education opportunities. Why is this important to the values of social work?
    a. Continuing education is necessary to maintain a level of competence in expertise areas that the social worker practices.
    b. Continuing education is required to maintain licensure, and licensure ensures that the social worker is regarded as a capable professional.
    c. Conferences and learning situations provide networking opportunities that can aid in interdisciplinary collaboration.
    d. Education is an ongoing personal journey.

112. Which criteria is NOT outlined in the NASW Code of Ethics in regards to evaluation?
    a. Social workers should be knowledgeable and use evaluation procedures responsibly.
    b. Social workers should report findings accurately using institutional review boards when appropriate.
    c. Clients must consent to evaluation.
    d. Single subject designs should be used to provide individualized evaluation.

113. Which is a type of evaluation tool?
    a. Independent variable
    b. Dependent variable
    c. Validity
    d. Target problem scaling

114. Which is NOT an activity performed by a social worker when referring clients for services?
    a. Rewarding clients for using functional coping skills
    b. Making contact with other providers through phone calls, meetings, letters, etc.
    c. Assisting clients with the completion of paperwork and ensuring clients qualify for the referred services
    d. Monitoring clients' progress to ensure services are effective

115. According to the NASW Code of Ethics, social workers must do which of the following related to culturally competent practice?
    a. Identify which thoughts and belief patterns or self-statements lead to the target problems.
    b. Use self-monitoring techniques.
    c. Emphasize strong boundaries.
    d. Be aware of their own biases and prejudices.

116. A social worker who is working to encourage her client to acknowledge and focus on his determination, ingenuity, and resiliency rather than his perceived "failures" he harbors for the financial strife he is in, is using which of the following approaches?
    a. The strengths perspective
    b. The re-centering method
    c. The bio-psychosocial perspective
    d. The learning theory

117. What is the general focus on the "launching family" stage in the basic family life cycle?
   a. Accepting new family members and transitioning from a marital system to a family system
   b. Selecting a lifestyle and a life partner
   c. Establishing independence as an adult and independence from one's family of origin
   d. Accepting the new independent role of an adult child and transitioning through the separation

118. In Skinner's theory of operant conditioning, the term *shaping* refers to which of the following?
   a. Placing a neutral stimulus before a reflex that occurs naturally
   b. Changing behavior through rewarding the person each time an approximation of desired behavior occurs
   c. Exploring superstitions that might impact willingness to make behavioral changes
   d. Giving a person a reward when the desired behavior is perfected

119. In the field of personality theories, which researcher proposed that personality develops as a result of striving to become the best one can be, combined with the importance of self-perception?
   a. Eric Ericson
   b. Sigmund Freud
   c. Carl Rogers
   d. Gordon Allport

120. Prescriptions used to treat psychopathologies typically work best when paired with which of the following?
   a. Lifestyle modifications
   b. The Paleo diet
   c. Relocation
   d. Service pets

121. Of the following drugs, which is most commonly prescribed in the United States and is used to treat thyroid problems?
   a. Synthroid
   b. Lexapro
   c. Thryonate
   d. Lithium

122. When creating an intervention plan, who should be treated as the expert on the client's life?
   a. The practitioner
   b. The client
   c. The client's parents
   d. The client's primary care physician

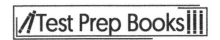
123. What is the primary difference between atypical and typical antipsychotics?
    a. Atypical antipsychotics were developed decades after typical antipsychotics and generally have fewer side effects.
    b. Typical antipsychotics were developed decades after atypical antipsychotics and generally have fewer side effects.
    c. Atypical antipsychotics were developed decades after typical antipsychotics and generally have more side effects.
    d. Typical antipsychotics were developed decades after atypical antipsychotics and generally have more side effects.

124. Which organizational theory is NOT considered a classical theory?
    a. Human Relations Theory
    b. Scientific Management Theory
    c. Administrative Theory
    d. Bureaucracy Theory

125. What does the term *therapeutic alliance* refer to?
    a. The relationship among social workers who work together at the same agency
    b. The relationship a social worker has with other professionals who work with their client
    c. The relationship between a social worker and a client
    d. The relationship between the client's problem and the therapeutic modality chosen

126. What is the goal of building rapport with a client?
    a. Laying the foundation for a relationship based on mutual trust, empathy, and acceptance
    b. Gaining an understanding of the client's presenting problem
    c. Deciding if the social worker wants to work with the client
    d. Completing the informed consent process

127. How can a social worker use transparency to reduce the impact of the power difference between the social worker and client?
    a. Share details about the social worker's own problems and difficulties.
    b. Withhold certain information and observations from the client.
    c. Explain that the client holds most of the power in the client-social worker relationship.
    d. Provide the client with as much information as possible about the treatment process.

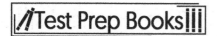

128. Alex is a social worker in the Emergency Room where Lucas, who is homeless, frequently visits for ailments of varying severity. The Emergency Room staff advises Alex that he must find somewhere for Lucas to go. Alex speaks at length with Lucas, who states that he has no friends or family with whom he is in contact. Lucas tells Alex that he has lived at shelters before and that he doesn't like the rules that must be followed. Lucas declines a bed at the local shelter. Alex discusses this with Lucas' doctor and nurse and both become adamant that Lucas must go to a shelter; sleeping on the street is not acceptable. Alex facilitates a discussion between medical personnel and Lucas in which Lucas maintains that he does not intend to go to a shelter. Eventually, Alex asks to speak privately with the medical personnel, and he advocates strongly on Lucas' behalf, stating that Lucas has made his decision. Was Alex's course of action correct?

    a. No. If the doctor felt that a shelter was necessary, then Alex's responsibility was to listen to the doctor and to convince Lucas to go to the shelter.

    b. Yes. Having a private conversation with the medical staff was the best solution, so that Lucas didn't hear the discussion.

    c. Yes. By advocating on Lucas' behalf, Alex was protecting his right to self-determination.

    d. No. Alex should have asked to call Lucas' relatives on his behalf to convince them to take him in.

129. All of the following are suggested industry strategies for setting and maintaining professional boundaries in social work EXCEPT which one?

    a. Limiting self-disclosure about personal life unless it directly relates to the client's goals

    b. Establishing clear agreements with clients during the initial sessions about the dynamics of the client-practitioner relationship

    c. Fostering positive dual relationships with clients to further support their emotional needs

    d. Exercising caution regarding the use of social media within the professional practice

130. Which of the following best describes what is meant by value suspension?

    a. The social worker acknowledging and controlling their personal values in social work practice

    b. The client evaluating and choosing to adopt one value system over another

    c. The client increasing their exposure to different values, beliefs, and morals as he or she gets older

    d. The client challenging someone else's existing values when engaging in a new relationship with that person

131. The Bricklin Perceptual Scales are typically utilized in what type of cases?

    a. Custodial cases

    b. Homicide cases

    c. Suicide cases

    d. Substance use cases

132. Which of the following is included in the biological section of a biopsychosocial assessment?

    a. Coping skills

    b. Marital problems

    c. Developmental history

    d. Educational background

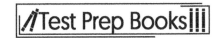

133. Which of the following is sometimes but not always included in a biopsychosocial assessment?
    a. Spiritual beliefs
    b. Psychiatric diagnoses
    c. Medical history
    d. Presenting problem

134. Which of the following is NOT a component of a mental status examination?
    a. Appearance
    b. Affect
    c. Speech
    d. Psychiatric history

135. Social workers help clients recognize stressors and problems in their lives, make plans for how to address them, and put the plan into action. What theoretical model describes this process?
    a. The cognitive behavioral model
    b. The problem-solving therapeutic model
    c. The psychoanalytic model
    d. The person-in-environment model

136. What is NOT part of the social worker's role in the intervention process?
    a. Active listening to verbal and nonverbal communication
    b. Collaborating with the client on their treatment plan
    c. Giving advice to the client
    d. Helping the client build their own support network

137. Which word describes the ability to be attuned to another person and understand their emotional experience without being consumed by it?
    a. Authenticity
    b. Sympathy
    c. Empathy
    d. Objectivity

138. What is the purpose of the emphasis on understanding systems within the field of social work?
    a. To help increase the amount of field experience that a social work student participates in because only so much can be learned in the classroom
    b. To better understand a client's place in society so that the social worker can help increase social understanding and make connections
    c. To learn about diversity within family and social systems so that all clients receive unbiased and respectful care
    d. To help the social worker advocate for clients on the local, state, and national levels by understanding the programs available

139. What are the core values of social work outlined in the *NASW Code of Ethics*?
    a. Service, social justice, dignity and worth of the person, importance of human relationships, integrity, and competence
    b. Ethical dilemmas, confidentiality, importance of supervision, self-disclosure, professionalism, and honesty
    c. Assessment methods, planning and documentation, treatment, monitoring and evaluation, follow-up, and termination
    d. Unconditional positive regard, mirroring techniques, confrontation and resistance, clarification, support, and reframing

140. Is it ever ethical for a social worker to limit a client's right to self-determination?
    a. No, a social worker must always support the decisions clients makes about their own lives.
    b. Yes, if the social worker believes that the client has broken a law.
    c. Yes, if the social worker believes that the client's judgement is impaired by a substance use disorder.
    d. Yes, if the social worker believes that the client's actions pose a serious, foreseeable, and imminent threat to themselves or others.

141. All of the following statements about self-disclosure are true EXCEPT:
    a. Self-disclosure can be harmful to clients.
    b. Self-disclosure is the best way to establish rapport with a new client.
    c. Most therapeutic situations do not require self-disclosure.
    d. Supervision can help a social worker determine when and if to use self-disclosure.

142. A social worker receives a friend request on Facebook from one of her clients. What is the best way for the social worker to respond?
    a. Accept the request to avoid offending the client.
    b. Accept the request but change the privacy settings to limit what the client can see.
    c. Deny the request and do not mention it to the client to avoid causing them embarrassment.
    d. Deny the request and explain to the client that the social worker has a policy of not connecting with clients on social media.

143. Under which of the following circumstances would terminating services to a client be unethical?
    a. The client has completed treatment and has no further need for services.
    b. The client has stopped paying for services, their failure to pay has been discussed, and they pose no imminent danger to self or others.
    c. The client suggests switching providers so that the client and the social worker can pursue a business opportunity together without a dual relationship.
    d. The social worker is leaving the agency; has notified their clients; discussed options for continuing treatment; and sought the transfer, referral, or continuation of services according to client preferences.

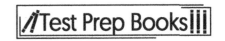
144. The process of social development as defined by Lev Vygotsky suggests that one's development in life is deeply impacted by:
    a. Income status
    b. Birth order and gender
    c. The variety of social institutions, such as family, school, or church, to which someone is exposed throughout life
    d. Physical stamina and overall health

145. John is a teenager. When he started high school, he participated in band, but he recently decided to quit and spend more time on sports. He has thought a lot about his sexuality and is considering coming out to his parents as bisexual. Which of Erikson's stages of social development is John currently dealing with?
    a. Trust vs. mistrust
    b. Industry vs. inferiority
    c. Intimacy vs. isolation
    d. Identity vs. role confusion

146. A teacher announces that recess is canceled because the students have been so disruptive. This is an example of which operant conditioning technique?
    a. Positive punishment
    b. Positive reinforcement
    c. Negative punishment
    d. Negative reinforcement

147. Which parenting style tends to have the most positive impact on children's health, happiness, and confidence?
    a. Authoritarian parenting
    b. Authoritative parenting
    c. Permissive parenting
    d. Uninvolved parenting

148. What is the purpose of an Institutional Review Board (IRB)?
    a. To review proposals for research involving human subjects to make sure that there are no ethical violations
    b. To periodically review and update the *NASW Code of Ethics*
    c. To audit social work organizations to ensure that their mission statements and policies are compatible with the *NASW Code of Ethics*
    d. To set academic standards for college and university social work degree programs

149. When is it legal and ethical to disclose confidential client information?
    a. After the client is deceased
    b. When responding to requests from the media
    c. For teaching or training purposes
    d. In order to defend oneself in court when being sued by a client

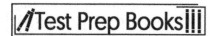

150. A client who is a minor discloses to a social worker that her father is physically abusive. What must the social worker do with this information?
    a. Encourage the client to call the police.
    b. Contact the client's parents to verify that the information is correct.
    c. Report the information to CPS immediately after the client meeting.
    d. Call the police.

151. A client discloses that he murdered someone five years ago. What must the social worker do with this information?
    a. There is nothing the social worker must do.
    b. Report the crime to the police.
    c. Terminate services with the client.
    d. Inform the client's wife that she might be in danger.

152. Which of the following statements about Attachment Theory is NOT true?
    a. Secure attachment is associated with better psychological health.
    b. Attachment describes the quality of the relationship that develops between an infant and its primary caregiver.
    c. Foster children are at an increased risk of developing an attachment disorder.
    d. Attachment only affects psychological functioning from birth to age five.

153. Which of the following behaviors could indicate abnormal or unhealthy sexual development?
    a. A kindergartener acting out oral sex with dolls
    b. A toddler masturbating
    c. A teenager questioning his sexuality
    d. A school-aged child embarrassed to get changed in the locker room

154. What is the meaning of *codependency* in the context of addiction?
    a. Two people misusing a substance together
    b. Having both a substance use disorder and a mental illness
    c. Being dependent on two different substances
    d. One person unintentionally enabling another person's substance misuse

155. What does *orientation* mean in the context of a mental status examination?
    a. The client's awareness of people, places, time, and events
    b. The client's sexual orientation
    c. The client's beliefs and feelings about treatment
    d. Informing the client of the purpose of the examination

156. A social worker wants to know more about a client's perceptions, needs, motivations, and conflicts. The social worker presents the client with a series of pictures and asks the client to use their imagination and tell stories about what might be happening in the pictures. Which assessment tool is the social worker using?
    a. Beck Depression Inventory (BDI)
    b. The Minnesota Multiphasic Personality Inventory (MMPI)
    c. Thematic Appreciation Test (TAT)
    d. Myers-Briggs Type Indicator (MBTI)

157. All the following are reasons a social worker might request a client's educational records EXCEPT:
    a. To determine if problems at home affect school performance
    b. To assess a client's level of intelligence
    c. To diagnose developmental disabilities
    d. To determine when a client's symptoms began

158. Which of the following statements regarding collateral data is NOT correct:
    a. Collateral data refers to information about the client that is not collected directly from the client.
    b. Medical, psychiatric, agency, employment, and school records are examples of collateral data.
    c. Social workers must obtain informed consent from the client to access collateral data.
    d. Collateral data cannot be subpoenaed because it is kept separate from a client's file.

159. To work effectively with clients from different cultural backgrounds, social workers should do all the following, EXCEPT:
    a. Avoid offending clients by not discussing their culture unless they bring it up first.
    b. Continuously reflect on one's own cultural attitudes, values, biases, and beliefs.
    c. Educate oneself about various cultures and the impact of discrimination.
    d. Develop cultural skills and knowledge about how culture affects treatment.

160. Which of the following statements is NOT true about a client's developmental level?
    a. It describes a client's ability to function in different domains at any given time.
    b. It can change over time.
    c. It is not as important as the client's age when choosing interventions.
    d. It can be delayed or advanced in some areas of functioning but not others.

161. All of the following statements are true about out-of-home placement EXCEPT:
    a. It is appropriate when the home is unsafe due to abuse or neglect.
    b. Individuals removed from dysfunctional homes are likely to have psychological or behavioral problems.
    c. Once an individual is removed from an unsafe home, their psychological and behavioral problems will begin to improve.
    d. Foster care is an example of out-of-home placement.

162. Establishing a marital relationship and joining two families together is the primary task of which stage of the family life cycle?
    a. Family with adolescents
    b. Newly married couple
    c. Launching family
    d. Family with young children

163. Which psychological defense mechanism is most associated with borderline personality disorder?
    a. Splitting
    b. Sublimation
    c. Denial
    d. Intellectualization

164. When a social worker suspects that a client is being abused by their romantic partner, the social worker should:
   a. Bypass rapport building and take action immediately.
   b. Prioritize addressing the client's medical needs and safety.
   c. Prioritize getting the client out of the relationship as soon as possible.
   d. Encourage couples therapy if the abuser is willing to participate.

165. A client finally quit her job after years of working for a demeaning, dishonest, and emotionally abusive boss. She states that she is a failure who can't hold down a job. The social worker remarks that from his perspective, she is a strong person who managed to excel for a long time under terrible circumstances and that her decision to leave was a healthy and rational one. What communication technique is the social worker using?
   a. Reframing
   b. Clarifying
   c. Validating
   d. Questioning

166. When asking a client about their sexual history, which of the following techniques is most appropriate?
   a. Using euphemistic language rather than technical terms, like "making love" instead of sex
   b. Asking about behaviors, like "having sex with men" rather than labels, like "homosexual"
   c. Asking yes and no questions, so the client does not have to discuss details
   d. Acknowledging that the social worker is also uncomfortable discussing these topics

167. Joshua, a social worker, is assessing a new client, Mr. G. In their initial meeting, Mr. G reports that he was referred by his medical doctor. He had gone to the doctor complaining of dizziness, sweating, irritability, sadness, and feeling like his heart was beating too fast. The doctor found Mr. G's blood pressure to be slightly elevated, but not enough to require medication. Otherwise, he is good health. In the course of their interview, Joshua discovers that Mr. G is a business owner who has lost a lot of income over the course of the pandemic. As a result, he has had to lay off several workers and take on the extra work himself. Mr. G's symptoms began a few weeks ago, shortly after his elderly mother moved in and he became her full-time caregiver. What is the most likely cause of Mr. G's issues?
   a. Hypertension
   b. Depression
   c. Psychosocial stress
   d. PTSD

168. If a person experiences major depression and alcohol use disorder at the same time, the two conditions are said to be:
   a. Comorbid
   b. Postmorbid
   c. Contraindicated
   d. Aggravated

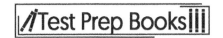

169. There are several different models of addiction. Which one considers addiction to be a chronic, progressive, relapsing disease?
    a. The biopsychosocial model
    b. The medical model
    c. The moral model
    d. The self-medication model

170. Which of the following is most important when determining whether an event is traumatic?
    a. The age at which the event occurs
    b. Whether a person is physically injured during the event
    c. The type of event
    d. The person's subjective experience of the event

Answer Explanations #1

1. A: While some children who are oppositional and defiant may refuse to conform to certain standards as a means to establish control, the child described in this scenario is more likely experiencing developmental delays due to the deficits in a number of areas. At one time, the state of Illinois required children to be able to tie their own shoes before being admitted to kindergarten. Although this is a crude measure of academic readiness, it probably served as a red flag, based on the fact that the vast majority of children can perform this task by age 5.

Pre-schools generally require that a three-year-old must be fully potty-trained before they will admit him or her to their program, again using a standard that the majority of children can achieve by that age. Language issues may have other causes, such as physiological symptoms, but being unable to meet these three standards is an indicator that the child is lagging behind others in attaining developmental milestones. Choices *B* and *D* refer to behavioral disorders of childhood that include symptoms of disregard/disrespect for others and sometimes include criminal behavior. Genetic deficiencies, Choice *C*, may contribute to a developmental delay, yet they could also be associated with physical issues passed genetically, such as deafness or dwarfism.

2. A: This description of states of adulthood is most commonly used in psychology and medicine. While some may question that early adulthood extends until age forty, with life spans increasing, this is a reasonable standard and is generally an acceptable conception in the fields of psychology and medicine as to how a lifetime is divided.

3. A: Parental history of mental illness is a biological feature and should serve as a red flag because some psychiatric conditions do have a genetic link, including—but not limited to—addictions and mood disorders. In addition, being raised by a parent impaired by mental illness or addictions often causes deep emotional scars that should be addressed in therapy. Income, education, and employment history are not considered biological factors; therefore, they are incorrect responses. The issues mentioned in *B*, *C*, and *D* can certainly have a biological impact, such as a scenario in which the child is deprived of good nutrition or medical care.

4. C: An official medical report brought by the client to their first session would be information from a collateral source. The other three examples show primary sources of information, as all of the information available is provided directly by the client. While the client is still the one physically giving the medical history report to the practitioner, it's considered a collateral source because it was officially documented and then obtained from a secondary source (the client's healthcare provider).

5. D: The Miller Analogies Test is a standardized test used for admissions in high IQ societies. The Myers-Briggs Type Indicator, the Beck Depression Inventory, and the Wechsler Adult Intelligence Scale are all commonly used psychometrics in social work.

6. B: While social workers look at an individual's clinical, psychosomatic, and environmental history, these are small components that make up a full spectrum of influences in the individual's history. The biopsychosocial lens allows the social worker to look at biological, psychological, and social factors together to make reliable diagnoses and plan treatments.

7. D: SMART stands for Specific, Measurable, Achievable, Relevant, Time-Specific. SMART objectives should have specific features that can be measured, are achievable for the client's abilities and

198

resources, are relevant to resolving the presenting problem, and have a timeframe for resolution in mind. Choice *D* is the only choice that includes all of these factors.

8. D: The six core purposes of the NASW Code of Ethics are:

- To establish the core values on which the mission of social work is based

- To provide a set of ethical standards for social workers, as well as specific information regarding different ethical dilemmas

- To help identify information that social workers should take under advisement when ethical conflicts may exist or when an ethical dilemma presents itself

- To provide standards that can be used by others to ensure accountability and responsibility by those in the profession

- To inform new social workers about core issues relating to the mission of social work and to the ethical standards of the field

- To provide the rules and standards that social workers can use to evaluate the conduct of others in the profession

9. C: No, informed consent has not been satisfied. Susan did not have a document outlining what therapy would entail, including the risks and limitations. She also did not have Claudia sign such a document to become part of the chart. Documentation of informed consent protects both the client and the social worker.

10. B: Personal gain refers to instances where a social worker engages in activity with a client that results in a monetary (or otherwise valuable) benefit to the social worker. This could involve situations such as referring a client to a business owned by the social worker or a friend/family member of the social worker, selling something to a client, or even asking a client for professional suggestions.

11. C: Culture is influenced by a person's race, ethnicity, immigration status, and traditions, to name a few. It can also include one's upbringing, class, and friendships, but these answers do not encompass all of the qualities listed in the question.

12. D: Ella is not engaging productively with her social worker and doesn't seem to want to be in the session or pursue change, showing low motivation and high resistance to intervention.

13. D: Sexual development is different for each person, and there is a wide range of variation in terms of achieving physical and emotional maturation. Sexuality is a very fluid and continuously changing process for most. The sexual practices one finds gratifying at age 16 may no longer be pursued at age 40. Some people do not seem to access their true sense of sexuality until mid-life. Others switch gears frequently throughout life when it comes to sexual preferences. This explains why *A* and *B* are incorrect. Choice *C* is also incorrect; in some cases, it may be helpful to share one's own experience with sexual orientation, but disclosing others' sexual orientation is inappropriate.

14. A: Gerontology covers a wide range of issues related to biological, social, and psychiatric features of aging. The study of gerontology is essential as the population ages and lives longer, healthier lives. How a population ages impacts the field of economics, psychology, medicine, even architecture. For example,

199

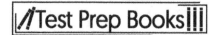

a two-story apartment complex in the middle of Iowa will probably not have an elevator. In Florida, where there is a large senior population, almost every apartment complex has an elevator to accommodate those in wheelchairs or those who have difficulty climbing steps.

15. B: Client advocacy is working on behalf of a client to remove barriers and obtain needed resources and/or services. Choice *A*, client empowerment, is helping clients to recognize and then use their strengths, resources, and systems to obtain goals. Choice *C*, crisis-intervention approach, is a short-term treatment usually lasting four to six weeks that is implemented when a client enters treatment following some type of traumatic event that causes significant distress. Choice *D*, case management, is helping to link clients with needed services and resources.

16. D: It is important that social workers always acquire client consent, even when working with involuntary clients. Guidelines about client consent are mentioned throughout the NASW Code of Ethics. When working with involuntary clients, social workers should help clients to recognize participation is still a choice, include a client's goals in a service plan along with mandated goals, and protect a client's right to self-determination.

17. A: The psychosocial approach is unique to the field of social work, allowing it to stand out from other professions. Choice *B* is related to the crisis intervention theory, whereby clients experience a state of disequilibrium and are out of balance. Choices *C* and *D* are related to Task Centered Practice, which emphasizes concepts of living and is a short term, practical, and evidence-based intervention.

18. B: Niklas Luhmann, a sociologist associated with communication theory, uses the term autopoiesis to describe social systems that are self-creating, which means they have the innate ability to produce and maintain themselves. Communications make up these systems and, in turn, generate other communications.

19. D: Maslow devised his last level during his later years and referred to it as Self-transcendence. Achievement of this goal relies on experiencing a greater sense of spiritual growth and practicing one's beliefs on a deeper level. Previously, self-actualization was the ultimate achievement in Maslow's hierarchy of needs. In later life, as he worked on his own spiritual evolution, he believed this went beyond the process of self-actualization and deserved to be added to his original model of human needs. Self-transcendence refers to elevating one's self to a state of spiritual enlightenment in which there is greater clarity and understanding of certain spiritual truths. Choices *A* and *B* are factors that contribute to the Self-transcendence Level, but these are not listed in Maslow's hierarchy of needs theory.

20. A: Self-image does change throughout the life cycle, and while this varies from individual to individual, age sixty represents a change in roles from being an actively engaged parent and successful member of the work force to an empty nester who will soon face retirement. In our society where youth, beauty, and wealth are revered, there is often a shortage of several of these when one enters the sixties. Even those who are financially fit will begin to experience physical changes, such as less energy, more body fat, and the onset of a variety of medical conditions that prevent one from doing some of the things that were once simple, such as lifting a three-year-old grandchild. Gracefully accepting these changes is difficult and painful. Choices *B*, *C*, and *D* all represent stages that consist of great change and challenging transition and often fail to correlate with a positive self-image.

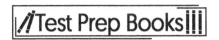

21. D: Denial is first so that the person has a moment to process the loss, followed by anger at others or self for causing the loss to occur. The grieving person in desperation tries to bargain with their God or others in hopes of bringing back that which was lost. As reality sets in, the person grieves the loss and experiences sadness and depression. Resolution occurs when the person accepts the loss and is ready to move on, with an understanding that in spite of that which is gone, they will be fine in the long run. The other responses do not outline the order correctly.

22. B: Typically, the problem has not actually started to impact a person or group until the secondary prevention stage. In the primary prevention stage, the practitioner helps the client identify potential causes for a problem and get rid of the problem's root cause. While actions aiming to stop specific social problems before they spread and cause further harm occur in the secondary prevention stage, the tertiary prevention stage involves actions that try to decrease the problem's severity, lasting effects, and duration through remedial service provisions.

23. D: To have an ethical dilemma, three conditions must be met. The first is that the practitioner must make a decision. If the situation does not require that a decision be made, then there isn't an ethical dilemma. The second is that there are different decisions that could be made or different actions one could take. The third condition is that an ethical ideal will be conceded no matter what decision is made.

24. C: The steps to resolving an ethical dilemma are as follows:

- Determine: Is there an ethical conflict or dilemma?
- Identify: What are the core standards and values involved in the situation?
- Rank: Take the values and ethical principles and rank them in order of importance regarding the situation
- Develop: Make a plan that correlates with the values and principles that were previously ranked as important to this situation. This may involve collaborating with colleagues or supervisors. When outlining the plan, identify any potential risks or adverse effects.
- Implement: Put the plan into motion, taking care to use social work practice skills that allow for ultimate sensitivity.
- Reflect: Evaluate the ethical decision-making process. How did all involved agencies and individuals fare? It is not uncommon for social workers to make use of ethical review committees or ethical consultations when facing dilemmas to gain assistance and perspective.

25. C: These medications are used to treat symptoms of depression. Atypical and typical antipsychotics are typically used to treat symptoms of schizophrenia or schizotypal behavior. Anti-inflammatory drugs are a type of pain reliever.

26. D: "A sudden, rapid, recurrent, nonrhythmic motor movement or vocalization" is a tic. Tics are the primary symptom of tic disorders, a group of neurodevelopmental disorders that includes Tourette's syndrome. Tics can change over time, be highly individual, and be simple or complex. Eye blinking and throat clearing are some of the more common examples of tics. Choice *A* is incorrect because unlike tics, motor stereotypies are rhythmic movements like arm flapping, which appear at a younger age, last longer, and tend to get worse during absorbing activities. Choice *B* is incorrect because unlike tics, compulsions in obsessive-compulsive disorder occur in response to a mental obsession. Choice *C* is incorrect because a spasm is an involuntary muscle contraction. Unlike spasms, tics can sometimes be suppressed to some extent, but suppressing them is often difficult and unpleasant.

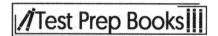

27. A: Selective mutism is categorized with anxiety disorders in the *DSM-5-TR*, and comorbidity with other anxiety disorders is common. The diagnosis is given when a person does not speak in certain situations, such as at school, for at least one month. The failure to speak must cause difficulty with functioning and cannot be explained by a communication disorder. The person speaks normally in other social situations. Choices *B*, *C*, and *D* are incorrect because they refer to other categories of disorders that are not related to selective mutism.

28. A: A data-driven intervention plan supports reliable, measurable, unbiased outcomes. Intervention plans should generally be detailed, and details should be clearly documented, which eliminates Choice *B*. Intervention plans shouldn't be cumbersome to develop or implement, which eliminates Choice *C*. Observations are helpful parts of developing and implementing interventions, but they shouldn't provide most of the information, therefore eliminating Choice *D*.

29. B: All professions, including social work, are built upon a foundation of values and guided by ethical codes. Rather than simply defining and explaining existing problems, the focus of the social work profession is providing care and improving society. As such, social workers must use and apply knowledge and skills from other fields, including sociology, philosophy, law, and psychology. Social workers should also distinguish between and cater to social and individual morality, recognize the interplay between these types of morality, and advocate when their absence creates social injustice.

30. B: During malpractice suits, the liability goes all the way up the chain of command. This means that not only the social worker at the heart of the lawsuit, but also any supervisors or persons above them, can be held liable and named in the lawsuit.

31. D: Although the agency has liability insurance, it's always best practice for a social worker to carry their own liability insurance. The liability insurance of the agency is going to protect the agency first and foremost. The social worker should always look out for their own best interest in cases involving questions of malpractice or the risk of lawsuit.

32. B: Determining possible solutions is the second step in the problem-solving process. Choices *B*, *C* and *D* are components of Task Centered Practice, which includes contracting and carefully planning task implementation, along with the social worker functioning as a collaborator to help clients identify issues, strengths, resources, and smaller tasks.

33. B: Short-term therapies typically only last six to twelve sessions. To ensure a client is prepared for closure of services, the social worker should start termination planning as soon as possible. Choice *A*, assessment, typically begins early in all interventions and not just specifically in short-term therapy. Choice *C*, educational services, can be included at any time, depending on the type of intervention. Choice *D*, metacommunication, is frequently addressed during conflict resolution.

34. D: The scapegoat role is typically used to define a role filled by a participant in group or family treatment. Social workers can fulfill many types of roles in practice. Choice *A*, the advocate role, can be defined as working on behalf of a client to remove barriers and obtain needed resources and/or services. Choice *B*, case management, is helping to link clients with needed services and resources. Social workers can also function as educators, Choice *C*, and frequently provide educational services to improve skills and increase knowledge.

35. C: Providing support and encouraging talking about the issue, but only at the chosen pace of the client, is the correct response. The person receiving a frightening diagnosis needs time to process

202

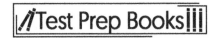

thoughts and feelings. Choice *A* would be a form of shaming the client about the smoking addiction and does nothing to help the individual make peace with the diagnosis. Choice *B* is inappropriate because family is not always the client's first choice for support, and the client should decide when and with whom to share this news. Choice *D* puts the therapist in a sticky situation in terms of boundaries. There may be some settings in which this could be helpful, but generally this is not an expectation of either client or therapist.

36. A: At some point, the adult child is expected to provide more care and support to the parent than the parent can provide to the adult child. This is a painful process for both parent and adult child. While most adult children are willing to lend a helping hand to parents, parents sometimes feel diminished and awkward as the roles shift. When assistance is in the form of direct care, such as bathing and dressing, it can be even more difficult for the parent to accept care from their child. Choices *B*, *C*, and *D* may each be true in terms of causing realignments of roles, but the process of caring for aging parents, who sometimes become quite childlike and difficult in later years, is at the core of relationship realignment.

37. B: The three symptoms noted are common experiences for persons diagnosed with Post Traumatic Stress Disorder (PTSD). Along with these, PTSD survivors can be triggered into a state of anxiety or panic when exposed to stimuli associated with the trauma such as smells, sensations, or sights. Those diagnosed with PTSD may be easily startled, and they can even have periods in which they feel they are re-experiencing the traumatic event. Choice *A*, claustrophobia, is a fear of small spaces. Choice *C* is incorrect; although persons with borderline personality disorder (BPD) may have a history of PTSD, the common symptoms of BPD don't align with the ones provided. Choice *D* can be a symptom of PTSD, but it is generally seen as a completely different diagnosis with a different set of criteria.

38. C: Defense mechanisms protect the ego from absorbing information it does not want to see, feel, or experience. This protective shield—which comes in many forms, such as rationalization, sublimation, or projection—helps reduce anxiety and guards against unwanted emotions like shame or guilt. Defense mechanisms can be helpful in reducing anxiety or can sometimes help one become immune to reality. Choices *A* and *B* imply that defense mechanisms are used to protect others from the truth about themselves, when this is not entirely accurate. Choice *D* suggests that defense mechanisms better allow one to exploit others. In some instances, this could apply, but for the most part, these mechanisms are acts of self-defense that keep the ego from accepting an unwanted truth.

39. C: Having thorough knowledge of local resources is better suited to the definition of case management. Choices *A, B,* and *D* are all related to providing educational services that can be performed in individual, family, small group, classes, or large group forums. Also, when providing these services, social workers determine skills, information, or knowledge that needs to be acquired by clients and also recommend resources such as books, articles, or websites.

40. C: Administering the intervention plan is part of the overall treatment process, not specifically evaluation. Identifying specific issues to be addressed; creating appropriate goals, objectives, and tasks; and using effective and relevant techniques and tools to measure success are all aspects of effective treatment evaluation.

41. A: Complementary goals benefit each other and are agreed upon by members of a system related to the same target problem. Choice *B* is the definition of shared goals, which are when members of a system choose the same goal that addresses an identified problem. Choice *C* refers to social worker's

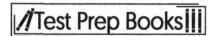

goals and ending treatment. Choice *D* refers to quantitative measures or the rate or occurrence of a behavior or problem.

42. D: Cohesion refers to an important function of group work, whereby members connect. The term is not necessarily a term used in family work. The other terms are all related to family therapy. When families are disengaged, Choice *A*, boundaries are rigid with little interaction and emotional engagement. Healthy boundaries, Choice *B*, around and within the family must exist for families to function effectively. Alliances, Choice *C*, are partnerships or collaborations between certain members of a family.

43. B: A flexible intervention plan can be tailored to the client's needs and can be updated as needs change. A tightly structured plan doesn't allow for this. An intervention plan certainly can be typed, but it's not necessary. The answer "five-dimensional" is not relevant to the question.

44. C: During a mental status exam (MSE), assessing how well the client pays attention is an example of cognition. Attention, level of concentration, memory, orientation, and judgment are examples of cognition during an MSE. Choice *A*, psychomotor behavior, involves eye contact, a handshake, posture, movement, and coordination. Mood and affect, Choice *B*, involve cooperation, appropriateness, stability, and demeanor, while thought patterns, Choice *D*, include flow of thought and the ability to be present and engage in relevant conversation.

45. C: Choices *A* and *B* provide examples of how client information can be stored, and Choice *D* provides an example of when client information can be stored. These are all personal managing options for the practitioner, but regardless of the manner or time of storage, it's essential that client information is stored securely in order to maintain privacy and confidentiality.

46. B: Attention-deficit/hyperactivity disorder is classified with neurodevelopmental disorders. Neurocognitive disorders typically include cognition disorders that originate from physiological degeneration in the brain. Neurological disorders aren't a classification in the *DSM-5-TR*. Section III covers areas for future research, and attention-deficit/hyperactivity disorder has already been documented.

47. A: Professional values for social workers focus on the general rights of those they serve, preserving and building social justice, and maintaining the strong moral base of the profession. While social workers should use scientifically sound practice and stay current with the latest in best practices through continuing education, a "solution-based" model, per se, is not necessarily appropriate in all situations for each client.

48. A: *Tarasoff vs. Regents of University of California* is the correct answer. In this 1976 case, the therapist failed to notify the intended victim of the threat of harm. After the client had stopped seeking treatment, he then attacked and killed Tarasoff, prompting her family to sue the University and therefore establishing the duty to warn. None of the other cases directly relate to duty to warn.

49. C: A social worker should always assess their own personal safety, as well as the safety of others, when deciding if a confidential disclosure should be discussed with the client. For example, a social worker is working with someone who has a history of violence toward women, and he discloses that he has been contemplating harming his neighbor who has turned down his advances. In this instance, it would be safer if the social worker didn't discuss the disclosure with the client. Given his history of violence, discussing the disclosure might put both the therapist and the neighbor at risk.

50. D: The Ethical Theory and Decision-Making Period occurred in the 1970s and 1980s, preceding the Ethical Standards and Risk Management Period of the 1990s. Choices *B* and *C* reversed the focus of each period, but it is true as stated in Choice *D* that the national Association of Social Workers updated the Code of Ethics during the Ethical Standards and Risk Management Period. Also during this time, there was a focus on the development of risk management strategies to protect clients and social workers from ethical violations within the field.

51. A: Pre-beginning is not a stage in group treatment. During the beginning stage, Choice *B*, social workers determine the group's purpose, members, objectives, and other logistical tasks, and then group formation occurs. During the middle stage, Choice *C*, most of the group work is done. During the end stage, Choice *D*, group members come to resolutions on the issues addressed during the group process.

52. D: Social workers may not prescribe medication. Social worker coordination can be provided during case management, Choice *A*, including linking clients with resources. Other types of coordination include wraparound services, Choice *B*, which are inter-organizational collaborations where agencies form shared goals for client(s). Service integration, Choice *C*, refers to different types of services provided simultaneously.

53. D: Engaging clients in treatment is a way to facilitate communication during treatment. Accurately recording case information contributes to effective treatment, Choice *A*; protects the agency from possible legal ramifications, Choice *B*; and protects patient confidentiality, Choice *D*, since only information necessary to the purpose of the documentation should be recorded.

54. A: A social worker's ability to perceive a client's feelings and communicate an understanding of those emotions back to the client are concepts of empathic communication. If a social worker shares common feelings with a client and is affected by those feelings in the same way, Choice *D*, it is a sympathetic response and not a desirable method of displaying empathy in treatment. Nodding, displaying genuineness, and engaging clients are ways to display empathic communication, but Choice *A* shows the main concepts.

55. C: The neighborhood in which one lives has great impact on things, such as education quality, exposure to crime, access to drugs or alcohol, and the type of role models one is exposed to. Social context shapes behavior, expectations, and morals. Choices *A*, *B*, and *D* are all true and reflect various aspects of social context that can significantly influence behavioral choices, such as differences from one culture to another and how these can be impacted by different social contexts.

56. C: Erikson devised eight stages of psychosocial development. He emphasized the importance of social context, asserting that family and environment are major contributors to child development. During maturation (aged sixty-five and above), ego integrity vs. despair is the struggle. Important life tasks, such as child rearing and career, are being completed. Reviewing and evaluating how one's life was spent and success over the course of one's life provides a sense of fulfillment, while failure emerges if one is dissatisfied with accomplishments, which leads to depression or despair.

57. A: Sue & Sue's Stages of Racial/Cultural Identity Development include the following: conformity, dissonance, resistance and immersion, introspection, and integrative awareness. In the conformity stage, individuals hold a strong preference for the dominant culture and display negative views, shame, or embarrassment regarding their own racial and/or cultural groups. In the dissonance stage, individuals reconsider or challenge their beliefs. For the first time, they appreciate positive aspects of their own

205

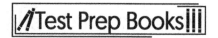

racial/cultural group. During the resistance and immersion stage, individuals have a pride of their racial and cultural group along with a preference for minority views and instead actively reject the views of the dominant culture. In the introspection stage, individuals become aware of the negative impact of the earlier resistance and immersion stage. At this point, they may realize that they do not actually disagree with all majority views or endorse all minority views, but find some sort of balance. Lastly, in the integrative awareness stage, individuals are able to appreciate both their own culture and differing cultures.

58. B: Spirituality tends to increase the likelihood of someone being connected to other people, the likelihood that the client might have a greater sense of purpose, and the likelihood of self-actualization. It also can provide hope to the hopeless, help reduce anxiety, aid in healing from emotional pain, and contribute toward a greater optimism. Being more artistic is not a factor connected to levels of spirituality.

59. A: Records must be kept in a secure and locked environment. Even though the office is always locked, a second form of security would be best. It is important to remember that cleaning staff or other individuals might have access to the office when neither social worker is there.

60. B: Documentation is the social worker's best friend. If it isn't documented, it didn't happen. Social workers deal with very sensitive situations, some of which end up in a court of law. If there is no documentation that something happened, there is no proof. Documenting any requests from clients—as well as whether those were honored and why or why not—is just as important as what happens during sessions.

61. C: Human dignity relates to an awareness of the value of each client and the intention to help each client improve their well-being and effectiveness at interacting with society. The strategies that Tom is using with Karen will help her assess her current strengths and weaknesses and community involvement and improve upon these so that she can become a healthier, more integrated member of society. Human relationship work strives to help clients understand and remove barriers in their current relationships to better meet personal goals. The core value of service centers around providing services to disadvantaged individuals and working to solve the causes of such disadvantages. Tom is acting with competence, performing duties that correspond to his training and experience, but this is not the specific value addressed with Karen's treatment.

62. B: The goal of cognitive restructuring is to help clients change irrational or unrealistic thoughts that result in a change in behaviors. Using self-monitoring to track situations, identifying situations that evoke dysfunctional thoughts and beliefs, and rewarding oneself for using functional coping skills are steps in the restructuring process, but not the ultimate goal.

63. D: It is normal for clients to have difficult feelings as termination approaches. This is not necessarily feedback toward the treatment process. Social workers can receive feedback from clients verbally/non-verbally, intentionally/unintentionally, or by the amount of progress toward goals.

64. B: In the first stage following a crisis event, clients experience an increase in feelings of stress and denial. They typically try to resolve the stressful reactions using past problem-solving and coping skills.

Second stage: Clients continue to experience higher levels of stress as the usual coping mechanisms fail. Clients may employ higher-level coping skills to alleviate the increasing stress levels, Choice *A*.

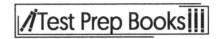

Third stage: Clients experience major emotional turmoil and possible feelings of hopelessness, depression, and anxiety, Choice *D*.

Fourth stage: Clients experience complete psychological and emotional collapse, or the individual finds a method to resolve the situation; however, there may be remaining emotional and psychological problems, Choice *C*.

65. C: Subjective data is when the client provides their perspective on what happened and the correlated feelings and experiences felt. The social worker may use the information to tease out facts related to the client's situation, which is known as objective data, Choice *B*. Measurable data, Choice *A*, and planning data, Choice *D*, are not relevant to the context of the question.

66. B: Conducting a needs assessment for the community allows the practitioner to see the current state of the community and determine if there are any areas for change. Choices *A*, *C*, and *D* may occur at a later stage, but they aren't the starting point for developing an intervention.

67. D: The prefix *cardi-* indicates the heart. Skin is usually indicated by the prefix *cutaneo-* or *derm-*. Stomach is usually indicated by the prefix *gastro-*. Liver is usually indicated by the prefix *hep-*.

68. B: The prefix *gastro-* indicates the stomach. Skin is usually indicated by the prefix *cutaneo-* or *derm-*. Liver is usually indicated by the prefix *hep-*. Heart is usually indicated by the prefix *cardi-*.

69. A: Angina pectoris can come on at any time and is a result of the heart not receiving enough oxygen. It's usually an indicator of heart disease.

70. A: Children have fewer resources for processing events of this nature because they have limited life experience and, therefore, fewer tools to help them adapt. Children are also less equipped to identify and share the emotions, memories, or thoughts they are experiencing than adults. The other responses are correct in that disorientation and disbelief are common in the beginning, and in the aftermath of disaster, other symptoms begin to emerge. Such events are indeed difficult to predict; therefore, one cannot easily prepare for trauma of this nature.

71. D: Culture is a complex and multi-faceted concept and is related to when, where, and with whom one was raised. Those in the mental health field should be constantly vigilant about a client's cultural practices because these strongly impact beliefs, ethics, and behavior. Choice *D* is the best answer because it does not constitute an aspect of cultural identity as easily as when, where, and how one was raised.

72. D: It is important to acknowledge the girl is not in any way at fault and that the act of sexual assault upon a minor is a felony. Choices *A*, *B*, and *C* plant a seed of hope that through sharing feelings in a safe setting, one can begin to move down the path to healing the emotional pain. It is helpful to normalize the experience to some extent so that the child realizes one in four girls are victims of some form of sexual abuse. The therapist should never blame the victim for abuse, regardless of the circumstances.

73. B: Amy should make a report to Adult Protective Services. Amy's job is not to prove or disprove that abuse or neglect is occurring; that is the job of Adult Protective Services. Amy has enough information to be concerned that something is not right about the situation and that Sofia may not be safe. A report should be made. Recall that mandatory reporting laws require social workers, and other professionals, to report any suspected abuse or neglect. This means that any professional who has a suspicion of abuse or neglect of a child or a vulnerable adult must legally make a report to either Child Protective Services or Adult Protective Services.

74. A: The six core values are: service, social justice, dignity and worth of the person, importance of human relationships, integrity, and competence.

75. D: HIPAA refers to the Health Insurance Portability and Accountability Act of 1996. HIPAA establishes that psychotherapy notes must be kept confidential by mental health professionals. This includes notes made during individual or group sessions, notes regarding conversations, notes pertaining to disclosures, and even notes that analyze situations involving the client.

76. D: The crisis is caused by the individual's reaction to the situation, not by the actual incident. Caplan theorized that individuals need to maintain homeostasis or remain in balance with their environment.

77. A: The furthering communication technique allows clients to know that the worker is listening and encourages more information. Questions that elicit short answers are called closed-ended questions, Choice *B*. Using facial expressions, body language, and postures to show that the worker is engaged and listening is called active listening, Choice *C*, and clarifying is when the social worker asks for clarification to ensure the client's message is understood, Choice *D*. All techniques are methods of facilitating communication with clients.

78. D: Examining the origins of the policies and procedures, including values and the related ideology, is an important step in the policy evaluation, not necessarily in the development process. When developing policies and procedures, front line workers should be involved because they are in the best position to determine how clients are affected. Additionally, policies should be clearly written and communicated and should be in the best interest of clients while still protecting agency and staff.

79. B: Indirect discrimination relates to laws and policies that are applied equally but have negative consequences for certain groups. The other three answers are examples of direct discrimination since the actions are based on individual biases rather than organizational decisions. In those three scenarios, people are purposefully discriminating against others. In Choice *B*, the school administrators may not have even considered the negative consequence for Jewish students.

80. B: This person's gender identity is bi-gender due to comfort in identification with both genders. Choice *A* is incorrect because the person does not appear confused about their sexual identity. Choice *C* is incorrect as bi-sexual refers to being attracted to both genders, and that information was not provided. Choice *D* is also incorrect. Transvestites enjoy dressing in attire of the opposite gender and engaging in stereotyped versions of the opposite gender.

81. D: Risk-taking behavior is purported to increase during adolescence by several theories including the need for excitement outweighing perceived consequences, the desire to gain status and acceptance among peers, and modeling adult behavior that may have been romanticized.

Social workers should work with adolescents who engage in risk-taking behavior to find healthy outlets to channel their talents or get them involved in more positive activities.

82. B: Good faith means that the social worker has a reasonable suspicion and has no alternative reasons for reporting other than concern.

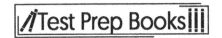

83. B: If Jane has been unable to rectify the situation through self-assessment, she should then turn to consultation with colleagues regarding her values conflict. If the consultation proves ineffective, she may ultimately need to consider termination and referring the client to another social worker. Social work as a profession prides itself on practitioners putting personal values aside, even when those values conflict with client values. Social workers must not engage in discriminatory practices or condone the discriminatory practices of others.

84. C: Cultural values and beliefs should be researched and learned when working with clients from a different culture. These values should then be used as strengths during goal development to aid the client in making the changes they desire.

85. C: Spirituality and religion are different concepts. Religion can be defined as an organized system of beliefs that others are expected to follow. Spirituality is a more personal process of self-growth and self-actualization. Spirituality in its purest form does not rely on an institution, religious leader, or set of rules to guide beliefs, making Choice *A* incorrect. Choice *B* is an example of a therapist overstepping boundaries and attempting to encourage others to accept their personal spiritual beliefs. There is no evidence to back up the statement that persons who do not attend church tend to be any angrier than anyone else.

86. B: This theory of addiction is based on the interplay of classical conditioning, operant conditioning, and social learning (observation). Choice *A* is not specifically a model of addiction, but rather a supposition as to why people abuse substances. *C* refers to the Moral Model of addictions in which the person addicted to drugs or alcohol is viewed as weak-willed. Choice *D* refers to a hybrid of the biopsychosocial model of addiction, which focuses on the role of the environment (such as cultural and social factors), and genetic theory.

87. A: Reaction formation is when a person displays an exaggerated version of the opposite emotion to what he or she is really feeling. For example, a person may display strong feelings of love toward someone, though internally and unconsciously he or she detests that person. Displacement is when the feeling someone has toward one person is displaced to another object or person, such as a dog or spouse. Projection happens when one's own feelings are viewed as actually being someone else's. Denial is the refusal to admit something exists, such as painful facts or situations.

88. A: Scapegoating a child occurs when a child is blamed for family problems and for things that are not their fault. This pattern of family dysfunction may happen in families where the problems are not being properly recognized or addressed, and members of the family seek to shift the blame. Affirming, undermining, or disavowing the child are not concepts connected to family dysfunction.

89. C: The definition of external validity is the ability of a study to be generalized to other people or circumstances. The other choices are all general research terms. Choice *A* refers to randomized controlled trials, which use participants or subjects who are chosen randomly to participate. Choice *B* is reliability, the consistency of a measure, or the likelihood the same result will be achieved each time it's used. Choice *D* is internal validity, which refers to cause and effect (i.e., are the effects of the study caused by the intervention?).

90. C: The Civil Rights Act was the earliest, enacted in 1964. The Child Abuse and Prevention Act, Choice *A*, was enacted in 1974; the Family Medical Leave Act, Choice *B*, in 1993; and the Patient Protection and Affordable Care Act, Choice *D*, in 2010. All of these acts were significant social welfare legislations.

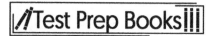

91. D: Social workers must overcome clients' feelings of anger or mistrust about treatment when motivating clients for participation in treatment, especially in the case of involuntary or non-voluntary clients. The other choices center on clients' self-perceptions, interactions, and experiences with others, including institutions or groups, which are all factors to consider when empowering clients.

92. B: Osteopenia is marked by a decrease in bone density. This is indicated by the prefix *osteo-*, meaning bone.

93. D: Danny is showing signs of alcohol problems that include inappropriate consumption levels, interference with his work responsibilities, and legal troubles related to the substance.

94. C: Reports indicate that about 70 percent of Americans take at least one prescription medication.

95. A: Service means addressing social problems. This refers both to individual problems and problems in the broader society. Social workers are encouraged to provide some services pro bono to give back to society and to help those who otherwise could not afford services. It also means that social workers should volunteer in some aspect outside of their paying positions.

96. D: Social workers operate from the values and goals that have been established for the profession. The core goals of social work are to improve social function, to resolve problems, to achieve desired change, and to meet self-defined goals. While some of these goals regard clients, they also apply to social workers themselves.

97. C: Issues involving a social worker's personal mental health are considered a form of impairment. Alcohol and drug addiction also fall into this category. With any issues regarding professional impairment, the social worker should seek consultation from colleagues and supervisors. It may be necessary to lessen the workload, and possibly to terminate some client relationships and make referrals.

98. C: Psychological or emotional abuse is when the abuser uses strategies of manipulation through shame, fear, and guilt to control the other's behaviors. It also involves verbal abuse, which takes the form of yelling, constant criticisms, belittling, threats, or name-calling. Physical abuse involves some type of physical harm. Vocal abuse is physiological disorder that occurs when a person damages their vocal cords. Critical abuse does not exist.

99. D: The stigma of mental illness can cause family members to become judgmental toward the individual who has been diagnosed, or he or she may have to deal with the misunderstandings of people outside the family. This is one of the reasons that dealing with a diagnosis of mental illness can be more complicated for a family than dealing with a diagnosis of physical illness. There is no ease associated with mental illness. Even though mental illness may involve some level of confusion or ambiguity, those are not terms that best answer the question.

100. B: While the use/abuse of alcohol, a history of mental illness, and a tendency to control others are all risk factors for abuse, the presence of a learning disorder is not associated with this. There are many factors that may indicate a potential abuser, but there are no foolproof ways to identify one apart from the evidence of abuse.

101. C: Social workers should assist clients in identifying and changing dysfunctional patterns when working with families. When preparing for termination, a social worker should help a client identify

210

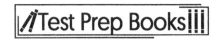

which skills the client lacked and other reasons that led to initiating services to help determine progress. The worker should also help the client find ways to continue building skills following the termination of services.

102. D: Goal Identification and Intervention Planning is the second phase of treatment. This is when goals, the treatment plan, and the contract are developed. During the first phase, Engagement and Assessment, the social worker focuses on rapport building and data gathering. The third phase, Implementation, is when interventions and tasks are implemented. During the last phase, Termination and Evaluation, the client and worker assess goal attainment and evaluation.

103. C: Single subject designs typically cannot be generalized to other clients or problems. The advantages of single subject designs include cost-effectiveness, ease of use, and immediacy of data.

104. A: These symptoms are indicators of physical neglect. Physical neglect can be the appearance of always being hungry, excessive sleepiness, or untreated medical problems. Other indicators of physical neglect are parents or caregivers demonstrating lack of interest or suffering from chronic illness. Usually, the home is an unsafe environment for victims who experience physical neglect.

105. A: The components of the biopsychosocial assessment drive the data pertinent to designing interventions that match the client's problems, such as client strengths and risk factors. In turn, these strengths and risk factors help guide the practitioner in the selection of a theoretical model to apply (in an effort to enhance client functioning and improve the client's overall well-being).

106. C: Resistance can appear any time during the intervention. Its presence is an important influence in how interventions are developed and managed.

107. D: Gambling disorder is the only non-substance related addictive disorder in the *DSM-5-TR*. Choice *A* is incorrect because internet gaming disorder appears in the *DSM-5-TR* as something that requires future study to determine if it exists and should be included as an official diagnosis. Choice *B* is incorrect because sex addiction is not a diagnosis in the *DSM-5-TR*. Hypersexuality is a symptom of several different disorders, but it is not a diagnosis on its own. Choice *C* is incorrect because kleptomania is a diagnosis categorized with disruptive, impulse control and conduct disorders, not addictive disorders.

108. B: Self-determination refers to everyone's right to live the life they choose. This doesn't mean that the choices made and life lived will be relatable or understood by others. Social workers strive to preserve self-determination, to allow clients to decide their own goals, and to assist clients in achieving those goals.

109. D: Sexual relationships between colleagues are permitted by the Code of Ethics. The only exception is that a sexual relationship between a supervisor and supervisee is not permissible because of the obvious authority and power that one individual has over the other.

110. D: Choice *D* is false because it was during the Values Period that discussion covered controversial issues like economic hardship, substance use, and race relations. Over time, social work values and ethics have evolved in five broad stages: the Morality Period, the Values Period, the Ethical Theory and Decision-Making Period, the Ethical Standards and Risk Management Period, and the Digital Period. The Morality Period occurred during the late nineteenth to early twentieth century. During this time, practitioners were concerned with the morality of clients, not the ethics of social workers. The goal of the field at the time was to build the ethics of individuals in poverty so they could get their lives on the

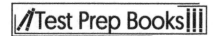

right track. As the period progressed, the focus shifted to the need for significant social reforms to reduce the impact of social problems such as poverty, unemployment, inadequate housing, health care, sanitation, and education.

111. A: Competence is the reason that social workers need to be continually educated. This is important so that the social worker can provide the services in which they are trained and remain up-to-date on research and practice. While the other answers may be true, they are not the strategy specifically implicated for being an effective social worker.

112. D: The NASW Code of Ethics does not indicate the use of single subject designs for evaluation. The code requires social workers to be knowledgeable about evaluation procedures, report findings accurately, use review boards when appropriate, and acquire client consent to participation in evaluation measures.

113. D: Target problem scaling is an evaluation tool that can be used when identified problems are difficult to quantify. The other terms are general research terms. Choice *A*, independent variable, is the variable changed or controlled when conducting an experiment or research. Choice *B*, dependent variable, is the variable dependent on the independent variable and observed for changes as the independent variable is manipulated. Choice *C*, validity, reflects whether a test, tool, or study is measuring what it intends to measure.

114. A: Rewarding clients for using functional coping skills is a step in cognitive restructuring, not an activity performed when referring clients for services. When referring clients, social workers must contact other providers through phone calls, meetings, or letters; assist clients with completion of paperwork; and monitor client progress to ensure services are effective and accessible.

115. D: According to the NASW Code of Ethics, social workers must be aware of their own biases and prejudices to successfully offer culturally competent practice. Choices *A* and *B* are steps in cognitive restructuring, including identifying which thoughts and belief patterns or self-statements lead to the target problems and using self-monitoring techniques. Choice *C* is a component of Scientific Management Theory, which emphasizes strong boundaries between the management who delegates tasks and the workers who perform the tasks.

116. A: Rather than focusing on problems and pathology, the strengths perspective, or strengths-based approach, in social work shifts the focus away from the traditional topics (problems and pathology), and instead, encourages social workers to focus on a client's strengths or assets and to build upon the client's inherent positive characteristics. In this example, the social worker is helping the client recognize his strengths, such as his determination, ingenuity, and resiliency, despite his financial challenges.

117. D: Family life cycle theories assume that individuals, as members of a family unit, pass through different stages of life. The main focus in the launching family stage is accepting the new independent role of an adult child and transitioning through the inevitable separation that comes with those changes. Also in this stage is the need for parents to face their own transition into middle or older age. Choice *A* describes a family with young children stage wherein couples must accept the new family member and shift from a marital system to a family system. Choices *B* and *C* describe the unattached young adult stage.

118. B: Changing behavior through rewards for approximation of desired behavior is the correct answer. Skinner demonstrated that behavior could be learned by rewarding actions that are similar to the

212

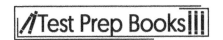

desired behavior. If one wants to teach a dog to chase and catch a Frisbee thrown to the end of a field, the dog must first be rewarded for sniffing the Frisbee, then grasping the Frisbee, and then catching it when thrown four feet, then six, then ten. This process is called successive approximation. Choice *A* refers to a classical conditioning. Choice *C* refers to superstitions, meaning that one can sometimes be confused as to which behavior is soliciting the reward. Some athletes wear the same pair of "lucky" socks each game, thinking this behavior leads to the reward of winning. In reality, the behavior that leads to the win can be anything from practicing harder to playing a team that is not highly skilled; therefore, the behavior is superstitious. Choice *D* is a poor form of teaching a person to learn a new behavior because it may take much trial and error before perfection is achieved.

119. C: Carl Rogers placed much emphasis on reaching one's greatest potential and the interplay between this potential and one's perception of self. Erikson and Freud theorized that one must achieve certain developmental challenges before moving to the next level of human growth. Allport, on the other hand, believed one's destiny depended on the possession of certain clusters of personality traits. Therefore, *A, B*, and *D* are wrong. Rogers focused on the concept that humans are driven by their own need to develop into the best person they are capable of becoming.

120. A: Prescription medications for mental disorders generally show the best results when paired with numerous, client-specific lifestyle modifications. These modifications may include changes to diet, a change of environment, or getting a service pet, but those examples on their own may not be the driving factor behind results.

121. A: It's important to know commonly prescribed drugs, as many clients may take these medications. This is relevant intervention and treatment plan information. Lexapro and lithium are used to treat mental disorders and aren't more commonly prescribed drugs. Thryonate is not a real drug.

122. B: The client is the expert on their own life and should be treated as such. Doing so also helps the practitioner involve the client in care. The client's parents and clinicians are important in providing collateral sources of information but shouldn't be viewed as the experts.

123. A: Atypical antipsychotics were developed in the 1990s and have been shown to have less severe side effects. Typical antipsychotics were developed in the 1950s. They can be used if atypical antipsychotics don't work for the client, but they usually have severe side effects.

124. A: Human Relations Theory is a neoclassical theory. It has roots in psychology and theorizes that higher levels of an employee's job satisfaction and morale lead to better performance and more loyalty to an organization. All other choices are classical theories. Scientific Management Theory emphasizes strong boundaries between the management who delegate the tasks and the workers who perform the tasks. Administrative Theory is a hierarchical system that uses five basic functions to be administered by management that relate to planning, coordination, and control. Bureaucracy Theory places emphasis on specialized areas with well-defined duties and uses a hierarchical, impersonal structure with heavy reliance on rules and procedures with the goal of maintaining control.

125. C: The therapeutic alliance refers to the relationship between the social worker and the client. A positive relationship is crucial to successful treatment. Social workers can build a positive relationship by being empathetic, competent, open, genuine, and respectful. The client must also be motivated and interested in treatment. The social worker should empower the client to participate as a partner in every stage of the helping process, including making decisions about what their treatment will look like.

213

126. A: The goal of building rapport with a client is to lay the foundation for a relationship based on mutual trust, empathy, and acceptance. A positive relationship is the basis of the helping process and the factor that promotes change and growth. During rapport building, the social worker and client can get comfortable with each other and start to build trust. The social worker can get a sense of how a client feels about seeking help and address any issues or concerns they have. If the social worker has trouble building trust with a client, they should seek supervisory assistance. The supervisor can help the social worker explore any feelings of countertransference that could be negatively affecting the helping relationship.

Choice *B* is incorrect because although the client's presenting problem might come up briefly during the rapport-building process, it is not the goal of rapport-building. Choice *C* is incorrect because the goal of rapport-building is not for the social worker to decide whether they want to work with a client. In general, ethics dictate that social workers should treat any client that they are competent to help. If a social worker is unable to build rapport with a client, they should seek supervision. Only in rare cases should a client be transferred to another social worker. Choice *D* is incorrect because informed consent is a requirement for beginning treatment and must be completed before the social worker focuses on building rapport.

127. D: As the expert, the social worker inherently has more power than the client, Choice *C*, and it is important to be aware of this and take steps to level the playing field. Transparency about the treatment process allows the client to understand themselves and their issues and participate more fully in their treatment. The social worker should give the client voice and choice in their treatment and should encourage feedback. The social worker should never withhold information from a client, Choice *B*, because this only reinforces the power difference.

The social worker should also be open about their own privileges and be willing to discuss how those privileges affect the relationship. Choice *A* is incorrect because the social worker should only share their own problems and difficulties in certain cases, and usually a supervisor should be consulted first. Self-disclosure can easily backfire and inadvertently reinforce the power imbalance. For example, a social worker might think that sharing their struggles with depression would reduce the power imbalance with a depressed client. However, the client might see the social worker and think, "I thought I was having so much trouble because of depression, but this social worker has depression too, and they are a successful professional. I guess I am just not trying hard enough."

128. C: Alex was correct in protecting Lucas' right to self-determination. Lucas had made it clear several times that he had tried going to a shelter in the past and did not like the restrictions. He preferred a freer life that allowed him permission to do as he pleased. If Lucas had been suffering from some sort of medical issue that would make him unsafe, then Alex would have needed to explain all the information to him so that he understood his choices. If Lucas still decided to avoid the shelter, then that would have been his right. Social workers should remember that clients have a right to lead their lives as they see fit, making their own decisions based on their values. Issues may arise when the values of clients do not align with how others believe clients should behave or live. Social workers must advocate on the behalf of clients with other professionals to ensure that their values are at the core of any plan. It is the job of the social worker to work with the client to aid in goal creation and identification that is congruent to the client's values.

129. C: Dual relationships are clearly outlined in the NASW Code of Ethics. The Code of Ethics states that social workers should not engage in dual relationships with clients or former clients in which

214

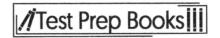

exploitation of the client may occur. The Code of Ethics does recognize that there might be situations where dual relationships are unavoidable. For example, a social worker might have two jobs, one of which involves providing group therapy to survivors of sexual abuse. It is possible that a member of the aforementioned therapy group could become an employee or client at the social worker's second place of work. In these types of situations, the Code of Ethics suggests that the social worker establish clear boundaries that are sensitive to the client/former client. The other options listed are suggested strategies for maintaining professional boundaries, among others.

130. A: Value suspension is the process of the social worker acknowledging and controlling their personal values in their social work practice, particularly in instances where their own moral codes, values, biases, and prejudices may differ from those of the client. To avoid conflict with the treatment he or she is providing to clients, the social worker should employ value suspension. Choice *B* describes a value conflict for the client and can occur as a result of Choice *C*. Value conflicts may occur when someone makes new friends, engages in romantic relationships, joins a new community, attends a new school, or accepts a new job.

131. A: The Bricklin Perceptual Scales are typically administered to children six years of age and older in custody cases to determine the child's perception of each caregiver.

132. C: Developmental history is part of the biological section of the biopsychosocial assessment. Choice *A*, coping skills, is part of the psychological section. Choices *B* and *D*, marital problems and educational background, are part of the social section.

133. A: The purpose of a biopsychosocial assessment is to get a holistic understanding of a client. Traditionally, this meant asking about current and past biological, psychological, and social function. It is becoming more popular to ask clients about other domains of function as well, especially spiritual and cultural, to make the assessment even more holistic. Social workers sometimes but not always include questions about spiritual beliefs, religion, and cultural traditions. On the other hand, psychiatric diagnoses, medical history, and presenting problem, Choices *B*, *C*, and *D*, are incorrect because they are always included in a biopsychosocial assessment.

134. D: A mental status examination provides information about a client's current mental state and function. Psychiatric history is part of the psychological section of the biopsychosocial assessment, not part of the mental status examination. Appearance, affect, and speech, Choices *A*, *B*, and *C*, are incorrect because they are all components of the mental status examination.

135. B: The problem-solving therapeutic model describes the role of the social worker in the problem-solving process. The goal is to help clients learn how to manage problems effectively and healthily. The client must learn how to identify a problem, stressor, or negative situation; understand and manage their reactions; plan how to respond; and carry out the plan. The social worker helps by guiding the client through these steps, modeling the process, and teaching the client skills they need to solve problems on their own.

136. C: The social worker's role involves active listening to verbal and nonverbal communication, Choice *A*, collaborating with the client on their treatment plan, Choice *B*, and helping the client build their own support network, Choice *D*. It can be tempting to give advice to clients; however, it is not appropriate for social workers to do this. The goal of treatment is to increase a client's ability to handle things on their own, not rely on the social worker for advice. Also, the social worker may think they are giving good advice when in reality they have misunderstood the client's situation.

137. C: Empathy describes the ability to be attuned to another person and understand their emotional experience without being consumed by it. Empathic communication is an extremely important skill for social workers to develop because it is the foundation of a positive relationship with clients. Empathy helps a social worker build initial rapport and then stay attuned to a client throughout the helping process. Empathy differs from sympathy, Choice *B*, which means feeling compassion for another person's experience without necessarily understanding it. Authenticity, Choice *A*, means being real and genuine and is also an important social work skill. Objectivity, Choice *D*, means trying to view a situation without bias.

138. B: The field of social work places an emphasis on understanding systems because once the practitioner understands a client's place in society, then he or she can help increase the client's social understanding and make connections to help meet treatment goals. Understanding the client from an individual, family, and social system perspective sets the foundation for an understanding systems. The other choices describe other emphases in the field of social work, such as the emphasis on field experience, the emphasis on advocacy at the local, state, and national levels, and the emphasis on maintaining effectiveness in practice.

139. A: The *NASW Code of Ethics* outlines the ethical standards for social work practice. It identifies the six core values of social work as service, social justice, dignity and worth of the person, importance of human relationships, integrity, and competence.

140. D: According to the *NASW Code of* Ethics, self-determination is one of the core values of social work. Social workers have an ethical obligation to respect and promote clients' rights to self-determination. It is ethical to limit a client's self-determination only if the social worker believes that the client is about to cause serious harm to self or others.

141. B: Self-disclosure can be used to connect with a new client, but it is not the best or only way to do so. Self-disclosure can be harmful and lead to boundary violations. For this reason, it is important to seek supervision when considering whether to use self-disclosure. In most situations, there are other ways to achieve the same outcome that carry less of a risk of harm to the client.

142. D: In order to maintain good professional boundaries, social workers should not connect with clients on social media. Ideally, the social worker would explain this policy at the start of treatment, but it's never too late to have a conversation with clients about boundaries and communication channels. Choices *A* and *B* are incorrect because they involve accepting the request. Choice *C* is incorrect because it is important to help the client understand that the reason for the denial is professional, not personal.

143. C: According to the *NASW Code of Ethics*, it is unethical for a social worker to terminate services to pursue a business, social, or sexual relationship with a client. Choice *A* is incorrect because it is unethical to continue services when the client is no longer in need. Choice *B* is incorrect because it is ethical to terminate a non-paying client who has been informed of the consequences of nonpayment if the client does not pose an imminent danger to self or others. Choice *D* is incorrect because the social worker is following the appropriate steps to terminate due to leaving the agency.

144. C: Vygotsky believed individuals are significantly shaped by the formal and informal social groups in which they interact. These institutions teach values, how to behave in relationships, how closely one

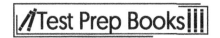

must follow rules and laws, and, in general, what is important in life. A child growing up hungry and neglected will have a very different view of life than one who is cherished and provided with love, support, and material needs. Choices *A*, *B*, and *D* all impact the quality of one's life, but Vygotsky leaned toward a more global explanation of social development that encompasses multiple social factors.

145. D: John is in the identity vs. role confusion stage. This stage takes place during adolescence and marks the transition from childhood to adulthood. It involves trying out new things and figuring out one's place in the world. Successful completion of this stage results in a solid sense of identity. Failure to complete this stage results in uncertainty about one's identity and role in society. Choice *A* is incorrect because trust vs. mistrust takes place during infancy and involves learning to trust others. Choice *B* is incorrect because industry vs. inferiority takes place during school age and involves learning to take initiative and work toward goals. Choice *C* is incorrect because intimacy vs. isolation takes place during young adulthood and involves learning to create and maintain fulfilling relationships outside the family of origin.

146. C: Negative punishment involves taking away a reward (recess) in order to discourage a problematic behavior (being disruptive). Positive reinforcement is providing a reward in response to a desirable behavior (e.g., rewarding the students who were behaving well). Negative reinforcement is taking away something undesirable in response to a desirable behavior (e.g., giving less homework because the class behaved well). Positive punishment is providing something undesirable in response to undesirable behavior (e.g., giving the class detention in response to the disruptive behavior).

147. B: Authoritative parenting involves high expectations and high support. It is democratic in that rules take into account the preferences of both parents and children. The emphasis is on nurturing discipline rather than punishment. This type of parenting tends to result in happy, capable, and successful children. On the other hand, authoritarian parenting involves high expectations and low support. Strict rules are set by the parents alone and enforced with punishment. This style results in children who are obedient and proficient but struggle with happiness, social competence, and self-esteem. Permissive parenting involves low expectations and high support. Parents are warm and nurturing but do not set rules or provide discipline. This style results in children who struggle with self-regulation, happiness, authority, and school performance. Uninvolved parenting involves low expectations and low support. Parents do not set rules and also do not provide nurturing and attention. This style results in the worst outcomes for children, particularly in terms of self-control, self-esteem, and competence.

148. A: IRBs are independent groups who ensure that research on human subjects is ethical. IRB approval is a requirement for this type of research.

149. D: If a social worker is sued by a client, then they have a right to release client information as part of their self-defense. This disclosure should be limited to the information required to defend themselves.

150. C: As mandated reporters, social workers are required by law to report suspected abuse or neglect to the appropriate authorities. Failure to do so is both unethical and illegal.

151. A: The social worker is not required to do anything with this confession. Social workers have a legal duty to warn and protect, which means that a social worker must take action if a client poses an imminent threat to self or others. That does not apply in this situation because the crime happened in the past, and there is no risk to anyone in the present.

217

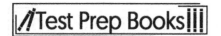

152. D: Although attachment develops during the first five years of life, it continues to affect psychological functioning throughout the lifespan. A secure attachment is associated with healthy adult relationships. Insecure, ambivalent, disorganized, or otherwise disordered attachment is associated with psychiatric disorders and difficulty with adult relationships. Choices *A, B,* and *C* are all true.

153. A: This demonstrates a preoccupation with sex and age-inappropriate knowledge of sexual behavior, both of which can indicate abuse. Often, children who have been abused act out what they have experienced through play. Choices *B, C,* and *D* are incorrect because they describe age-appropriate sexual behavior. Masturbating, exploring sexuality, or being concerned with nudity are all normal behaviors that indicate healthy sexual development.

154. D: Codependency describes one person (often a spouse or other family member) unintentionally enabling someone's substance misuse by making excuses for their behavior, giving them money, denying that they have a problem, or otherwise protecting them from consequences. Choice *A* is incorrect because the codependent partner does not need to be using a substance. Choice *B* describes a co-occurring disorder, not codependency. Choice *C* is incorrect because it describes a polydrug addiction.

155. A: In the context of a mental status examination, *orientation* refers to a client's orientation to reality. This means the client's understanding of who they are, where they are, when they are (time and date), and what has happened recently. A client who can answer all these questions correctly is considered "oriented x4." Inability to answer these questions correctly indicates that the client's mental status is not optimal; the client is disoriented. The client's sexual orientation, the client's beliefs and feelings about treatment, and informing the client of the purpose of the examination, Choices *B, C,* and *D*, are incorrect because they are not related to a client's orientation to reality.

156. C: A Thematic Appreciation Test (TAT) is used to explore a client's perceptions, needs, motivations, conflicts, and desires. The pictures are intentionally ambiguous and the client's reactions to them can uncover subconscious information that the client may not be aware of. Choice *A*, Beck Depression Inventory (BDI), is a relatively short test that asks a series of questions to determine the level of depression symptoms the client is currently experiencing. Choice *B*, The Minnesota Multiphasic Personality Inventory (MMPI), is an extensive personality test that asks a series of questions to assess the client's level of psychopathology. Choice *D*, Myers-Briggs Type Indicator (MBTI), is a personality test that asks a series of questions to assign clients a personality type based on four dimensions (extraverted/introverted, sensing/intuition, thinking/feeling, and judging/perceiving). The result is an MBTI type; for example, INTJ.

157. B: Educational records are a type of collateral data that can provide helpful information about a client's current and historical functioning. Educational records are not an appropriate way to assess a client's level of intelligence. Although academic performance can be correlated with intelligence, there are many other factors that can affect a client's behavior at school. To assess intelligence, social workers should use an evidence-based assessment tool, such as the Stanford-Binet Intelligence Scale. Choices *A*, *C*, and *D* are incorrect because they are examples of how educational records can be used appropriately. Educational records can reveal if and how events in other areas of a client's life affect their school performance, Choice *A*. They can assist in the diagnosis of developmental disorders in children and adults, Choice *C*. They can also help pinpoint when a client's symptoms began, Choice *D*.

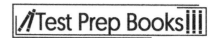

158. D: When a social worker collects collateral data about a client, that data becomes part of the client's file. This means that the data is subject to the same privacy standards as the rest of the client's file. One risk of collecting collateral data is that it can be subpoenaed, and a social worker can be ordered by a judge to release it to the court. This possibility should be explained to the client along with other risks and benefits of giving permission for the social worker to access collateral data. Choices *A*, *B*, and *C* are incorrect because they are accurate statements.

159. A: Some social workers may be reluctant to point out cultural differences due to fear of offending a client, but this is misguided. Comfort in talking about cultural differences is a critical component in working with diverse populations. It is important to remember that cultural differences can be significant without being visually obvious. In addition, significant diversity exists within cultures, and different people relate to their cultural experiences in different ways. It is beneficial to talk about these issues with all clients to strengthen the relationship, avoid misunderstanding, and create an effective and appropriate treatment plan.

160. C: Developmental level refers to someone's ability to function in different domains at any given time. It considers physical, psychological, and social functioning. It is important to assess a client's developmental level throughout the helping process, as it can change over time. A person's developmental level can be delayed or advanced across the board or only in certain areas. For example, a person can be physically mature but socially delayed. Understanding these nuances is critical to providing effective treatment, which is why developmental level is more important than chronological age when selecting interventions.

161. C: Out-of-home placement is destabilizing for the person removed from the home. In the short term, their psychological and behavioral problems are likely to become more pronounced. This can include mood problems, aggression, and acting out. The ultimate goal of out-of-home placement is to improve the health and functioning of the displaced person, but it is important for social workers to be aware that things often get worse before they get better.

162. B: In the newly married couple stage, a couple learns how to live together and how to adjust their other relationships to accommodate a partner. In the family with adolescents stage, the main task is allowing more autonomy for the adolescents. In the launching family stage, the primary task is accepting that children are now independent adults and transitioning to an adult-adult relationship with them. In the family with young children stage, the primary task is transitioning from a marital system to a family system.

163. A: Splitting is a tendency to see self and others as either all good or all bad due to an inability to integrate the good and bad in people. It is associated with borderline personality disorder. Sublimation is channeling negative emotions into adaptive behavior (for example, writing poetry when depressed). Denial involves refusing to acknowledge negative thoughts, feelings, or behaviors. Intellectualization involves explaining away negative emotions with fact-based, intellectual arguments.

164. B: When working with victims of domestic violence, the priorities are ensuring the client's safety and addressing their medical needs. Social workers should also educate themselves on the dynamics of domestic violence, including the cycle of violence, motivations of the abuser, and effects on the victim. Choice *A* is incorrect because a client is unlikely to accept help from someone they don't trust, and victims of abuse often have particular difficulty with trust. Choice *C* is incorrect because leaving an abusive relationship is extremely dangerous and requires careful safety planning. Choice *D* is incorrect

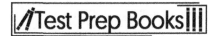

because research consistently demonstrates that couples therapy is counterproductive in abusive relationships and can actually increase the abuse.

165. A: This is an example of reframing. The social worker is offering a different perspective on the client's situation. Reframing can remind clients that there are ways of looking at their situation that can be more positive and motivating. Choice *B* is incorrect because clarifying involves paraphrasing and asking questions to ensure understanding. Choice *C* is incorrect because validating means acknowledging and empathizing with a client's situation. Choice *D* is incorrect because questioning involves drawing a client out and gathering information.

166. B: Questions about sexual history should be framed in terms of behaviors rather than labels. Labels can be perceived as judgmental and may be understood in different ways by different people. For example, a male client might consider himself heterosexual and also occasionally have sex with men. Asking about behaviors provides a clearer picture of what is actually going on. Choice *A* is incorrect because euphemistic language is also open to different interpretations, can be perceived as judgmental, and communicates that the social worker is not comfortable discussing the topic in a straightforward manner.

A term like "making love" could be especially inappropriate because it conflates sex and love, which may or may not be the client's experience. This type of language could be especially confusing for a client who has been sexually abused. Choice *C* is incorrect because yes and no questions do not give the client the opportunity to provide context and details. Choice *D* is incorrect because if the social worker is uncomfortable discussing these topics, the client is likely to feel uncomfortable as well. Social workers should practice asking these types of questions with clear language and relaxed body language to communicate to clients that it is ok to talk about these issues.

167. C: Mr. G is exhibiting the symptoms of psychosocial stress. Psychosocial stress is the body's reaction to a perceived threat. It can be caused by a single stressful event, but more commonly manifests in the context of prolonged exposure to stress. Under stress, the body releases activating hormones like cortisol that help the body respond in the short term. However, under chronic stress, the body continues to release these hormones and is unable to return to homeostasis.

If the body is stuck in this activated state for long periods of time, symptoms like Mr. G's begin to occur. Mr. G had already been experiencing increased stress due to his business problems. The additional responsibility of caring for his mother increased his stress levels even more, causing him to develop symptoms and seek help. Choice *A* is incorrect because hypertension, or high blood pressure, is a symptom of psychosocial stress, not the cause. His doctor evaluated his blood pressure and determined that he needed psychosocial rather than medical help. Choice *B* is incorrect because although he is experiencing sadness and irritability, his symptoms taken together do not indicate a mood disorder as much as a stress response. Choice *D* is incorrect because his symptoms have had a short duration and do not include re-experiencing or avoidance, which are typical with PTSD.

168. A: Comorbid disorders are disorders that occur at the same time. Choice *B* is incorrect because postmorbid means happening after an illness began. If someone develops depression and then later develops alcohol use disorder (AUD), the AUD would be postmorbid. Choice *C* is incorrect because contraindicated means not indicated. For example, taking Tylenol is contraindicated for people with AUD because both alcohol and Tylenol can damage the liver. Choice *D* is incorrect because aggravated

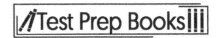

means made worse. For example, if someone is depressed and drinking makes their symptoms worse, drinking aggravates their depression.

169. B: The medical model considers addiction to be a chronic disease that is present even after a person becomes sober. It is the model promoted by AA. The biopsychosocial model considers addiction in the context of the complex interplay of person and environment. The moral model considers addiction a sin or character flaw. The self-medication model views substance use as an attempt to relieve symptoms of a psychiatric disorder.

170. D: A person's subjective experience of an event determines whether it is traumatic, not the facts about the event. A traumatic event overwhelms a person's ability to cope. It may or may not actually be life threatening, but it is perceived to be. Choice *A* is incorrect because even though overwhelming events in childhood are more likely to be traumatic, trauma can happen at any age. Choice *B* is incorrect because trauma is about the perception of danger rather than the fact of injury. Choice *C* is incorrect because even though certain events like natural disasters or interpersonal violence are more likely to be traumatic, any event perceived as overwhelming and threatening can result in trauma.

Practice Test #2

1. What does it mean for a social worker to be congruent in their communication with a client?
   a. The social worker maintains professional detachment and objectivity.
   b. The social worker and the client have the same understanding of the client's problems.
   c. The social worker matches the client's body language and speaking style.
   d. The social worker's verbal and nonverbal communication is real and genuine.

2. All the following are guidelines social workers should follow when requesting feedback from clients, EXCEPT:
   a. Pay attention to informal feedback in the form of verbal and nonverbal cues.
   b. Use a standard feedback form for every client.
   c. Request feedback at different times throughout the treatment process.
   d. Clearly explain the purpose of the feedback and how it will be used.

3. Which social work interviewing technique is used to bring together important points that have been discussed, reflect on progress made, and ensure that the social worker and client are on the same page at the end of a session?
   a. Asking open-ended questions
   b. Validating
   c. Clarifying
   d. Summarizing

4. Which of Erikson's stages of development is associated with school-aged children?
   a. Autonomy vs. shame and doubt
   b. Intimacy vs. isolation
   c. Industry vs. inferiority
   d. Trust vs. mistrust

5. A woman tells her social worker that she is worried about her seven-year-old son. She caught the boy talking to himself, and he explained that he was talking to his imaginary friend. The woman is afraid that this means her son is mentally ill. What should the social worker tell the woman?
   a. This behavior suggests that the boy is being neglected or abused.
   b. This behavior indicates that the boy is experiencing psychosis.
   c. This behavior is normal for very young children but is concerning at age seven.
   d. This behavior is normal for the boy's age and development.

6. According to Piaget's theory of cognitive development, people reach the formal operations stage at age eleven. The formal operations stage is characterized by all of the following EXCEPT:
   a. Magical thinking
   b. High-level abstract thinking
   c. Planning for the future
   d. Hypothetical thinking

7. According to Kohlberg's theory, at which level of moral development do people conform to established rules and laws of society?
    a. Preconventional
    b. Conventional
    c. Postconventional
    d. Adult

8. A client states that he is being followed and the police will not take his reports seriously. Because of this, he concludes that the police or government are responsible. The evidence he gives is that he often sees the same cars on his street and the same people in his local coffee shop. He does not accept any of the more plausible explanations for his experiences. He has no other symptoms and is otherwise functioning normally. The belief that he is being followed is an example of:
    a. Schizophrenia
    b. Hallucination
    c. Delusion
    d. Disorientation

9. Which of the following tools is most useful for taking a family history?
    a. Ecogram
    b. Genogram
    c. Medical records
    d. Family tree

10. A social worker notices that one of her clients sometimes comes to therapy restless, talking quickly, and with dilated pupils. Other times he appears irritable and tired. He has been sniffling constantly for two months, which he attributes to a lingering cold. He has been getting into trouble for missing work. He used to be involved in several community groups but has stopped participating. His wife recently confronted him about the fact that he is often up late into the night then falls asleep randomly during the day. She checked their bank account and discovered that he has been spending large amounts of money that he refuses to explain. What is the most likely explanation for this client's behavior?
    a. Psychosocial stress
    b. Alcohol use disorder
    c. Cocaine use disorder
    d. Narcolepsy

11. A social worker is providing therapy to a 10-year-old boy whose parents are going through a divorce. He recently had a doctor's appointment at the suggestion of the school nurse who said the boy was coming to her office several times a week complaining about a sore tummy. The doctor did a full evaluation and determined that the boy is healthy and has no signs of gastrointestinal illness. The boy continues to complain about tummy aches frequently and the social worker has observed that these episodes appear genuinely painful. The social worker does not believe that the boy is faking his symptoms. What is the most likely explanation for the tummy aches?
    a. A medical condition missed by the doctor
    b. Factitious disorder
    c. Hypochondria
    d. Somatization

223

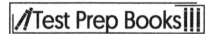

12. A social worker notices that one of her colleagues often seems stressed and tired. Several times, she thinks she smells alcohol on his breath but isn't sure. One day, she sees him drinking at his desk. He is responsible for providing clients with transportation. What is the first thing the social worker should do?
   a. Inform her supervisor about her colleague's drinking.
   b. Report the employee to the police for driving under the influence.
   c. Bring her concerns directly to her colleague and assist him in taking remedial action.
   d. Report her colleague to the state board of social work.

13. What is the most important factor that contributes to beneficial outcomes between a social worker and a client?
   a. A social worker's competence
   b. A positive therapeutic relationship between the social worker and client
   c. The type of therapy used
   d. A client's motivation and engagement in treatment

14. During which stage of the helping process should the social worker discuss the limits of confidentiality and clarify the roles of the social worker and the client?
   a. Engagement
   b. Assessment
   c. Planning
   d. Termination

15. A social worker notices that she feels tense and defensive around one of her clients, and she is not sure why. She talks about this in supervision and realizes that the client reminds her of someone she used to work for and had a difficult relationship with. This is an example of what?
   a. Projection
   b. Transference
   c. Countertransference
   d. Dual relationship

16. A child refuses to do his homework, so his mother takes away his phone as a consequence. What type of operant technique is this?
   a. Positive reinforcement
   b. Positive punishment
   c. Negative reinforcement
   d. Negative punishment

17. The phallic stage of Freud's psychosexual model of development is characterized by all of the following EXCEPT:
   a. The genitals becoming the focus of pleasure and gratification
   b. Oedipus and Electra complexes possibly emerging
   c. Potty training being a source of internal conflict
   d. Experiencing this stage between ages three and six

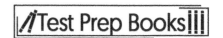

18. Which reinforcement schedule is most effective at producing the desired behavior and least susceptible to extinction?
   a. Continuous
   b. Variable ratio
   c. Fixed ratio
   d. Fixed interval

19. What is an example of a negative punishment technique?
   a. A time-out
   b. A token economy
   c. Spanking
   d. Cancelling chores

20. Social work interviews should always be focused and purposeful. Which of the following is NOT one of the three purposes of a social work interview?
   a. To gather information about a client
   b. To determine a client's level of honesty
   c. To provide or update a client's diagnosis
   d. To provide therapy to a client

21. Dan is seeing a social worker about his depression. They have met for a couple of sessions during which the social worker asked a lot of questions and had Dan complete the Beck Depression Inventory. Together they have come up with goals for Dan, and now they are talking about different ways they could accomplish those goals. The social worker has suggested some evidence-based interventions, and they are determining which one would work best for Dan's situation. Which phase of treatment is Dan in?
   a. Engagement
   b. Evaluation
   c. Planning
   d. Implementation

22. What is the focus of problem-solving approaches, such as brief, solution-focused therapy?
   a. To understand how thoughts, feelings, and behaviors influence each other
   b. To explore unconscious and subconscious motivations and drives
   c. To find practical solutions to current problems
   d. To help clients identify their values and act in accordance with them

23. Encouraging a client to take a more active role in their treatment is likely to result in all the following, EXCEPT:
   a. A more equitable relationship between client and social worker
   b. More positive treatment outcomes
   c. The client feeling empowered
   d. The client feeling overwhelmed

225

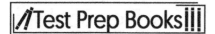

24. A normally developing child will demonstrate all of the following behaviors and abilities by age one EXCEPT:
    a. Having knowledge of at least 50 words
    b. Responding to their name
    c. Smiling socially
    d. Sitting up on their own

25. Which theorist is most known for their work on children's cognitive development?
    a. Erikson
    b. Freud
    c. Skinner
    d. Piaget

26. According to Levinson's theory of adult development, the early adulthood stage, which takes place from roughly age 17 to 45, is characterized by all of the following EXCEPT:
    a. It overlaps with the early adulthood transition and the midlife transition.
    b. It is the time of adult life with the most energy and highest stress.
    c. Many become mentors to younger people during this stage.
    d. Important activities include establishing a family and career.

27. Mary is a 22-year-old woman who has just graduated from college. She states that she feels like a failure for being single. She and her family expected that she would find a husband at school, just like all her friends did. Now, she is living back at her parents' home in a community where everyone her age is starting a family. Her younger sister Tara is already engaged at age 20, and Mary's parents have been making comments about how it will look if Mary is still single by the wedding. Which theory of development best explains Mary's distress?
    a. Neugarten's social clock theory
    b. Erikson's stages of psychosocial development
    c. Freud's theory of psychosexual development
    d. Levinson's seasons of life theory

28. Sarah is a fifteen-year-old high school student who says her parents are making her go to therapy even though she does not want to. What kind of client is Sarah?
    a. Voluntary
    b. Involuntary
    c. Non-voluntary
    d. Mandated

29. What should social workers be aware of when working with involuntary clients?
    a. Goals are set by the court, not the client and social worker.
    b. Motivation is likely to be high due to fear of legal consequences.
    c. Social workers should help clients see that they still have choices.
    d. There is no difference between working with voluntary and involuntary clients.

30. At the beginning of treatment, a social worker and client agreed on a rule that the client would show up for sessions on time. Recently, the client has been showing up later and later. They had a conversation about it and agreed that if the client was more than fifteen minutes late, the session would be cancelled. The client arrives twenty minutes late for the next session but is extremely apologetic, saying that they were stuck in traffic. The social worker does not want to negatively affect the therapeutic relationship. What should the social worker do?
    a. Remind the client of their agreement and cancel the session.
    b. Do not cancel the session because the traffic was out of the client's control.
    c. Warn the client that the next time this happens, the session will be canceled.
    d. Compromise by doing a half session.

31. When would role-play NOT be a helpful technique?
    a. When a supervisor is teaching a social worker a new skill
    b. With older clients, because it will seem childish
    c. When helping a client improve their communication skills
    d. When trying to reduce the impact of a traumatic event through repetition

32. A social worker is working with a client who has great difficulty saying "no" to his boss's requests, even when the requests are unreasonable and result in the client being overwhelmed by extra work. The social worker shows the client a video of a conversation between a boss and an employee in which the boss is pushy, but the employee remains assertive. What type of modeling is this?
    a. Live modeling
    b. Symbolic modeling
    c. Covert modeling
    d. Participant modeling

33. Which of the following statements about intimate partner violence (IPV) is NOT correct?
    a. IPV is almost exclusively seen in heterosexual relationships.
    b. IPV is driven by an abuser's need for power and control.
    c. Leaving an abuser is difficult and may take multiple attempts.
    d. IPV can involve physical, sexual, psychological, and economic abuse.

34. A social worker volunteers to travel to the site of a natural disaster to provide crisis intervention and support to the victims. When he returns home, he notices that he is having difficulties readjusting to his normal routine. He has trouble sleeping, feels anxious and irritable, and has frequent intrusive thoughts about the disaster. What is he most likely experiencing?
    a. Burnout
    b. Compassion fatigue
    c. Vicarious/secondary trauma
    d. Major Depressive Disorder

35. At what age can minors obtain social work services without the permission of a parent or guardian?
    a. Sixteen
    b. Seventeen
    c. Eighteen
    d. Age varies according to state law

36. Which of the following describes the most appropriate way for a social worker to ensure confidentiality of psychotherapy notes?
    a. Take the notes home every day.
    b. Store the notes in a secure location separate from client records.
    c. Do not take notes during psychotherapy sessions.
    d. Use clients' initials or an assigned number rather than their full name.

37. Joanna is working with a social worker to address her alcohol use, which has become a problem. At the moment, total abstinence is not something she feels prepared to try, but she still wants to take steps to improve her health and reduce negative consequences from drinking. What should the social worker do?
    a. Use motivational interviewing to show her why abstinence is necessary.
    b. Suggest inpatient alcohol rehabilitation programs.
    c. Suspend therapy until she achieves abstinence.
    d. Explore harm reduction approaches.

38. Which of the following statements about harm reduction techniques is NOT correct?
    a. They are cost-effective.
    b. They are evidence-based.
    c. They normalize unhealthy behavior.
    d. They meet people where they are.

39. A community that has been hit hard by the opiate overdose crisis is considering implementing harm reduction measures to improve the health and safety of its residents. All the following are evidence-based harm reduction techniques they should consider, EXCEPT:
    a. Opening a needle exchange where drug users can trade in used needles for clean ones
    b. Increasing jail time for people convicted of drug possession
    c. Making suboxone, methadone, and other medication-assisted treatment more available
    d. Providing Narcan and overdose reversal training to community members

40. Teaching coping skills can help clients with anxiety in all the following ways, EXCEPT:
    a. Eliminating the anxiety
    b. Recognizing and managing day-to-day symptoms
    c. Learning deep breathing and relaxation techniques
    d. Replacing unhealthy coping mechanisms

41. When a client presents with co-occurring substance use disorder and mental illness, what should be treated first?
    a. The substance use disorder should be treated first.
    b. The mental illness should be treated first.
    c. Both should be treated at the same time.
    d. It depends on the substance being abused and the mental illness.

42. What is the medical term for problems with understanding, speaking, reading, or writing due to brain injury?
    a. Aphasia
    b. Agnosia
    c. Acalculia
    d. Prosopagnosia

43. All the following statements about dementia are accurate EXCEPT:
    a. It is a cognitive disorder common in elderly people.
    b. It can cause mood changes including irritability and apathy.
    c. It starts suddenly and progresses quickly.
    d. It causes problems with memory.

44. What is the first thing a social worker should do to assist a client with sexual dysfunction?
    a. Ask whether the client has experienced sexual abuse.
    b. Refer the client for a medical evaluation.
    c. Assess the client for depression and anxiety.
    d. Ask about medications, lifestyle, and stress.

45. Which class of medication can cause tardive dyskinesia?
    a. Antidepressants
    b. Mood stabilizers
    c. Antipsychotics
    d. Antianxiety medications

46. A client with bipolar disorder requires regular blood tests to check his kidney and thyroid function as well as his blood levels of a medication. Which medication is this client taking?
    a. Lithium
    b. Lamictal
    c. Seroquel
    d. Wellbutrin

47. Juan is a social worker helping his client Karen, who came to treatment because she frequently has angry outbursts and doesn't understand why. Juan wants Karen to do some homework, including keeping a log of when the outbursts occur, what was happening, how she was feeling, and what she was thinking. Karen is reluctant because she says she wants to stop having outbursts and doesn't want to write about them. How can Juan explain that self-monitoring would be beneficial to her treatment?
    a. Keeping the log will increase her discipline and make her feel empowered.
    b. Doing homework is required for her treatment plan.
    c. Writing about the outbursts will cause them to happen less frequently.
    d. It will clarify what causes the outbursts and what can be done to reduce them.

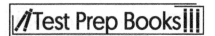
48. A social worker is acting as a mediator in a family conflict. She wants to bring attention to how the way the family communicates might contribute to the conflict. She asks them to talk about how they communicate with and react to each other both verbally and nonverbally. What is the term for this type of communicating about communication?
    a.   Metacommunication
    b.   Empathic communication
    c.   Miscommunication
    d.   Structured communication

49. When a social worker acts as a conflict mediator, what is their goal?
    a.   Listen to all parties in the conflict without suggesting solutions.
    b.   Determine who is right and who is wrong.
    c.   Suggest solutions that will benefit all parties.
    d.   Teach strategies to live with the conflict rather than resolve it.

50. When a client is in crisis, what is the first thing a social worker should do?
    a.   Teach them coping skills.
    b.   Determine what caused the crisis.
    c.   Ensure their safety.
    d.   Mobilize their social supports.

51. Which type of drug is Effexor?
    a.   SSRI
    b.   Benzodiazepine
    c.   Stimulant
    d.   SNRI

52. Which of the following drugs has the highest potential for abuse?
    a.   Abilify
    b.   Ativan
    c.   Celexa
    d.   Geodon

53. In an initial meeting with a social worker, Mr. M states that he has been taking Prozac for ten years for depression. He explains that he has tried to stop taking the medication, but always begins taking it again after a couple of days because he feels so terrible. Why is Mr. M experiencing adverse effects when he stops taking Prozac?
    a.   Stopping the antidepressant is causing his depression symptoms to return.
    b.   He is addicted to Prozac and experiencing withdrawal symptoms.
    c.   He is dependent on Prozac and experiencing discontinuation symptoms.
    d.   He is psychologically dependent on Prozac and experiencing psychosomatic symptoms.

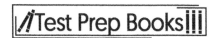

54. A social worker is treating a client named Sarah who has just been prescribed a monoamine oxidase inhibitor (MAOI) for depression. Sarah wants to make sure that she understands how to take the medication safely. What is the most important thing for the social worker to discuss with Sarah?
    a. Dietary restrictions
    b. Physical activity
    c. Timing of doses
    d. Tardive dyskinesia

55. All the following are important steps in problem formulation EXCEPT:
    a. Defining the problem in specific terms
    b. Determining when the problem started
    c. Determining what the client did to cause the problem
    d. Determining how serious the problem is

56. All of the following must be documented in client records EXCEPT:
    a. Detailed accounts of all conversations with clients, whether they are relevant to treatment or not
    b. Goals for treatment, written as SMART goals and periodically reviewed and updated
    c. All assessments conducted with the date, result, and rationale for the assessment included
    d. Records of consultations with supervisors or other professionals, including the date, result, and rationale of the consultation

57. A social worker realizes that one of her clients makes her feel very uncomfortable, but she can't pinpoint why. What should she do first?
    a. Discuss the feelings with a trusted colleague.
    b. Transfer the client to another social worker.
    c. Obtain supervision to discuss the feelings.
    d. Ignore the feelings and maintain professionalism.

58. Accepting a gift from a client is a common ethical dilemma in social work. Which core values of social work are in conflict in this case?
    a. Service vs. social justice
    b. Self-determination vs. competence
    c. Importance of human relationships vs. competence
    d. Importance of human relationships vs. integrity

59. What is an advanced directive?
    a. Any verbal or written statement a client makes about what types of care they wish to receive when dying
    b. A legal document that includes directions about the care a client wishes to receive when dying
    c. Another name for a Do Not Resuscitate (DNR) order
    d. A document written by a physician regarding which types of care are appropriate for a dying client

60. A woman tells a social worker that she is concerned about her sixteen-year-old son. She states that his interests are totally unstable, and she worries that he might have a personality disorder. A couple of months into the school year, he started dressing in all black, wearing eyeliner, and hanging around with a new group of friends. Then, six months later, he decided to join the soccer team, started wearing preppy clothes, and even started using different slang. Lately, all he wants to do is hang out with his teammates, frequently missing family dinners because he is with his friends. On one or two occasions, she thought she smelled beer on his breath, but she wasn't sure. What should the social worker do?

    a. Suggest that the son come in for a personality disorder assessment.
    b. Suggest that the son see a drug and alcohol counselor.
    c. Make a report to child protective services because the son shows signs of being abused.
    d. Provide reassurance and psychoeducation about adolescent development.

61. Which of the following is NOT an effective way for parents to support their children's social development?

    a. Modeling positive social interactions by treating other people with respect
    b. Encouraging empathy by helping children consider others' perspectives
    c. Showing unconditional support by taking the child's side in social conflicts
    d. Speaking openly about values and listening to the child's opinion

62. A social worker is telling her supervisor about a recent play therapy session with a four-year-old boy. During the session, the boy announced, "I have a pee pee," pulled down his pants, and pointed to his genitals. He then stated, "Daddy does too, but you don't because you're a girl." The social worker is concerned that the boy's behavior might be a sign of sexual abuse. What should the supervisor tell her?

    a. She should make a report to child protective services with the information she has.
    b. She should tell the mother that the father might be abusing the boy.
    c. She should assess the child for developmental delay, as four is too old for this behavior.
    d. She should not worry because the boy is displaying typical behavior for a four-year-old.

63. A licensed clinical social worker is at home supervising a play date between his six-year-old daughter and Amanda, another six-year-old girl who has just moved to town. Amanda picks up two dolls and simulates oral sex. The social worker asks what she is doing, and she replies with a sexually explicit description of the activity. Amanda then asks the social worker if he wants to engage in the activity with her. Should the social worker make a report to child protective services?

    a. No, because the incident happened at home and not in the course of practicing social work.
    b. Yes, because the child displayed signs that indicate sexual abuse.
    c. No, because it is normal for children this age to be curious about sex.
    d. Yes, but only after trying and failing to resolve the issue with Amanda's parents.

64. Which of the following is NOT an appropriate intervention for intimate partner violence?

    a. Safety planning
    b. Batterer intervention programs
    c. Couples counseling
    d. Individual counseling

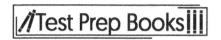

65. All of the following are important reasons for social workers to engage in self-care EXCEPT:
    a. To reduce the risk of burnout and compassion fatigue
    b. To maintain work/life balance
    c. To maintain well-being
    d. To reduce the need for supervision

66. All of the following are things that social workers can do to increase transparency in the social worker-client relationship EXCEPT:
    a. Clarify the roles of the social worker and client.
    b. Clarify the process and purpose of treatment.
    c. Create balance by sharing personal information with the client.
    d. Give clients choices and decision-making power wherever possible.

67. A social worker attends a conference about art therapy and decides it would be a good addition to the services she offers in her private practice. She attends a training course and receives a certificate of completion. She then updates her website to reflect that she is now an art therapy practitioner. Is this ethical?
    a. Yes, because she attended a conference and completed a training course.
    b. Yes, because the training course provided a certificate of completion.
    c. No, because art therapy practitioners must complete an internship after training.
    d. No, because she didn't consult with a supervisor/consultant with art therapy experience.

68. According to Freud, what type of problem will be experienced in adulthood by a child whose parents are too strict about toilet training?
    a. Binge eating disorder
    b. Disorganization and messiness
    c. Excessive cigarette smoking
    d. Rigid and obsessive thinking

69. Carol Gilligan created an adaptation of Lawrence Kohlberg's theory of moral development based on her research of women's moral development. What was the main change she made to Kohlberg's original theory?
    a. Women view morality more in terms of relationships than men do.
    b. Women go through the same stages in a different order than men.
    c. Women achieve a higher level of moral development than men.
    d. Women go through additional stages that men do not.

70. What progression do almost all theories of spiritual development have in common?
    a. Persecution to salvation
    b. Egocentrism to universalism
    c. Resistance to obedience
    d. Atheism to theism

233

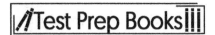

71. A social worker has a client who is a young, black male living in a mostly white, suburban community. Growing up, the young man behaved like the white children around him. After a series of racist incidents, he has become more aware of race and more interested in exploring his black identity. Lately, he has pulled away from his white friends stating that they are "nothing but hillbillies and racists." He started wearing traditional African clothing and threw out all his books and music produced by white people, stating that black culture is superior. According to Atkinson, Morten, and Sue's theory of racial and cultural identity development, which stage is the young man currently experiencing?
   a. Dissonance
   b. Conformity
   c. Resistance and immersion
   d. Synergistic articulation and awareness

72. Jim is a 42-year-old man who is married with two young children. Three weeks ago, he survived a house fire. He had to run through flames to get out, resulting in minor burns but no other injuries. Since then, he has been having difficulty concentrating and making decisions. He has been tearful, feeling down, and not finding enjoyment in his hobbies. Sometimes he feels strange, like he's not quite in his body and he's living in a dream or a videogame. All these symptoms started three weeks ago. What would be best diagnosis for Jim at this point?
   a. Major depressive disorder
   b. ADHD
   c. PTSD
   d. Acute stress disorder

73. Which of the following risk factors is the strongest predictor of a suicide attempt?
   a. Substance use
   b. Previous suicide attempt
   c. Social isolation
   d. Diagnosis of depression

74. Which of the following is NOT a warning sign that may indicate a depressed client is at risk of attempting suicide?
   a. Requesting more frequent therapy appointments
   b. Sudden and marked increase in mood
   c. Giving away possessions
   d. Threatening to attempt suicide

75. What subgroup of personality disorders is referred to as "odd and eccentric?"
   a. Cluster A
   b. Cluster B
   c. Cluster C
   d. Cluster D

76. A middle-aged male client frequently gets angry, yells at his wife, then feels regretful afterwards. All the following are anger management techniques that might help this client, EXCEPT:
   a. Counting to ten before responding
   b. Leaving the situation momentarily to calm down
   c. Recognizing that anger is not a useful emotion
   d. Deep breathing exercises

234

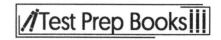

77. A client just received a major promotion at work. She is also getting married next month and preparing to welcome her first child several months after that. Which type of technique would be most helpful for the client at this moment?
    a. Harm reduction techniques
    b. Stress management techniques
    c. Limit-setting techniques
    d. Anger management techniques

78. A social worker is helping a client who is experiencing a lot of stress at work. The social worker asks the client about specific triggers, and together they identify the following sources of stress: the client is not sure if their boss is happy with their work, the client has trouble managing their time, and the client is worried that one of their coworkers might get a promotion instead of them. What is the next thing the social worker should do to help the client manage their stress?
    a. Teach the client deep breathing techniques.
    b. Ask the client what evidence they have that their coworker will be promoted.
    c. Reassure the client that everyone gets stressed at work.
    d. Help the client identify which parts of the situation they can control.

79. Monica is a young woman who was born in the United States to Mexican parents. She has friends from several different Latin American backgrounds. She considers herself Chicana, and her ethnicity is an important part of her life. According to Ferdman and Gallegos's model of Latino identity development, which lens or orientation best describes Monica's relationship to her ethnic identity?
    a. Undifferentiated
    b. Subgroup identified
    c. White identified
    d. Latino identified

80. The disability rights movement challenged prevailing ideas about disabilities and the people who live with them. According to the disability rights perspective, what is disability?
    a. A permanent deficit caused by a medical condition
    b. A gift that confers superior abilities
    c. A consequence of the breakdown of the nuclear family
    d. A barrier caused by an intolerant and unaccommodating society

81. A social worker meets with a new client who has multiple issues. The man is homeless and living on the street. He has a substance use disorder and a psychotic disorder, neither of which are currently being treated. He is also estranged from his adult son and wants to reconnect. What resource should the social worker connect the client with first?
    a. Housing
    b. Addiction counseling
    c. Psychiatric treatment
    d. Family counseling

82. A social worker is meeting with a new client who states that her main goal is to expand her social circle, with a secondary goal being to work toward a promotion at work. During the assessment, the client reveals that she has diabetes, but her blood sugar is not well-managed because she cannot afford her insulin. The social worker tells her that they need to get her medically stabilized before they can work on her other goals. The client is unhappy with this, saying that she came to treatment to work on her social and professional issues, not her medical condition. How should the social worker respond?
   a. Agree to work on the professional goals first because a promotion and increase in pay will make insulin affordable.
   b. Transfer the client to another therapist who will be comfortable with her priorities.
   c. Tell her that according to Maslow's hierarchy, her priorities are incorrect.
   d. Explain how managing the diabetes will facilitate her other goals and vice versa.

83. A man reluctantly goes to see a social worker after his wife tells him she is going to divorce him if he won't consider therapy. The man walks in and demands to know what the social worker's qualifications are. He expresses doubt that she could possibly understand him given his "genius IQ," but says it doesn't really matter since he's just trying to get his wife off his back. He says his wife is the one who should be in therapy, since she consistently fails to cook, clean, and maintain the home to his standards. He goes on to talk about how powerful and successful he is and how the only real problem in his life is that people constantly envy him. What diagnosis should the social worker consider for this client?
   a. Delusional disorder
   b. Antisocial personality disorder
   c. Narcissistic personality disorder
   d. Abusive personality disorder

84. What is pica?
   a. The compulsion to pull out one's hair
   b. A communication disorder also called "stuttering"
   c. A symptom of psychotic disorders also called "word salad"
   d. The consumption of non-food items like chalk, paint, or ash

85. Harmful use of substances; cutting, burning, or scratching oneself; hitting one's head against a wall; and not following medical advice are all examples of what type of behavior?
   a. Abusive behavior
   b. Self-injurious behavior
   c. Depressed behavior
   d. Violent behavior

86. Mr. C has been smoking cigarettes for twenty years. A friend recently told Mr. C that she quit and is feeling better. Since then, he has been wondering if he should quit too, or at least reduce the amount he smokes. He knows that smoking isn't healthy but can't imagine giving it up. He is considering talking to his friend again and asking her why and how she decided to stop. What stage of change is Mr. C in?
   a. Pre-contemplation
   b. Action
   c. Maintenance
   d. Contemplation

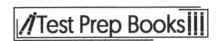

87. Which of the following is NOT a social work role related to death and dying?
    a. Helping clients come to terms with a terminal diagnosis
    b. Educating clients about advanced directives and other options related to end-of-life care
    c. Encouraging a client to consider hospice care once their diagnosis becomes terminal
    d. Providing compassionate support and respect to the client and the client's family

88. All the following are ways that organizations and social workers can increase social worker safety EXCEPT:
    a. Having a procedure in place to report unsafe clients or settings without fear of reprisal
    b. Identifying other professionals who could assist the social worker in an emergency
    c. Using the same safety procedures in every practice setting
    d. Limiting the amount of personal information about a social worker that is available online

89. A social worker in private practice meets with a new client and learns that he has a very different worldview than she does. The client makes several statements about his beliefs that leave the social worker feeling uncomfortable. She is concerned that empathizing with the client would involve compromising her own values. What should the social worker do first to address this?
    a. Reflect on her personal values and determine if she can put them aside to remain professionally objective.
    b. Consult with a trusted friend for advice on how to work with the client without compromising her own values.
    c. Refer the client to another social worker whose values are more like the client's and who could therefore provide better care.
    d. Update her intake procedure to screen out clients with certain values to avoid this conflict happening in the future.

90. Social workers sometimes collaborate with other types of professionals on interdisciplinary teams. In these situations, it is helpful for the team to create a written agreement about how the group will function. This document serves all the following purposes EXCEPT:
    a. Clarifying the roles of each professional and how they will participate in the group
    b. Clarifying the professional values and perspectives of each team member
    c. Determining which profession's code of ethics is most relevant to the client's needs
    d. Agreeing on a decision-making process, including how conflicts will be handled

91. Out-of-home displacement can be traumatic. All the following factors increase the likelihood of trauma in this situation EXCEPT:
    a. Being older at the time of displacement
    b. Being displaced by a traumatic event, such as war
    c. Being separated from friends and family
    d. Having to move multiple times

92. Which psychotherapy modality is most effective for clients with borderline personality disorder?
    a. Psychodynamic therapy
    b. Dialectical behavior therapy
    c. Exposure and response prevention therapy
    d. Cognitive behavioral therapy

93. A young man who recently graduated from college and moved home to his parents' house is seeking treatment from a social worker to address his anxieties about starting his career. During the conversation, the social worker notices that the client views his situation in "all-or-nothing" terms, fixates on minor details, and tends to catastrophize. What type of treatment would be most helpful for this client?

    a. Eye Movement Desensitization and Reprocessing (EMDR)
    b. Psychodynamic therapy
    c. Cognitive behavioral therapy
    d. Family therapy

94. Which type of psychotherapy is based on the work of Sigmund Freud?

    a. Psychodynamic therapy
    b. Emotion-focused therapy (EFT)
    c. Structural family therapy
    d. Cognitive behavioral therapy

95. According to Maslow's hierarchy of human needs, all of the following statements about self-actualization are accurate EXCEPT:

    a. It is an ongoing process.
    b. It is the highest level of the original pyramid model.
    c. Most people reach it by middle adulthood.
    d. It involves developing one's full potential.

96. What is Mary Ainsworth's Strange Situation Protocol used to assess?

    a. Social anxiety in adolescents
    b. Cognitive development in toddlers
    c. Resilience in adults
    d. Attachment in infants

97. What is an example of an invisible disability?

    a. Down's syndrome
    b. Tourette's syndrome
    c. Chronic fatigue syndrome
    d. Paraplegia

98. A young man is seeing a social worker for relationship problems. The man states that he is constantly afraid that his girlfriend is going to leave him despite no evidence that this is the case. He fears that she does not feel as strongly for him as he does for her. He doesn't want to be clingy and demanding, but he can't help himself and frequently seeks reassurance that she still wants to be with him. What type of attachment style does the young man's attitude and behavior suggest?

    a. Secure
    b. Anxious
    c. Avoidant
    d. Disorganized

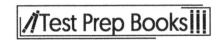

99. A client expresses that he does not understand why he engages in a particular behavior. The behavior goes against his moral values, makes him uncomfortable, and causes shame and guilt. According to psychoanalytic theory, which term describes the client's behavior?
    a. Preconscious
    b. Unconscious
    c. Ego-syntonic
    d. Ego-dystonic

100. According to cognitive behavioral approaches, what causes negative feelings and problematic behaviors?
    a. Chemical imbalances in the brain
    b. Thoughts, assumptions, and beliefs
    c. Unprocessed trauma
    d. Early childhood experiences

101. A social worker has a client who is trying to develop healthy habits. Every time the client engages in a healthy habit, the social worker gives him a token as a reward. What type of intervention is this?
    a. Behavioral
    b. Psychoanalytic
    c. Empowerment
    d. Cognitive

102. Cognitive behavioral therapy often uses homework to practice the self-monitoring skills taught in sessions. A common homework assignment is keeping a thought log. Which of the following is NOT a component of a thought log?
    a. Negative feelings and emotional states that arise
    b. Times in the past when the client felt the negative feelings
    c. Thoughts that accompany the negative feelings
    d. Behaviors that accompany the negative feelings

103. Mary is a 52-year-old woman whose husband is 63. She tells a social worker that she has become increasingly frustrated with her husband because, since he turned 60, "he has been using his age as an excuse." She gives the following example: she asked him to go pick something up at the grocery store that they needed urgently. The store did not have the exact brand and product she requested, so her husband came home. She asked him why he didn't buy a similar item, ask a store associate for help, go to another store location, or even just call her to ask what she would like him to do. He said he got confused at the store and couldn't think of any of those things. The woman states that he still gets all the television trivia questions right, so obviously he is mentally fine and just doing things like this to annoy her. What is the most likely explanation for husband's change in behavior?
    a. He is developing dementia and possibly Alzheimer's disease.
    b. He is showing signs of an acute injury, possibly a stroke.
    c. He is gaslighting her to maintain power and control.
    d. He is showing signs of normal age-related cognitive decline.

104. How do people's relationships tend to change in old age?
    a. Their social circle expands.
    b. Their relationships become more superficial.
    c. They have more positive interactions within their social circle.
    d. Family relationships become less important.

105. A client states that he is open to romantic and sexual relationships with people of all genders. Which word best describes his sexual orientation?
    a. Pansexual
    b. Bisexual
    c. Transgender
    d. Asexual

106. A woman is concerned about her teenage child, who was assigned female at birth and recently came out as transgender. Her child has begun dating a female classmate; the mother is confused and frustrated, telling the social worker, "I don't understand why he had to transition to date a girl when he could have just stayed a girl and been a lesbian." What should the social worker tell the mother?
    a. It is common for teenagers to go through phases like this, and she should be patient.
    b. Internalized homophobia is making the son think he needs to change his gender to date the girl.
    c. The son is probably feeling neglected and acting out for attention.
    d. The mother is confusing gender identity and sexuality; they are unrelated.

107. Rachel and Sarah have both contracted with the same outside supervisor for individual supervision. After one of Sarah's supervision sessions, she pulls Rachel aside to ask her for advice. She admits that she has a "big crush" on the supervisor and it's making it hard to participate fully. What advice should Rachel give to Sarah?
    a. These feelings are totally normal, and they will probably pass. You should stay aware of your feelings, but don't act on them.
    b. You should terminate supervision so you can think through these feelings without the pressure of a professional relationship.
    c. You should keep doing supervision with him and try to determine whether these feelings are real and if they are mutual.
    d. You should talk to your supervisor about these feelings. It could give insight into patterns in your personal and professional relationships.

108. Josh is hired as a manager in a large social work agency. The agency recently received negative feedback from clients and employees regarding safety. He is assigned to review the agency's policies and flag anything that could be contributing to the problem. Which of the following policies should he flag as most likely to create an unsafe environment?
    a. If a client needs to meet with a social worker after normal business hours, the social worker must arrange for at least one other person to be in the office.
    b. There is a "three strikes, and you're out" rule regarding client outbursts; services will be terminated after three incidents of yelling, violence, or abusive behavior.
    c. Social workers may only communicate with clients during business hours via work phone or email. Using social media or other personal channels is not allowed.
    d. Group supervision is provided for free by the agency. If an employee wants individual supervision, the agency can provide recommendations but not funding.

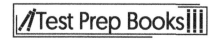

109. The *NASW Code of Ethics* recommends that social workers practice self-care. Neglecting self-care can result in a variety of personal and professional problems. Which of the following is NOT an example of practicing good self-care?
    a. Having clear boundaries that separate a social worker's personal and professional lives
    b. Creating healthy routines involving meditation, nutrition, and regular exercise
    c. Venting to a loved one or trusted friend about clients that are particularly challenging
    d. Recognizing warning signs of burnout and using supervision to address them

110. Sandra is a social worker who has worked for 10 years at an agency serving survivors of domestic violence. In this time, her workload has been steadily increasing, but her pay and benefits have remained the same. She has had four different managers in the past two years. Increasingly, over the past year, she has been dreading going into work. Her anxiety has been getting worse and causes trouble sleeping. She often has nightmares about things her clients have gone through. She stopped dating and reduced her socializing some time ago because she has started to feel fearful and panicky around men. She used to find it easy to empathize with her clients, but lately she feels frustrated and bombarded by their suffering. What is the most likely explanation for Sandra's feelings?
    a. Compassion fatigue
    b. Burnout
    c. Stress
    d. Secondary trauma

111. A social worker is conducting group therapy with women who struggle with alcohol misuse. One woman says that it seems like the local addiction treatment center was made for men, and the rest of the group agrees. The social worker helps them identify the specific ways that the treatment center is not meeting their needs as women. The social worker reminds them of previous group discussions about the unique strengths and abilities they have as women, and together they discuss how they wish the treatment center would acknowledge and build on these strengths. The group decides to work together to advocate for the creation of more inclusive treatment services and asks the social worker for help finding resources to support their efforts. What type of approach is the social worker using?
    a. Harm reduction
    b. Crisis intervention
    c. Empowerment
    d. Behavioral

112. Which of the following statements about client contracts is NOT correct?
    a. They can be modified over the course of treatment.
    b. They contain information about timing, attendance, and cancellation of treatment sessions.
    c. They function as a legal document.
    d. They include client goals.

113. A client has a long list of goals they want to work on. The social worker is using partializing techniques to help the client decide which ones to pursue first. Which theoretical construct would be most helpful in this situation?
    a. Maslow's hierarchy of needs
    b. Erikson's stages of psychosocial development
    c. Freud's stages of psychosexual development
    d. Systems theory

241

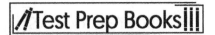

114. What does the term *partialization* mean in social work practice?
    a. Combining aspects of different treatment modalities
    b. Breaking complex problems into more manageable parts
    c. Clarifying the responsibilities of the client and social worker
    d. Asking a client to play the part of another person

115. What is a technique used in assertiveness training?
    a. Not taking no for an answer
    b. Using "you" statements
    c. Indirect communication
    d. Using "I" statements

116. In the stages of change model, what is considered an "unofficial" stage that is often but not always a part of the change process?
    a. Relapse
    b. Rehabilitation
    c. Self-actualization
    d. Preparation

117. A social worker asks a client to imagine that they wake up tomorrow and their problem has magically disappeared. The social worker asks what would be different, how they would know things had gotten better, and what they would do. What type of question is this?
    a. Scaling question
    b. Seeking exceptions question
    c. Miracle question
    d. Clarification question

118. Alexa is a young woman receiving treatment from a social worker for anxiety. Alexa is hopeful that she can get better and knows that changing some of her behaviors is in her best interest. She acknowledges being nervous about change but has consistently been willing to take small steps in the right direction. She sometimes comes to her weekly sessions five minutes late due to her school schedule, but she participates fully and does not miss sessions. Based on this information, what are Alexa's levels of motivation and resistance?
    a. High motivation/high resistance
    b. Low motivation/low resistance
    c. Low motivation/high resistance
    d. High motivation/low resistance

119. Which of the following is NOT an indication of a client's resistance to change?
    a. Minimizing the problem
    b. High self-confidence
    c. Skipping therapy
    d. Refusal to try new behaviors

120. A social worker asks a client about how he has reacted to problems in the past and what he tends to do when problems arise. What is the social worker assessing?
    a. Coping skills
    b. Communication skills
    c. Motivation
    d. Resistance

121. When Liam was born, the doctor said, "It's a boy!" Throughout his life, Liam identifies as a man and uses he/his pronouns. Which term best describes Liam?
    a. Transgender
    b. Cisgender
    c. Normal
    d. Non-binary

122. Which of the following is NOT a problem commonly associated with poor body image?
    a. Eating disorders
    b. Psychotic disorders
    c. Social isolation
    d. Emotional distress

123. Which statement is most accurate about self-esteem throughout the lifetime?
    a. Self-esteem rises steadily from childhood to old age.
    b. Adolescents are the age group with the highest self-esteem.
    c. Self-esteem falls steadily until late middle age then rises until death.
    d. Self-esteem falls in adolescence, rises in adulthood then declines in old age.

124. All of the following are age-related changes that put older adults at an increased risk of depression EXCEPT:
    a. Relationships becoming more superficial
    b. Declining physical health
    c. Losing professional roles
    d. Reduced community participation

125. Research on spirituality has demonstrated all of the following EXCEPT:
    a. People who embrace spirituality live longer.
    b. People who embrace spirituality are happier.
    c. Spirituality without religion is not as beneficial.
    d. Spirituality provides benefits through hope, connection, and healing.

126. Social workers are increasingly expected to use evidence-based practice methods. Evidence-based practice integrates all of the following information sources to inform treatment decisions EXCEPT:
    a. Client characteristics, culture, and preferences
    b. Scientific research evidence
    c. Knowledge and experience of the clinician
    d. Traditional use of potential interventions

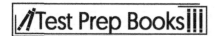

127. A social worker is conducting research to determine the effectiveness of a new tool for measuring symptoms of depression. The tool asks a series of questions and assigns each participant a number from 0 to 10, with 10 indicating the highest level of depression and 0 indicating no evidence of depression. The tool is used multiple times for each participant and produces consistent results; however, the results do not accurately reflect each participant's depressive symptoms. What can be said about this tool?
   a. It lacks reliability.
   b. It lacks validity.
   c. It has internal validity but not external validity.
   d. It has external validity but not internal validity.

128. A research study is designed to evaluate the impact of a new homework policy on the GPA of high school juniors in a bilingual charter school. What is the dependent variable in this study?
   a. Homework policy
   b. GPA
   c. High school juniors
   d. Bilingual charter school

129. A licensed clinical social worker in private practice is considering restructuring her fees to include a sliding scale based on income. She also plans to reserve a few hours a week to provide treatment pro bono (free of charge) to clients who would otherwise be unable to pay for services. Would this fee structure be ethical?
   a. The sliding scale would be ethical, but pro bono services would be unethical.
   b. Pro bono services would be ethical, but the sliding scale would be unethical.
   c. Both the sliding scale and pro bono services would be ethical.
   d. Neither the sliding scale nor pro bono services would be ethical.

130. The *NASW Code of Ethics* provides specific guidance on social workers' responsibilities to several types of people. According to the *NASW Code of Ethics*, social workers have professional ethical responsibilities to all the following people and groups EXCEPT:
   a. The broader society
   b. Social workers' clients
   c. Social workers' families
   d. Social workers' colleagues

131. A social worker is creating a new website to promote her private practice. She has identified several current clients who she believes could provide testimonials endorsing her services. She plans to discuss the risks and benefits of providing a testimonial with each client, answer any questions they have, and ask them to sign a written permission form if they agree to provide a testimonial. She will make it clear to each client that choosing not to provide a testimonial will not negatively impact their past, current, or future access to her services. Is her behavior ethical?
   a. It is ethical because she is providing full informed consent.
   b. It is unethical because she is not giving all her clients an equal chance to participate.
   c. It is ethical because testimonials allow potential clients to make more informed choices.
   d. It is unethical because asking current clients for testimonials is never ethical.

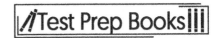

132. Which of the following is an indication that a client has an avoidant coping style?
    a. Laughing about their problems
    b. Relying on others to manage their problems
    c. Getting upset and lashing out
    d. Using drugs or alcohol to feel better

133. When determining which level of care is needed for a client, a social worker should look for an option that ensures the client's health and safety, and is also:
    a. The option with the most robust services
    b. The least expensive option
    c. The highest level of care available
    d. The least restrictive environment

134. A client disagrees with his diagnosis of schizophrenia. He states that he does not experience hallucinations or delusion. He is frustrated that the police sent him to a social worker instead of investigating his report of harassment. He explains to the social worker that his problem is not schizophrenia. Rather, his problem is that Genghis Khan has been reincarnated into the form of the local news anchor and sends him threatening messages through the TV. What is this client most likely experiencing?
    a. Anosognosia
    b. Synesthesia
    c. Prosopagnosia
    d. Denial

135. In the trauma-informed care framework, what are the three "E's" of trauma?
    a. Engagement, education, empowerment
    b. Event, experience, effects
    c. Empathy, emotions, esteem
    d. Ethical, evidence-based, effective

136. Social workers often use the SOAP format to document client interactions. What does the "P" in the acronym stand for?
    a. Psychological
    b. Presenting problem
    c. Plan
    d. Physical

137. What is the relationship between gender and self-esteem?
    a. Men tend to have higher self-esteem than women during middle adulthood.
    b. Women tend have higher self-esteem than men during adolescence.
    c. Gender does not affect self-esteem.
    d. Women tend have higher self-esteem than men throughout the lifespan.

138. Which of the following alterations in self-image is NOT associated with trauma?
    a. Feeling like a bad person
    b. Developing gender dysphoria
    c. Feeling like the world is unsafe
    d. Having difficulty trusting others

245

139. Phil tells a social worker that he is worried about behavior changes in his 68-year-old mother. She started dieting and exercising as a New Year's resolution and lost a lot of weight. At weekly family dinners, she would not partake in the meal, instead bringing an apple cut into tiny pieces for herself. Recently, she stopped attending entirely and has been withdrawing from friends as well. Phil convinced her to get a medical check-up. She was healthy with normal blood tests, although the doctor did tell her she should not lose any more weight. Phil thinks his mother might still be losing weight, but he is not sure because she has been wearing baggy sweatsuits instead of her usual stylish clothes. He is worried that the doctor missed something serious. What should the social worker recommend?

    a. A second opinion from a medical doctor
    b. An assessment for age-related cognitive decline
    c. An assessment for bipolar disorder
    d. An assessment for anorexia nervosa

140. A client tells a social worker that, growing up, his father was "like a drill sergeant." The father made the rules, and the children obeyed without question. He insisted on respect, hard work, and discipline. Punishments were frequent. Reflecting on his upbringing, the client states that it made him excel, but he never learned to be happy. What parenting style did the client experience from his father?

    a. Permissive
    b. Authoritarian
    c. Authoritative
    d. Uninvolved

141. In which of the following situations can a social worker disclose a client's confidential information to a third party without the client's written permission?

    a. When the social worker is seeking reimbursement from the client's insurance company
    b. When the social worker is consulting with an expert about the client
    c. When the parents of a minor client request access to their child's records
    d. When the social worker is updating an interdisciplinary team about the client's progress

142. A licensed clinical social worker is qualified for all the following activities EXCEPT:

    a. Prescribing medication
    b. Opening a private practice
    c. Diagnosing mental illness
    d. Providing psychotherapy

143. A social worker in private practice recently published a book about motorcycle repair. She updates the "qualifications" section of her practice's website to reflect that she is a published author. She does not include a link to the book or suggest that her clients purchase it. Is this ethical?

    a. Yes, because she is not encouraging her clients to purchase the book.
    b. No, because her clients could feel pressured to buy the book.
    c. Yes, because it provides potential clients with more information about her.
    d. No, because the book is not related to her qualifications as a social worker.

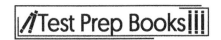

144. Ellen is a social worker who treats clients with trauma histories. She has noticed that many of her clients benefit from therapeutic massage, and she has identified a local massage therapist named Julie with extensive training in trauma-informed care. All of the clients Ellen has referred to Julie have had positive experiences, and many have suggested Julie to other people in their social networks. One day, Julie emails Ellen to thank her for all the business she has been sending her way. Included in the email is a coupon for a free massage. Ellen has back problems that occasionally make it difficult to sit through sessions with her clients. Her doctor strongly suggested massage, but Ellen has been unable to afford it. Is it ethical for Ellen to book the free massage?

    a. Yes, because it was recommended by her doctor, and it would improve her ability to sit with her clients.

    b. Yes, because it was offered as a thank you for past referrals, not an incentive to make more referrals.

    c. No, because giving or receiving money or services in exchange for referrals is a conflict of interest, which is unethical.

    d. No, because getting a massage from the same person as her clients would be a dual relationship, which is unethical.

145. A client has a specific problem they want to work on. The client's insurance will pay for twelve sessions with a social worker. Which type of treatment would NOT be suitable for this client?

    a. Task centered

    b. Psychoanalytic

    c. Cognitive behavioral

    d. Brief, solution focused

146. Insurance companies often show a preference for cognitive behavioral therapy (CBT) over other types of interventions for all the following reasons EXCEPT:

    a. CBT is the most researched psychotherapy.

    b. CBT is effective for a wide range of problems.

    c. CBT is effective for all clients.

    d. CBT is time limited.

147. A social worker is running a psychoeducation group for men with substance use disorders. During the first meeting, one of the participants states, "everyone knows junkies can't be trusted." How should the social worker respond?

    a. Discuss stigmatizing language and provide alternative vocabulary.

    b. Ask the participant why he believes this to be true.

    c. Pull the participant aside and explain that the word "junkie" is offensive.

    d. Do not react and see how the rest of the group responds.

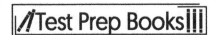
148. Andre is a social worker who recently started work at a large agency with a much higher volume of clients than his previous job. His caseload always includes at least 25 clients and sometimes as many as 50. In the beginning, he was struggling to remember details about his clients and felt that this was negatively affecting his ability to build rapport. He started jotting down little personal details in each client's records that he could refer to before each meeting. He noted things like favorite foods, religious beliefs, friends' and relatives' names, jokes made by clients, and unusual things about each client's appearance to help him remember who they are as people, not just where they are in the treatment process. Andre explains this new system during supervision. How should his supervisor respond?
   a. Clarify the ethical standards for documentation and help him find a new way to remember clients.
   b. Congratulate him on using good problem-solving skills to overcome his difficulties.
   c. Ask to see his client records to ensure these personal details are being documented appropriately.
   d. Suggest other strategies he could try in addition to the personal notes to help remember clients.

149. Which of the following is NOT one of the core values of the social work profession?
   a. Service
   b. Competence
   c. Confidentiality
   d. Social justice

150. According to the *NASW Code of Ethics,* one of the core values of social work is "the importance of human relationships." All the following are ways social workers can uphold this value EXCEPT:
   a. Helping clients improve their communication with loved ones
   b. Advocating for parental leave policies at their agencies
   c. Building rapport and a strong therapeutic alliance with clients
   d. Becoming the support system for clients who do not have one

151. A social worker is trying to decide whether to use self-disclosure with one of her clients. She and the client are both single mothers and she thinks disclosing this might help her client feel less alone. She has considered the potential benefits and harms to the client, but she is still not sure what to do. What should she do next?
   a. Test the waters by making a small self-disclosure and see how the client reacts.
   b. Ask the client if it would be helpful to hear about the social worker's experience.
   c. Err on the side of caution and do not make the disclosure.
   d. Obtain supervision to determine if the disclosure is professionally justified.

152. Which of the following pieces of information about a client is an example of subjective data?
   a. The client's mother died six months ago.
   b. The client is 43 years old.
   c. The client reports feeling sad and lethargic.
   d. The client scored 21 on the Beck Depression Inventory.

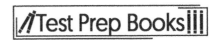
153. A social worker is evaluating Mr. X, a 48-year-old white, male client whose physician referred him after a recent check-up found no medical basis for his symptoms. Mr. X reports that his wife died unexpectedly six weeks ago. Initially, he was sad and preoccupied with thoughts about her, but he was coping with the support of friends. About three weeks ago, he started feeling much worse. He has been feeling down, tired, and hopeless every day. He reports trouble sleeping, loss of appetite, and trouble concentrating. He no longer feels any pleasure from his favorite hobbies. He says that he feels guilty, like he's letting everyone down, even though he can't provide any evidence that he has done anything wrong. According to the *DSM-5-TR*, what is the most appropriate diagnosis for Mr. X?
   a. Bereavement disorder
   b. Dysthymia
   c. Major depressive disorder
   d. Adjustment disorder with depressed mood

154. All the following are indications of ego strength EXCEPT:
   a. Not experiencing negative moods
   b. Setting and respecting boundaries
   c. Learning from mistakes
   d. Healthy coping mechanisms

155. If someone is diagnosed with renal disease, which organ is not functioning properly?
   a. Liver
   b. Stomach
   c. Gall bladder
   d. Kidneys

156. Hepatitis refers to inflammation or infection of which part of the body?
   a. Brain
   b. Liver
   c. Intestines
   d. Thyroid

157. Jason is a social worker who is meeting a new client for the first time. The client is a woman named Hilda with intellectual disabilities whose mother is her court-assigned legal guardian. Hilda is able to communicate well, care for herself, and work a part-time job. She and her mother sought the guardianship because Hilda is unable to manage her finances, but otherwise her mom stays out of her business. Hilda comes to the initial meeting and begins telling Jason her story. What is the best way for him to respond?
   a. Tell Hilda that he wants to hear more, but first he needs her mom to sign some papers.
   b. Wait for Hilda to finish telling her story, then explain the informed consent documents and have her sign them.
   c. Talk to Hilda about how treatment works, her rights, and situations where he must share her information with her mom. Get her mom's informed consent and Hilda's assent.
   d. Excuse himself for a moment. Ask his supervisor to make a determination about whether Hilda or her mom should provide informed consent.

158. Which of the following activities is NOT part of the informed consent process with clients in social work?
    a. Using a genogram or ecomap to assess the client's environment and relationships
    b. Explaining the purpose, timeline, and risks and benefits of treatment
    c. Clarifying the client's right to confidentiality and its limitations
    d. Discussing if and how technology will be used in treatment and the associated risks and benefits

159. What is the purpose of an Institutional Review Board?
    a. To review journal articles submitted to peer-reviewed academic journals
    b. To investigate accusations of social worker misconduct
    c. To approve and monitor research studies that involve human subjects
    d. To ensure social work degree programs meet ASWB standards

160. Which of the following are examples of unethical dual relationships in social work?
    I. A supervisor requiring his supervisees to participate in his research study
    II. Attending the same church as a client
    III. Terminating with a client to pursue a business opportunity together
    IV. Hiring a client to assist with an event
    V. Referring a client to a former colleague
    VI. Providing treatment to two members of the same family

    a. I, III, and VI
    b. I, III, and IV
    c. II, V, and VI
    d. II, IV, and V

161. What is the primary role of a geriatric social worker?
    a. To assist clients undergoing weight-loss surgery
    b. To counsel clients undergoing genetic testing
    c. To help clients live well as they age
    d. To support clients on the autism spectrum

162. Social workers can assist with all of the following aspects of genetic testing EXCEPT:
    a. Advocating for affordable, accessible testing options
    b. Discussing the risks and benefits of testing
    c. Providing post-testing counseling
    d. Diagnosing genetic disorders

163. According to family life cycle theories, what is the primary task that needs to be accomplished during the launching-family stage?
    a. Finding one's lifestyle and life partner
    b. Establishing a marital system
    c. Accepting adult children's independence
    d. Transitioning from a marital system to a family system

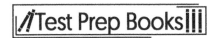
164. Research has shown that people who become caregivers for their aging parents are at increased risk for all of the following EXCEPT:
    a. Cognitive decline
    b. Depression
    c. Substance use disorders
    d. Heart disease

165. Two months ago, Ms. M was in a bad car accident. She was not seriously injured, but since then, she has refused to get back behind the wheel. She has been having trouble sleeping due to nightmares and recently started drinking wine to fall asleep. Although she is usually a calm and relaxed person, lately she has been jumping at the slightest noise. She used to love playing with her children, but recently she feels numb and disconnected from them. What is most likely the primary explanation for Ms. M's behavior changes?
    a. Alcohol Use Disorder
    b. PTSD
    c. Depression
    d. Anxiety

166. A social worker is meeting a new client with a previous diagnosis of schizophrenia. When asked about their diagnosis, the client states that they don't know much about the disorder except that it is caused by demons and bad spirits. The social worker explains what schizophrenia is, what causes it, how it affects people, what symptoms they might experience, how it's treated, and what community resources are available. What is this type of explanation called?
    a. Partializing
    b. Psychotherapy
    c. Psychoeducation
    d. Assessment

167. At what stage in the group therapy process does most of the group's therapeutic work occur?
    a. Preparation
    b. Beginning
    c. Middle
    d. End

168. A large social work agency is preparing for their annual visit from an independent group that assesses the organization's functioning. Last year, the agency received positive feedback about their client outcomes, and the managers are hoping that this year will be no different. What is this type of assessment called?
    a. Internal audit
    b. Program evaluation
    c. External audit
    d. Special audit

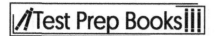

169. A social work researcher is conducting unstructured interviews with twenty patients in the cancer wing of a hospital. What type of research is this?
    a. Qualitative research
    b. Quantitative research
    c. Case study
    d. Naturalistic observation

170. What is NOT included in a treatment plan?
    a. The problems that are going to be addressed
    b. The goals that are going to reduce the impact of the problems
    c. The interventions that are going to be used
    d. Proof that the interventions are evidence-based

Answer Explanations #2

1. D: Congruence in social work practice means that the social worker's verbal and nonverbal communication is both real and genuine. Incongruence means there is a disconnect between what the social worker is feeling, thinking, and showing. For example, relaxed body language and smiling while saying that one is happy is congruent, while furrowing one's brow and crossing one's arms while saying one is happy is incongruent. Congruence is a critical skill for social workers to develop because it forms the basis of an authentic and trusting relationship. It is also important to be able to recognize congruence and incongruence in a client's communication because that can reveal discrepancies between what a client says and what they actually feel.

2. B: Regular feedback from clients is essential to improving social work practice and growing as a professional. When soliciting formal feedback, tailor the communication method to individual clients' preferences and abilities. For example, a client with limited literacy should not be given a form to fill out. For this reason, using the same standard feedback form for every client is not recommended. In addition to formal feedback, it is important to pay attention to clients' informal feedback. For example, failure to progress as expected can be considered informal feedback that something is not working as well as it could. Negative feedback is just as important as positive feedback because it provides an opportunity to learn and improve. Because of this, social workers should seek feedback at various times during treatment, not just when things are going well. Additionally, feedback should always be documented, and the client's confidentiality should be respected.

3. D: Summarizing is an interview technique in which the social worker restates the important points of a discussion. Summarizing can be done at any time, but it is especially effective at the end of a session to make sure that the social worker and client are on the same page about how the session went and what the next steps are. Summarizing also helps focus the discussion on important issues to address while highlighting the progress that has been made. Choice A is incorrect because asking open-ended questions is a technique used to elicit additional information from a client. Choice B is incorrect because validating is a technique used to affirm a client's feelings and statements about their experiences. Choice C is incorrect because clarifying is an interview technique that involves paraphrasing what a client has said and asking questions to make sure the social worker understands.

4. C: Industry vs. inferiority is the developmental stage that children go through during their school years, from age six until puberty. This is when children learn to initiate projects, follow through with them, and feel proud of their accomplishments. To complete this stage successfully, children must be encouraged and supported in their endeavors. On the other hand, if their attempts to take initiative are criticized or restricted, children will doubt themselves and feel inferior to their peers. Choice A is incorrect because autonomy vs. shame and doubt is the stage from age one to three when children start to become independent from their primary caregiver. Choice B is incorrect because intimacy vs. isolation takes place during young adulthood when people develop committed intimate relationships outside of their family of origin. Choice D is incorrect because trust vs. mistrust is the stage from birth to age one when babies develop the ability to trust others if their needs are met by their caregivers.

5. D: The social worker should reassure the woman that her son's behavior is normal for his age and developmental level. Many children develop imaginary friends around this time, and it does not indicate the presence of a disorder or problem. Although children talk to and play with their imaginary friends, they usually understand that they are not actually real people. The behavior can be distressing for

253

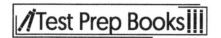

parents, and social workers can help by providing empathy and psychoeducation. In the absence of other concerning symptoms, a seven-year-old having an imaginary friend is not an indicator of abuse/neglect, Choice *A*; psychosis, Choice *B*; or abnormal development, Choice *C*.

6. A: Magical thinking is associated with the preoperational stage of cognitive development, which occurs between ages two and seven. Magical thinking involves believing events are connected when they are not. Because young children are egocentric, they often believe that they have more influence over the events around them then they actually do. For example, a child calls his sister a name. The sister gets sick. The child believes his sister got sick because he called her a name. As children develop cognitively, magical thinking is replaced by more logical thinking and a better understanding of cause and effect. The formal operations stage is the final stage of Piaget's model. It represents the most mature thinking processes. People who have reached this stage are able to think abstractly at a high level, Choice *B*; effectively plan for the future, Choice *C*; and think hypothetically, Choice *D*. This level of cognitive development allows people to take on adult roles and responsibilities.

7. B: Kohlberg theorized that people go through three main levels of moral development, subdivided into six stages. The second level (stages three and four) is conventional morality. At this level of moral development, people conform to the rules of society. They follow the rules both to be seen as a good person by others and because they believe that rules are important to society. Choice *A* is incorrect because the preconventional level is the first level of moral development and lasts until age nine. At this level, children are focused on avoiding punishment and seeking rewards. Choice *C* is incorrect because the final level of moral development is postconventional. At this level, people are motivated by concern for the general welfare of others and develop their own set of principles based on a broad understanding of ethics. Choice *D* is incorrect because adults can be at either the conventional or postconventional level; many adults do not make it past conventional morality.

8. C: A delusion is a fixed belief that is false and does not change in the face of evidence to the contrary. Choice *A* is incorrect because the client is functioning normally and does not have other symptoms. People with schizophrenia often experience delusions, but not everyone with delusions develops schizophrenia. Choice *B* is incorrect because the client is not seeing things that are not there. Instead, he is interpreting things he sees in a delusional way. Choice *D* is incorrect because disorientation refers to confusion about people, time, place, and events.

9. B: A genogram is a tool that can be used to identify patterns in a family. It is a visual representation of a client and their family that tracks generational patterns of behavior, emotions, relationships, psychosocial functioning, and tendencies. Choice *A* is incorrect because an ecogram is a visual representation of a client and various aspects of their environment. Choice *C* is incorrect because medical issues are only one of many components of a family history. Choice *D* is incorrect, because it does not cover the depth and breadth of information that a genogram does.

10. C: Cocaine use disorder is most likely because of the client's combination of physical symptoms (sniffling, dilated pupils, restlessness, talking quickly, irritability, sleep disturbance, mood, and attitude changes) and increasing negative life consequences (missing work, arguing with wife, overspending, withdrawal from previous activities). Choice *A* is incorrect because his behavior is causing problems rather than the circumstances of his life causing stress. Choice *B* is incorrect because, although alcohol use disorder shares similar negative consequences, the physical signs are different. The sniffling, dilated pupils, and talking quickly are especially indicative of cocaine use. Choice *D* is incorrect because

254

narcolepsy is a medical condition that causes daytime sleepiness, but not any of the other issues he is having.

11. D: Somatization is when a person's psychological distress manifests as physical symptoms. People experiencing somatization are not aware that their symptoms have a psychological origin and often seek medical treatment, only to be told that there is nothing wrong with them. The stomach aches are most likely a manifestation of the boy's distress about his parents' divorce. Choice *A* is unlikely because the doctor did a full workup to rule out gastrointestinal issues, and because the symptoms occurred in conjunction with the divorce. Choice *B* is unlikely because factitious disorder involves faking symptoms or intentionally making oneself sick out of a desire for attention. The social worker believes that the boy is genuinely experiencing stomach pain and there is no evidence that he is causing or faking his symptoms. Choice *C* is unlikely because there is no indication that the boy is experiencing health anxiety or excessive worry about his symptoms.

12. C: The *NASW Code of Ethics* requires social workers who know of a colleague's impairment to go directly to that colleague first. If the situation does not get resolved, it is then possible to pursue other channels, but only after going directly to the colleague in question.

13. B: The quality of the therapeutic relationship is the most consistent factor associated with good therapeutic outcomes. The other choices are still important but secondary to a strong therapeutic alliance.

14. A: Clarifying roles and explaining the limits of confidentiality should be done early in the helping process during the engagement period. This is also the time for rapport building and laying the groundwork for a trusting therapeutic relationship. These conversations may need to be revisited periodically during other stages of the helping process.

15. C: Countertransference is when a social worker has a strong emotional response to a client. For example, the client might remind the social worker of someone from their past. It is important for social workers to be aware of countertransference and to work through it with the help of supervision if needed. Choice *A* is incorrect because projection is a psychological defense mechanism. Choice *B* is incorrect because transference refers to a client's unconscious association of a social worker with someone from the client's past. Choice *D* is incorrect because dual relationships are when a social worker has more than just a helping relationship with a client, such as a client who is a member of the same PTA as the social worker. Dual relationships should be avoided. If avoiding a dual relationship is not possible, a social worker should take steps to protect the client from harm and establish clear boundaries.

16. D: Operant conditioning describes how people learn through consequences. Negative punishment involves taking away a desirable stimulus (the phone) after an undesirable behavior (refusing to do homework). Choice *A* is incorrect because positive reinforcement involves rewarding a desirable behavior. For example, if the child does his homework, he is allowed extra video game time. Choice *B* is incorrect because positive punishment involves providing an undesirable stimulus in response to an undesirable behavior. For example, the boy refuses to do his homework, so his mother yells at him. Choice *C* is incorrect because negative reinforcement involves removing an undesirable stimulus in response to a desirable behavior. For example, the child does his homework, so his mother will stop hassling him.

17. C: According to Freud's theory of human psychosexual development, children go through five stages, each of which is defined by a focus on a different part of the body as a source of pleasure. The third stage is the phallic stage, which takes place between ages three and six, Choice *D*. During this period of development, children explore their bodies and become interested in their genitals as a source of pleasure, Choice *A*. Children develop what Freud called a pseudosexual interest in the parent of the opposite gender. The child sees the same gender parent as a competitor or rival for the opposite gender parent's love and sexual attention. This leads to one of Freud's major concepts: the Oedipus and Electra complexes, Choice *B*. In Greek mythology, Oedipus killed his father and married his mother.

The Electra complex refers to a girl wanting to kill her mother and marry her father. These desires are symbolic; Freud was describing an internal tension in children this age where sexual desire for one parent creates tension and conflict with the other. Freud's theory has largely fallen out of favor among professionals. For one, there is very little evidence to support it. Also, his theories are centered on the male, heterosexual experience in atomic family units, which is not necessarily representative of how most people grow up today. It is easy to see these limitations when one considers how his theory would apply to a single-parent family or a family with homosexual parents, a homosexual child, or a transgender child. Choice *C* is the correct answer because potty training is not part of the phallic stage; it occurs during the second stage, the anal stage, which takes place from ages 18 months to three years.

18. B: Reinforcement schedules refer to how frequently a desired behavior is rewarded. A variable ratio reinforcement schedule means that the reward is sometimes given in response to the behavior but not every time, so it is unpredictable. Variable ratio produces the strongest behavioral response, and the learned behavior is less susceptible to extinction than it would be using a different reinforcement schedule. This is why casinos operate using variable ratio reinforcement. The gambler continues to put money in the slot machine hoping for a reward, knowing that the reward could come at any time. Variable ratio produces the most enduring behavior change. Choice *A* is incorrect because continuous reinforcement involves rewarding the behavior every time it occurs.

An example would be giving a dog a treat every time it obeys a command. Continuous reinforcement is effective for teaching a new behavior, but it is less effective than variable ratio. Once the reward is no longer given, the behavior is susceptible to extinction. Choice *C* is incorrect because fixed ratio means rewarding the behavior after a certain number of attempts. An example would be paying a farm worker $100 for every three bushels of fruit picked. Fixed ratio is less effective than variable ratio because it produces a less steady behavioral response. There is a slowdown after each reward; for example, the worker is likely to take a quick break after completing three bushels. Choice *D* is incorrect because fixed interval means that the reward is given after a certain amount of time has passed, regardless of the number of attempts at the behavior. Fixed interval produces less behavioral response and more of a pause after the reward is given. An example would be giving a lab animal a treat every five minutes in response to the animal pushing a button. The animal will push the button a lot around the five-minute mark, but much less the rest of the time.

19. A: A time-out is an example of a negative punishment technique. Negative punishment involves taking away something desired in response to undesired behavior; a time out takes away play and interaction as punishment for an undesired behavior. Choice *B* is incorrect because a token economy is an example of positive reinforcement. A reward (a token) is given in response to a desired behavior. Choice *C* is incorrect because spanking is an example of positive punishment. A punishment (spanking) is given in response to an undesired behavior. Choice *D* is incorrect because cancelling chores is an example of negative reinforcement. Something undesirable (chores) is taken away in response to a

256

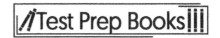

desired behavior. It is important to note that the use of the terms *positive* and *negative* in this context does not mean "good" and "bad." It refers to whether something is given or taken away in response to a behavior.

20. B: Interviewing is a critical social work skill with three main purposes: information gathering, Choice *A*, diagnosis, Choice *C*, and therapy, Choice *D*. The same interview can serve more than one function. For example, during a therapeutic conversation, a client might reveal information that leads to a change in diagnosis. Interviews should be planned but also flexible to respond to the client's needs as they arise. Choice *B* is correct because determining if a client is being honest is not one of the purposes of social work interviewing. Sometimes social workers are concerned that their clients are lying to them or otherwise withholding information. In this situation, a social worker must reflect on why the client might be reluctant to open up and how the social worker's behavior could be contributing to the problem. Supervision can be helpful in these cases. It is not helpful or appropriate to use an interview to try to "catch" a client in a lie or omission.

21. C: Dan is in the planning phase of treatment. Different sources provide different labels for the phases of treatment in social work (for example, planning is also referred to as goal identification and intervention planning), but there is general agreement on how the treatment process progresses. It starts with engagement, Choice *A*, which involves rapport-building, then moves to assessment, where strengths, needs, barriers, and problems are identified. Based on information gathered during engagement and assessment, a treatment plan with goals and an intervention is created. Next is implementation, also called intervention, Choice *D*, in which the intervention is used to achieve the client's goals. In the final phases, the client's progress is evaluated, Choice *B*, and the process of termination and preparing the client for life post-treatment is completed.

22. C: Problem-solving approaches focus on helping a client identify problems in their life and develop practical solutions for managing them. These approaches are generally brief and present-focused; they do not delve into the past and the origins of a problem, but instead focus on concrete solutions that can be implemented immediately. Brief, solution-focused approaches have become increasingly popular due to funding constraints, pressure from insurance companies, and client preferences. Choice *A* is incorrect because it describes cognitive behavioral approaches. Choice *B* is incorrect because is describes psychodynamic approaches. Choice *D* is incorrect because it describes acceptance and commitment therapy.

23. D: Encouraging clients to take an active role in their treatment benefits the client, the treatment plan, and the therapeutic relationship. Social workers may worry that asking a client to participate in problem formulation, goal setting, and treatment planning could make the client feel overwhelmed, but it is likely to make them feel empowered. One of the main goals of treatment is to improve a client's ability to identify and manage challenges on their own. Treatment is an opportunity for the client to practice this skill with the guidance of the social worker. Some clients will need more assistance than others in this process, and social workers must be patient and attuned to the needs of each individual.

24. A: Normally developing children are not expected to know at least 50 words by age one. Most children begin saying things like "mama" and "dada" around nine months. This is also when the child recognizes and responds to their own name, Choice *B*. The child gradually learns words for familiar objects over time, reaching a vocabulary of at least 50 words by age two. Not speaking at all by age two is a red flag that may indicate a developmental delay. Choice *C* is incorrect because babies begin smiling socially around two months of age. Choice *D* is incorrect because sitting up unassisted is a skill babies

257

develop between six and nine months of age. It is important to remember that every child is unique, and although human development occurs on a predictable schedule, individual children may reach milestones at slightly different times and speeds. That said, social workers must be familiar with normal human development in order to recognize signs of potential delay and disability. Social workers should also be able to provide psychoeducation to parents about their child's development.

25. D: Piaget is most known for his work on children's cognitive development. He introduced the idea that children are not merely miniature adults; they go through a process of maturation during which different cognitive skills and abilities develop. He identified four stages of cognitive development through which children move from concrete, egocentric thinking to abstract, logical, and hypothetical thinking. This has implications for what adults can reasonably expect from children. For example, children do not learn cause and effect until the concrete operations stage between the ages of seven and eleven; a five-year-old who does not fully grasp the consequences of his actions is not being willful, he has just not learned that skill yet. Choice *A* is incorrect because Erikson is most known for his theory of social development. Choice *B* is incorrect because Freud is most known for his work on personality and psychosexual development. Choice *C* is incorrect because Skinner is most known for his work on learning through operant conditioning.

26. C: Unlike other developmental theorists who focus on childhood, Levinson studied adults and concluded that development continues throughout the lifespan. His contribution is important because it is a reminder that people grow and change as they face challenges throughout the course of life. Levinson's seasons of life theory describes adult development as a progression though stages and transitions, which overlap. The stages are stable periods while the transitions involve dynamic growth and change. The early adulthood stage is the second stage in Levinson's model. It begins with the early adulthood transition and ends with the midlife transition, overlapping with both, Choice *A*. During this period, from ages 17-45, adults are at their physical peak and have high energy. They also experience the most stress, Choice *B*, due to the demands of establishing a career and a family at the same time, Choice *D*. During this stage, many people seek out older, more experienced individuals to guide them as mentors. People generally do not become mentors themselves until they reach the following stage, which Levinson calls middle adulthood.

27. A: Bernice Neugarten theorized that every community has a "social clock" that sets expectations for when certain important life events will occur, such as getting married and having children. People who do not achieve these milestones "on time" experience distress because they feel like they are disappointing people around them. Seen through this lens, Mary is distressed because her social clock is "ticking"; she feels like she has run out of time to find a husband and start a family because of the norms in the community in which she lives. At 22, Mary is clearly not too old biologically, and in many other communities she would not be expected to even be thinking about marriage and children.

However, in Mary's community, she stands out in a way that causes her stress and fear about the future. Choice *B* is incorrect because according to Erikson, Mary is in the intimacy vs. isolation stage and has until roughly age 40 to find a partner. Choice *C* is incorrect because Freud's theory focuses on sources of sexual pleasure. According to Freud, Mary is in the genital stage of psychosexual development, which lasts until death and involves seeking pleasure through heterosexual sex. This theory does not accurately explain Mary's situation because her distress is related to her social position, not her access to a sexual partner. Choice *D* is incorrect because according to Levinson, Mary is just completing her early adulthood transition and has until age 45 to establish a family.

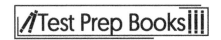

28. C: Sarah is a non-voluntary client because she was pressured into treatment by something other than the legal system. Choices *B* and *D* are incorrect because involuntary or mandated clients are required by the legal system to attend treatment. Choice *A* is incorrect because voluntary clients come to treatment on their own without outside pressure. When working with non-voluntary or involuntary/mandated clients, motivation, lack of trust, and anger can be issues. In these cases, it is particularly important that the social worker is patient, empathetic, and focused on the client's own needs and goals in addition to those imposed by outside forces.

29. C: Unlike voluntary clients, involuntary/mandated clients are attending treatment due to external pressure. Working with these clients presents unique challenges, making Choice *D* incorrect. Because these clients did not choose to pursue treatment, their motivation is likely to be low. Fear of legal consequences may motivate a client to do the bare minimum to avoid punishment, but this is different than the intrinsic motivation for change typical of voluntary clients. Therefore, Choice *B* is incorrect. It is important for social workers to emphasize that involuntary/mandated clients still have choices. They can choose to participate or not and accept the consequences, and they can choose to pursue their own goals in addition to those imposed by the courts; therefore, Choice *A* is incorrect. Social workers must work harder to engage and motivate involuntary clients, as their resistance is likely to be high and their trust low. Being empathetic, acknowledging the client's situation, clearly explaining what will happen during treatment, and encouraging the client to make choices where possible are the best ways to form a positive relationship with these clients.

30. A: Social workers are often reluctant to set and enforce rules, boundaries, and limits with their clients because they do not want to punish them or negatively affect the relationship. This is misguided because rules, limits, and boundaries create a predictable environment where clients feel safe and can learn to self-manage. In order to be trustworthy, social workers must do what they say they will do, and this includes enforcing agreed-upon rules. In this example, the social worker should remind the client of their agreement about lateness and cancel the session. The social worker should be empathetic and clear that this is a consequence of an action, not a punishment or an indication that the social worker does not like the client. Setting limits might be difficult in the moment, but over time, this will strengthen the therapeutic relationship and allow the client to learn and grow.

31. D: It is not helpful to role-play traumatic events; encouraging a client to relive trauma is irresponsible because it is very likely to be re-traumatizing. In most other situations, role-play is a helpful technique with multiple benefits. It encourages active learning and participation, helps clients see a situation from different perspectives, provides concrete examples of theoretical concepts, and improves conversation and communication skills. Choice *A* is incorrect because role-play is useful in supervision as well as in treatment. Choice *B* is incorrect because role-play can be useful for clients of all ages. Choice *C* is incorrect because role-play is an excellent way to practice communication skills.

32. B: This is an example of symbolic modeling because the model (the employee) is seen in a video doing the desired behavior (saying "no" assertively). Modeling is a useful technique that helps clients learn or improve skills through observation and imitation. Choice *A* is incorrect because live modeling involves watching a person do the desired behavior in real life. Choice *C* is incorrect because covert modeling involves asking the client to imagine someone performing the desired behavior and describe it in detail. Choice *D* is incorrect because participant modeling involves a real person modeling the desired behavior, then instructing the client to model it as well.

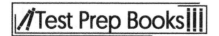

33. A: IPV does not discriminate based on sexuality. It occurs in all types of intimate relationships and across all racial, cultural, and socioeconomic groups. The other answer choices are true statements about IPV.

34. C: Vicarious/secondary trauma results from working with clients who have experienced trauma and witnessing the effects of that trauma. The symptoms can develop quickly and are similar to the symptoms experienced by the traumatized client. Choice *A* is incorrect because burnout is a state of exhaustion, emotional fatigue, and a sense of incompetence that develops cumulatively over time. Choice *B* is incorrect because compassion fatigue refers to a combination of the symptoms of burnout and secondary trauma that also develop over time. Choice *D* is incorrect because the symptoms arose in response to the trauma exposure and have only persisted for a short time.

35. D: Different states have different laws regarding minors' ability to seek services independently.

36. B: Psychotherapy notes must be kept in a secure location separate from clients' files. The notes should contain only information directly related to the clients' problems and the service provided. Choice *A* is incorrect because it is not appropriate to take notes home. Choices *C* and *D* are incorrect because they are not effective ways to maintain confidentiality.

37. D: Harm reduction approaches envision behavior change along a continuum where positive changes are possible at any point. This approach meets people where they are and celebrates changes that improve health and reduce harm, regardless of whether total abstinence is the desired goal. A harm reduction approach would be most beneficial for Joanna at this time because she is motivated to start addressing her drinking but is not ready to consider total abstinence. Focusing on small, achievable, positive changes will both improve her day-to-day life and help sustain her motivation. Choice *A* is incorrect because Joanna is motivated to address her drinking, but she is not in a stage of change where abstinence feels possible. Focusing on abstinence right now is likely to increase her resistance and fear and decrease her motivation for change. Choice *B* is incorrect because inpatient rehabilitation is the highest level of care, and nothing in the question indicates that she requires this level of treatment. Choice *C* is incorrect because Joanna has clear goals (improve health and reduce negative consequences) that therapy could help her achieve, and nothing in the question indicates that she is too impaired from drinking to benefit from therapy.

38. C: Harm reduction techniques are cost-effective, Choice *A,* and generally inexpensive. They are supported by extensive research and scientific evidence, Choice *B*. Harm reduction techniques meet people where they are, Choice *D,* and work on making positive behavioral changes from there, regardless of whether the end goal is abstinence. Some people worry that harm reduction techniques normalize or even promote unhealthy behaviors, but research evidence and practical experience clearly show the opposite. Harm reduction promotes health and safety for individuals, groups, and communities.

39. B: Harm reduction has gotten more attention in the context of the opiate overdose crisis since it is practical, easy to implement, and extremely effective. Needle exchanges, Choice *A*; medication-assisted treatment, Choice *C*; and overdose prevention, Choice *D,* are strategies with impressive track records of success. Increasing jail time for drug possession is not an example of a harm reduction approach because it is punitive and it increases rather than reduces the negative consequence" of drug use for the individual and the community. Incarceration has many negative effects on a person's health and life, and it is not a treatment for substance misuse.

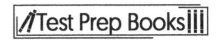

40. A: Teaching clients new skills is an important role of social workers. Coping skills help clients respond in healthy ways to problems that arise in their lives. The goal of coping is not to eliminate the problem, but rather to develop strategies to manage day-to-day symptoms, Choice *B*. Strategies that can be especially helpful for people with anxiety disorders include deep breathing and relaxation techniques, Choice *C*. Some people with anxiety develop unhealthy coping mechanisms, such as substance use, avoidance, isolation, and self-harm. These techniques might provide relief in the moment but cause additional problems and even increase anxiety in the long run. Replacing these with healthy coping mechanisms, Choice *D*, will help clients feel better, improve their health, and gain confidence in their ability to make positive changes.

41. C: Co-occurring substance use and mental disorders are common, and best practice is to treat them at the same time. This is called integrated treatment. Choices *A* and *B* are incorrect because it is best to treat both issues at the same time. Choice *D* is incorrect because integrated treatment produces the best outcomes regardless of which substance or mental illness a person is experiencing.

42. A: Aphasia is a communication disorder caused by brain injury that causes problems with understanding and producing language. Someone with aphasia may have difficulties with speaking, understanding, writing, reading, or any combination of these. It is often associated with damage from a stroke. Choice *B* is incorrect because agnosia is difficulty recognizing familiar objects. Choice *C* is incorrect because acalculia is difficulty with simple math. Choice *D* is incorrect because prosopagnosia is difficulty recognizing familiar faces. All four of these disorders are medical issues diagnosed by a physician, not a social worker. However, social workers often provide support to clients dealing with these issues.

43. C: Dementia is a cognitive disorder common in elderly people, Choice *A*, which causes changes in mood, Choice *B*; memory, Choice *D*; and thinking. Dementia is a chronic condition that starts gradually and progresses slowly over time. When these symptoms appear suddenly and progress quickly, they are more likely to be caused by delirium rather than dementia.

44. B: Sexual dysfunction describes problems with sexual desire, performance, or both. It can be caused by medical, psychological, and lifestyle factors. The first thing a social worker should do to assist a client with sexual dysfunction is refer them to a physician for a medical evaluation. It is important to determine if there is a medical problem first, before exploring other potential causes. If problems persist after medical explanations are ruled out, then it would be appropriate to explore psychological factors, Choices *A* and *C*, or lifestyle factors, Choice *D*, that may be contributing to the problem.

45. C: Antipsychotics can cause tardive dyskinesia, especially when they are taken at high doses for a long time. Tardive dyskinesia causes involuntary movements of the face, mouth, tongue, and sometimes other body parts. Sometimes these symptoms go away when the drug is discontinued, but sometimes they persist indefinitely. It is very important for people taking antipsychotics to be monitored for tardive dyskinesia so that the medication can be changed before the symptoms become irreversible. Choices *A*, *B*, and *D* are incorrect because none of these classes of drugs cause tardive dyskinesia.

46. A: Lithium is a mood stabilizer often prescribed to treat bipolar disorder. Lithium has a narrow therapeutic index, which means that the difference between therapeutic and toxic levels of the drug is small. People taking lithium must get regular blood tests to make sure their lithium levels stay in the therapeutic range. Lithium can sometimes cause problems with the kidneys and thyroid, so it is also recommended to monitor the function of these organs during lithium treatment. Choices *B*, *C*, and *D* are

261

incorrect because none of these drugs have a narrow therapeutic index or a risk of kidney and thyroid damage, so none of them require regular blood tests and monitoring.

47. D: When assigning homework, it is important for social workers to clearly explain why it is important and how it connects to the client's goals. Keeping a log of the outbursts will reveal patterns that Karen may not be aware of and clarify why the outbursts occur. This information will allow Karen and Juan to collaborate on a treatment plan that will effectively reduce the outbursts. By explaining this, Juan is making a connection between doing homework and achieving her goal of reducing the outbursts. Logging behaviors, feelings, and thoughts is an example of client self-monitoring. Self-monitoring techniques can be used to translate vague, subjective experiences (e.g., "I have outbursts, but I don't know why") into data that can be acted on (e.g., "When I feel disrespected, I lose control; it happens more frequently and severely if I am hungry or tired").

In this example, an intervention might focus on techniques for managing the feeling of being disrespected as well as creating a routine that ensures she is well-rested and eating regularly. Choice A is incorrect because even though doing the homework is likely to make Karen feel more involved and empowered in her treatment, telling her this without explaining why the homework is important is not likely to increase her motivation to do it. Also, increasing discipline is not one of the goals of her treatment. Choice B is incorrect because telling Karen that homework is required for her treatment plan does not help her understand why it is important. It also makes the treatment plan sound like something imposed on her rather than something she is collaborating on. Choice C is incorrect because the goal of tracking the outbursts is not to reduce the outbursts but to understand why they occur so that they can intervene effectively.

48. A: Metacommunication means communicating about communication. It involves bringing awareness to the way we communicate rather than the information we are communicating. Developing this skill can help clients express themselves more effectively, understand other peoples' reactions, and reduce or prevent misunderstanding and miscommunication. Metacommunication is particularly helpful in conflict resolution situations because often the conflict has as much to do about how something is said as what is actually said. Choice B is incorrect because empathic communication is about being accepting, genuine, and offering unconditional positive regard. Choice D is incorrect because structured communication refers to planned communication, such as a formal interview with preplanned questions.

49. C: Social workers often mediate conflicts both informally and formally. The goal of a mediator is to generate solutions to the conflict that will work for everyone involved. Mediators do not simply listen without suggesting solutions, Choice A. It is not their role to take sides or determine who is right and wrong, Choice B, but rather to find a solution that meets everyone's needs. The goal of conflict mediation is to resolve the conflict, not live with it indefinitely, Choice D. If a social worker is unable to help the parties come to a mutually agreeable solution, it may be necessary to seek the services of a professional mediator.

50. C: When clients are in crisis, safety is always the first priority. Until safety is addressed, other interventions cannot be helpful. After ensuring client safety, the social worker should help them return to their previous level of functioning. This can involve teaching coping skills, Choice A; mobilizing social supports, Choice D; and providing resources. Crisis intervention is generally brief and focused on stabilizing the client. Exploring what caused the crisis, Choice B, is not necessary during this acute situation. Instead, crisis intervention is focused on the client's immediate needs.

51. D: Effexor (generic name Venlafaxine) is an SNRI, a serotonin and norepinephrine reuptake inhibitor. This means it increases the levels of serotonin and norepinephrine in the brain. Effexor and other SNRIs are primarily used to treat depression. Choice *A* is incorrect because SSRIs are also prescribed primarily for depression but have a different mechanism of action; they are serotonin reuptake inhibitors. Choices *B* and *C* are incorrect because they are not antidepressants and have different mechanisms of action than Effexor.

52. B: Ativan is a benzodiazepine, which is primarily prescribed for anxiety but can be used for other purposes as well. Benzodiazepines have a high abuse potential. Over time, people develop a tolerance and require higher and higher doses to get the same effect. Long term use is associated with cognitive impairment. Withdrawal from benzodiazepines is life threatening and requires medical detox. On the other hand, benzodiazepines are extremely effective when taken occasionally for anxiety or panic. For these reasons, Ativan and other benzodiazepines are generally recommended for short-term or occasional use. Choices *A*, *C*, and *D* are incorrect because none of these drugs are considered to have abuse potential.

53. C: Mr. M is dependent on Prozac and is experiencing discontinuation symptoms. Over time, the body adjusts to psychotropic medication and stopping it suddenly can cause adverse effects. This can happen with Prozac and other SSRIs after about a month of daily use, and Mr. M has been taking the drug for ten years. People vary in whether and to what extent they experience discontinuation symptoms, but it is generally unpleasant and can last for weeks or months. To reduce these symptoms, it is recommended that people who want to stop taking a psychotropic medication work with a psychiatrist to slowly taper their dose down over time. Choice *B* is incorrect because there is a difference between being dependent on a drug and being addicted to it. Mr. M is not experiencing negative life consequences or drug cravings, which are hallmarks of addiction. Just as people with diabetes are not addicted to insulin, Mr. M is not addicted to Prozac. Choice *D* is incorrect because antidepressant discontinuation syndrome is a documented physical phenomenon, it is not psychological or psychosomatic.

54. A: The social worker must make sure that Sarah understands the dietary restrictions that come along with MAOIs. She needs to avoid foods with high levels of the amino acid tyramine, especially aged foods, cheeses, smoked or pickled fish, wine, beer, liver, dry sausage, fava beans, and brewer's yeast. Eating these foods while taking an MAOI can cause dangerously high blood pressure, requiring emergency medical treatment. Because of this risk, other types of antidepressants are often tried before MAOIs. However, MAOIs are effective drugs as long as patients are careful with what they eat. Choices *B*, *C*, and *D* are incorrect because MAOIs do not affect physical activity, do not have special indications about timing of doses, and do not cause tardive dyskinesia.

55. C: Problem formulation describes the process that social workers go through with their clients to determine exactly what the problem to be treated is. It sounds obvious, but it can be difficult to identify exactly what issue treatment should focus on. The process involves working with a client to define the problem, Choice *A*; determining its onset, Choice *B*; describing the history of the problem, when it occurs, and how it has progressed over time; and determining how severe it is, Choice *D*. It is important that the client is involved in the process of problem formulation and that the problem is discussed through a strengths-based, person-in-environment lens. Choice *C*, determining what the client did to cause the problem, implies that the client is to blame for the problem, which is inconsistent with a strengths-based, person-in-environment approach, unhelpful for treatment, and harmful to the client.

56. A: Documentation should only include information directly relevant to treatment. It is not appropriate to include subjective impressions or extraneous information. The other choices describe information that should be documented.

57. C: The social worker is experiencing countertransference, and the first thing she should do is bring it up in supervision. These feelings should not be ignored as they can be therapeutically useful. Her supervisor can help her explore the countertransference and gain insight into what the client is unconsciously trying to elicit in her and why.

58. D: Importance of human relationships and integrity are in conflict. Rejecting the gift could negatively affect the social worker-client relationship. Accepting the gift, especially an expensive one, could compromise the social worker's professional integrity and boundaries. Generally, it is considered appropriate to accept a gift that is inexpensive or handmade.

59. B: Advanced directives are written, legal documents that contain a person's preferences for care when they are dying. They can include directions about treatments the person wants or doesn't want. This way, a person's wishes can be followed even once they are no longer able to communicate them. Having an advanced directive in place allows terminally ill clients as much control over their treatment options as possible and prevents disagreement among family members about which type of care should be pursued.

60. D: The social worker should reassure the mother and provide her with psychoeducation regarding adolescent development. The son is exhibiting typical behavior for a sixteen-year-old, indicating normal, healthy development. Adolescence is a time when people try on many different identities and experiment with how they present themselves to the world. Spending more time with peers than family is part of the process of individuation that teens go through as they establish their own identity separate from their family. It is also normal for teens to experiment with drugs and alcohol at this age. If the mother is worried, she should talk to her son about substance use, but nothing in the example indicates that he needs drug and alcohol treatment, Choice *B*. Choice *A* is incorrect because personality disorders involve longstanding patterns of dysfunctional behavior. The son's behavior indicates adolescence, not disorder, and nothing indicates that the son is experiencing distress. Choice *C* is incorrect because there is no indication that the son is being abused or neglected. Although certain kinds of "acting out" can be red flags for abuse, the son's behavior reflects normal adolescent development.

61. C: Parents are often tempted to intervene in their children's social conflicts by taking sides or attempting to solve the problem for the child. Although understandable, this impulse does not assist with children's social development. Children need to learn how to manage social conflicts on their own. Parents can support their child by modeling good social skills and respectful interaction with others, Choice *A*. They can encourage empathy by helping the child consider situations from multiple different perspectives and practice walking a mile in someone else's shoes, Choice *B*. They should also initiate conversations about values, rules, and morals and encourage children to share their own opinions on these topics, Choice *D*. When a child experiences social conflict, the parent can reinforce these skills and help the child think through the best way to resolve the conflict. Jumping in to solve the problem for the child may feel like support to the parent, but it communicates to the child that they are not competent to solve the problem on their own, leading to insecurity and underdeveloped social skills.

62. D: The supervisor should reassure the social worker that the boy's behavior is normal and developmentally appropriate, and it does not indicate abuse or sexualization. Children between ages

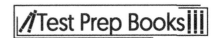

two and five are curious about their bodies and do not feel embarrassed about nudity. It is normal for children this age to learn names for their genitals and to understand that males and females have different bodies. Nothing about the boy's behavior warrants a report to child protective services, Choice A. The fact that the child knows his father also has a "pee pee" does not indicate that the father is abusing the boy. It would not be appropriate to tell the child's mother that the father might be doing something inappropriate based on the information given, Choice B. Choice C is incorrect because the boy's behavior is totally normal and expected for his age. If the behavior were to persist into the child's elementary school years, it would start to become a cause for concern about the child's development.

63. B: The social worker should make a report to child protective services because Amanda's behavior is very concerning. She shows red flags that indicate sexual abuse. It is not normal for a six-year-old to know sexually explicit language, Choice C. Children who have been sexually abused often fixate on the experience and act it out through play, as Amanda did with the dolls. The fact that Amanda asked the adult male social worker if he wanted to engage in sexual activity with her is particularly concerning because it indicates that she expects this behavior with adult men. Engaging much older or younger children in sexualized play is another red flag for sexual abuse.

The fact that the child recently moved to town does not affect the decision to make a report (the report should be made regardless), but it does mean that Amanda could be in even more danger due to not being socially integrated. The fact that the incident happened at the social worker's home, outside of his social work practice, is irrelevant, Choice A. Social workers are mandated reporters, which means that they are legally and ethically required to report suspected abuse any time they encounter it, regardless of whether they are working at the time. Choice D is incorrect because the social worker should not talk to Amanda's parents before making the report. He has no way of knowing whether the abuse is ongoing or who the perpetrator(s) is/are. If family members are involved, the social worker could be putting Amanda in more danger by talking to the parents about his suspicions.

64. C: Couples counseling is not appropriate in cases of intimate partner violence. There is evidence that couples counseling puts victims in danger of further abuse. The other choices describe appropriate interventions.

65. D: Self-care is not intended to reduce the need for supervision. In fact, supervision can be a component of a social worker's self-care routine because it helps them address work stress and practice more effectively.

66. C: Sharing personal information with a client is not an appropriate way to promote transparency and instead can be harmful to clients. Transparency allows the client to feel like an equal in the helping process and reduces the negative impact of the power differential between social worker and client.

67. D: It is not ethical for the social worker to call herself an art therapy practitioner because she has not completed all of the steps required to practice ethically in a new area. In addition to study and training, she would also need to consult with and receive supervision from professionals with experience in art therapy. This is important because it provides ongoing support to the social worker as she begins treating clients in this new modality. The other choices are incorrect because attending a training and receiving a certificate is not sufficient to gain competence in a new area, and an internship is not required to practice art therapy.

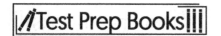

68. D: Freud theorized that children develop into sexually mature adults by progressing through five stages, each defined by which body part is the main source of pleasure. He believed that if the child's gratification was overly restricted or indulged during any of the stages, they would develop a fixation leading to certain predictable problems in adulthood. Toilet training occurs during the anal stage. Freud believed that a child whose parents are overly strict about toilet training will develop a fixation leading to an anal-retentive personality. Freud describes this personality type as overly controlled with rigid and obsessive thinking. On the other hand, if parents are too hands-off with toilet training, the fixation will manifest in an anal-expulsive personality marked by disorganization and messiness, Choice *B*. According to Freud, binge eating disorder, Choice *A*, and excessive cigarette smoking, Choice *D*, are oral fixations that develop as a result of parents being too strict or indulgent during the weaning process in the oral stage.

69. A: Carol Gilligan was Lawrence Kohlberg's research assistant and later become a preeminent scholar in her own right. She criticized Kohlberg's theory, which was based on men, as being sexist. Women did not often reach the postconventional stage, according to Kohlberg's theory, and Gilligan refused to believe that this was due to women being morally inferior. Her research on women's morality led her to adapt the theory to explain women's moral development. Kohlberg's theory emphasizes individual rights and justice as the highest possible moral values.

Carol discovered that women conceive of morality in terms of their connections with others and consider caring the highest moral value. While men's morality is more individualistic, women's is more relational. Gilligan did not believe that women or men were more or less likely to achieve a higher level of moral development, Choice *C*. Her theory used the same stages Kohlberg did, Choice *D,* in the same order, Choice *B*. During the preconventional stage, women are concerned with self-interest and survival. In the conventional stage, they emphasize being selfless and taking care of others. In the postconventional stage, women take control of their own lives while still placing a strong emphasis on caring and relationships.

70. B: Almost all theories of spiritual development are based on the same basic themes. As people develop spiritually, they move from an egocentric and self-centered orientation to a more integrated, universal orientation. This means that spiritual growth encourages people to be less focused on themselves and their egos, instead seeing themselves as part of a whole and focusing on the common good. Choices *A* and *B* are incorrect because persecution and salvation, as well as resistance and obedience, are common themes in certain religious groups but not in theories of spiritual development. Spiritual development is distinct from religion, meaning that people develop spiritually whether they identify with a particular religious group or not. Similarly, spiritual growth is not dependent on a belief in God(s) and does not require a progression from atheism to theism, Choice *D*.

71. C: Atkinson, Morten, and Sue theorized that minority youths go through five stages of racial and cultural identity development. Their theory formed the basis of many later theories of racial, ethnic, and cultural identity development. The first stage in their theory is *conformity*, Choice *B*, where the minority individual identifies with the majority (white) culture and values it above their own. This was the stage the young man was in while growing up in the white community. The second stage is *dissonance*, Choice *A*, where something happens that causes the person to question their allegiance to the majority culture.

The young man was in this stage when the racist incidents occurred and prompted him to think more about his identity as a black man. The third stage, which the young man is currently in, is *resistance and immersion*. In this stage, the person becomes heavily aligned with their minority identity and devalues the majority culture. The fourth stage is *introspection*, where the person begins questioning their total rejection of the majority culture. The final stage is *synergistic articulation and awareness*, Choice *D*, when the person can see and appreciate strengths in themselves, their minority culture, and also the majority culture.

72. D: Jim experienced a traumatic event (house fire) and has been experiencing symptoms of traumatic stress for three weeks, which is consistent with acute stress disorder. Choice *A* is incorrect because, although Jim has been experiencing symptoms of depression for at least two weeks, the depression seems to be caused by traumatic stress. Traumatic stress symptoms overlap with the symptoms of many mental illnesses, but the client should be diagnosed with a trauma and stress-related disorder rather than a mental illness. Similarly, Choice *B* is incorrect because Jim's inattention and difficulty with decision-making seem related to trauma, not ADHD. ADHD is a lifelong condition, but Jim's symptoms were not present before the house fire. Choice *C* is incorrect because Jim has been experiencing symptoms for only three weeks. According to the *DSM-5-TR*, the main difference between acute stress disorder and PTSD is the duration of the symptoms; acute stress disorder is diagnosed within four weeks of the trauma, and PTSD is diagnosed if the symptoms persist for at least one month. If Jim's symptoms are still present after another week, his diagnosis should be changed to PTSD.

73. B: The biggest risk factor for suicide is a history of one or more suicide attempts. Risk factors are characteristics that are associated with an increased risk of suicide. Choices *A*, *C*, and *D* are risk factors for suicide as well, but none of them are as strong a predictor as past attempts. It is important to understand that there is no way to be certain that a client will or will not attempt suicide. Social workers must consider risk factors, protective factors, warning signs, and other assessment data and make the best judgement that they can about the most appropriate level of care and treatment plan for each client.

74. A: Requesting more frequent therapy appointments is not a warning sign for suicide. In fact, having access to healthcare and supportive relationships with providers are protective factors that reduce the risk of suicide. Choice *B* is incorrect because a sudden increase in mood can indicate that the client has made the decision to end their life and is feeling relieved. Choice *C* is incorrect because giving away possessions can indicate that the person is planning for their death. Choice *D* is incorrect because threats or statements about wanting to attempt suicide are warning signs that should always be taken seriously.

75. A: Cluster A personality disorders are described as "odd and eccentric." Cluster A includes paranoid personality disorder, schizoid personality disorder, and schizotypal personality disorder. People with these diagnoses often exhibit behavior that is considered unusual and socially awkward. Choice *B* is incorrect because this set of personality disorders are described as "dramatic and erratic." Choice *C* is incorrect because this set of personality disorders are described as "anxious and fearful." Choice *D* is incorrect because there is no such thing as "Cluster D" personality disorders.

76. C: Many clients struggle with anger management. Social workers can help by teaching anger management techniques. The goal of using these techniques is to learn to recognize and respond to anger in a healthy way, not eliminate it. Anger is a useful signal that something in one's life needs attention. It is not inherently "bad;" however, responding to anger in unhealthy ways can cause problems with relationships and physical health. Social workers can help by teaching anger management techniques, including counting to ten before responding, Choice *A*; leaving the situation momentarily to calm down, Choice *B*; deep breathing exercises, Choice *D*; avoiding all-or-nothing thinking; meditation;

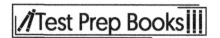

and exercise (with a physician's approval). Different techniques will work for different clients based on their needs and preferences. It is important to practice these techniques regularly so that they become natural responses. Social workers should also develop their capacity to manage their own anger so that they can model healthy behavior for their clients.

77. B: This client could benefit from stress management techniques because she is dealing with three major stressors (promotion, marriage, and a child) in a short period of time. Many people think of stress as being caused only by negative events, but positive and anticipated events can also cause a great deal of stress and disruption. Clients might feel confused about why they are stressed when things are going so well. Social workers can help by educating clients about how the fight-or-flight response works and teaching techniques to return to baseline more quickly. Common stress management techniques include deep breathing exercises, meditation, yoga, and journaling. Choice *A* is incorrect because the client is not trying to reduce the risk of harm from a specific behavior. Choice *C* is incorrect because there is no indication that the client is struggling with boundaries or rules. Choice *D* is incorrect because there is no indication that the client is having trouble with anger.

78. D: There are three main steps to take when helping a client manage stress: identify triggers, identify which parts of the situation the client can control, and teach techniques to manage the stress from things that are outside the client's control. The client in the example has already identified their stress triggers. The next step is to determine what the client can control. In this example, the client can control their uncertainty about how their work is perceived by having a conversation with their boss or requesting a performance review. The client can control their time management issues by developing new skills in that area. The client cannot control whether their colleague receives a promotion. Choice *A* is incorrect because any needed stress management techniques should be taught after identifying and working on the parts of the situation the client can control. Choice *B* is incorrect because encouraging the client to speculate about their coworker shifts attention away from the parts of the situation that are within the client's power to change. Choice *C* is incorrect because reassuring the client that everyone gets stressed at work minimizes the client's problem without offering any solutions.

79. B: Ferdman and Gallegos's theory of Latino identity development is not a linear model in which people progress from one stage to the next. Instead, it involves six different lenses or orientations through which Latino people come to view their identity. Which lens they adopt is dependent on several factors, including their family, their peer group, and their experiences growing up, going to school, and interacting with social institutions. The model shows that Latino identities are multifaceted, involving a variety of ethnic, racial, and cultural identities. Monica views her ethnicity through the "subgroup identified" lens. This means that she recognizes the existence of multiple Latino races, and as a Mexican American, she identifies as Chicana. Choice *A* is incorrect because the undifferentiated lens describes people who consider themselves "colorblind," who are aligned with the dominant culture, and who attribute their struggles to personal failure rather than discrimination. Choice *C* is incorrect because the white identified lens describes people who recognize the existence of Latino and white races and identify as white. Choice *D* is incorrect because the Latino identified lens describes people who recognize the existence of Latino and white races and identify as Latino.

80. D: The disability rights movement transformed the conversation around disability, challenging the prevailing notion that people are disabled by medical conditions, Choice *A*, and reframing it as people being disabled by a society that fears them and refuses to accommodate them. People with disabilities had been largely left out of the discourse about their own lives, with other people making decisions on their behalf. Disability rights activists challenged this, adopting the slogan, "nothing about us, without

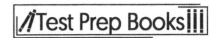

us." While non-disabled people viewed the problem of disability as a medical one with a medical solution, activists taught that the obstacles they faced had less to do with the nature of their medical condition and more to do with trying to navigate a society that would not accommodate them. Disability activists recognize that there are strengths associated with disability as well as challenges; however, they do not consider disability a gift or superior status, Choice *B*. Choice *C* is incorrect because the movement sees society and social institutions as disabling, not the breakdown in nuclear families.

81. A: Housing should be the first priority, along with other basic needs like access to food, water, and sanitation. When prioritizing the needs of clients with multiple issues, social workers should use Maslow's hierarchy of human needs to guide their decision-making process. The pyramid is a visual representation of human needs from the most basic to the most complex. The most basic needs must be addressed before higher ones can be considered. The man in the example will not be able to benefit from family counseling, Choice *D*, addiction treatment, Choice *B*, or psychiatric treatment, Choice *C*, while also constantly searching for his next meal and a safe place to spend the night.

82. D: The social worker should provide psychoeducation on diabetes and explain how managing the condition will facilitate her social and professional goals. The social worker should also explain how leaving the diabetes untreated will create obstacles, making it more difficult to achieve her current goals and creating new problems at the same time. Showing the client Maslow's hierarchy could be helpful depending on the client's learning style. However, the goal is not to convince the client that the therapist is right and she is wrong, Choice *C*, but rather to help her draw connections between her physical health and other aspects of her life. Transferring the client to another social worker should not be the first response because it does not help the client to understand and improve her situation, Choice *B*. The social worker could compromise by agreeing to pursue some aspects of her social or professional goals and her medical condition simultaneously. However, this should not be framed as pursuing a promotion so the client can pay for insulin, Choice *A*. This is backwards; the social worker should find other resources to make the insulin affordable so that the client is healthy enough to pursue a promotion.

83. C: The man displays clear signs of narcissistic personality disorder, including grandiosity, entitlement, lack of empathy, and a belief that he is better than other people and envied by them. People with NPD rarely seek treatment for their narcissism. They usually come to the attention of clinicians for other reasons, like the man in the example. Choice *A* is incorrect because there is not enough information to determine whether his statements about himself ("genius IQ," for example) are delusional in nature. In any case, these statements are better explained by grandiosity and inflated sense of self than fixed, false beliefs that do not change in the face of evidence to the contrary. Choice *D* is incorrect because abusive personality disorder is not a recognized diagnosis. People can behave abusively whether they have a diagnosable condition or not.

84. D: In the *DSM-5-TR*, pica is a feeding and eating disorder that involves consuming nonfood items like chalk, paint, pebbles, or ash for at least one month in a way that is not developmentally appropriate or culturally condoned. It can occur in the context of another disorder, or it can be a diagnosis by itself. It is important that individuals with pica get treatment to avoid medical complications. Choice *A* is incorrect because compulsively pulling out one's hair is called trichotillomania. Choice *B* is incorrect because child-onset fluency disorder is also called stuttering. Choice *C* is incorrect because word salad describes disorganized speech, not pica.

85. B: Self-injurious behavior (SIB) is an umbrella term for behaviors that involve harming oneself. SIB is highly stigmatized and misunderstood. SIB does not indicate that a client is suicidal, but SIB and suicidality can co-occur. It is important to assess clients for both issues and create a treatment plan to reduce the risk of harm while helping clients develop healthier coping mechanisms. Choices *A* and *D* are incorrect because the behaviors are directed at the self, not another person. Choice *C* is incorrect because although SIB sometimes arises in the context of depression and other psychiatric disorders, SIB is not necessarily depressed behavior.

86. D: According to the stages of change model, Mr. C is in the contemplation stage. He is thinking about the possibility of reducing or quitting, but he is feeling ambivalent about it and is unsure how to proceed. In this stage, social workers can help clients think through the pros and cons of making a change, identify obstacles to change and how to get past them, and move into the preparation stage when they are ready. Choice *A* is incorrect because in pre-contemplation, the person is not thinking about change at all. Choice *B* is incorrect because the action stage involves acting on a plan to change. Choice *C* is incorrect because maintenance refers to maintaining a changed behavior.

87. C: Social workers' role in death and dying includes education, support, and respect. It does not include encouraging clients to choose one option over another. It would be appropriate to educate a terminal client about their options, including hospice care, but advocating for one course of action is not ethical.

88. C: Social workers who practice in different settings (school, home, office, prison, etc.) should consider how each setting might affect their safety differently. It would not be appropriate to use the exact same safety procedures in every setting. For example, a school social worker should know which staff members to call for help in the event of an emergency and how to contact them. A social worker doing a home visit would need a different safety plan, such as having a cell phone to call 911 if necessary.

89. A: When there is a conflict between a social worker's values and their client's values, the social worker should first engage in self-reflection about her values and whether she is able to put them aside to remain professionally objective. Choice *B* is incorrect because a trusted friend is not qualified to advise on social work ethics and discussing the client would be a violation of his privacy. Choice *C* is incorrect because referring the client to another social worker should only be done in extreme cases where the social worker has already engaged in self-reflection, consulted with a supervisor, and still cannot remain objective. Choice *D* is incorrect because asking clients about their values on an intake form is unethical unless this information is required for treatment. Additionally, screening clients based on their values is discrimination, which is unethical.

90. C: Interdisciplinary teams function best when the team comes to an agreement about how the group will operate, including the roles, values, and expected contributions of each team member. The agreement should also include a process for decision-making and handling conflicts if they arise. Choice *C* is correct because choosing one set of professional values for the entire team to follow would defeat the purpose of interdisciplinary collaboration. The purpose is to provide multiple professional perspectives on a client's situation.

91. A: Out-of-home displacement can be extremely traumatizing. Certain factors increase the likelihood that a displaced person will experience trauma. These include being displaced by a traumatic event, such as war, natural disaster, or violence, (Choice *B*); being separated from friends and family, Choice *C*; and

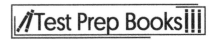

having to move multiple times, Choice *D*. Many people believe that children are naturally resilient and easily recover from trauma, but research shows that this is not the case. In fact, the younger someone is when they experience a trauma, such as out-of-home displacement, the more likely they are to experience negative effects throughout their lifetime. Social workers should be aware that children experiencing displacement may require special attention. Social workers should also be aware that adult clients who experienced displacement as a child might still be affected by it years later.

92. B: When choosing which psychotherapy modality to use with a client, social workers must consider their competency, the client's needs, agency policy, insurance requirements, and the research evidence. Some types of therapy have been shown to be more effective for certain disorders. Dialectical behavior therapy is an evidence-based psychotherapy treatment for borderline personality disorder (BPD). It was developed by Marsha Linehan, a clinician who also has a BPD diagnosis, and it is considered the best modality for these patients. Choice *A* is incorrect because psychodynamic therapy is aimed at uncovering unconscious motivations and desires that affect behavior. Choice *C* is incorrect because exposure and response prevention therapy is used to treat phobias and obsessive-compulsive disorder. Choice *D* is incorrect because cognitive behavioral therapy helps draw connections between thoughts, feelings, and behaviors.

93. C: The young man would benefit most from cognitive behavioral therapy (CBT). CBT teaches clients how their thoughts, feelings, and behaviors influence each other. Specifically, CBT teaches clients how changing their thoughts by challenging cognitive distortions can help them feel better and act the way they intend to. The young man in the example is experiencing distress and exhibiting multiple cognitive distortions (all-or-nothing thinking, overgeneralizing, and catastrophizing). CBT would help him reframe the cognitive distortions into more realistic and accurate thoughts, which should reduce his anxiety. For example, the man might think, "if I don't get this job, I'll never succeed in life, and I should just give up."

CBT would help him consider the evidence and reframe this thought to something like, "if I don't get this job, I will be disappointed, but there will be many other opportunities for me to pursue, and eventually I will probably find something that is a good fit." Choice *A* is incorrect because EMDR therapy is used to process traumatic events and reduce the accompanying trauma symptoms. Choice *B* is incorrect because psychodynamic therapy explores childhood experiences and unconscious motivations and drives. Choice *D* is incorrect because although the client is living with his parents, there is no indication that family dynamics are contributing to his difficulties.

94. A: Psychodynamic therapy is based on Freud's work. Psychodynamic and psychoanalytic approaches are based on the idea that personality is shaped by childhood experiences and by conflicts between unconscious drives and societal norms. In Freud's view, the personality is made up of the id, ego, and superego. The id represents sexual and aggressive drives, the superego represents morals and societal norms, and the ego manages the conflict between the id and the superego. Psychodynamic therapy uses various techniques, including free association and dream analysis, to explore parts of the personality that people are not normally conscious of. Choice *B* is incorrect because EFT helps clients become more comfortable with their emotions instead of avoiding or fearing them. Choice *C* is incorrect because structural family therapy explores family relationships, communication, and boundaries. Choice *D* is incorrect because CBT brings awareness to how thoughts, feelings, and behaviors influence each other.

95. C: According to Maslow's hierarchy of human needs, the highest level of the original pyramid is self-actualization, Choice *B*. Maslow later added an additional level called self-transcendence, but the original model is much more well-known and commonly used in practice. Self-actualization is only possible once all the lower-level needs have been satisfied. Maslow understood self-actualization to be an ongoing process of becoming truly and fully oneself, Choice *A*. It involves developing one's full potential as noted in Choice *D*, finding one's calling, truly living in accordance with one's values, and utilizing all of their abilities. This is the state that humans aspire to, but very few achieve it. In fact, only about one in one hundred people regularly operate at this level.

96. D: Mary Ainsworth researched attachment between mothers and their infants. She devised the Strange Situation Protocol where the mother and child are in an unfamiliar room, the mother leaves for a short period of time, and then she returns. The child is observed to see how they behave in response to the mother's absence and how they react when she reappears. From this research, Ainsworth identified several different attachment styles. A securely attached infant will explore the room when the mother is present and turn to the mother when they are afraid. Securely attached infants prefer the mother to a stranger (in this case the observing researcher), becoming upset when the mother leaves and happy when she returns.

Ainsworth also identified two different forms of insecure, or anxious, attachment. Anxious-ambivalent attachment is indicated when the child is extremely distressed when the parent leaves but does not seek comfort from the parent when she returns. Anxious-ambivalent children do not explore the room much, regardless of whether the mother is present. Anxious-avoidant attachment is indicated when a child avoids the mother and shows no response to her leaving or returning. Anxious-avoidant children also do not explore much in either condition. Since Ainsworth's work, attachment theory has been further developed and additional subtypes have been identified; however, the Strange Situation Protocol is still used by attachment researchers today. Choices *A, B,* and *C* are incorrect because the Strange Situation Protocol is used only to assess attachment in infants.

97. C: Chronic fatigue syndrome (CFS) is an example of an invisible disability. Invisible disabilities are conditions that cause problems with everyday functioning even though they are not immediately obvious to others. Invisible disabilities are common, and their impact can be devastating. People with invisible disabilities must deal with their symptoms while also dealing with reactions of confusion, anger, and disbelief from others. For example, many people with chronic pain or limited mobility need to park in a handicapped parking spot. When they exit their vehicle without a cane, crutch, or wheelchair, other people may react with anger and aggression.

Even health professionals are not always trained in identifying and understanding the impact of invisible disabilities. It is important for social workers to know how to support people with these conditions and assist them in educating their loved ones and the rest of their care team about their condition and needs. Social workers must also remember not to make assumptions about anyone's abilities, including their clients. Choice *A* is incorrect because Down's syndrome is associated with specific facial features that make it readily apparent to others. Choice *B* is incorrect because Tourette's syndrome involves vocal and/or motor tics that are apparent to others. Choice *D* is incorrect because paraplegia means that a person's lower body is paralyzed. People with paraplegia need assistive mobility devices, making their disability visible to others.

98. B: The young man is exhibiting behavior and attitudes suggestive of an anxious attachment style. Anxious attachment develops when an infant's primary caregiver meets the child's needs inconsistently. The infant is left trying to figure out why they get the response they need sometimes but not other times. Insecurity, poor self-esteem, and fear of abandonment are common. Although attachment styles develop in the first few years of life, they continue to affect people throughout the lifespan. The

272

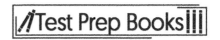

attachment with the original caregiver becomes the person's internal model for relating to others. The young man is desperate for his girlfriend's love but also afraid that it will be taken away.

The social worker can help the man gain awareness about this pattern, where it came from, and how to manage it without negatively affecting his relationship. The social worker can also model a secure attachment in the therapeutic relationship. Choice *A* is incorrect because securely attached adults tend to be comfortable in relationships. Choice *C* is incorrect because adults with avoidant attachment styles tend to fear intimacy and push people away in relationships. Choice *D* is incorrect because disorganized attachment develops because of abuse, neglect, and other serious problems in the original caregiver relationship. Adults with disorganized attachment styles tend to behave erratically in relationships, exhibiting characteristics of both anxious and avoidant styles at the same time.

99. D: The client's behavior is ego-dystonic because it goes against his ego, the part of his personality that manages the conflict between primal drives and social norms. Ego-dystonic behavior causes a person to feel guilty, unsettled, and anxious. If the behavior was in line with his ego and did not produce feelings of guilt and distress, it would be considered ego-syntonic, Choice *C*. Choice *A* is incorrect because the preconscious is the part of the mind that holds all the thoughts and feelings that a person is not currently focusing on but can be readily accessed when needed. Choice *B* is incorrect because the unconscious is the part of the mind that holds thoughts and feelings that a person has no conscious awareness of.

100. B: Cognitive behavioral approaches conceptualize a relationship among thoughts, feelings, and behaviors such that unwanted feelings and behaviors are caused by distorted, inaccurate, and overly negative thoughts, assumptions, and beliefs. The goal of cognitive behavioral therapy (CBT) is to teach clients to change the thought patterns that drive how they feel and behave. People are often not aware of their own limiting beliefs and habits of thinking. CBT first teaches clients to become aware of their thought patterns through self-monitoring, often including homework. Then, the therapist works with the client to practice challenging unhelpful thoughts, assumptions, and beliefs, and replacing them with statements that are more accurate and helpful. Choice *A* is incorrect because psychiatry, not psychotherapy, conceptualizes problems as resulting from chemical imbalances in the brain. Choice *C* is incorrect because although CBT can be used to treat trauma, it focuses on the thoughts, assumptions, and beliefs related to the trauma. This is different from psychotherapies like EMDR, which see the trauma itself as the source of the problem and processing the trauma as the solution. Choice *D* is incorrect because CBT focuses on solving problems in the present without going deeply into past experiences.

101. A: The social worker is using a token economy, which is an example of a behavioral approach. Behavioral approaches are based on the theories of Skinner and Pavlov, who believed that all behavior is learned. Learning occurs through punishment and reinforcement (both positive and negative). To teach a new behavior, the social worker provides incentives and rewards to motivate the client. Choice *B* is incorrect because psychoanalytic approaches are based on Freud's "talking cure," in which unconscious motivations are uncovered through unstructured talking with the therapist, free association, and dream interpretation. Choice *C* is incorrect because empowerment approaches involve helping clients develop their self-efficacy and access the resources they need to meet their own needs. Choice *D* is incorrect because cognitive approaches focus on changing thought patterns to influence feelings and behavior. Cognitive and behavioral approaches can be used on their own. They have also been found to be very effective when used together, as in cognitive behavioral therapy.

102. B: Homework including thought logs, also sometimes called emotion logs, is a critical part of CBT. The goal of CBT is to change how a client thinks, which takes a lot of time, practice, and self-awareness. Keeping a thought log encourages clients to practice their new skills outside of therapy sessions. This thought log is usually a worksheet that clients fill out whenever they notice they are feeling bad. They write down details about how they are feeling, Choice A; what thoughts they are having in response to their feelings, Choice C; and what behaviors they are doing at the time, Choice D. A thought log does not include references to the past; it is focused on the present. CBT is based on the idea that a client does not need to interrogate their past to find solutions to present problems.

103. D: The man is showing signs of normal age-related cognitive decline. After age 60, adults tend to experience a gradual decline in certain cognitive functions. Older adults lose fluid intelligence, which is the ability to think through new situations. This explains why the man became confused at the grocery store. On the other hand, crystallized intelligence, which includes learned information and behavior, remains stable. This is why the man can still answer all the trivia questions. The disconnect between these two abilities has led the man's wife to conclude that he is faking his confusion. The social worker can help by providing psychoeducation on normal aging, identifying areas where that the couple might need support, and connecting them with community resources.

Choice A is incorrect because the man is showing very subtle cognitive changes indicating normal aging. Dementia and Alzheimer's disease present with much more serious and obvious cognitive problems. The woman is very sensitive to the change in her husband because they are so close, but it is unlikely that his behavior would cause concern from other people. Choice B is incorrect because a stroke or another acute brain injury would present with much more severe symptoms that come on suddenly. Choice C is incorrect because there is no indication that the husband is abusive and trying to make his wife doubt her perceptions.

104. C: As people age, their social lives tend to change. Older adults tend to have fewer social connections than younger people. However, despite having a narrower social circle, Choice A, they report more positive interactions within that social circle. This is because older adults prioritize spending time with the people they truly care about and with whom they have positive and meaningful relationships, Choice B. Family relationships become more important as people age, Choice D, and older adults report more enjoyable interactions with family than younger people. All of these changes together are referred to as social aging and are considered normal.

105. A: Pansexual is the term for someone who experiences sexual and romantic attraction to people of all sexes and genders. This differs from bisexuality, Choice B, which means attraction to two genders, usually men and women. Pansexual is a broader term that encompasses the entire spectrum of gender and sex, including non-binary and intersex individuals. The word bisexual has been around longer than pansexual. For this reason, some people might call themselves bisexual despite being attracted to all genders and sexes. People should be allowed to describe their sexuality with whatever terms are comfortable for them. Social workers should be familiar with these terms and concepts and explore what they mean to their clients in order to provide the most effective support. Choice C is incorrect because transgender is a term that describes gender identity, not sexuality and attraction. Transgender people identify with a gender that is different from the sex they were assigned at birth. Choice D is incorrect because asexual means not experiencing sexual attraction. Asexual people are not interested in having sex with other people; however, they may still experience romantic or emotional attraction and a desire for intimate, non-sexual relationships.

106. D: The mother expressed a common misconception about gender identity and sexual orientation. They are distinct and unrelated concepts. The child identifying as transgender does not say anything about their sexuality. Transgender people can have any sexual orientation, just like cisgender people. Choice *A* is incorrect because although it is typical for teenagers to explore their sexuality, it does not mean that they are going through a phase that they will eventually snap out of. It can be harmful for parents to assume that their child is heterosexual and cisgender and dismiss anything else as a "phase." Choice *B* is incorrect because gender identity and sexuality are unrelated. People do not decide to change their gender to avoid being homosexual. Choice *C* is incorrect because expressing one's gender identity is normal behavior and not an indication of dysfunction or attention-seeking.

107. D: Sarah's feelings are an example of transference, which means that she is projecting something onto her supervisor. Transference can occur when working with clients and it can also occur in the supervisory relationship. Exploring the transference with her supervisor could strengthen their professional relationship as well as help her understand patterns in her other relationships. Choice *A* is incorrect because although her feelings are not unusual, suppressing them would not be helpful. Choice *B* is incorrect because she should explore these feelings in the context of supervision. Also, it would still be a dual relationship to pursue a romantic attachment with a former supervisor. Choice *C* is incorrect because supervision is not an appropriate place to explore the possibility of a romantic relationship.

108. B: This policy is a red flag for potential safety issues because it requires a client to display unsafe behavior three times before action is taken. A better policy would be to have a clear process for employees to report any unsafe client behavior as soon as it occurs and a clear set of steps for addressing it. All employees should be familiar with this procedure and have confidence that using it will not result in penalty or reprisal from the agency.

109. C: Self-care is extremely important for social workers to be productive at work and fully engaged in their personal lives. In addition to the practices outlined in choices *A*, *B*, and *D*, self-care can include things like journaling, having supportive relationships with colleagues, and taking time off to relax and recharge when appropriate. Choice *C* is incorrect because discussing clients with a friend or family member is a violation of client privacy. While it can be helpful to let friends and family know if one is feeling overwhelmed at work, it is unethical to disclose information about clients and their treatment.

110. A: Sandra is experiencing compassion fatigue, which includes a combination of the symptoms of burnout and secondary trauma. Burnout involves total exhaustion and feelings of professional inadequacy and hopelessness. Secondary trauma involves experiencing the same symptoms as one's clients who have been exposed to trauma, such as nightmares and hypervigilance. Both burnout and compassion fatigue tend to develop slowly over time, while secondary trauma is more likely to develop quickly in response to a specific trauma experienced by a client. Stress is a more general term and can be either helpful or harmful depending on the circumstances. Stress is certainly a part of what Sandra is feeling, but compassion fatigue is more accurate.

111. C: The social worker is using an empowerment approach. The goal of empowerment approaches is to help clients access the resources they need to achieve their goals. This approach is strengths-based, meaning it focuses on building clients' abilities, resilience, power, and resources, rather than reducing their deficits. Empowerment approaches believe that every client has the ability to make the changes they want to make when they have access to the resources they need. This approach takes into account the impact of discrimination on groups and individuals; clients are encouraged to connect with others who have similar experiences and goals and work together to advocate for their collective needs. The

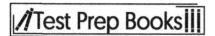
role of the social worker is to help clients identify and build on strengths and access resources. Choice *A* is incorrect because harm reduction seeks to improve health and reduce harms associated with a behavior. Choice *B* is incorrect because crisis intervention approaches focus on stabilizing clients in acute crisis situations. Choice *D* is incorrect because behavioral approaches use incentives to motivate individuals to change their behaviors.

112. C: A client contract is an agreement between the social worker and client about treatment expectations. It is usually a written document, but it can also be more informal, depending on agency policies. Although the social worker and client create it collaboratively and agree to commit to it, it is not a legal document. This means that it is not legally binding or enforceable. The client and social worker should agree on what the consequences will be if either party breaks the agreement, with the understanding that the consequences will not involve the legal system. Social workers should explain the purpose of the contract in a way that each of their clients understands.

It is especially important that clients understand their role in the creation of the contract; that is, clients do not merely sign it, they co-create it. The contract should include the client's goals, Choice *D*, written as SMART goals. SMART stands for specific, measurable, achievable, realistic, and timely. The contract describes how progress on these goals will be tracked and what the process will be for modifying or adding to the treatment plan, Choice *A*. The contract should also contain expectations for when and where sessions will occur, what happens if a session is missed or cancelled as in Choice *B*, how long treatment will last, and any financial arrangements that have been made.

113. A: When using partializing techniques to help clients prioritize their treatment goals, Maslow's hierarchy of needs is a useful theoretical construct. Maslow's hierarchy conceptualizes human needs in the form of a pyramid with the most basic on the bottom and the most complex at the top. To build a strong and stable pyramid, you start at the foundation and move up as each level is completed. The base of the pyramid includes physiological needs like food, air, and water. The next level is safety, then love and belonging, followed by esteem. At the top of the pyramid is self-actualization. If a client is facing food insecurity and wants to make new friends, then food insecurity should be the priority. Choice *B* is incorrect because Erikson's stages of psychosocial development describe human development in terms of eight life stages, each defined by a specific conflict that needs to be resolved to progress to the next stage successfully.

The theory can help social workers understand what concerns a client is likely to have based on their life stage, as well as identify areas where a client is more or less advanced than expected. However, the theory has been criticized for cultural and gender bias and would not be particularly helpful in prioritizing the goals of an individual client. Choice *C* is incorrect because Freud's stages of psychosexual development describe human personality development in terms of five stages of sexual maturation. The theory has always been controversial and would not be helpful in prioritizing client goals. Choice *D* is incorrect because systems theory describes how systems function and interact. It can help in understanding how changes in one part of a system can affect the rest of the system; for example, when a child develops a serious illness, the rest of the family will be affected. Systems theory is very important in social work, but it does not directly address how goals should be prioritized.

114. B: Partialization means breaking complex problems into more manageable parts. Clients sometimes come to treatment with multiple complex issues, and it can be challenging to know where to start. Partializing techniques can help the client and the social worker feel less overwhelmed by creating a logical, organized treatment plan. The social worker can help the client translate their issues into SMART

276

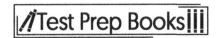

goals, determine which goals are most important to the client, predict which goals will be easier or quicker to achieve, and decide which goals to tackle first. Social workers can also teach clients to use partializing techniques outside of sessions when they are facing complex problems and feeling overwhelmed and unsure of how to proceed. Choice A is incorrect because it describes holistic practice. Choice C is incorrect because it describes role clarification. Choice D is incorrect because it describes role play.

115. D: Assertiveness training involves teaching clients to communicate their feelings and needs directly in a way that is respectful of others. Social workers can help clients develop their skills in this area by identifying situations in which the client has trouble being assertive, teaching them strategies, and practicing until assertive communication becomes more natural. Replacing "you" statements, Choice B, with "I" statements is a common technique. "You" statements involve blame and put people on the defensive, while "I" statements focus on the feelings of the speaker. For example, the statement, "You always come home late! You obviously don't care about me," could be replaced with "I get worried when you come home late, because I'm afraid something has happened to you."

The "I" statement is much more likely to lead to a constructive conversation where both people get their needs met. It is critical for social workers to understand that assertiveness is not the same as aggressiveness. Choice A is incorrect because not taking no for an answer is an example of aggressiveness and not respecting others' rights and boundaries. Choice C is incorrect because assertiveness is about communicating directly. People are often afraid to communicate difficult or negative feelings directly because they don't want to make the other person feel bad. In the long run, avoiding these conversations usually leads to more problems. Assertiveness training teaches people how to communicate directly without alienating or harming other people.

116. A: Relapse is considered an unofficial stage in the stages of change model because it is so common among people trying to change their behavior. When a person relapses, they move back to one of the previous stages. It is important for clinicians to destigmatize relapse, framing it as part of recovery rather than a failure. Choices B and C are not part of the model, officially or unofficially, and Choice D is an official stage of change.

117. C: The miracle question helps a client imagine a life without their current problem. It provides insight into a client's goals and helps the client think past their perceived limitations. It is particularly helpful with clients who struggle to articulate what a better future would look like. Choice A is incorrect because scaling questions ask clients to rate something on a scale of 1-10. Choice B is incorrect because seeking exceptions questions ask clients about exceptions to the rule, such as moments when they were not experiencing their presenting problem. Unlike the miracle question, seeking exceptions questions are concrete, not hypothetical. Choice D is incorrect because clarifying questions are used to check that the social worker has understood the client and to make the client feel heard.

118. D: Alexa demonstrates high motivation and low resistance. Evidence of high motivation includes feeling hopeful about getting better, acknowledging the need for change, being willing to take small steps to change behavior, participating fully in sessions, and not missing sessions. Most clients show at least some degree of resistance. In Alexa's case, she is fearful, but she acknowledges her fear and still wants to change. Coming to sessions a little late could indicate resistance, but in this case, her tardiness is clearly explained by her school schedule, and she is diligent about attending and participating. Choices A, B, and C are incorrect because they do not describe Alexa. Choices A and B are unlikely to describe most clients because typically motivation and resistance have an inverse relationship.

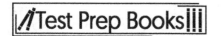

119. B: High self-confidence indicates motivation rather than resistance to change. It is important for clients to believe that they can improve their lives. Social workers can help clients increase their self-confidence by focusing on their strengths, resources, and goals, and by celebrating every small step in the right direction. Choices *A*, *C*, and *D* are incorrect because they are all indications that a client is resistant to change. When clients exhibit resistance, the social worker should explore the resistance and where it is coming from. Then, they should assess which stage of change the client is in and tailor their interventions accordingly with the goal of moving the client towards readiness for change.

120. A: Coping skills are the strategies people employ to deal with their problems. Asking about how clients handled problems in the past and identifying patterns in how they react to difficult situations can reveal how healthy their coping skills are. Choice *B* is incorrect because communication skills are assessed by paying close attention to a client's verbal and nonverbal communication in the context of their culture and history. Choices *C* and *D* are incorrect because motivation and resistance are assessed by observing a client's behavior and determining which stage of change they are in.

121. B: Liam is a cisgender man. Cisgender means that a person's gender identity matches their biological sex. A cisgender man has male genitalia, one X chromosome and one Y chromosome, and male sex hormones, and identifies as a man. Transgender, Choice *B,* means that a person does not identify with the gender they were assigned at birth. For example, if Liam had male genitalia, chromosomes, and hormones, but identified as a woman, he would be transgender. Choice *C* is incorrect because labeling cisgender people "normal" and people of other genders "abnormal" is transphobic and contributes to the stigma against the transgender community. Social workers have an ethical obligation to fight against these stigmatizing beliefs to promote social justice and the inherent dignity of every person. Choice *D* is incorrect because non-binary means that a person does not identify as either a man or a woman, but rather as a mix of both or neither. Some non-binary people consider themselves gender fluid, meaning that their gender identity is not fixed and changes over time or in different situations. In general, some people experience the same gender identity throughout their lives, while other people's identities might shift or change.

122. B: Psychotic disorders are not commonly associated with poor body image. People with psychotic disorders can have positive or negative body image, but poor body image does not lead to psychotic disorders or symptoms. On the other hand, poor body image is strongly associated with other types of distress, including emotional distress, anxiety, depression, and eating disorders. Eating disorders can arise as the result of negative body image and vice versa. Poor body image tends to be accompanied by low self-esteem and self-confidence, which can cause people to withdraw from social relationships. People who feel ashamed about the way they look may start to believe that they do not deserve to be treated well. They may treat themselves poorly and seek others who treat them poorly as well.

123. D: Every individual has a unique life course, and many factors influence a person's self-esteem at any given time. However, it is possible to make general statements about human self-esteem across the lifespan. Research has shown that people tend to start with high self-esteem in childhood, which declines through adolescence. Adolescence is a time of identity confusion, puberty, and more shaky self-esteem. As people enter adulthood and become more stable, their self-esteem starts to rise. It continues to rise throughout adulthood until reaching its highest point around age 60. At this point, people are comfortable with themselves and the social roles they occupy. Finally, in late adulthood, after age 70, self-esteem declines sharply. This corresponds to the age when physical health is declining, people lose status, their social roles change, and their networks become smaller.

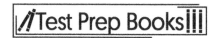

124. A: As people enter old age, a combination of factors can put them at increased risk of depression. Declining physical health and age-related cognitive decline make daily activities more difficult, and more serious health problems may start to arise. Older people experience many social losses, including the loss of status associated with working and a reduction in community participation. Although older adults have fewer social connections over time, the connections they maintain tend to be strong, meaningful relationships, not superficial ones. Gerontologists generally recommend that older adults maintain these relationships and also find other ways to continue participating in community and social life as a way to reduce their risk of depression.

125. C: Research has demonstrated that spirituality has a positive impact on people's health and happiness. Spirituality is different from religion. Religion is organized around a specific doctrine. Spirituality is a much broader term encompassing a variety of practices related to mind, body, and spirit. Some people's religion and spirituality are related, while other people consider themselves spiritual but not religious. The benefits of spirituality are not dependent on membership of any particular religion. On average, people who embrace spirituality live longer and report being happier. These benefits come from the hope that faith provides, the social connections gained through participating in spiritual practices, and the opportunities for healing emotional pain.

126. D: Evidence-based practice is a process of taking into account research evidence, clinical knowledge, and client characteristics to choose the most appropriate intervention or treatment. It provides better outcomes for clients and increases the legitimacy of the profession. Before evidence-based practice was emphasized, these decisions were made based on authority, common sense, and tradition, as in Choice *D*.

127. B: The tool lacks *validity*, meaning that it is not measuring what it intends to measure. The fact that the tool produces consistent results means that it is measuring something, just not depressive symptoms. Choice *A* is incorrect because *reliability* means producing consistent results. The tool has reliability, but not validity. Choices *C* and *D* are incorrect because *external validity* means that the results from the study participants can be applied to the general population. *Internal validity* means that participant results are caused by the intervention and not by some other factor.

128. B: GPA is the dependent variable, meaning that it is expected to be increased or reduced in response to changes in the independent variable, which is the homework policy. The study controls and manipulates the independent variable (homework policy) in order to see how it affects the dependent variable (students' GPAs). Choice *C, high school juniors*, refers to the study sample and Choice *D, bilingual charter school*, refers to the population from which the study sample is selected.

129. C: The *NASW Code of Ethics* provides guidance on how to set fees for social workers in private practice. It states that fees must be "fair, reasonable, and commensurate with services," and that fees should take into consideration "a client's ability to pay." Offering reduced fees on a sliding scale to low-income clients is one way to set fees ethically and fairly. The *NASW Code of Ethics* was updated in 2017 to include guidance on offering pro bono services. Specifically, the section on the social work value of service encourages social workers to offer at least some services pro bono. Pro bono means "for the public good," and in this context refers to providing services without charging a fee. For these reasons, both a sliding scale and pro bono services are ethical and even encouraged in the profession.

130. C: According to the *NASW Code of Ethics*, ethical responsibilities fall into the following six categories: to their clients, their colleagues, and greater society, as well as in practice settings, as

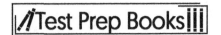

professionals, and to the profession itself. Each of these six responsibilities is discussed extensively in the "Ethical Standards" section of the *Code of Ethics.* The *Code* also provides guidance on how to manage conflicts among these responsibilities. For example, a social worker's primary responsibility is to their client, but this must be balanced with their responsibility to the greater society. Although social workers, like anyone else, certainly have personal responsibilities to their family members, the profession does not set specific ethical standards related to social workers' family relationships.

131. D: According to the *NASW Code of Ethics*, it is unethical for social workers to ask current clients for testimonials. This would be a misuse of social workers' power and influence over their clients. Even though she plans to tell them that refusing will not affect their treatment, her clients could still feel pressured to participate. To avoid the potential for manipulation, coercion, and undue influence, the *Code of Ethics* instructs social workers to avoid soliciting testimonials in general and especially from current clients.

132. D: Using alcohol or drugs to feel better is an example of avoidant coping. Other examples include over-focusing on work, withdrawing and isolating, and avoiding thinking about problems. Choice *A* is incorrect because humor is a healthy coping mechanism. Choice *B* is incorrect because it indicates a dependent coping style. Choice *C* is incorrect because it indicates an aggressive coping style. While these unhealthy coping styles may provide some short-term relief, in the long term they are likely to create additional problems.

133. D: In social work, level of care refers to different treatment options along a continuum from least (outpatient) to most (inpatient) restrictive. Social workers must offer clients the least restrictive option that still ensures their health and safety. For example, if a client could be treated with outpatient therapy, it would not be appropriate to recommend a partial hospitalization program. Clients may need to go up or down levels of care as their needs change over time. Choices *A* and *B* are incorrect because these options might not be appropriate for a client's needs. Choice *C* is incorrect because the highest level of care is not necessarily the better option, depending on a client's needs.

134. A: Anosognosia is the term for lack of insight, and it can be a feature of many psychiatric disorders. The client does not realize that he is ill and perceiving reality differently from those around him. Anosognosia is different from denial, Choice *D*, in that the client is not being stubborn or willfully ignoring his illness. Instead, his brain is literally unable to recognize that something is wrong. Choice *B* is incorrect because synesthesia is a neurological difference where one type of sensory input automatically triggers another. This sensory mixing can take different forms. For example, some people see colors when they hear sounds, associate numbers and letters with colors, or "taste" words. It is not considered a mental disorder. Choice *C* is incorrect because prosopagnosia, also called face blindness, is an inability to recognize faces. It can occur from birth or be acquired after brain injury.

135. B: In the trauma-informed care model, the three "E's" of trauma are event, experience, and effects. This means that trauma is caused by one or more *events*, that a person *experiences* it as threatening to their life or self, and that it has negative *effects* on a person's well-being and functioning. The three "E's," first introduced by SAMHSA, are widely considered to be the basic definition of what trauma is and how it occurs. Choices *A*, *C*, and *D* are incorrect because they are not included in the three "E's" concept.

136. C: The SOAP format is commonly used by social workers and other types of health care professionals when documenting meetings with clients. The acronym stands for: subjective, objective, assessment, plan. *Subjective* information includes a client's feelings and perceptions, *objective* includes facts and observations, *assessment* includes a summary of the combined subjective and objective data, and *plan* includes the treatment plan that follows from the assessment. Choices A, B, and D are incorrect because they are not part of the acronym. Information related to psychological and physical functioning and the presenting problem could appear under any of the four sections of a SOAP note.

137. A: Research has shown that although men and women tend to follow the same basic pattern of self-esteem throughout the lifespan, certain differences can be observed. Self-esteem tends to be high in early childhood, and then decline through later childhood and adolescence. In adulthood, self-esteem steadily rises in both men and women; however, men tend to have higher self-esteem than women during this period. As adults continue to age, the difference between men's and women's self-esteem decreases; by very old age, women's tends to be higher than men's. Gender is one factor that affects self-esteem throughout the lifespan, but it is important to remember that these are population trends, and every individual is unique.

138. B: Gender dysphoria means feeling like one's gender does not match the sex they were assigned at birth. Gender dysphoria does not develop as a response to trauma; this is a pernicious myth about which social workers should be informed. The myth assumes that trauma, especially sexual trauma, causes people to develop gender dysphoria, but this is not true. On the other hand, transgender people are at a much higher risk of experiencing trauma due to stigma and discrimination. Although trauma does not change someone's gender, it does have profound effects on other aspects of their sense of self.

People who have been through traumatic events often feel unsafe in their bodies and environments. They come to view the world as being a fundamentally dangerous place. Particularly for survivors of interpersonal trauma, there may be a deep sense of betrayal. Survivors may feel like other people cannot be trusted. They may also develop a belief that they are bad or otherwise deserving of the trauma they suffered. They may feel broken, damaged, or fundamentally different from other people. It is common for trauma survivors to engage in self-harming and self-destructive behaviors in response to these alterations in self-esteem. Social workers can help trauma survivors heal their self-image by processing their trauma and challenging the maladaptive self-beliefs that came from it.

139. D: Phil's mother should be assessed for anorexia nervosa. Anorexia nervosa is an eating disorder characterized by excessive weight loss, fear of weight gain, and body image distortion. The woman exhibits many telltale signs of the disorder, such as food rituals, dressing in clothes that conceal body shape, social withdrawal, and weight loss. Many people, including family members and even professionals, have biases about which types of people develop eating disorders. The stereotype of eating disorder sufferers being young, underweight, white females is dangerous because eating disorders can affect anyone. In the example, even though Phil knows his mother is dieting, he assumes her excessive weight loss must be caused by a medical condition or age-related cognitive decline. Social workers must be aware of their own biases and stereotypes about different conditions in order to accurately identify people who are suffering. There is no evidence that the woman's behavior is due to mood changes in bipolar disorder. The woman does not have a history of bipolar disorder, and it is extremely rare to suddenly develop the condition that late in life. Also, the woman's symptoms are better explained by an eating disorder than a mood disorder.

140. B: The client's upbringing is an example of authoritarian parenting. This parenting style involves the parent as dictator of the house, making all the rules and decisions. Children are meant to obey and face

281

punishment for questioning or failing to abide by the rules. Authoritarian households tend to have high expectations and low warmth. Children brought up in this environment are often capable but unhappy. Choice *A* is incorrect because permissive parenting is basically the opposite of authoritarian parenting. Permissive parents do not set or enforce many rules—and when rules are broken, there do not tend to be serious consequences. Children in permissive households are free to behave as they wish. Permissive households tend to be low on expectations and high on warmth. Children brought up by permissive parents tend to experience difficulties at school, at work, and in relationships.

Choice *C* is incorrect because authoritative parenting involves high expectations and high warmth. There are rules and structure, but children are given some input into the rules and decisions that affect them. There are consequences to breaking rules, but punishments are not too severe. Children raised in authoritative households tend to experience the most positive life outcomes. Choice *D* is incorrect because uninvolved parenting is often seen in dysfunctional families. It involves inconsistent rules and consequences without warmth or guidance for children. This parenting style tends to leave children confused about how they are supposed to behave. Children raised by uninvolved parents tend to experience problems throughout the lifespan.

141. C: Minor clients do not have the ability to provide informed consent unless they are legally emancipated. Unemancipated minors require consent from their parent or guardian to access services. The age at which a minor can access services without parental involvement varies by state. Even though the child is the client, the parent is legally allowed access to the child's records, and they decide who the records will be shared with because they are the one providing informed consent. It is considered best practice for social workers to seek a minor's assent to treatment and to make sure they understand the limits to their confidentiality. When parents request their child's treatment information, social workers should let the child know before sharing with the parents if possible. Choices *A, B,* and *D* are incorrect because social workers must get written permission from a client to share their information with insurance companies or other payers; consultants, colleagues, and supervisors; interdisciplinary teams; and any other third party requesting the client's information.

142. A: Licensed clinical social workers are qualified or licensed to diagnose and treat mental illness. They can provide psychotherapy to individuals, groups, families, and couples in a variety of settings, including their own private practice. Licensed clinical social workers cannot prescribe medication. For this reason, social workers who diagnose and treat mental illness often have professional relationships with psychiatrists and other prescribers to whom they can refer their patients for medication management.

143. D: It would be unethical to include "published author" in a section about her qualifications as a social worker because the book is totally unrelated to social work. It does not matter that she is not providing a link or encouraging her clients to purchase the book, although these actions would also be unethical. The basic problem is that she is implying that the book is a professional accomplishment rather than a personal one. This would be like someone getting a doctorate in computer science and then adding "doctor" to their social work business card – it is false advertising because of the implication that the doctorate is related to social work.

144. C: It is unethical to give or receive any kind of compensation for a referral. Ellen cannot accept the free massage because it creates a conflict of interest. If she accepts the massage, it could communicate to Julie that they have an unspoken agreement whereby Ellen gives Julie clients, and Julie gives Ellen discounts. When making referrals, a social worker should only be considering what is best for the client,

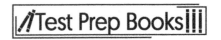

not what the benefit to the social worker might be. Choice *A* is incorrect because her medical situation does not change the fact that accepting the massage would be unethical. Choice *B* is incorrect because the ethical standard applies to any type of referral. Choice *D* is incorrect because getting a massage from the same person a client goes to is not an unethical dual relationship; it is unethical because it creates a conflict of interest.

145. B: Insurance companies, agencies, and clients often prefer treatment that is shorter in duration. In the example, the client has a specific problem to work on in a brief period of time, so treatment should be practical and focused on the present. Psychoanalytic approaches would not be suitable because they require a long duration of treatment and focus on exploring past experiences, dreams, unconscious desires, and the origins of problems. Choices *A, C,* and *D* are brief interventions that focus on solving current problems. Task-centered approaches, Choice *A,* involve translating goals into a series of tasks that the client completes to solve their problem. Cognitive behavioral approaches, Choice *C,* involve identifying distorted thought patterns with more helpful ones resulting in behavior change. Brief, solution-focused approaches, Choice *D,* find practical, concrete solutions for present problems.

146. C: Cognitive behavioral therapy (CBT) is one of the most popular forms of psychotherapy, particularly among insurance companies and other third-party payors. This is because it has been researched more than any other psychotherapy, Choice *A.* Research has been shown it to be effective, evidence-based treatment for a wide range of problems and disorders, Choice *B.* Unlike some forms of psychotherapy, it is structured and time limited, Choice *D.* For these reasons, CBT is often considered the gold standard for psychotherapy interventions. However, CBT is not necessarily effective for all clients. In particular, clients with learning difficulties and psychotic disorders are unlikely to benefit from CBT. It is important for social workers to be aware of the limitations of CBT and advocate for alternatives when CBT would not be effective.

147. A: Psychoeducation involves providing information to help clients understand their problems. Psychoeducation helps clients learn about the nature of the problem, its causes and effects, and different treatment options and resources that are available. One purpose of psychoeducation is to provide clients with the vocabulary they need to talk about their experiences. In the example, the participant used the word *junkie*, which is stigmatizing, ill-defined, and not a useful way to describe a person's situation. Because this is the first group meeting, it is important for the social worker to set the tone, make it clear that stigmatizing language is unhelpful and unwelcome in the group, and provide alternative vocabulary to foster a more effective discussion.

Choice *B* is incorrect because it challenges the participant's beliefs rather than addressing the real issue, which is the participant's choice of words. Choice *C* is incorrect because the situation is an opportunity to get the whole group on the same page about language. Also, pulling the participant aside might make them feel singled out and does not reassure the rest of the group that this type of language will not be used in the future. Choice *D* is incorrect because this is the first meeting of the group, so the social worker should create a safe atmosphere and establish rules and expectations for the group. A failure to react communicates that stigmatizing language is acceptable, which could make other participants feel unsafe and unwilling to participate.

148. A: The supervisor should explain to Andre that it is unethical to include extraneous personal information about clients that is unrelated to treatment in a client's record. Client records are not merely notes to aid the social worker. Under certain circumstances, they can be seen by the client, other professionals, or the courts. A good general rule is to not include anything in a client file that one would

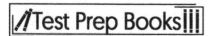

not want to read aloud in court. Although Andre's method clearly helped him with memory, it is not ethical, and the supervisor must help him find a different solution to replace his current one.

149. C: According to the *NASW Code of Ethics*, the core values of the social work profession are service, integrity, dignity and worth of the person, importance of human relationships, competence, and social justice. Confidentiality is an important concept in social work, but it is not one of the six core values.

150. D: Becoming a client's support system is not a way to uphold the value of the importance of human relationships. The social worker should instead assist a client in building and strengthening their own support system. The social worker can do this by helping the client to identify people who already support them, identify others who could potentially support them, assist them in strengthening these relationships, provide education on healthy relationships, and act as a partner to the client throughout the treatment process.

151. D: The social worker should obtain supervision to discuss the situation. She should only proceed if they determine together that it is professionally justified. In general, social workers should always consult a supervisor before making a self-disclosure. Choice *A* is incorrect because it still involves a self-disclosure that the social worker is unsure about. Choice *B* is incorrect because it is not the client's decision whether the social worker uses self-disclosure. Choice *C* is incorrect because it does not help the social worker determine if self-disclosure would help the client. It also does not provide the social worker with an opportunity to improve their services by learning how to manage the situation if it comes up again in the future.

152. C: "The client reports feeling sad and lethargic" is subjective data. Choices *A*, *B*, and *D* are incorrect because they are examples of objective data. Social workers use both objective and subjective data when assessing, diagnosing, and treating clients. In this question, it could be that the client reported feeling sad and lethargic (subjective evidence of depression), which prompted the social worker to assess the client using the BDI (objective data). Taken together, the client's score on the BDI and his reported feelings provide strong evidence to support a treatment plan for depression.

153. C: According to the *DSM-5-TR*, Mr. X meets the full criteria for major depressive disorder. For at least two weeks, he has been experiencing at least five depressive symptoms, and at least one symptom is depressed mood or loss of interest/pleasure. This represents a change from his previous functioning and is not related to a medical disorder. In a previous edition of the *DSM* (*DSM-IV*), major depressive disorder was not diagnosed within two months of a death. This was called the "bereavement exclusion," which has been eliminated in the *DSM-5-TR*. This is due to the recognition that, although grief and depression share some features, they are distinct conditions. Clients who meet the full criteria for depression should be offered appropriate treatment regardless of whether the depression occurred in the context of grief. Choice *A* is incorrect because bereavement disorder is not a diagnosis. Choice *B* is incorrect because dysthymia is chronic depression that occurs over at least two years. Choice *D* is incorrect because adjustment disorder with depressed mood is diagnosed when someone experiences depressive symptoms in response to a psychosocial stressor but does not meet the full criteria for major depressive disorder.

154. A: Ego strength refers to a person's ability to be resilient in the face of stressors, cope with problems, and return to their baseline after emotional upset. Choice *A*, not experiencing negative moods, is NOT an indication of ego strength. Everyone experiences negative moods, but people with high ego strength recognize that moods don't last forever, avoid getting overwhelmed by them, and

284

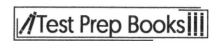

learn and grow from negative experiences. Choices *B*, *C*, and *D* are incorrect because they are all indicators of high ego strength.

155. D: Renal disease refers to kidney disease. The kidneys are the main component of the renal system and work to filter impurities from the blood. The prefixes *ren-* and *neph-* both refer to kidneys; a person with renal disease sees a nephrologist for medical treatment. People with kidney problems may require dialysis, diet changes, medication, or other medical interventions. Kidney problems can also affect how certain medications are metabolized in the body, which may mean that the person requires a different dosage than a person with healthy kidneys. Choices *A*, *B*, and *C* are incorrect because they are not part of the renal system.

156. B: Hepatitis affects the liver. There are several different kinds of hepatitis including hepatitis A, hepatitis B, hepatitis C, and alcoholic hepatitis. There are vaccines to protect against A and B. C is a particular concern among people who inject drugs or receive blood transfusions. C is now curable, but the treatment can be expensive. Unlike A, B, and C, alcoholic hepatitis is not caused by a virus and can be cured by abstinence from alcohol. The prefix *hep-* refers to the liver; a person with hepatitis sees a hepatologist for medical treatment. Choices *A*, *C*, and *D* are incorrect because they refer to other organs.

157. C: Hilda's mother is her court-appointed legal guardian, which means that Hilda cannot legally provide her own informed consent for treatment. The social worker should still have the informed consent conversation with Hilda (including the role of her mother), make sure she understands, and seek her assent. Then, the social worker should have a similar conversation with her mother and have her mother sign the informed consent documents. Choice *A* is incorrect because even though Hilda can't provide informed consent, she should still be given all of the relevant information in language that she understands. It is especially important for her to understand the limits of her confidentiality and her mother's access to her records. Choice *B* is incorrect because Hilda cannot legally sign the informed consent. Also, the social worker should not listen to Hilda's entire story before obtaining Hilda's assent and her mother's consent. Choice *D* is incorrect because consulting a supervisor is not necessary; the legal, ethical, and organizational standards are clear that Hilda's mother must provide informed consent.

158. A: Genograms and ecomaps are tools commonly used by social workers to assess a client's environment and relationships. Ecomaps help a social worker and client understand how various forces in the client's life impact their functioning. Genograms help uncover patterns in the family and how they affect the client. These assessment tools are used during the treatment process, not during informed consent. Social workers are required by law to get informed consent from clients before starting treatment. The purpose of informed consent is to provide information about the treatment process, the role of the social worker and client, the client's rights and any limitations to those rights, as well as whether and how technology will be used.

159. C: Institutional Review Boards (IRBs) approve and monitor research studies that use human subjects. The *NASW Code of Ethics* encourages social workers to contribute to the development of knowledge in the profession, and doing research is one way to accomplish this. Social workers conducting research on human subjects have an ethical obligation to protect those subjects from harm and must obtain IRB approval before beginning the study. IRBs can approve a study, recommend changes, and monitor the study process for any ethical concerns that may arise.

160. B: Dual relationships involve having two different relationships with someone at the same time or at different times. In social work, it is best to avoid dual relationships whenever possible. Sometimes dual relationships are unavoidable, especially in smaller communities. When a dual relationship occurs, it is important to determine whether it is ethical and act accordingly. A supervisor requiring his supervisees to participate in his research study is unethical because the supervisor is using his power over his supervisees in a coercive way.

It is unethical to require anyone to participate in a research study, and doing research on your subordinates creates a conflict of interest. Terminating with a client to pursue a business opportunity together is unethical because it is unethical to have a business relationship with a client. Additionally, terminating services for this purpose is unethical and could harm the client. Hiring a client to assist with an event is unethical for the same reasons; it creates a conflict of interest and interferes with the treatment process. Attending the same church as a client is an example of a dual relationship that might be unavoidable, especially in small communities. However, it is ethical as long as it does not interfere with treatment. Referring a client to a former colleague is not a dual relationship and is not unethical as long as it benefits the client. Providing treatment to two members of the same family is not a dual relationship and not unethical as long as the social worker clarifies their role related to each client.

161. C: Geriatric social workers primarily work with older people and specialize in helping their clients live well as they age. Geriatric social workers help people adjust to the biopsychosocial changes that come with aging. They may also work with their clients' families and caregivers. Geriatric social work is a growing field; the population is aging, people are living longer, and people's expectations about old age are changing. Geriatric social workers play an important role in advocating for opportunities for older people to access connection, activity, and meaning in their communities. Choice *A* is incorrect because geriatric social work is not related to bariatric surgery. Choices *B* and *D* are incorrect because, although geriatric social workers assist their clients with a wide range of potential issues, they specialize in aging, not genetic testing or autism.

162. D: As genetic testing becomes more popular, social workers are increasingly called to support clients undergoing genetic testing. Social workers' roles can include conducting biopsychosocial assessments for people with genetic disorders, assisting them to access resources and support, counseling clients who are deciding whether to undergo testing, providing psychoeducation and counseling to clients after testing, and assisting clients with genetic disorders in making family planning decisions. Essentially, social workers can be involved in all aspects of genetic testing except conducting the test itself and diagnosing genetic disorders. Social workers can connect clients with genetic testing services and help them understand their diagnosis, but providing the actual diagnosis is not the social worker's role.

163. C: Family life cycle theories describe the development of family systems in terms of stages that families progress through over time. During the launching-family stage, the children have grown up and are establishing themselves as independent adults. The relationship between parents and their children shifts to accommodate these new roles. During this stage, the parents might also start taking on caregiver roles as their own parents age. Choice *A* is incorrect because finding a suitable lifestyle and life partner happens during the first stage: unattached young adult. Choice *B* is incorrect because establishing a marital system occurs during the newly-married couple stage. Choice *D* is incorrect because transitioning from a marital to a family system happens during the family-with-young-children stage. Family life cycle theories can provide insight into the challenges that families commonly confront at different times. However, these models are based on a very narrow view of what a family is, and do not take into account the many different types of families common today. It is important for social workers to remember that each individual and family is unique.

164. A: Adults who become caregivers for their aging parents are at an increased risk of depression, substance use, and heart disease. Cognitive decline is not associated with caregiving. In the United States, it is common for adults to care for their elderly parents at a time when they are still supporting their children. This dual responsibility causes stress and demands on time, financial resources, and energy. Relationships between adult children and their aging parents can become strained, especially if the parent is not appreciative of the caregiving. On the other hand, family relationships can be strengthened, and more closeness can develop among the generations. Social workers can help caregivers by connecting them with resources, support, coping skills, and burnout prevention strategies.

165. B: Ms. M appears to be suffering from PTSD caused by the car accident. PTSD involves symptoms of re-experiencing (nightmares), avoidance (not driving), arousal and reactivity (jumpy), and cognition and mood (numb). Choice *A* is incorrect because her alcohol use appears to be secondary to her PTSD. People sometimes use substances to cope with symptoms of PTSD. If Ms. M continues drinking to fall asleep, she might develop an Alcohol Use Disorder; however, that is not the primary cause of her other behavioral symptoms. Choices *C* and *D* are incorrect because although she is showing signs of depression and anxiety, they appear to be caused by the PTSD rather than Major Depressive Disorder or General Anxiety Disorder.

166. C: This type of explanation is called psychoeducation, and it is an important component of social work. Psychoeducation involves providing clients with information about their problems and disorders. When clients understand the nature of their problem, its cause and effects, and the treatment options available, it helps them feel more in control and make better decisions. In the example, the client believes their schizophrenia is caused by demons, so logically the way to get better would be to remove the demons. To solve a problem effectively, a client must understand it.

Once the client understands that schizophrenia is caused by biological, psychological, and social factors, they will be more likely to pursue appropriate treatments. Choice *A* is incorrect because partializing is the process of breaking complex issues into smaller, more manageable components. Choice *B* is incorrect because psychotherapy is the general term for treatments that involve talking and listening to a client about their problems. Psychoeducation can happen during psychotherapy. Choice *D* is incorrect because assessment is the process of gathering information about a client to inform their treatment plan. In the example, the social worker is in the process of assessing the client when they provide the psychoeducational explanation about schizophrenia. Assessment is about collecting information, while psychoeducation is about providing information.

167. C: Group therapy progresses through three general stages: beginning, middle, and end. The focus of the group changes as it transitions from one stage to the next. Preparation, Choice *A*, is not technically a stage in the group process, but there is important work for the social worker to do before the group begins. The social worker must make decisions about the type, duration, participants, and purpose of the group. During the beginning stage, Choice *B*, the social worker takes an active role in setting the tone and norms of the group. Participants tend to be more hesitant in this stage because they have not yet formed relationships with each other. During the middle stage, most of the group's therapeutic work occurs. By this point, the group should be cohesive and focused on accomplishing its goals. The participants are most active at this stage, and the social worker takes a less active role. Finally, the end stage, Choice *D,* occurs once the group has accomplished its goals and is ready for termination. The social worker helps the group review its accomplishments and process feelings related to the group ending.

168. C: An external audit is when a third party assesses an organization's functioning. External audits are conducted regularly to monitor the performance of an agency. The specifics of what is assessed can vary based on the organization's size and programs. Choice *A* is incorrect because an internal audit is an organizational assessment performed by staff within the agency. Choice *B* is incorrect because a program evaluation is an assessment of one specific program, not the entire organization. Choice *D* is incorrect because a special audit is an assessment that is recommended for a specific reason, such as noncompliance.

169. A: Qualitative research involves collecting data from interviews and open-ended surveys. These types of data can give an in-depth view of the experiences of a small number of participants but can't be generalized to a larger population. Choice *B* is incorrect because quantitative research involves collecting data from multiple choice questions, assessment instruments, and other tools that generate numerical data. Choice *C* is incorrect because a case study involves only one research subject. Choice *D* is incorrect because naturalistic observation involves observing subjects in their natural environment without interacting or being detected.

170. D: Social workers must use evidence-based interventions, but it is not necessary to prove this on a treatment plan. Instead, a treatment plan is a contract between a social worker and a client that includes the problem or problems that are going to be addressed, Choice *A*; the goal or goals that are going to reduce the impact of the problem, Choice *B*; the roles of the client and social worker in the treatment process; the interventions that are going to be used, Choice *C*; how progress will be monitored; situations where the contract would need to be renegotiated; and information about when, where, and how often the client and social worker will meet.

Practice Test #3

To keep the size of this book manageable, save paper, and provide a digital test-taking experience, the 3rd practice test can be found online. Scan the QR code or go to this link to access it:

testprepbooks.com/bonus/aswbmasters

The first time you access the test, you will need to register as a "new user" and verify your email address.

If you have any issues, please email support@testprepbooks.com

Index

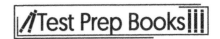

Dear ASWB Masters Test Taker,

We would like to start by thanking you for purchasing this study guide for your ASWB Masters exam. We hope that we exceeded your expectations.

Our goal in creating this study guide was to cover all of the topics that you will see on the test. We also strove to make our practice questions as similar as possible to what you will encounter on test day. With that being said, if you found something that you feel was not up to your standards, please send us an email and let us know.

We would also like to let you know about another book in our catalog that may interest you.

ASWB Clinical	**ASWB Bachelors**
amazon.com/dp/1637756828	amazon.com/dp/1628458836
(paid link)	(paid link)

As an Amazon Affiliate, TPB Publishing earns from qualifying purchases.

We have study guides in a wide variety of fields. If the one you are looking for isn't listed above, then try searching for it on Amazon or send us an email.

Thanks Again and Happy Testing!
Product Development Team
info@studyguideteam.com

FREE Test Taking Tips Video/DVD Offer

To better serve you, we created videos covering test taking tips that we want to give you for FREE. **These videos cover world-class tips that will help you succeed on your test.**

We just ask that you send us feedback about this product. Please let us know what you thought about it—whether good, bad, or indifferent.

To get your **FREE videos**, you can use the QR code below or email freevideos@studyguideteam.com with "Free Videos" in the subject line and the following information in the body of the email:

- a. The title of your product
- b. Your product rating on a scale of 1-5, with 5 being the highest
- c. Your feedback about the product

If you have any questions or concerns, please don't hesitate to contact us at info@studyguideteam.com.

Thank you!

Ask for noise-cancelling headsets during test.   Schedule appt to test

Pay   ASWB → Get authorization to
$230   purchase practice test
for $85   **Index**

//Test Prep Books‖‖

- ASWB Exam 170 multiple choice (20 questions being pretested for possible inclusion as scored questions on future ASWB exam.

- Pretest if not affect your score on exam - only the 150 remaining questions will count toward your score. (Pretest + score questions mixed together.)

Master's - MSW - Practice of master's social work including the application of specialized knowledge + advanced practice skills.

I. Human Development, Diversity + Behavior in the Environment   (Major Content Area)

1B. Concepts of Abuse + Neglect (~~Com~~ Competency Area w/in Main Content Area)

    KSAs for Concepts of Abuse + Neglect
    - Indicators + dynamics of abuse + neglect throughout the lifespan
    - the effects of physical, sexual + psychological abuse on indiv., families, groups, org. + communities
    - the indicators, dynamics + impact of exploitation across the lifespan (e.g. financial, immigration status, sexual trafficking)
    - the characteristics of perpetrators of abuse, neglect, + exploitation

II. Assessment, Diagnosis + Treatment Planning.

300

Tips:
- Use test answer eliminator under Tools to strike out options that are incorrect.
- Arrive 30 mins early
- Layer up (cold in testing room)
- Ask for noise-cancelling headsets
- Find location of test ctr. before test day.

* Remember exam question basics (Pg 24 of Exam Book) uses a 3 or 4 option multiple choice format w/ these parts:
- Stem - main body of question that poses the problem to be answered.
- Options - The possible answers
- Key - This correct answer
- Distractors - The incorrect answers
* See example pg. 25 ⚠ They sound plausible but there is only one answer to the question.

→ Capitalized or bolded words in the STEM provide info important to test taker. pay close attention to qualifiers like BEST, FIRST, NEXT & MOST.

2 Kinds of questions - STEMS have either a direct question or incomplete statement that leads to the or they contain a vignette - a short scenario or situation question itself.

Usually require the test-taker to remember specific info. See ex. (Pg 26)

5 several thinking processes: some cognitive skills are defined + applied to ASWB test questions - divided in 3 basic cognitive levels: RECALL; APPLICATION; REASONING
You will encounter all 3 on exam by the mix will depend on the category of the examination you're taking.

* Masters will have more application + reasoning questions than recall questions
See pgs 27-29 (Recall, Application - Examples)
See pgs 30 - 33 (Reasoning)